# Complete Buddhist Poetry: Verses and Chants from the Pali Canon

*Bodhi Path Press*

GRAPEVINE INDIA

Published by

**GRAPEVINE INDIA PUBLISHERS PVT LTD**

www.grapevineindia.com

Delhi | Mumbai

email: grapevineindiapublishers@gmail.com

Ordering Information:

Quantity sales: Special discounts are available on quantity

purchases by corporations, associations, and others.

For details, reach out to the publisher.

First published by Grapevine India 2024

# THERAGATHA

# VERSES OF THE ELDER MONKS

# CANTO I. PSALMS OF SINGLE VERSES
# PART I

I Subhuti

Reborn in the time of our Buddha at Savatthi, in the family of councillor Sumana, younger brother of Anathapiṇḍika, he was named Subhuti. Now on the day when the Jeta Grove, purchased by his uncle, was presented to the Exalted One, Subhuti was present, and when he heard the Norm, he found faith and left the world. Receiving ordination, he mastered the two categories (of Vinaya rules). Thereafter a subject for exercise in meditation was given him to learn, and he went into the forest and practised it. Developing insight on the basis of love-jhana, he won arahantship. And he, teaching the Norm without distinctions or limitations, became chief among the brethren who cultivated universal amity. And because, while going round for alms, he fell, at house after house,  into love-jhana, taking his alms when he emerged from reverie, this was judged to bring great reward to his almoners, and he became chief among them that were held worthy of gifts. Wherefore the Exalted One said: 'Subhuti, bhikkhus, is the chief of my bhikkhu-disciples in universal amity, and chief among such as are held worthy of gifts. …

So this great Brother, travelling about the land for the good of the many, came in due course to Rajagaha. King Bimbisara heard of his coming, and went to salute him, bidding him, 'Here, your reverence, be pleased to dwell, and I will make you a dwelling-place.' But, going thence, he forgot. The Brother, receiving no shelter, meditated in the open air. And because of the Brother's dignity, the god rained not, so that the people were oppressed with the drought and raised a tumult at the door of the king's house. The king asked himself for what reason the god rained not, and judged it must be because the Brother was in the open. So he had a leaf-hut made for him, and saluted him, saying, 'Be pleased, lord, to dwell in this leaf-hut,' and so departed. The Brother entered, and seated himself cross-legged on the couch of hay. Then the rain began to drip drop by drop, not in a torrent. But the Brother, wishing to allay the people's fear of drought, declared the absence of any danger to himself from without, or from within, by uttering the verse:

Well-roofed and pleasant is my little hut,

And screened from winds—Rain at thy will, thou god!

My heart is well composed, my heart is free,

And ardent is my mood. Now rain, god! rain.

Thus verily did the venerable Brother Subhuti utter his Psalm.

And the verse was his confession of Anna.

II Kotthita the Great

Reborn in this Buddha-age at Savatthi, in a very wealthy clan of brahmins, he was named Kotthita. When he was come of age he had learned the three Vedas, and perfected himself in the accomplishments of a brahmin. He heard the Master preach the Norm, found faith, and entered the Order. Practising insight from the day of his ordination he attained arahantship, together with thorough mastery of the form and meaning of the Norm. As proficient herein he used to question the great Theras and Him-of-the-Ten-Powers about them. Hence it came that he was held chief of those who were thus proficient. Then the Master, having shown his attainments in the Vedalla-Sutta, ranked him chief of those who were proficient in insight.

He, on a later occasion, conscious of the bliss of emancipation, broke forth in this verse:

Whoso, serene and calm, dead to the world,

Can utter wisdom's runes, with wit unswelled.

Unruffled—he doth shake off naughty things

As they were forest leaves by wind-god blown.

Thus verily did the venerable Brother Mahn-Kotthita utter his psalm.

III Kankha-Revata

(Revata the Doubter)

He was reborn in the days of our Exalted One in a wealthy family of Savatthi. And as he stood in the outermost ring of those who went after dinner to hear Him-of-the-Ten-Powers preach, he believed, and thereupon entered the Order. And he attained arahantship by way of practising jhana; and so proficient in jhana did he become, that the Master pronounced him chief of the bhikkhus who practised it.

His task accomplished thus, this great Brother reflected on the inveterate tendency of his mind to doubt, now wholly overcome, and praised the might and wisdom of the Exalted One, whereby his mind was now calm and steadfast, saying:

Behold how great the wisdom is of Them

Who Thus-have-come! As fire at midnight hour,

Givers of light, givers of sight are they

To those that pass, subduing all their doubt.

Thus verily did the venerable Brother Kankha-Revata utter his psalm.


IV Punna of the Mantanis


He was reborn in the days of our Exalted One, in an eminent brahmin clan, at the brahmin village of Donavatthu, not far from Kapilavatthu. He was sister's son of the Elder Kondanna, and was named Punna. And after performing all the duties of his novitiate, he put forth every effort till he had accomplished the highest duties of a recluse. He thereupon went with his uncle to dwell near the Master, leaving the neighbourhood of Kapilavatthu. And thoroughly intent in practice, he not long after became an arahant.

Now Punna came to have a following of 500 clansmen who had also left the world. And because he himself had  acquired the ten bases of discourse, he taught his followers therein till they, too, became experts and arahants. They thereupon desired him to take them to the Master. But he, judging it unfitting to go surrounded by them, bade them go on, and promised to follow them. They, being all fellow-countrymen of Him-of-the-Ten-Powers, walked the sixty yojanas to Rajagaha, and, in the great Vihara of the Bamboo Grove, found him and did obeisance to him. Now, when bhikkhus come to Buddhas, the Exalted Ones, it is customary for friendly greetings to be exchanged. Wherefore the Exalted One asked them: 'I hope, brethren, that you are well and have pleasantly rested: Whence come ye?' 'From your own country, lord,' they replied. Then he asked if there were a bhikkhu who knew the Ten Subjects, saying: ' Who, brethren, of such fellow-countrymen of mine is capable, himself a simple liver, to discourse on the simple life?' 'Punna, lord, the venerable son of the Mantanis.'

And when the Master went from Rajagaha to Savatthi, Punna went thither and, in the Fragrant Chamber, was taught the Norm. And Sariputta, desiring to meet him, went after him to Dark Wood, whither he had gone to meditate on the Master's words, and found him resting beneath a tree. And they discoursed of those words, and had joy of each other, Punna winning his heart by the parable of the posting by chariot.

Now the Master proclaimed Punna chief among the bhikkhus in preaching the Norm. And he one day, reflecting near the Master on the emancipation he had won,  bethought him: 'Verily to me and many others, delivered from the round of sorrow, how great a help is communion with good men!' And with joy and enthusiasm he uttered this verse:

 Aye with the good consort, with them

 Who know, who understand, who see the Good. Great is the Good and deep and hard to see,

 Subtle and delicately fine, to which

 The wise and brave do penetrate, e'en they

 Who strenuous live and lofty vision gain.

Thus verily did the venerable Punna of the Mantanis utter his psalm. And the Brother explained that the psalm contained his affirmation of aanna.


V Dabba (Of the Mallas)

He came to birth in the family of a clansman of the Mallas, at Anupiya. As a child of seven, he saw the Master when the latter visited his country and home, and was so attracted that he asked his grandmother, his mother having died at his birth, if he might leave the world under the Master. She brought him to the Master, who bade a bhikkhu ordain him. And the boy, being one in whom past causes and an aspiration were taking effect, realized the Four Paths in succession, in the very act of having his curls cut off.

 And when the Master left the Mallas' country for Rajagaha, Dabba, meditating alone, and desirous of devoting his body to the service of the Order, considered that he might both apportion night's lodging and direct to meals. The Master sanctioned his doing so, and his success herein, and his supernormal power herein, lighting the brethren to their lodgings with his shining finger, is told in the Pali narrative.

But it was after the baseless calumny, wherewith the bhikkhas who followed Mettiya and Bhummajaka sought to ruin him, had been condemned by the Order, that the Brother, conscious of his virtuous compassion for others, uttered this verse:

 Once hard to tame, by taming tamed is now

 Dabba, from doubts released, content, serene.

 Victor is Dabba now, and void of fears;

 Perfected he and staunch in steadfastness.

Thus verily did the venerable Brother Dabba utter his psalm.

## VI Sita-Vaniya

This is the psalm of the venerable Brother Sambhuta. He was reborn at Rajagaha as the son of an eminent brahmin, and named Sambhuta. With his three friends, Bhumija, Jeyyasena and Abhiradana, he heard the Exalted One preach the Norm, and left the world to enter the Order. While practising the systematic meditation of 'mindfulness respecting the body,' he stayed continually in Sita-Vana (Cool Wood), and thus became known as Sita-Vaniya (Cool Woodlander).

And seeing bhikkhus passing by on their way to see the Exalted One, he said: 'Friends, worship the Exalted One for me with speech of mine, and say to him thus' (showing the Master his uninterrupted concern with the Norm):

There is a brother who to Cool Wood gone doth dwell

Alone, content, in meditative ecstasy,

Victorious, no more by creeping dread dismayed,

He mindful watcheth over sense with courage high.

Thus verily did the venerable Brother Sita-vaniya utter his psalm.

VII Bhalliya

He, with his elder brother Tapussa, was born in the time of our Exalted One, in the city of Pokkharavati, as the son of a caravan-driver. As they were conducting a caravan of carts in a pleasant glade, a muddy place checked their progress. Then a tree-fairy, one of their own kin, showed himself, and said: 'Sirs, the Exalted One hath just attained enlightenment, and for seven weeks abideth fasting in the bliss of emancipation, seated at the root of the King's Stead tree. Serve him with food; this will long make for your good and happiness.' They, with joyful eagerness, waited not to prepare food, but took rice-cakes and honey, and, leaving the high road, ministered to the Exalted One.

Now when the Exalted One had set rolling the wheel of the Norm at Benares, he stayed in due course at Rajagaha. There Tapussa and Bhalliya waited on him and heard him teach. The former became a lay-follower, the latter left the world and mastered the six forms of abhinna.

One day when Mara appeared to the Brother in fearsome terrifying shape, Bhalliya, manifesting how he had passed beyond all fear, uttered a psalm to Mara's discomfiture:

Whoso hath chased away the Death-king and his host,

E'en as a mighty flood the causeway of frail reeds,

Victor is he, self-tamed. Fear cometh never more.

His is the Goal supreme, and utter steadfastness.

Thus verily did the venerable Bhalliya utter his psalm.'


VIII Vira

Reborn in this Buddha-age at Savatthi, in the family of a minister to King Pasenadi, he was named Vira. And when, as befitted his name, he had acquired athletic accomplishments, he became a warrior. Marrying with his parents' consent, a son was born to him. Thereupon, seeing the trouble in the perpetuation of life, he left the world in anguish, and putting forth every effort soon acquired sixfold abhinna. Now when, as arahant, he was living in the bliss of fruition, his former wife tried to lure him back in various ways. But the venerable Vira said:

'This woman, desiring to seduce me, is like one wishing to shake Mount Sineru with the wing of a gnat.' And he showed her how futile it was by his psalm:

Once hard to tame, by taming now is tamed

Vira, from doubts released, content, serene;

Victor is Vira, free from creeping dread;

His is the goal supreme, and steadfast strength.

The woman, hearing him, was deeply moved, and thought:

'My husband has won to this-what good is domestic life to me ?' And she went forth among the Sisters, and soon acquired the Three-fold Lore.

IX Pilinda-Vaccha

Reborn at Savatthi as a brahmin's son, before the Exalted One became a Buddha, they named him Pilinda, Vaccha being the name of his clan. He became a recluse, and acquired the charm called the Lesser Gandhara, deriving therefrom great renown. But when our Exalted One became Buddha the charm ceased to work. He having learnt that the Greater Gandhara spell stopped the Less,  concluded that Gotama the recluse knew the former, and he waited on him in the hope of acquiring it, asking if the chance might be granted him. The Exalted One answered: 'You must leave the world.' He, fancying that this was a preparation for the charm, did so. To him the Exalted One taught the Norm, and gave him exercise in meditation, so that he, the conditions being ripe, attained arahantship.

Now one who, in consequence of Pilinda's guidance in a former birth, had gone to heaven as a deva, waited on him morning and evening out of gratitude. Hence the Brother was distinguished as one dear to the gods, and was ranked chief among the brethren who were such by the Exalted One.

And Pilinda one day, sitting among the brethren, and reflecting on his success, declared to them how the charm had brought him to the Exalted One uttering this psalm:

O welcome this that came, nor came amiss!

O goodly was the counsel given to me!

'Mong divers doctrines mooted among men

Of all 'twas sure the Best I sought and found.

X Punnamasa

Reborn in this Buddha-age as the eon of Samiddbi, a brahmin of Savatthi, he left the world when a son was born to him, and entering the Order under the Exalted One, took the Four Truths as his exercise in meditation, and became an arabant. His former wife sought to seduce him from his faith, visiting him adorned, and with her child. But the brother, showing his utter detachment, uttered this psalm:

All longings as to this or other life

Have I put far from me, as one who hath

Beta'en himself to truth, whose heart's at peace,

Who, self-subdued, in all things undefiled,

Discerns the world's incessant ebb and flow.

Then the woman thinking, 'This holy man cares not for me nor for the child; I am not able to persuade him,' went away.

# CANTO I. PSALMS OF SINGLE VERSES
## PART II

XI Gavaccha the Less

Reborn as a brahmin at Kosambi, and hearing the Exalted One preach, he entered the Order. At that time the bhikkhus of Kosambi had become contentious. Then Gavaccha the Less, not taking part with either side, remained steadfast in the Exalted One's admonition, and developing insight, attained to arahantship. And seeing in the bhikkhus' quarrelsome tastes what might have been the downfall of his own good, he reflected with joy and enthusiasm on his own contrasted state, saying:

Abundantly this brother doth rejoice,

For the blest truths the Buddha hath revealed

Are his, and he hath won the Path of Peace,

And his the bliss where worldly cares are stilled.


XII Gavaccha Major

He was reborn in this Buddha's days as the son of Samiddhi, a brahmin of the village of Nalaka in Magadha. And he entered the Order because Sariputta had done so, and he knew that Sariputta was very wise. After he had attained arahantship, and was enjoying the bliss of emancipation, he uttered his psalm to encourage his fellow-disciples to make efforts:

In wisdom strong, guided by virtue's rule, intent,

To concentration's rapture given, yet vigilant;

Partaking of such fare as brings thee only good:

So in the faith, with passions quenched, await the hour.


XIII Vanavaccha

In this Buddha-age he took rebirth at Kapilavatthu, in the brahmin clan of the Vaccha's. He was born in the forest, his mother being taken with travail while walking in the forest which she had yearned to see. He became one of the future Buddha's playmates in the sand. And because he loved the woods, he was known as Woodland-Vaccha. Later on, when he had entered the Order, it  was in the forest that he strove for and won arahantship. And it was in praise of the forest life that he uttered his psalm, replying to the brethren who asked him: 'What comfort can you get in the forest?' 'Delightful, my friends, are forest and mountain!'-

Crags with the hue of heaven's blue clouds,

Where lies enbosomed many a shining tarn

Of crystal-clear, cool waters, and whose slopes

The 'herds of Indra' cover and bedeck:

Those are the braes wherein my soul delights.


XIV Sivaka

(A Novice attending Brother Vanavaccha.)

In this Buddha—era he was born as the son of Vanavaccha's sister. When his mother heard that her eldest brother Vanavaccha had left the world, had graduated in the Order, and was dwelling in the forest, she said to her son: 'Dear Sivaka, you should leave the world under the Elder, and wait on him; the Elder is getting old now.' He, at this sole bidding of his mother, and because of his previous aspirations, did so and, ministering to his uncle, dwelt in the forest. One day, when he had gone to the outskirts of the village on some errand, he fell very ill. And when medicine did not cure him and he came not, the Elder, wondering at the reason, went and found him ill. Administering remedies and tending him the Elder, when dawn was nigh, said: 'Sivaka, since the time when I left the world, I have not sojourned in the village. Let us go hence into the forest.' Sivaka answered: 'Sir, even if my body stay now by the village, my heart is in the forest, wherefore though I lie here yet shall I go thither.' Then the Elder took hold of his arm and led him to the forest exhorting him. He, made steadfast by that admonition, won arahantship.

Thereafter he uttered his psalm, combining his master's words and his own, expressing both his love of seclusion and his achievement, his obedience to his master and the winning of anna:

The teacher spake me thus: 'Sivaka, hence

Let's go!' Here in the town my body dwells;

My thoughts are to the forest gone. So thus,

Prostrated though I be, yet do I go.

No bond is there for those who understand.


XV Kunda-Dhana

In the age of our Exalted One, he was reborn at Savatthi as a brahmin's child, and called Dhana. Knowing the  three Vedas by heart, he when advanced in years heard the Master preach, and left the world. Now King Pasenadi of Kosala becama interested in him and provided him with necessaries, so that he had not to go round for alms. But it was when the great Subhadda invited the Master and his company to dine with her, that Kuṇḍa-Dhana revealed his powers and attainments, as it is written in the Commentary on the Aṅguttara-Nikaya. And it was to the brethren that he recited this verse:

Five cut thou off; Five leave behind, and Five beyond all cultivate!

He who the Fivefold Bond transcends—a Brother

Flood-crossed is he called.


## XVI Belatthasisa

In this Buddha-age he was reborn at Savatthi in a brahmin's family, and before the Exalted One became a Buddha he left the world to join the ascetic Order of Kassapa of Uruvela, and tend the sacred fire. And when Kassapa was tamed by the Buddha, he was one of the thousand ascetics who obtained arahantship on hearing the sermon on Burning.

He thereafter became the tutor of the 'Treasurer of the Norm.' And one day, reflecting on the pure bliss of fruition and his own earlier discipline, in rapture he uttered a psalm:

E'en as the high-bred steer with crested buck Lightly the plough adown the furrow turns,

So lightly glide for me the nights and days

Now that this pure untainted bliss is won.


## XVII Dasaka

He, by his karma, was reborn in the age of our Exalted One at Savatthi, as the child of a slave of Anathapiṇḍika,  and was by him appointed as gate-porter of the Vihara. Hearing of his virtuous conduct and his wishes, his master made him a freed man, and said, how happy it was to leave the life of the world. He was ordained accordingly; but from that time he grew slothful and slack of effort, taking no steps to roll back the round of rebirth, and sleeping much after meals. At sermon-time he would get into a corner on the outskirts of the congregation, and sit snoring. Now the Exalted One, contemplating his antecedents, spoke the following verse to him in order to stir up agitation:

Who waxes slothful and in diet gross,

Given to sleep and rolling as he lies,

Like a great hog with provender replete—

The dolt comes back again, again to birth.

Hearing this, Dasaka grew agitated and, developing insight, not long after realized arahantship. Thereafter he thought 'the verse of the Exalted One became as a goad to me,' and he repeated the verse. Thus, though uttered as a protest concerning food, it became the declaration of his anna.


XVIII Singala-Pitar

Reborn in this Buddha-age of wealthy parents at Savatthi, he married and named his son Singala(ka), himself becoming known as Singala's father. At a later time he threw off domestic ties, and left the world for the Order. The Exalted One, contemplating his inclinations, gave him the meditative exercise of the idea of a skeleton. Taking it he dwelt among the Sakiyans at Suṁsumaragira, in the Bhesakala Wood. Now in that wood a woodland sprite, judging that the Thera would soon grasp the fruition he laboured after, uttered this verse:

Lo! in the forest of Bhesakala

A brother dwells, heir of the Buddha's grace,

Suffusing through and through this earthy frame

With thought intent, austere, of skeleton. Beshrew me, if he do not swiftly drive

All passion of the senses clean away!

Hearing that verse the brother thought 'this fairy said this to me to call forth effort,' and willing unfaltering endeavour, he developed insight and attained arahantship. Thereafter he recalled the fairy's words, and breathed forth that very verse as the confession of his anna.

XIX Kula

Reborn in this Buddha-age at Savatthi of a brahmin family, he entered the Order, but from want of mental balance could not concentrate on a given idea. Now one day going to the town for alms, he saw men conducting running water wherever they wished by digging channels. Within the town he marked out of the corner of his eye how the fletcher fixed the arrow-shaft in his lathe, and leaving with full bowl he saw the chariot-makers planing axle and tire and hub. So entering the Vihara he dined; then during siesta he pondered on these three modes of taming things, making them his goad, and applying them to his own need of self-mastery. So striving he not long after won arahantship. And connecting those object-lessons with his own heart's taming, he confessed anna in this verse:

The conduit-makers lead the stream,

Fletchers coerce the arrow-shaft,

The joiners mould the wooden plank;

The self—'tis that the pious tame.


XX Ajita

He was reborn, when our Master was living, at Savatthi, as the son of the brahmin who was price-assessor to the king of Kosala. He became an ascetic as follower of Bavari, the learned brahmin, who dwelt in the Kapittha park on the banks of the Godhavari. Now Bavari sent him, together with Tissa and Metteyya, to the Master. And Ajita was so satisfied with the Master's answers to his questions, that he entered the Order. Choosing a form of mental exercise he developed insight, and attained arahant-ship. Thereupon he uttered his song of victory in this verse:

All unafraid of death, nor fain to live,

I shall lay down this compound frame anon, With mind alert, with consciousness controlled.

# CANTO I. PSALMS OF SINGLE VERSES
## PART III

XXI Nigrodha

He in this Buddha-age was reborn in an eminent brahmin's family at Savatthi. And on the day when Jeta Grove was presented, he saw the majesty of the Buddha and was satisfied, so that he entered the Order. When he had stirred up insight, he soon became able to exercise the six forms of supernormal thought. And pondering, in the bliss of fruition, on the advantages of the doctrine which leads us away from rebirth, he uttered this verse as the expression of anna:

No fear have I of fearsome things, for He,

Our Master, knoweth well th' ambrosial lore. The Path where fear nowise a footing finds,

Along that Path the brethren hold their way.


XXII Cittaka

He was born in this Buddha-age at Rajagaha, as the son of a brahmin of great possessions. And when the Master was staying in the Bamboo Grove, Cittaka went to hear him, and found faith and so entered the Order. Choosing ethical conduct as his exercise, he entered a wooded spot, and there in devotional practice induced jhana. Thereby developing insight he soon attained arahantship. Thereupon he went to salute the Master. Asked by the brethren, 'Have you been strenuous, friend, in your forest sojourn?' be uttered his psalm, to show he had been so, and to declare anna:

Peacocks of sapphire neck and comely crest

Calling, calling in Karaṅvia woods; By cool and humid winds made musical: They wake the thinker from his noonday sleep.


XXIII Gosala

He was born in this Buddha-age in a wealthy Magadhese family. He came to know Sona-Kutikanna; and when he heard that the latter had left the world, he grew agitated, and thought: 'If he who has so great an estate shall leave the world, why not rather I?' And entering the Order, he took for exercise the subject of ethical conduct, and seeking a suitable haunt, dwelt on the uplands not far from his native village. Now one day his mother, who daily dispensed alms, gave him, on his round, rice-porridge prepared with honey and sugar. This he took and ate in the shade of that hill under a bamboo thicket. With bowl and hands washed, and refreshed by the appropriate fare offered him, he put forth insight without toil and, with mind intent on the ebb and flow of all things, attained the topmost meditation of the Paths, winning arahantship, with mastery of the form and meaning of the doctrine. Desirous to go up to the hilly region that he might dwell in bliss while he lived, he made known his own experience in this verse:

Lo! I who in the bamboo thicket dined

Off rice and honey, who now comprehend,

Him worshipping, the ebb and flux of all

These factors of my life, will hie me back

Up on my hill, to foster there the growth

Of heart's detachment, lone and separate.


## XXIV Sugandha

He was reborn in this Buddha-age of wealthy parents at Savatthi. And because of his aspiration in the past, when he presented Kassapa Buddha with a Fragrant Chamber of sandal-wood, that he might in one life be reborn with a fragrant body, he, on the day of his birth—and his mother before that day—filled the house with fragrance. Then said his parents: 'Our son is come bringing his own name!' and they called him Sugandha (Aroma). When grown up, he was induced to leave the world by the preaching of the Thera Maha-Sela. And within seven days he attained arahantship. Confessing anna he uttered this verse:

Scarce have the rains gone by since I went forth,

Yet see the seemly order of the Norm!

The Threefold Wisdom I have I gotten now

And done all that the Buddha bids us do.


## XXV Nandiya

Born in this Buddha-age at Kapilavatthu, in the house of a Sakiyan raja, his parents said: He is born bringing us bliss; and they called him Nandiya (Beatus). Grown up, he went forth, when Anuruddha and the rest left the world under the Master. And because of his studies and his resolve made in the past, he soon attained arahantship. Thereafter he dwelt with Anuruddha the Thera and his friends, in the Eastern Bamboo Wood. There Mara, the Evil One, wishing to frighten him, appeared in a terrifying shape. But the Thera drove him away with the words, 'O Evil One! what canst thou do with those that have transcended thy realm? 'Tis thou that thereby wilt meet with defeat and ruin.'

To him whose thought is ever newly born

From splendour of the Path, and eke hath touched

The Fruit—if such a Brother thou assail'st,

Black-hearted sprite, to misery thou must go.


## XXVI Abhaya

He was reborn in this Buddha-age as the son of King Bimbisara. The circumstances of his rebirth will be set forth later. Nataputta the Jain leader taught him a dilemma to set the 'Samana Gotama,' but in the Master's reply he recognized the defeat of the Jain and the supreme enlightenment of the Exalted One. Thereafter, when the king died, Abhaya grew anxious and left the world for the Order. Through the preaching of the Sutta on the parable of the hole in the yoke, he reached the First Path; again, stirring up insight, he realized arahantship. Thereupon, glorying in that which he had won, he confessed anna saying:

Of him, the Buddha, kin o' th' sun, I heard

The word most eloquent, and hearing pierced

The subtle truth of things, as 'twere the tip

Of hair by cunning bowman's art transfixed.


## XXVII Lomasakangiya

When Kassapa was Buddha, this brother left the world and followed him. Now after the Master had preached the Sutta on Happy-Lonely, a certain bhikkhu talked with Lomasakangiya about it. And our Thera, being unable to explain it, uttered the wish: 'May I in the future become able to teach thee the Happy-Lonely!' The other answered: 'May I ask thee!' Of these two the former, when our Buddha lived, was reborn at Kapilavatthu, in the house of a Sakiyan raja. And he was very delicate, and covered with fine hair, and therefore he was called Lomasakangiya. The other was reborn at that time among the gods, and named Candana.

Now when Anuruddha and the other Sakiyan youths left the world, Lomasakangiya would not. Then Candana, to stir him up, came to him and asked concerning the Happy-Lonely. The other knew not what he meant. Then Candana reminded him. So Lomasakangiya went to the Exalted One and asked him if it was true that he had made that resolve in the past. 'Ay, youth,' replied the Exalted One; 'and the meaning of it is to be understood in more than fifty points of detail.' Then Lomasakangiya said: 'Wherefore, lord, let me be ordained.' And the Exalted One sent him to get his parents' permission. He asked his mother, but she feared for his health, saying: 'My dear, thou art delicate. How canst thou leave the world?' Then Lomasakangiya uttered this verse:

Dabba and Kusa grass and pricking stems

And all that hurts in brush and underwood

Forth from my breast I'll push and thrust away,

And go where I the growth may cultivate

Of heart's detachment, lone and separate.

Thereupon his mother said, 'Well then, my dear, go forth.' And he gained the Master's consent to be ordained. After doing the preliminary exercises he went to enter the forest. And the bhikkhus said to him: 'Friend, you are delicate. What can you do here? 'Tis cold in the forest.' But he repeated his verse, and entering the forest, devoted himself to meditation, and soon acquired the six forms of supernormal thought. When he won arahantship he confessed anna in the same verse.


XXVIII Jambugamika's Son

He was reborn in this Buddha-age at Campa as the son of a lay-adherent named Jambugamika, and became called after his father. While studying as a novice in the Order, he dwelt at Saketa, in the Anjana Grove. Then his father, thinking, 'I wonder if my son remains devoted to his life in the Order or not?' wrote the following verse to examine him, and sent it to him:

And art thou then not gratified by gear?

And art thou then not charmed thyself t' adorn?

And is this fragrant odour, virtue-fraught,

Wafted by thee, and not by other folk?

When he had read this he thought: 'My father is suspicious that I want worldly vanities. Even to-day I have not got beyond the level of the common man!' Filled with anxiety, he strove and wrestled, so that he soon acquired the six abhinnas. And taking the verse his father sent him as a goad, he finally realized arahantship. And both to confess anna and honour his father, he recited the verse.


XXIX Harita

Reborn in this Buddha-age at Savatthi, as the son of a wealthy brahmin, his parents wedded him to a brahmin's daughter suitable in birth, beauty and every other respect. And he, enjoying his lot with her, was one day, while he contemplated the perfection of her beauty, admonished by the order of things, that such beauty must needs ere long be crushed out by decay and death. Nay, when but a few days had passed by, his wife was bitten by a black snake and died. Overwhelmed by anguish he sought the Master and, hearing the Norm, severed his domestic ties and left the world. Now while he was training himself ethically, he could not make straight his heart. And going for alms into the village, he saw a fletcher applying his tools and making straight the shaft of an arrow. Then, he thought: 'These men make even a senseless thing straight; why do I not make straight my heart?' So he turned back and, seated for siesta, stirred up insight. And lo! the Exalted One, seated in the air above him, admonished him by this verse:

Now bend aloft thyself; e'en as his bolt

The fletcher, so do thou, O Harita,

Make straight thy heart and ignorance cut away.

Hearing him, the Thera developed insight, and soon became an arahant. He thereupon confessed anna with this same verse.


XXX Uttiya

He was born in this Buddha-age at Savatthi, as the son of a brahmin, and leaving the world on the quest of the Ambrosial, he became a Wanderer. One day on his travels he came where the Exalted One was preaching, and entered the Order. From the impurity of his moral principles he could not win the goal. And seeing other bhikkhus who had won confessing to anna, he asked the Master for a lesson in brief. The Master answered, 'It follows that you, Uttiya, must purify the rudiments,' and he taught him them in brief. Uttiya, accepting the lesson, called up insight, but in the process he fell ill. In his anxiety he put forth every effort, and attained arahantship. Inasmuch as he won to perfect attainment in the face of such a condition, he confessed anna, with reference to his illness:

Since sickness hath befallen me, O now

Let there arise in me true mindfulness.

Sickness hath now befallen me—'tis time

For me no more to dally or delay.

# CANTO I.

# PSALMS OF SINGLE VERSES  PART IV

XXXII Suppiya

He in this Buddha-age was reborn, in consequence of his actions, in a despised class, as one of a clan of watchmen in a cemetery at Savatthi. Converted by the preaching of the Thera Sopaka his friend, he entered the Order and attained to the highest, declaring this in his psalm while he yet was striving for arahantship:

O would that I who hourly waste, might change For that which ne'er decays—who ever burn,

Might change for that cool bliss-e'en for the Peace

That passeth all, Safety beyond compare!


XXXIII Sopaka

(A Boy-Bhikkhu.)

He was reborn in this Buddha-age at Savatthi, of a very poor woman. In her travail his mother fell into a long deep swoon, so that her kinsfolk said 'She is dead!' And they bore her to the cemetery, and prepared to cremate the body. But a spirit prevented the fire burning by a storm of wind and rain, so they went away. Then was the child born hale while the mother died. And the spirit, in human shape, took the infant and placed it in the watchman's house, nourishing it for a time with suitable food. After that the watchman adopted it, and the child grew up with his own son Suppiya (Ps. XXXII.). And because of his birth in the cemetery, he became known as Sopaka, 'the Waif.' When he was seven years' old it came to pass that the Exalted One early in the morning spread out his Net of Insight to contemplate what folk might be brought in. And seeing what the net enclosed, he went to the cemetery. The boy, impelled by his antecedents, approached the Master with a gladdened mind and saluted him. The Master taught him, so that he asked to leave the world, and when bidden to gain his father's consent, fetched the latter to the Master. The father saluted, and asked the Master to admit the boy. And the Master had him admitted, and assigned to him the study of fraternal love. He, taking this exercise and dwelling in the cemetery, soon acquired the corresponding jhana. And making that his base, he fostered insight and realized arahantship. As arahant he showed in his verse to the other bhikkhus dwelling there the principle of the love exercises, bidding them make no difference between those who were to them friendly, indifferent, or hostile. For all alike their love should be one and the same in its nature, and should include all realms, all beings, at all ages:

E'en as she would be very good

Towards her only child, her well-beloved son,

So too ye should be very good

Towards all creatures everywhere and everyone.


## XXXIV Posiya

He was reborn in this Buddha-age at Savatthi, as the son of a very wealthy councillor, and the younger brother of the Thera Sangamaji. When he was grown up he married; but when a son was born to him, he, being impelled by the order of things belonging to the last span of life, grew anxious concerning birth and the like. So he left the world and dwelt alone in the forest, exercising himself in the Four Truths. And soon after he won arahantship.

Then he went to Savatthi to worship the Exalted One, and came to his home. There his former wife entertained him and, unaware of his disposition, was desirous of drawing him back by her attractions. The Thera thinking 'Alas! the fool of desire has designs even on such as me,' said no word, but rose up and went away into the forest. And the bhikkhus there said to him: 'Why, friend, you are come back too quickly; have you not seen your people?' The Thera told them what had taken place, and recited a verse:

Best when not near, both now and evermore,

Are such as these for him who understands.

Forth from the township to the woods I went,

Thence to my home once more I came; but thence

Rising I gat me forth again, nor e'er

Did this same Posiya let fall a word.


## XXXV Samannakani

He was reborn in this Buddha-age as the son of a Wanderer, and was converted to the religious life when lie saw the Exalted One perform the twin-miracle. And through jhana he attained arahantship.

Now a Wanderer named Katiyana, whom he had known as a layman, had lost all support from the laity since the Buddha had arisen, and was destitute. He came to the Thera and said: 'You of the Sakiyans, who have won much fame and support, live happily, but we are distressed and destitute. What should one do to compass happiness both in this life and the next?' The Thera said: 'Happiness not of the world:— this, for one who undergoes the suitable procedure to get it, and who gets it, is alone to be called unqualified happiness.' And to illustrate this by his own attainment, he uttered this verse:

Happiness he who seeks may win an he practise the seeking—

Honour he gaineth beside, and growth of renown shall befall him—

So he but practise the road called Straight, even the Ariyan,

The Noble Eightfold Path whereby we may reach salvation.


XXXI Gahvaratiriya

He was reborn in this Buddha-age at Savatthi, in a brahmin's family, and named Aggidatta. When grown up he saw the Exalted One work the twin-miracle, and, being convinced, he entered the Order. Taking a subject for meditation, he went to the Ratira forest, and became known as Gahva-Ratiriya. Growing in insight, he in a short time attained arahantship. Thereupon he went to worship the Exalted One at Savatthi. His kinsfolk, hearing of his coming, bestowed liberal gifts upon him. And when he wished to go back to the forest, they said: 'Sir, the forest is full of peril through the gadflies and mosquitoes. Stay here!' But the Thera, devoted to detachment, replied, 'Life in the forest suits me,' and confessing anna he uttered this verse:

In the great forest, in the mighty woods,

Touched though I be by gadfly and by gnat,

I yet would roam, like warrior-elephant,

In van of battle, mindful, vigilant.


XXXVI Kuma's Son

Reborn in this Buddha-age in the Avanti country, at the town of Veḷukaṇḍa in the family of a housefather, he was called Nanda. But his mother's name was Kuma, whence he was known as Kuma's son. He entered the Order after hearing the venerable Sariputta preach, and studied on the slope of the frontier hills; but it was only after he had gone to hear the Exalted One that he was able so to correct his exercises, as to realize arahantship. As arahant he saw that the other bhikkhus showed excess in bodily needs, and he admonished them in the doctrine, saying:

O goodly are the things our ears now hear!

O goodly is the life we here may lead!

O good it is always to lack a house! Now questioning on things of high import,

Now showing all due thanks and reverence:

Such is the calling of the true recluse,

Of him who owneth naught of anything.


## XXXVII The Comrade of Kuma's Son

Reborn in this Buddha-age at the town of Veḷukaṇḍa, of a wealthy family, and named Sudanta—some say Vasuloki—he became the dear friend of Kuma's son. When the latter left the world, he thought: 'That can be no mean religion which Kuma's son has entered.' So he went and heard the Master preach. Thereupon he was filled with a much more fervent desire and entered the Order, dwelling with Kuma's son on the frontier hills devoted to religious exercises.

Now at that time many bhikkhus touring in various districts, going and coming, halted at that station, so that there was much noise. And Sudanta, disturbed in his concentration of mind, made his trouble the goad for the taming of his thoughts, and uttered this verse:

To divers regions back and forth they fare

Heedless of heart upon their rounds, and balk

The mind's due concentration. What, forsooth,

Shall all this vagabondage bring to pass?

Hence is it meet that clamour be subdued,

Nor harass him who fain would meditate.


## XXXVIII Gavampati

He was reborn in this Buddha-age as one of the four lay-companions of the Thera Yasa, who, when they heard of Yasa's renunciation, imitated him, and also won arahantship. Thereafter he dwelt in the Anjana Grove at  Saketa, experiencing the bliss of emancipation. Now at that time the Exalted One came also with a great company of bhikkhus to the Anjana Grove, and the accommodation was insufficient, many of the bhikkhus sleeping around the vihara on the sandbanks of the River Sarabhu. Then in the middle of the night the stream rose in flood, and a great cry arose from the younger brethren. The Exalted One hearing it, sent for the venerable Gavampati, and said: 'Go, Gavampati, arrest the rising stream, and put the bhikkhus at ease.' And the Thera by his mystic power did so, and stopped the stream afar so that it stood up like a mountain-peak. Thenceforth the might of the Thera became known. One day as the Master sat teaching in the midst of a great assembly he saw Gavampati, and in compassion for the world praised his virtues in this verse:

Who by his might reared up the Sarabhu,

Who standeth self-reliant and unmoved,

Who hath transcended every tie, Gavampati,

Him mighty seer the very gods acclaim,

Surpasser of the coming back to be.


## XXXIX Tissa

He was born in this Buddha-age at Kapilavatthu, as the son of the Exalted One's aunt, and named Tissa. He left the world to follow the Exalted One, and dwelling in a woodland settlement, was proud because of his rank, being  irritable and captious in his conduct, so that he did not do his duties with zeal. Then the Master, surveying him one day with celestial vision from afar, while he was sleeping with open mouth at siesta, came over him above, shedding glory down upon him, and wakening him with these words:

As one downsmitten by impending sword,

As one whose hair and turban are aflame, So let the Brother, mindful and alert,

Go forth, all worldly passions left behind.

When the Thera heard this, his heart was filled with anguish, and he abode intent on insight. Noting this, the Master taught him the 'Sutta of Thera Tissa,' which is in the Saṁyutta collection.' At the close of it Tissa was established in arahantship. And to confess anna and honour the Master, he uttered that same verse.


## XL Vaddhamana

Reborn in this Buddha-age at Vesali, in the family of a Licchavi raja, he became as a pious lad a servitor to the Order. Later, after he had been ordained, he also was subject to sloth and torpor, and was also aroused by the Master with this verse :

As one downsmitten by impending sword,

As one whose hair and turban are aflame,

So let the Brother, mindful and alert,

Go forth, all lust of living left behind.

# CANTO I. PSALMS OF SINGLE VERSES
## PART V

XLI Sirivaddha

He was reborn in this Buddha-age at Rajagaha, in the house of a prosperous brahmin. Previous causes induced him, when King Bimbisara met the Master, to take orders, and he went to a certain forest near the hills Vebhara and Paṇḍava, and there dwelt devoted to religious exercises. And there arose once a great storm, and the lightnings entered the cave. But the wind from the pregnant clouds assuaged the heat and fever oppressing the Thera, so that by the more suitable temperature his heart grew concentrated, and he was able to exercise such insight that he won arahantship. So he, with anna as a pretext, broke forth into this utterance touching himself:

The lightnings flash e'en in the rocky cave,

Smiting Vebhara's crest and Paṇḍava, And, in the mountain-bosom hid, a child

Of that incomparable Master sits

Ardent in contemplative ecstasy.


XLII Khadira-Vaniya

(Revata)

He was reborn, in this Buddha-age, in the kingdom of Magadha, at the village of Nalaka, as the son of Rupasari, the brahminee. When he was grown up his mother desired he should marry, but he heard of Sariputta's renunciation, and said: 'If my elder brother Upatissa has laid aside this wealth, I too will vomit back his vomit,' and he went to the bhikkhus and, announcing himself as the younger brother of the 'General of the Norm,' he asked for ordination. When he had won arahantship in the Acacia Wood, he went to Savatthi to salute the Exalted One and his brother, staying a few days at the Jeta Grove. Then the Master, seated in the conclave of the Ariyans, assigned 'Revata the Acacia-woodlander the first place among forest bhikkhus.'

At another time he went to his native village and fetched away his three nephews, the sons of his three sisters, Cala, Upacala, and Sisupacala. named respectively, Cala, Upacala, and Sisupacala., and ordained them. One day the Thera was ill, and Sariputta heard of it, and said: 'I will make inquiry after Revata's state and treatment.' And seeing him coming far off, Revata admonished the three novices to be heedful, saying:

Come, Cala, and you, Upacala too,

Sisupacala also, take good heed,

Be on your guard, for he who comes to you

Is as a wondrous archer splitting hairs.

And when they heard him the novices went forth to meet the General of the Norm, and while he conversed with their uncle, sat near composed and intent. When he approached them, they rose up, bowed, and remained standing. The Thera asked them at which vibara they were each dwelling, and they replied: 'At such an one.' Then, instructing the boys, he said: 'My little brother has indeed taught the lesser duties belonging to the Norm,' and thus praising Revata, he departed.


## XLIII Sumangala

He was reborn in this Buddha-age at a hamlet near Savatthi, in a poor family. Grown up, he earned his living in the fields, furnished with a little sickle, plough, and spade. Now one day when King Pasenadi of Kosala was bestowing a great offering on the Exalted One and the Order, he went, taking milk and butter, along with men who were taking woodwork. Seeing the attentions and honours paid to the Brethren and Sisters, he thought: These Sakiyan recluses live in sheltered lodgings and in delicate robes-what if I too were now to leave the world?' And he approached a certain great Thera and made known his intention. The Thera out of compassion admitted him, and sent him into the forest with an exercise. But in solitude he pined and wavered, and departed to his native village. Then as he went along he saw the peasants ploughing the fields in soiled garments, covered with dust blown by hot winds. And he thought: 'Truly these fellows earn their living in great misery!' And feeling anxious, his insight approaching maturity, he set himself to do the exercises that had been given him, going to the roots of a tree, and biding in seclusion. Thus he finally won arahantship. Thereafter, to celebrate his own emancipation from the ills of life, he broke forth into this psalm:

Well rid, well rid, O excellently rid

Am I from these three crooked tasks and tools,

Rid o' my reaping with your sickles, rid

Of trudging after ploughs, and rid's my back

Of bending o'er these wretched little spades.

 Though they be ever here, ay, ever here,

Enough of them, I say, for me, enough!

Go meditate, Sumangala, ay, go

And meditate, Sumangala, and bide

Earnest and diligent, Sumaṅgala!


XLIV Sanu

He was reborn in this Buddha-age at Savatthi, in the family of a lay-follower, after the father had left his home. The mother, naming him Sanu, brought him when he was seven years old to the bhikkhus for ordination, deeming she would thus ensure for him supreme happiness. Now Sanu, the Novice became very learned, a teacher of doctrine, and practised in the jhana of love, being beloved by gods and men. And as we know from the Sanu-Sutta (Saṁyutta Nikaya, i. 208) his mother, in his previous birth, was a Yakkha. Now as time went on Sanu lost his intellectual discernment and grew distraught, and longed to go a-roaming. Then his previous mother perceived this, and warned his human mother saying: 'Your son has a fancy to roam, wherefore bid him rouse himself. Tell him what the Yakkhas say:

Do nought of evil, open or concealed,

If evil thou now doest or wilt do,

Thou'lt not escape from ill, e'en though thou flee.

Thus saying, the Yakkha-mother disappeared. But when the human mother heard, she was overwhelmed with grief. Then Sanu the novice, taking his robe and bowl, set out early and came to his mother. At sight of her sorrow he said: 'Mother, why do you weep?' When she told him why, he said this verse:

Mother, they weep for the dead, or the living they may not see.

But for him, O mother, who lives, who is here, why mournest thou me?

His mother answered him from the Suttas, "This is death, O bhikkhus, that one should reject the training and turn again to lower things,' and with this verse:

They mourn for son who lieth dead, or him

Who is alive but whom they no more see.

And him they mourn, who though he did renounce

The world, my son, doth hither come again,

For though he live again, yet is he dead.

Drawn forth from burning embers, O my dear,

Dost thou on embers wish to fall again?

When he heard her, anguish seized on Sanu the Novice, and making firm his insight, he soon won arahantship. And thereupon thinking, 'My victory is due to that verse,' he repeated it as his psalm.

XLV Ramaniyaviharin

Reborn in this Buddha-age at Rajagaha, as the son of a leading citizen, he lived in youthful wantonness. One day he saw the king's officers arresting an adulterer, and growing agitated, he listened to the Master teaching, and left the world. As a bhikkhu, but still susceptible to fleshly lusts, he made himself a well-garnished chamber, well furnished as to food and drink, seat and couch; and so he ever dwelt. For this reason he was known as Ramaniya-viharin (Pleasant-lodge Brother). But his previous indulgence making the recluse's life too hard for him, he felt unworthy to accept the offerings of the faithful and said: 'I will roam.' On his way he sat down beneath a tree. And as carts were passing by on the road, one ox being weary stumbled at a rough place and fell. The carter loosened its yoke, gave it hay and water and so allayed its fatigue; then he harnessed it again and they went on. And the Thera thought: 'Even as this ox having stumbled has arisen and draws his own load, so doth it behove me, who once have stumbled in the forest of vice, to arise and carry out the duty of a recluse.' And thoughtfully turning back, he told what he had done and seen to Thera Upali, was by him absolved from his fault, and helped back into right ways. And not long after he attained arahantship. Thereafter enjoying the bliss of freedom, he set forth his lapse and return in this verse:

E'en though he trip and fall, the mettled brute

Of noble breed will steadfast stand once more.

So look on me as one who having learned

Of Him, the All-Enlightened One, have gained

True insight, am become of noble breed,

And of the Very Buddha very child.


XLVI Samiddhi

He was reborn in this Buddha-age at Rajagaha, in a clansman's family. From the time he was born the wealth of his family increased, and he himself, handsome and virtuous, became known as Samiddhi (Prospero). He saw the power of the Buddha when the latter was met by Bimbisara, won faith in him, and left the world, abiding devoted to meditation. When the Exalted One was staying at the Tapoda Park, Samiddhi one day was musing in exquisite joy on his good fortune as a bhikkhu. Then Mara the Evil One, unable to bear it, made a fearful noise near him, as if the very earth were splitting. The Thera told this to the Exalted One. The latter bade him persist where he was and think no more about it. He obeyed, and soon after won arahantship. Mara, unaware of it, once more created a fearful noise. But the Thera felt no fear: 'Undaunted by all such Maras, not once have I turned a hair!' And confessing anna, he uttered this verse:

In trust and hope forth from my home I came

Into the homeless life. And there in me

Have mindfulness and insight grown, and tense

And well composed my heart and mind. Make thou

Whatever shams thou list, thou'lt harm me not.

And Mara, thus rebuked, said, 'The recluse knows me,' and vanished from that place.


## XLVII Ujjaya

He was reborn in this Buddha-age at Rajagaha, as the son of a brahmin graduate. Grown up and proficient in the Three Vedas, he saw no kernel in them, and being urged by maturity of conditions, he went to the Bamboo Grove, and when he had heard the Master preach, he left the world. Meditating in the forest on ethical conduct, he was not long in winning arahantship. Thereupon he approached the Master, saluted him, seated himself on one side and, by praising the Exalted One, confessed anna in this verse:

Buddha the Wake, the Hero hail! all hail! Thou who from every bond art wholly free!

Strong in the lore I learnt of thee, I live From fourfold venom cleansed, sane, immune.


## XLVIII Sanjaya

He was reborn in this Buddha-age, at Rajagaha, as the son of a wealthy brahmin. Grown up, he followed the example of Brahmayu, Pokkharasati and other well-known brahmins, who found faith in the Master and reached the First Path. Later he entered the Order and acquired the  six abhinnas. Then, confessing anna, he uttered this verse:

Since I went forth from home to homeless life,

Ne'er have I harboured conscious wish or plan

Un-Ariyan, or linked with enmity.


## XLIX Ramaneyyaka

Reborn in this Buddha-age at Savatthi in a wealthy family, his heart was moved when the Jeta Grove was presented, and he left the world. Dwelling in the forest he meditated on ethical conduct, and, because of his attainments and charm, he became called Ramaneyyaka (Gratus, Gratulus).

Now one day Mara the Evil One, wishing to disturb him, made a fearful noise. The Thera, hearing it, was with his habitual courage unafraid, and knew it was Mara. And to show his contempt he uttered this verse:

Not all the clitter-clatter of your noise,

No more than chirp and squeal of forest sounds, Avail to make pulse throb or mind distraught,

For one the aim to which my heart is given.

This verse became the Thera's confession of anna.


L

Vimala

He was reborn in this Buddha-age at Rajagaha, of a wealthy family, and (because of a wish he had uttered over a pious act when Kassapa was Buddha) his body was as pure as a dewdrop on a lotus-leaf, or as that of the Bodhisat in his last birth. Wherefore he was named Vimala (Immaculatus). When grown up he was filled with faith on seeing the Buddha at Rajagaha, and leaving the world, took a form of study and went to dwell in a mountain cave in Kosala.

Now one day a vast storm-cloud spread over the firmament and the rain fell, allaying heat and feverishness, so that the Thera was able to concentrate till he had won arahantship. Thereupon rejoicing over his accomplished task, he broke forth in this psalm:

The burdened earth is sprinkled by the rain,

The winds blow cool, the lightnings roam on high.

Eased and allayed th' obsessions of the mind,

And in my heart the spirit's mastery.

This verse was the Thera's confession of anna.

# CANTO I. PSALMS OF SINGLE VERSES
## PART VI

LI-LIV Godhika, Subahu, Valliya, Uttiya

In the time of our Buddha, these four, companions in a former birth when Kassapa Buddha was on earth, were reborn at Pava as the sons of four Malla rajas, and there  was whole-hearted friendship between them. They went on some embassy to the King at Kapilavatthu. At that time the Master too had gone thither, and was staying in the Banyan Park, where he convinced the Sakiyan rajas by his twin-miracle Then the four saw the same and believed. They entered the Order, and not long after attained arahantship with thorough mastery of the letter and spirit of the Norm. Now after they had received much honour and support from the King and his ministers, they dwelt in the forest. Then King Bimbisara, when they went to Rajagaha, called on them and invited them to spend the rains, building for each of them a chalet, but carelessly omitting to have the huts roofed. So the Theras dwelt in those huts unsheltered. But at the time of the rains, the god rained not. And the king, wondering thereat, remembered his neglect, and had the chalets thatched with plaster and painted, and held an opening festival, besides giving gifts to the Order. The Theras did the King the favour of entering, and forthwith attained to the suffusion of universal love. Then from the north and the east arose a great storm-cloud, and just as the Theras emerged from their ecstasy, the rain fell. Then Godhika, aroused by the thunder of the storm, uttered this verse:

God rains as 'twere a melody most sweet.

Snug is my little hut, sheltered, well-roofed.

The heart of me is steadfast and at peace.

Now an it pleaseth thee to rain, god, rain !

And Subahu:

God rains as 'twere a melody most sweet.

Snug is my little hut, sheltered, well-roofed,

Well hath my mind the body's nature grasped. Now an it pleaseth thee to rain, god, rain!

And Valliya:

God rains as 'twere a melody most sweet.

Snug is my little hut, sheltered, well-roofed.

Herein earnest and strenuous I dwell.

Now an it pleaseth thee to rain, god, rain!

And Uttiya:

God rains as 'twere a melody most sweet.

Snug is my little hut, sheltered, well-roofed.

Herein I dwell unmated and alone. Now an it pleaseth thee to rain, god, rain!


LV Anjana-vaniya

He was reborn in this Buddha-age at Vesali, of the family of a raja of the Vajjians.
When he was grown up, a threefold panic had arisen in the Vajjian territory—to
wit, the fear of drought, of sickness, and of non-human foes. This is all told in
the Commentary on the Ratana-Sutta. When the Exalted One quieted the panic at
Vesali, and a great concourse heard him preach, this raja's son heard him also, and
winning faith, left the world.

When he had fulfilled the preliminary training, he dwelt in the Anjana Wood at
Saketa. And when the rains drew near, he procured a worn castaway couch, and
placing it on four stones and enclosing it above and around with grasses, he set
up a door to it, and so got a sheltered retreat for the rainy season. After only one
month his strenuous study won for him arahantship. Thereafter, feeling the bliss
of emancipation, he roused himself, and contemplating his victory with rapture
uttered this verse:

Deep in the leafy glades of Anjana

My couch into a little hut I made.

The threefold wisdom have I made my own,

And all the Buddha's ordinance is done.


LVI Kutiviharin

His story (in this life) is like that of Anjana-vaniya, with this difference: while
striving for insight he was walking by the fields, and took shelter from the rain in
the little empty hut of the field-watchman, and there won arahantship. Thereupon
the watchman came and said: 'Who is in the hut?' The answer was: 'A bhikkhu is
in the hut,' and the rest of the verse:

Who's in my little hut? A brother 'tis,

Who in thy little hut, all passions tamed,

Hath throughly set his mind. Know this, O friend,

'Twas not for naught thou mad'st thy little hut!

Then the watchman said: 'Luck indeed for me, good luck indeed is mine, that your honour should have come into my little hut and be sitting there!'

And the Exalted One heard their converse by his celestial hearing, and discerned the watchman's pleasure. And he addressed these verses to him:

Within the hut a brother dwells, peace in his heart, purged of all taint.

 Fruit of this deed shall be to thee: lord of the gods thou'll come to be

 Six times, ay, seven, lord of the gods, ruler over celestial realms,

 Thereafter all thy passions tamed, a Silent Buddha thou shalt be.

From that time the Thera began to be called Kutiviharin.


LVII Kutiviharin (2)

His story resembles that of the Anjana Wood Thera, with this difference: When he had left the world under similar circumstances, he pursued his religious studies in a very old hut. And he thought: 'This old hut is now rotten; I ought to make another.' So he turned his mind to new action. Then a spirit, seeking salvation, sought to agitate him by uttering this verse, simple in words but profound in meaning:

 This was an ancient hut, say'st thou? To build

 Auother hut, a new one, is thy wish?

 O cast away the longing for a hut!

 New hut will bring new pain, brother, to thee.

When he heard these words, the Thera grew anxious, and with effort and endeavour establishing insight, soon won arahantship. Thereupon he repeated the verse as that which had spurred him on to victory, and as the confession of his anna. Because he had attained while in the hut, he, too, became known as Kutiviharin.


LVIII Ramaniyakutika

His story resembles that of the Anjana-Woodlander, with this difference: he dwelt in a hut beside a hamlet in the Vajjian territory. It was a pretty pleasing little chalet, with floor and walls well prepared, surrounded by park and tank, and with its enclosure of smooth pearly sand. And the Thera's excellent virtues enhanced its attractiveness. He there won arahantship, and there continued to dwell. Now when people came to see the vihara (settlement), they could see the hut. One day a few fast women came by, and seeing the attractiveness of the hut said:

'The recluse living there might be a youth we could fascinate.' So they accosted him, saying: 'Delightful, sir, is your dwelling-place. We too are delightful to see, just in the prime of our youth,' and they began to show off their raiment and so forth. But the Thera set forth his passionless state in this verse:

Delightful is my little hut, the gift

Most fair of faithful, pious folk.

What need of maidens then have I? Nay, go

Thither to them, ye women, who have need of you.

By this 'not needing' saying, the declaration of the Thera's arahantship is implied.


## LIX Kosalaviharin

His story resembles that of the Anjana-Woodlander, with this difference: after his novitiate, he dwelt in the forest by a village in the kingdom of Kosala, near the dwelling of a lay adherent. The latter, seeing him camped under a  tree, made a little hut and gave it him. There the Thera attained arahantship. Then filled with rapture at his emancipation, he uttered this psalm:

Strong in my faith I left the world. Now here

Within the woods a hut is made for me;

And I with zeal and ardour meditate,

With watchful wit and clarity of mind.

This was his confession of anna, and because he dwelt so long in Kosala, he became known as the Kosala settler.


## LX Sivali

He was reborn in this Buddha-age as the son of Suppavasa, the king's daughter. When his mother was not able to bring forth and lay seven days in great suffering, she said to her husband: 'Before I die I will give a gift.' And she sent him to the Master, saying: 'Go tell of my state to the Master, and invite him; and what he says, mark well and come and tell it me.' He did her bidding, and the Master said: 'May Suppavasa, daughter of the Koliyas, be happy. May she, happy and healthy, give birth to a healthy child.' The raja heard, saluted the Exalted One and set out for the village. Even before he came, Suppavasa was delivered of a son. The persons  who had surrounded her with tearful faces went forth delighted to tell the raja. He saw them coming and thought: 'That which He of the Ten Powers told me has been fulfilled.' And he went to the princess and told her what the Master had pronounced. Then she bade him show hospitality to the Buddha and the Order for seven days. And saying, 'The child is born, bringing gladness of heart to all our kin,' they named him Sivali (Auspicious).

By the seventh day from his birth he was able to do anything. Sariputta, General of the Norm, conversed with him on that day, and said: 'Does it not behove one who has overcome such suffering as you have done to leave the world?' 'Sir,' babbled the infant, 'I would leave the world.' Suppavasa saw them talking, and asked the Thera what he had said. 'We spoke of the long suffering he has overcome. With your leave I will ordain him.' She replied: 'It is well, sir; ordain him.' And Sariputta, ordaining him, said: 'Sivali, you want no other exhortation than the cause of the long suffering you have overcome. Think on that.' 'Sir,' replied the child, 'yours was the burden of ordaining me; but I will find out what I am capable of doing.' At the moment when the first lock of his hair was cut off, he was established in the fruition of the First Path, when the second was cut, in that of the Second Path, and so for the third and fourth. ...

Other teachers say that after Sariputta had ordained him, he went the same day, and taking up his abode in a secluded hut, meditated on his woefully delayed birth, and so, his knowledge attaining maturity, descended into the avenue of insight, casting out all the intoxicants (of the mind) and thus attaining arahantship. Thereupon experiencing the bliss of emancipation, he in emotional rapture uttered this psalm:

Now have they prospered, all my highest aims,

To compass which I sought this still retreat.

The holy lore and liberty, my quest,

All lurking vain conceits I cast away.


LXI Vappa

He was reborn in this Buddha-age at Kapilavatthu, as the son of a brahmin Vasettha. Now when Asita the seer had declared that the young noble Siddhattha would become omniscient, Vappa with four other sons of brahmins, Kondanna at their head, became recluses. When Asita's prophecy had been fulfilled, Vappa heard the Buddha preach and thought: 'I will win salvation.' He was present during the six years when the Great Being made his ascetic struggles; thereupon disgusted when the latter again took solid food, he went to Isipatana, and there met the Master then starting the Wheel of the Norm a-rolling and was converted. On the fifth day he and his four mates won arahantship. Thereupon reflecting on the might of the Master and the blindness of the world, and how the Ariyan state bestowed vision, he said this verse:

He who doth see can see another seer,

Him too who hath no eyes wherewith to see,

He who himself sees not, can ne'er discern

Either the eye that sees not, or the seer.


## LXII Vajji-putta

He was born in this Buddha-age at Vesali, in the family of a councillor, and was named Vajji-son. He saw the majesty of the Exalted One when the latter came to Vesali, believed, entered the Order, and after his novitiate dwelt in a wood near Vesali. Now a festival took place at Vesali, and there was dancing, singing and reciting, all the people happily enjoying the festival. And the sound thereof distracted the bhikkhu, so that he quitted his solitude, gave up his exercise, and showed forth his disgust in this verse:

Each by himself we in the forest dwell,

Like logs rejected by the woodman's craft.

So flit the days one like another by,

Who more unlucky in their lot than we?

Now a woodland sprite heard him, and had compassion on the bhikkhu, and thus upbraided him, 'Even though you, bhikkhu, speak scornfully of forest life, the wise desiring solitude think much of it,' and to show him the advantage of it spoke this verse:

Each by himself we in the forest dwell,

Like logs rejected by the woodman's craft.

And many a one doth envy me my lot,

E'en as the hell-bound him who fares to heaven.

Then the bhikkhu, stirred like a thoroughbred horse by the spur, went down into the avenue of insight, and striving soon won arahantship. Thereupon he thought, 'The fairy's verse has been my goad!' and he recited it himself.


## LXIII Pakkha (The Cripple)

Reborn in this Buddha-age among the Sakiyans, in the township of Devadaha, in the family of a Sakiyan raja, he was named Young Sanmoda. But inasmuch as, when a boy, he suffered from rheumatism, and at times walked like a cripple, he grew to be called Pakkha (=cripple), and retained the name after his recovery. He was present when the Exalted One visited his kinsfolk, won faith in him, entered the Order, and dwelt in the forest. Going one day to the village for alms, he sat down beneath a tree. Then a kite, seizing some flesh, flew up into the sky. Him many kites attacked, making him drop the meat. Another kite grabbed the fallen flesh, and was plundered by another. And the bhikkhu thought: 'Just like that meat are worldly desires, common to all, full of pain and woe.' And reflecting hereon, and how they were impermanent and so on, he carried out his mission, sat down for his afternoon rest, and expanding insight won arahantship. Thereupon making the base of his emotion his goad, he confessed anna in this verse:

They fly at what is fall'n, and as it lies,

Swooping in greed they come again, again....

But what 'twas meet to do, that have I done,

And what is verily delectable,

Therein was my delight: thus happily

Has happiness been sought after and won.


LXIV Vimala-Kondanna

He was reborn in this Buddha-age as the son of Ambapali, his father being King Bimbisara. She named the child Vimala, but afterwards he was known as Vimala-Kondanna. He was convinced by the Buddha-majesty of the Exalted One at Vesali, left the world for the Order, and attained arahantship. He declared his anna in this verse:

By the bright Banner came I here to birth

In her called of the Tree. And by the  That smites the flag, is the great Flag o'er-thrown.


LXV Ukkhepakata-Vaccha

He was born in this Buddha-age at Savatthi, as the son of a brahmin of the Vaccha family. He heard the Master preach, entered the Order, and went to dwell at a village settlement in Kosala. Through the bhikkhus who came there from time to time he mastered the doctrine, although he did not know how to distinguish what was Vinaya, what Suttanta, and what Abhidhamma. This too, however, he learnt from questioning Sariputta, so that, whereas other bhikkhus were versed in Vinaya, or in some other part of doctrine, he had learnt the Pitakas by heart, even before the Council, when they were recited. And soon after attaining this proficiency, he won arahantship. Thereafter he became a teacher, and one day, addressing himself as another person, he uttered this verse:

That heaped wealth by Vaccha's toil thrown up By steady increment these many years,

That doth he to the laity declare,

Seated in honour, filled with splendid joy.


LXVI Meghiya

Reborn in this Buddha-age at Kapilavatthu, in the family of a Sakiyan raja, he was named Meghiya. When grown up, he entered the Order and ministered to the Exalted One while he was residing at Calika on the River Kimikala. And seeing a pleasant mango-wood he desired to dwell there. Twice the Exalted One refused, but at his third request, let him go. There, however, being consumed by evil thoughts as by flies, he got no concentration of mind, so he returned and told the Master. The latter said, 'When the heart, Meghiya, is not ripe for emancipation, five things conduce thereto,' and admonished him. Whereupon Meghiya attained arahantship, and announced his anna in this verse:

He, the great Hero, counselled me, whose mind

Hath all transcended that our minds may know.

And I, hearing the Norm, held close to Him

In loving pupillage and piety. The threefold wisdom have I made my own,

And all the Buddha's ordinance is done.


LXVII Ekadhamma Savaniya

He was reborn in this Buddha-age at Setavya, in the family of a councillor. When the Exalted One visited Setavya, and stayed in the Singsapa Wood, he went to listen to him, saluting, and sitting down at one side. The Master contemplated his inclinations, and taught him the Norm in the verse:

Impermanent indeed are all component things

And he, influenced by his past resolve (to leave the world when the Norm was revived), discerned the truth more plainly, left the world, and studying the notions of ill and of the absence of soul, acquired insight and won arahantship. And because, by one hearing of the Norm alone, his destiny was fulfilled, he acquired the name of Once-Norm-hearer (Ekadhammasavaniya). His anna he confessed in this verse:

Burnt up in me is all that doth defile,

And rooted out all life's continuance;

Slain utterly the cycle of re-birth:

Now is there no more coming back to be.


LXVIII Ekudaniya

He was reborn in this Buddha-age at Savatthi, as the son of a wealthy councillor. Come to years of discretion, he was convinced by the majesty of the Buddha, at the presentation of the Jeta Grove, and left the world. Fulfilling his novitiate, and dwelling in the forest, he came to the Master to learn. And at that time the Master, seeing  Sariputta rapt in contemplation near him, broke forth into this psalm:

He who doth dwell on highest plane of thought, etc.

And the brother hearing him, even when once more far away, and for a long time in the forest, kept repeating the psalm ever and anon, so that it became customary to call him 'Ekudaniya,' 'One-Psalm-er.'

Now one day he got unity and concentration of mind, and so, insight expanding, he won arahantship. And dwelling in the bliss of emancipation, he was once invited by the Treasurer of the Norm to be tested in exposition, with the words: 'Friend, expound the doctrine to me.' And from long dwelling in mind over that verse, he uttered it then again:

He who doth dwell on highest plane of thought,

With zeal unfaltering, Sage, Arahant,

In wisdom's branches trained:— such as he is,

No sorrows may beset him, who with mind

Calm and serene and clear abideth aye.

This became the confession of his anna.


LXIX Channa

Reborn when our Exalted One was alive in the house of King Suddhodana, of a slave, he was called Channa. A contemporary of the future Buddha, he found faith in the Master when the latter returned to meet his kinsfolk. He thereupon entered the Order. Out of his affection for Him, egoistic pride in 'our Buddha, our Doctrine' arose, and he could not conquer this fondness, nor perform his duty as novice. When the Master had passed away, and his injunction that the higher penalty be imposed on Channa was carried out, the latter suffered anguish, extirpated his fondness, and soon after attained arahantship. Thereafter, blissful in his emancipation, he expressed his rapture in this psalm:

I heard the Truth which that Great One had taught,

And felt its mighty virtues, known by Him

Who all things with supernal insight knew. The Path for winning things ambrosial

I found. Past-master He in sooth to guide

Into the way of blest security.


LXX Punna

Reborn in this Buddha age in the Sunaparanta country, at the port of Supparaka, in the family of a burgess, he was named Punna. Arrived at years of discretion, he went with a great caravan of merchandise to Savatthi, when the Exalted One happened to be there. And he went to hear the Master at the Vihara with the local lay-followers. There he believed, and left the world. And for a time he won favour among the teachers and preceptors by his skill in dialectic. Then one day he went to the Master, and asked for a lesson, so that he, hearing propositions pairwise, might therewith go to dwell in Sunaparanta. To him the Exalted One uttered a 'Lion's Roar' of a lesson, to wit: 'Now there are objects, Punna, cognizable by the eye, etc.' So Punna departed, and studying concentration and insight, acquired the three forms of higher cognition.

When he won arahantship he won over many people to the faith, even 500 lay-brethren and as many lay-sisters.

And as he lay near final death he confessed anna in this verse:

Only virtue here is highest; but the wise man is supreme.

He who wisdom hath and virtue,

He 'mong men and gods is victor.

# CANTO I. PSALMS OF SINGLE VERSES
## PART VIII

LXXI Vacchapala

He was born in this Buddha-age at Rajagaha, as the son of a rich brahmin, and was named Vacchapala (calf-herd). He saw when the Master met Bimbisara, the selfsubmission of Uruvela-Kassapa to the Exalted One, and believing, entered the Order. In a week he had so developed insight as to have acquired sixfold abhinna.

As arahant he extolled in sheer happiness his attainment of Nibbana in this verse:

Is there a man who can the truth discern

Tho' it be very subtle and refined,

Who, skilled to measure spiritual growth,

Is yet of lowly and of gentle mind,

Who shapes his life by rule of Them that Wake: For him Nibbana is not hard to find.

And this was the Brother's confession of anna.


LXXII Atuma

Now he was reborn in this Buddha-age at Savatthi, as the son of a councillor, and was named Atuma. When he was adolescent his mother proposed to find him a wife, and consulted with kinsfolk. But he, being impelled by the fullness of conditions, said: 'What have I to do with house-ways? Now will I leave the world.' But though he went to the Brethren and was ordained, yet did his mother seek to corrupt his pious wish. Then he declared his inclination in this verse:

As the new bamboo-stem, even when grown

To its full knotted height, can scarce emerge,

So I by all this bringing home of brides—

Give me your leave! Gone forth e'en now am I.

And even as he stood speaking to his mother, insight grew in him, and casting off the defilements, he became an arahant.

## LXXIII Manava

He was reborn in this Buddha-age at Savatthi, in the house of a brahmin grandee. For seven years he was reared within the precincts of home, and when at seven years old he was taken out on the estate, he saw an aged person, a diseased person, and a corpse for the first time. When he was told about these things, he was filled with dread, went to the Vihara, heard the doctrine, and gained his parents' consent to enter the Order. Thereupon he won insight and arahantship.

Him thus having arrived thereat the Brethren asked:

'How is it you were stirred to come forth at so tender an age?' He thereupon, confessing anna, signalized his going forth in this verse:

I saw an aged one, and one afflicted with disease,

And then I saw one dead, with all his span of life consumed.

Thence I forth going left the world to live the other life,

And from me put away the enticing sweets of sense-desire.

Now, because he left the world while so young, the Thera was always called Boy (Manava).


## LXXIV Suyamana

Reborn in this Buddha-age at Sali, as the son of a certain brahmin, he grew up expert in the Three Vedas. Feeling repelled by domestic life, and inclined to jhana, he met the Exalted One at Sali, believed, was ordained, and attained arahantship as soon as his head was shaved.

Thereupon he signalized his putting away the hindrances, and confessed anna in this verse:

With sensuous desires, with enmity,

With sloth of mind and torpor of the flesh

A brother hath no truck, and in his heart

Turmoil of any kind and doubt are dead.


## LXXV Susarada

He was reborn in this Buddha-age at Sariputta's native place, in a brahmin's family, and was called Susarada (Dullard), because he was slow in growing. He was converted by the teaching of that Thera and in due time, as a bhikkhu, became an arahant, and confessed his anna in this verse:

O goodly is the sight of cultured minds! Doubt is cut off, and wisdom grows apace.

E'en of a fool they make an able man;

Hence goodly is the intercourse with saints.


## LXXVI Piyanjaha

He was reborn in this Buddha-age at Vesali, in the family of a Licchavi noble (raja). When grown up he was ever mad for war and an unconquered fighter, ever sacrificing what was near and dear, so that he became known as Piyanjaha—Love-renouncing. But when the Master came to Vesali, Piyanjaha found faith in him, entered the Order, dwelt in the forest, developed insight and won arahantship. As arahant he thought, 'How different is worldly success from Ariyan success!' and by this insight confessing anna, he uttered this verse:

Where men are arrogant, see thou lie low. Where they are low in mind, lift up the heart.

Dwell thou where other folk care not to dwell,

Wherein men find delight, take thou no joy.


## LXXVII Hattharoha-Putta

(Elephant-rider's Son.)

Reborn in this Buddha-age at Savatthi, in the family of an elephant-driver, as he grew up, he became proficient in managing elephants. One day, as he was training an elephant by the river, he was impelled by maturing conditions to think: 'What is all this elephant-taming to me? Better is it to tame one's self.' So he went to the Exalted One, heard the Norm, believed, entered the Order, and exercised himself in insight on a basis of ethical meditation. And as a skilful elephant-trainer restrains savage ways by his hook, so he by meditation suffered not his thoughts to wander away from his exercise, saying this verse:

Once roamed this heart a field, a wanderer

Wherever will, or whim, or pleasure led.

To-day that heart I'll hold in thorough check,

As trainer's hook the savage elephant.

And so acting, his insight expanded, and he realized arahantship.

## LXXVIII Mendasira

He was reborn in this Buddha-age at Saketa, in the family of a burgess. Because his head resembled that of a ram, he acquired the nickname of Menḍasira (= ram's head). While the Exalted One was staying at Saketa in the Anjana Wood, Menḍasira came to believe in him, entered the Order, and practising calm and insight,  acquired sixfold abhinna. He could thus recall former births, and concerning these he uttered this verse:

Full many a round of rebirth have I run

Nor found a clue. Lo! now from me who sore

Have suffered is the load of ill withdrawn.

And this was his confession of anna.


## LXXIX Rakkhita

Reborn in this Buddha-age in the township of Devadaha, in the family of a Sakiyan noble (raja), he was named Rakkhita (Guarded). He was one of those five hundred young nobles who, as having renounced the world, were given by the Sakiyan and Koliyan rajas as escort to the Exalted One. The latter had converted these youths by the lesson of the Kunala-jataka—a lesson against the danger of sensuality. And connecting this lesson with his exercises, he developed insight and attained arahantship. Thereafter, reflecting on his own renunciation of the corruptions, he uttered his verse confessing anna:

All passion have I put away, and all

ill will for ever have I rooted out;

Illusion utterly has passed from me;

Cool am I now. Gone out all fire within.


## LXXX Ugga

Reborn in this Buddha-age in Kosala, at the town of Ugga, as the son of a councillor, he was named Ugga. When he had attained to years of discretion, he went to hear the Master, who had come to that town, found faith in him, entered the Order and finally won arahantship. He thereupon set forth his severance of the round of rebirth, confessing anna in this verse:

All action wrought by me and bringing birth,

Whether 'twas of great potency or small,

Shattered and ended is it utterly.

Now is there no more coming back to be.


LXXXI Samitigutta

Reborn in this Buddha-age at Savatthi, as the son of a brahmin, he was named Samitigutta. Hearing the Master preach, he entered the Order and attained entire purity of conduct. As the consequence of his action in a former life, he was attacked by leprosy and his limbs crumbled off piece by piece. He dwelt in the infirmary. And one day the General of the Norm went on his round of inquiry, asking after this and that sick bhikkhu. Seeing Samitigutta, he gave him an exercise on the contemplation  of feeling, saying 'My friend, in so far as there is what we call process of the five constituents, the whole of suffering is a matter of feeling. But if just the constituents be absent, suffering is absent.' So saying, he went on; but the patient, set up by the lesson, developed insight and realized sixfold abhinna. Thereupon he remembered the evil action in former births for which he was now overcome by disease. And extolling the fact that all was now done with, he uttered this verse:

Whatso of evil wrought in bygone days,

In former births by me, just here and now,

'Tis that whereby I lie and suffer sore—

But other ground for ill exists no more!


LXXXII Kassapa

Reborn in this Buddha-age at Savatthi, as the son of a brahmin of north-western origin, he was named Kassapa. His father died while he was a child, and his mother brought him up. When one day he heard the Exalted One preach at the Jeta Grove, he was then and there impelled by maturing conditions to enter the First Path. And going to his mother, he asked her permission for his ordination.

Now when the Master had ended the rainy season with the Parivara festival and was starting on his country tour, Kassapa was anxious to go with him. And first he went to take leave of his mother. She let him go with this admonition:

To any place where alms are easy got,

Where'er 'tis safe and free from peril, there

Go thou, my boy; vex not thy life with care.

Then the Thera thought: 'My mother wants me to go where I shall be free from care. Come then, for me 'tis right to win a place entirely and absolutely free from care.' And, striving, he set up insight and soon won arahantship. Thereupon, inasmuch as his mother's words had been his spur in winning it, he repeated that very verse.

## LXXXIII Siha

Reborn in this Buddha-age in the country of the Mallas, in the family of a raja, he was named Siha (Leo). Seeing the Exalted One, he was attracted by him, saluted him and sat down at one side. The Master discerned the trend of his mind and taught him the Norm, so that he believed, entered the Order, and, taking his exercise, dwelt in the forest. His thoughts were distracted by many objects and he could not concentrate. The Master saw this and, standing over him, uttered this verse:

O Siha! persevere in earnestness;

By night and day abide unfaltering.

Engender the good Norm within thy heart.

Swiftly renounce that piled up base of birth.

Hereby the Thera was able to expand insight and win arahantship. And, confessing anna, he repeated the verse.

## LXXXIV Nita

Reborn in this Buddha-age at Savatthi as the son of a brahmin, he was called Nita. When grown up he thought: 'These Sakiyan recluses are very lucky in that they are well provided with all necessaries. It is a happy life, that of a member of the Order.' So he entered it to get pleasure from it, paid scant attention to his exercise, ate his fill, spent the day in idle talk, and slept all night long. But the Master discerned the ripeness of his antecedents, and gave him this verse in admonition:

Thou all the night to slumber given o'er,

Who lov'st the day 'mid chattering crowds to spend:—

Dost deem that thou this way at any time,

Poor silly fool, of ill shalt make an end?

Agitated by the Master's words, he settled to develop insight, and not long after attained arahantship. He then confessed anna in repeating this verse.

LXXXV Sunaga

He was reborn in this Buddha-age in the village of Nalaka as the son of a brahmin, and was a friend of Sariputta before the latter left the world. Hearing the General of the Norm preach, he too left the world, being established on the plane of insight. Anon he won arahantship. Thereupon, in course of teaching the bhikkhus, he confessed anna in this verse:

Expert to grasp the image conjured up, Versed in the secret of the life detached,

Practised in contemplation, clear in mind:—

Well may he win to rapture unalloyed.


LXXXVI Nagita

He was reborn in this Buddha-age at Kapilavatthu, in the family of a Sakiyan raja, and named Nagita. When the Exalted One was staying in that place, he preached the Lump of Sweetness discourse. Thereby Nagita was induced to enter the Order, whereupon he attained arahantship. Then, thrilled with rapture over the truth of the Master's teaching and the effective guidance of the Norm, he burst out in this psalm:

Outside our Order many others be, who teach

A path never, like this one, to Nibbana leading.

But us the Exalted One, the blessed Master's self

Instructs as 'twere by just the palm o' th' hand outspreading.


LXXXVII Pavittha

Reborn in this Buddha-age in the kingdom of Magadha, in a brahmin's family, and being naturally inclined to the life of a recluse, he became a Wanderer. His training ended, he wandered forth, and heard of Upatissa and Kolita (= Sariputta and Moggallana) joining the Buddha's Order. And he thought: 'That methinks must be a  better Order since such great sages enter it.' And he went and heard the Master, believed, and was ordained. Soon after he realized arahantship, and thus confessed anna:

The factors of the self are throughly seen;

All bases of new being broken down.

Slain utterly the cycle of rebirth.

Now is there no more coming back to be.


## LXXXVIII Ajjuna

He was reborn in this Buddha-age at Savatthi, in the family of a councillor, and named Ajjuna. When grown up he came into contact with the Jains, and entered their Order very young, thinking among them to win salvation. But finding there nothing to satisfy him, he met the Master, believed, entered his Order, and anon won arahant-ship. Then in rapture at his attainment, he burst forth in this verse:

O wonder that I found the power to draw

Myself forth from the waters on dry land.

Borne drifting on the awful flood I learnt

To know the Truths, their truth to understand.


## LXXXIX Devasabha

Reborn in this Buddha-age as the son of the raja of a district, he succeeded to his title when quite young. But  when being awakened (buddho) he went to hear the Master teach, he resigned his title, entered the Order, and anon won arahantship. Then joy arose in him when he reflected on the corrupting things he had put away, and he burst forth in this psalm:

Transcended is the miry bog of lusts.

Past doom infernal am I safely come

From flood and fetter dire to liberty,

And shed is every form of self conceit.


## XC Samidatta

Reborn in this Buddha-age at Rajagaha as the son of a brahmin, he was called Samidatta. When arrived at years of discretion, he heard of the Buddha's puissance, and went with laymen to the Vihara to hear him. He believed and entered the Order, but from the immaturity of his knowledge he continued for a little while without application. Finally, on again hearing the Master teach, he became devoted and intent, and won arahantship.

Later on the bhikkhus asked him: 'How now, friend, have you reached the state of the elect?' And he, showing the guiding efficacy of the doctrine, and his own attainment in the Norm and minor doctrines (dhammanudhamma), confessed anna in this verse:

The factors of my life well understood

Stand yet a little while with severed root.

Slain is the round of living aye renewed.

Now is there no more coming back to be.

# CANTO I. PSALMS OF SINGLE VERSES
# PART X

XCI Paripunnaka

He was reborn in this Buddha-age at Kapilavatthu, in the family of a Sakiyan raja. And because of the completeness of his gifts and fortune he became known as Paripunnaka. His means allowed him to enjoy at all times food of a hundred essences. But he, hearing that the Master partook of mixed scraps, said: 'Though he be delicately bred, the Exalted One lives thus, contemplating the bliss of Nibbana. Why should we in our greed become epicures? Let us, too, seek for that bliss of Nibbana!' Thus agitated he renounced his home, entered the Order, and, taking his exercise of meditation on the body from the Exalted One, he in due course attained arahantship. Thereupon he burst forth into this psalm:

Never as 't were some dish of hundred essences.

Could I o'errate what I partook to-day,

When He, the all-seeing Gotama, the Buddha blest,

Himself revealed to me the holy Norm.


XCII Vijaya

He was reborn in this Buddha-age at Savatthi, in a brahmin's family, and named Vijaya. When he had learnt the brahmin wisdom, he left the world as an ascetic, and dwelt in the forest practising jhana. Then he heard of the Buddha's mission and was glad, and went to salute and hear him. Thereupon he entered the Order and soon won arahantship, confessing anna in this verse:

In whom the intoxicants are dried up;

Whose happiness dependeth not on food;

Whose range is in the Void and the Unmarked

And Liberty:— as flight of birds in air

So hard is it to track the trail of him.


XCIII Eraka

He was reborn in this Buddha-age at Savatthi, as the son of an eminent person, and was named Eraka. He had beauty and charm, so that in all that he had to do he was in the most highly favoured position for doing it. His parents wedded him to a maiden suitable for beauty, virtue, years, and accomplishments. But anon, because it was his final life, he grew agitated at continued being, and sought the Master. After hearing him teach the Norm, Eraka left the world. And the Master gave him an exercise, but for some days he remained mastered by evil thoughts. Then the Master, knowing the course of his thoughts, admonished him in a verse. And he, on hearing it, thought: 'Unfitly have I acted; I, fool, that I should have continued full of bad thoughts when learning from such a Master.' And in distress he devoted himself to gaining insight, and soon won arahantship. Thereupon he confessed anna by repeating that verse:

Woeful are worldly wishes, Eraka!

No weal in worldly wishes, Eraka!

Whoso desireth joys of sense desireth ill.

Whoso desires not joys of sense desires no ill.


XCIV Mettaji

Reborn in this Buddha-age in the kingdom of Magadha as the son of a brahmin, he was named Mettaji. Grown up, he saw the evil of worldly desire, and became an ascetic dwelling in the forest. Hearing of the Buddha's advent, and impelled by antecedent causes, he sought the Master and asked him concerning his progress and regress. The answer given convinced him that he should enter the Order, whereupon he won arahantship. And in this verse he extolled the Master:

All glory to the Exalted One,

Our splendid Lord, the Sakiyas' son!

For he the topmost height hath won,

And well the Norm supreme hath shown.


XCV Cakkhupala

He was reborn in this Buddha-age at Savatthi, as the son of a landed proprietor named Maha-Suvanna, and received the name of Pala. He was also called Pala major, because his younger brother was called Pala minor. And the parents bound the sons in domestic bonds. But the Master came to the Jeta Grove, and there Pala major heard him, and leaving his brother to manage the property entered the Order. After five years of novitiate, he went with sixty bhikkhus to perfect his studies. And they chose a woodland spot near a border village, where the villagers were lay-followers, and he, dwelling in a leaf-hut, practised the duties of a recluse.

He was attacked by ophthalmia, and a doctor prescribed for him. But he did not follow the advice, and the disease grew worse. 'Better,' he thought, 'is the allaying of the moral torments (kilesa) than that of eye-disease.' Thus he neglected the latter and worked at his insight, so that eyes and torments perished at the same time. And he became a 'dry-visioned' arahant.

Now the village patrons asked the bhikkhus what had become of the Thera, and, hearing of his blindness, they  ministered to his wants full of compunction. Then those bhikkhus having also won arahantship, they proposed that they should return to Savatthi to salute the Master; but the Thera said: 'I am weak and blind, and the journey is not without risk. I should hinder you. Do ye go first and salute for me the Master and the great Theras, and tell Pala minor of my state that he may send a servant to me.' At length they consented to go, after taking leave of their patrons and providing him with a lodging. And they carried out his bidding, and Pala minor sent his nephew Palika. And the bhikkhus ordained Palika, because the road was not safe for a solitary layman. He went and announced himself to the Thera, and set out with him. Midway, near a village in the forest, a woodcutter's wife was singing. And the novice was smitten by the sound, and, bidding his uncle wait, went and dallied with her. The Thera thought: 'Now I heard a woman singing, and my novice stays long. Is he not evilly employed?' The youth returned, saying: 'Let us go, sir.' And the Thera said: 'What! hast thou been vile?' The novice at length confessed, and the Thera said: 'One so evil shall hold no staff for me. Get thee hence!' 'But the way is perilous, and you are blind. How will you go?' 'Fool! even if I lie down and die, yet will I get on, but not with such as thee.' Then he uttered this verse:

All blind am I and perished are mine eyes

And through the jungle's wilderness I fare.

E'en then I'll go, and were it lying down,

But not with child of evil as my mate.

Then the other, conscious of his evil action, weeping with outstretched arms, plunged into the forest. But the efficacy of the Thera's virtue made Sakka's throne hot, and the god, in the shape of a man journeying to Savatthi, took his staff and brought him that evening to Savatthi to the Jeta Grove. And Pala minor ministered to him all his days.


XCVI Khandasumana

Reborn in this Buddha-age at Pava in the family of a Malla raja, he was named Khaṇḍasumana (Jasmine), because on his birthday the jasmine was in bloom. He heard the Exalted One while the latter was staying in Cunda's mango grove at Pava, entered the Order, and acquired sixfold abhinna. Thereupon he remembered his own former births: how he had offered a plant of jasmine at the tope of Kassapa Buddha when all the plucked flowers went to form the king's own offering; and, discerning how this act had guided him to Nibbana now, he said this verse:

One flower in pious offering brought

Did win me years on years of pleasant life

In heavenly worlds; the balance hath availed

To bring me perfect peace and purity.


## XCVII Tissa

Reborn in this Buddha-age at the town of Roguva in a raja's family, at his father's death he succeeded to the title. As an absent ally of King Bimbisara, he sent him presents of jewels, pearls, and robes. The king sent him in return the life of the Buddha on a painted panel, and the Conditioned Genesis on a gold plate specially inscribed.

When he saw these, because he had resolved under former Buddhas and because it was his last birth, he pondered on going forward and turning back, setting the order of the doctrine in his heart and growing uneasy till he came to this conclusion: 'Now have I seen the likeness of the Exalted One, and have learnt the order of his doctrine at the same time. Full of ill are worldly desires. What have I to do with the life in houses?' And he abdicated, entered the Order, and, taking his earthen bowl and followed, as was Prince Pukkusati, by a lamenting populace, he left the town and went to Rajagaha. There he dwelt in the Sabbasoṇḍika Cave, and visited the Exalted One. And learning of him, he won arahantship. Thereupon alluding to his experiences, he uttered this psalm:

Renouncing costly vessels wrought in bronze,

In gold, I grasped this earthen bowl.

The second time was I anointed then.


## XCVIII Abhaya (2)

Reborn in this Buddha-age at Savatthi in a brahmin family, he was called Abhaya. After he had heard the Master teach and had entered the Order, he went one day for alms into the village and saw a woman attractively dressed. This disturbed his mental composure, so that he returned to the Vihara thinking: 'Looking on a visible object has corrupted me. I have done amiss.' Thus repudiating that consciousness, he so developed insight as to win arahantship.

Thereupon he reviewed his moral slip and his recovery in this verse:

Sight of fair shape bewildering self-control, If one but heed the image sweet and dear,

The heart inflamed in feeling doth o'erflow

And clinging stayeth. Thus in him do grow

The deadly taints that bring new living near.


XCIX Uttiya

Reborn in this Buddha-age at Kapilavatthu in the family of a Sakiyan raja, he was named Uttiya. Come to years of discretion, he witnessed the power of the Buddha when the latter came to visit his kin, believed in him, and entered the Order. As a student he visited the village one day for alms, and on the way he heard a woman singing, and his concentration gave way, desire and passion arising in him. Checking himself by the power of reflection, he entered the Vihara much agitated, and seating himself for siesta-meditation, he so developed insight that he won arahantship. Thereupon he mentioned his release from the ills of rebirth, through disgust at the corruptions, in this verse:

Sound of sweet voice bewildering self-control,

If one but think upon the image dear,

The heart inflamed in feeling doth o'erflow

And clinging stayeth. Thus in him do grow

The deadly taints that bring Saṁsara near.


C Devasabha (2)

Reborn in this Buddha-age at Kapilavatthu in the family of a Sakiyan raja, he was named Devasabha. When grown up he believed when he saw the Master appeasing the quarrel between Sakiyans and Koliyans, and was established in the Refuges. Again, he went when the Master was staying at the Banyan Park, this time entering the Order. He won arahantship, and dwelling on the bliss of his emancipation, he burst forth in rapture with this psalm:

Whoso supreme endeavour doth put forth,

 Whose range is in the fourfold heedfulness, He with fair flowers of Liberty enwreathed,

Sane and immune, will reach the perfect peace.

Thus the Thera confessed anna.

# CANTO I. PSALMS OF SINGLE VERSES
## PART XI

CI Belatthakani

Reborn in this Buddha-age at Savatthi in a brahmin's family, he was named Belatthakani. When after hearing the Master teach he had entered the Order, and was practising calm and insight in a forest of Kosala, he grew very slothful and was also rough of speech. Hence he did not evoke the right state of mind for his exercises. Now the Exalted One considered his maturing insight, and stirred his heart by this admonitory verse:

Though layman's life be left, yet if the task

Remain undone, the mouth harsh furrows plough,

The paunch be full, the mind all slack with sloth:—

Like a great hog with provender replete,

He cometh back, again, again to birth.

Then he, seeing the Master as if seated before him, was thrilled with agitation at his discourse, and establishing insight, was not long in winning arahantship. And through the divers expressions of the psalm, he declared his anna.


CII Setuccha

Reborn in this Buddha-age as the son of the raja of a district, he was unable to maintain his country's independence, and lost his throne. Wandering about the land unhappy, he saw and heard the Exalted One, entered the  Order, and won arahantship. And inveighing in his psalm against worldliness, he thus in divers ways confessed anna:

By vain conceits deluded, and their wits

Corrupted by the varied things of sense;

Flushed by their gains, by dearth thereof upset,

They fail to win the concentrated mind.


CIII Bandhura

Reborn in this Buddha-age at the town of Silavati as the son of a councillor, he was named Bandhura. And going one day on some business to Savatthi, he went with the laity to the Vihara, heard the Master, believed and entered the Order, and in due time won arahantship. Now to render service to his raja and so show his gratitude for his success, he went to Silavati and preached the Norm to the raja, declaring to him the Four Truths. The raja became a convert, built a great Vihara in the township, calling it Sudassana, and bestowed it on the Thera with many honours and offerings. The latter handed over everything to the Order, and going on his rounds as before, conceived the wish to go to Savatthi. The bhikkhus said: 'Sir, stay with us. If you lack in what you require, we will make it good.' He replied: 'I have no need, friends, of anything out of the way; I keep going on anything I get. I am content with the savour of the Norm,' and uttered this psalm:

Nay, 'tis not this I need, who live in bliss,

Regaled by sweetest nectar of the Norm.

Drinking those drops peerless, supreme, shall I

Forsooth my tongue with poison now acquaint?


## CIV Khitaka

Reborn in this Buddha-age at Savatthi in a brahmin's family, he heard, when grown up, of the great supernormal powers of Moggallana the Great. And he thought: 'I, too, will become so gifted.' And impelled by prior causes he entered the Order under the Exalted One, and by exercising himself in the training for calm and insight, acquired in due course sixfold abhinna. Then he, enjoying the various forms of supernormal movement, continued to bestow favour on beings by the wonder of those acts and by the wonder of training. When the bhikkhus asked him: 'Khitaka, friend, do you employ supernormal power?' he uttered this verse:

Buoyant in sooth my body, every pulse

Throbbing in wondrous bliss and ecstasy.

Even as cotton-down blown on the breeze,

So floats and hovers this my body light.


## CV Malitavambha

Reborn in this Buddha-age in the town of Kurukaccha as a brahmin's son, he was converted by the preaching of Pacchabhu, the great Thera, and entered the Order. Working at exercises for insight, he abode in any place where, of the four necessaries of life, only suitable food was hard to get; but where such food was easily got and the rest difficult to find, he went away. So continuing, because he had the antecedents, and was of the nature of the Great Men, he expanded insight, and in due course became an arahant. Thereupon, reflecting on his attainment, he broke forth in this verse:

Where I am straitened let me never dwell, Let me go thence, if life too pleasant prove.

Ne'er will the man with eyes to see abide

Where aught may hinder in the quest supreme.


## CVI Suhemanta

Reborn in this Buddha-age in the Border country as the son of a wealthy brahmin, he went to hear the Exalted One teach the Norm in the deer park at the town of Sankassa. Leaving the world he joined the Order, and became a reciter of the Three Pitakas, becoming in due course possessor of sixfold abhinna. Thereupon he thought: 'I have won all that a disciple may win. What if I were now to do a service to the brethren?' So he lectured to them and solved their difficulties. And one day he addressed them and other intelligent persons concerning himself in this verse:

A hundred tokens show, a hundred marks

Betray wherein the hidden meaning lies.

Whoso hath eyes to see but one, a dullard is,

Who can discern the hundred, he is wise.

Thus the Thera magnified before the Brethren his attainment of analytic knowledge that was so excellent.


## CVII Dhammasava

Reborn in the kingdom of Magadha in a brahmin's family, and impelled by maturity of conditions, he preferred the religious to the household life. Seeking the Exalted One on the South Hill, he heard him teach the Norm, whereupon he entered the Order, and in due course became an arahant. And reflecting with joy upon his career, he broke forth in this psalm, confessing anna:

I pondered well, then sought the life that lay

Beyond the walls and bonds of household life.

The Threefold Wisdom have I made my own,

And all the Buddha's ordinance is done.

CVIII Dhammasava's Father

He followed his son's example, saying: 'My son left the world when he was young; why should not I leave it?' So he, too, sought the Master, and in due course realized arahahtship and uttered his psalm:

A hundred years was I and eke a score,

When forth I went and knew my home no more.

The Threefold Wisdom have I made my own,

And all the Buddha's ordinance is done.


CIX Saṅgha-Rakkhita

Reborn in this Buddha-age in a wealthy family at Savatthi, he found faith, and entering the Order took an exercise, and joined another bhikkhu, both dwelling in the forest. Not far from where they abode, a doe in the thicket had  given birth to a fawn. Tending it, her love kept her from going far from it, and lacking grass and water close by she was famished. Seeing her the Thera said: 'Ah, surely this world bound in the bonds of craving suffers sore, unable to cut them!' And taking this feeling as a goad, he developed insight and won arahantship. Thereupon, discerning that his companion was cherishing many wrong thoughts, he admonished him through the parable of the doe, and uttered this verse:

Not yet doth he, though in retreat he dwell,

Con o'er the system by that Blest One (planned)

Who showed compassion for our highest good.

Still are his powers relaxed and uncontrolled,

Like woodland doe all tender grown and weak.

Now hearing these words that bhikkhu grew agitated, and expanding insight, in due course won arahantship.


CX Usabha

Reborn in this Buddha-age in a wealthy family, in the kingdom of Kosala, he found faith in the Master when the latter accepted the gift of the Jeta Grove. Finishing his novitiate, he dwelt in the forest at the foot of the mountain. Now at the time of the rains, the clouds had emptied themselves in the crests of the hills and trees; bushes and creepers became filled with dense foliage. Then the Thera, going forth one day from his cave, saw the loveliness of the woods and the mountains, and considered seriously: 'These trees and creepers are unconscious, yet by the season's fulfilment they have won growth. Why should not I who have attained a suitable season win growth by good qualities?' And he uttered this verse, which became his confession of anna, for he fortnwith strove and won arahantship:

The trees on high by towering cloud refreshed

With the new rain break forth in verdant growth.

To Usabha who for detachment longs,

And hath the forest sense of things, doth come

[From this responsive spring] abundant good.


CXI Jenta

He was reborn in this Buddha-age in the kingdom of Magadha at the village of Jenta, as the son of the raja of a district. While still young, his mind, impelled by maturity of conditions, inclined to leaving the world, and he turned the matter over and wondered what he should do. So doubting he heard the Master preach. From that day he became devoted to the religious life, and entered the Order. Happily working and with swift insight, he realized arahantship; then reflecting on his attainment and how he had been perplexed, he joyously uttered this verse:

Hard is the life without the world, and hard

In sooth to bear house life. Deep is the Norm;

Hard too is wealth to win. Thus difficult

The choice of one or other how to live.

Behoves me bear unceasingly in mind

[And see in everything] Impermanence.


CXII Vacchagotta

Reborn in this Buddha-age at Rajagaha as the son of a wealthy brahmin, and because there were four Theras named Vaccha, he was called Vacchagotta. Come to years of discretion, and expert in brahmin learning, he, as a seeker after emancipation, found no pith in those studies, and became a wandering recluse. As such he met and questioned the Master. Satisfied with the answers, he entered the Order, and in due course acquired sixfold abhinna. Reflecting with joy upon his career, he uttered this psalm:

The Threefold Lore is mine, and I excel

In Jhana-ecstasy, adept in calm

Of balanced mind. Salvation have I won,

And all the Buddha-ordinance is done.


## CXIII Vanavaccha (2)

Reborn in this Buddha-age as the son of a wealthy brahmin at Rajagaha and named Vaccha, he found faith when King Bimbisara conferred with the Master. And entering the Order he attained arahantship. As arahant he dwelt in the woods devoted to detachment; hence he came to be called Woodland Vaccha (Vanavaccha). Now it happened that the Thera, in order to do a kindness to his kinsfolk, went to Rajagaha, and dwelt there a little space, telling them of his mode of life. They begged him, saying: 'Sir, do us the kindness of dwelling in the near Vihara, and we will wait upon you.' The Thera showed them in this verse both his love of the mountains and the life of detachment:

Crags where clear waters lie, a rocky world,

Haunted by black-faced apes and timid deer,

Where 'neath bright blossoms run the silver streams:

Those are the highlands of my heart's delight.

This verse became the Thera's confession of anna.


## CXIV Adhimutta

Reborn in this Buddha-age in a brahmin family at Savatthi and named Adhimutta, he became discontented at finding no pith in the brahmin wisdom, and while he was seeking to escape during his last span of life, he saw the majesty of the Buddha at the presentation of the Jeta Grove. Entering the Order, he in due course won arahantship. Thereupon he admonished those bhikkhus dwelling with him who were very corpulent, in this verse:

If ye to this gross body give such heed,

Greedy its pleasures to enjoy, the while

Life's energies do ebb away, O whence

Shall come perfection in the holy life?


## CXV Mahanama

Reborn in this Buddha-age at Savatthi in a brahmin family, and named Mahanama, he heard the Exalted One teaching the Norm, and gaining faith, entered the Order. Taking an exercise, he dwelt on the hill called Nesadaka. Unable to prevent the rising up of evil thoughts and desires, he exclaimed: 'Of what worth is life to me with this corrupted mind?' And disgusted with himself he climbed a steep crag of the mountain, and made as if he would throw himself down, saying, 'I will kill him,' speaking to himself as to another and uttering this verse:

Lo thou! how to a wretched end art come

By this steep crag, this famous Hunter's Hill,

Its many crests begirt by sal-tree woods,

[And all its glens with tangled verdure] clothed!

In the act of upbraiding himself thus, the Thera evoked insight and won arahantship. And this verse became his confession of anna.


CXVI Papapariya

Reborn in this Buddha-age in a brahmin family at Rajagaha, he became proficient in the three Vedas. And being of the Parapara clan, he was called the Parapariyan, and taught mantras. He saw the wisdom and majesty of the Master at the Rajagaha Conference, and entered the Order, in due course winning arahantship. Reflecting on his career, he broke forth in joy with this psalm:

Avoiding truck with contact's sixfold field,

Guarding the gates of sense, master of self,

The general root of misery vomiting,

From every poison-taint am I immune.

This verse became his confession of anna.

CXVII Yasa

Reborn in this time of our Exalted One as the son of a very wealthy councillor at Benares, he was exceedingly delicately nurtured, and had three mansions for the different seasons, all of which is told in the Khandaka. Impelled by antecedent conditions, he saw one night the indecorum in his sleeping attendants and, greatly distressed, put on his gold slippers and left both house and town, gods opening the doors for him. So he went towards Isipatana, exclaiming: 'Alas! what distress! Alas! what danger!' Now at that hour the Exalted One, who was staying at Isipatana in order to do him kindness, was walking to and fro out of doors, and said: 'Come, Yasa, here is there neither distress nor danger.' Yasa filled with joy put off his slippers, and sat down beside the Exalted One. The Master talked to him by a graduated discourse, and when he had finished teaching the Truths, Yasa became a convert. And while the Exalted One taught the Truths to his father who had come to seek him, Yasa realized arahantship.

Then the Exalted One held out his right arm to Yasa, saying, 'Come, bhikkhu !' And at his merely saying the words, Yasa's hair was shorn two fingers' length, and he was equipped with the eight necessaries. Reflecting on his career, he rejoiced over those words calling him to his present state, 'Come, bhikkhu!' and uttered this psalm:

With perfumed skin and delicately clad

And head ablaze with gems, natheless my way

I found and made the Threefold Lore my own; And now the Buddha-ordinance is done.


CXVIII Kimbila

Reborn in this Buddha-age at Kapilavatthu in the family of a Sakiyan raja, and named Kimbila, he inherited immense wealth. The Master saw the maturity of his insight while staying at Anupiya, and in order to arouse him, conjured up a beautiful woman in her prime, and showed her to him passing to old age. Then Kimbila greatly shaken uttered this verse:

As bidden by some power age o'er her falls.

Her shape is as another, yet the same.

Now this my self, who ne'er have left myself,

Seems other than the self I recollect.

He thus, considering the fact of impermanence, was yet more strongly agitated, and going to the Master heard the Norm, believed, entered the Order, and in due course won arahantship. Thereupon he emphasized how he had formerly looked on things as permanent by repeating the verse, thereby confessing anna.


CXIX Vajji-putta (2)

(The Vajjian)

Reborn in this Buddha-age as the son of a Licchavi raja at Vesali, he became known as the Vajjian's son, because his father was one of the Vajjians. While yet a youth and engaged in training elephants, he, inclined by fullness of cause to seek Release, went to the Vihara at the hour when the Master was to preach, and having heard, entered the Order, and in due course acquired sixfold abhinna.

At a later time, shortly after the Master had passed away, Vajjiputta formed an agreement with the chief Theras to preserve the Dhamma intact, and travelled with them from place to place. One day he saw the Venerable Ananda, who was still a student only, surrounded by a large congregation, teaching them the Norm. And to call forth endeavour in him to reach the higher Paths, he uttered this verse:

Come thou and plunge in leafy lair of trees,

Suffer Nibbana in thy heart to sink!

Study and dally not, thou Gotamid!

What doth this fingle-fangle mean to thee?

Hearing this and speech of others, dispelling poisonous odours, Ananda grew agitated, and most of the night walked to and fro meditating. Then, with insight worked up, he entered his dwelling, and in the act of lying down on his couch, he won arahantship.


CXX Isidatta

Reborn in this Buddha-age in the kingdom of Avanti at Veḷugama, as the son of a caravan guide, he became (by correspondence) the unseen friend of Citta, a house-father at Macchikasaṇḍa. The latter wrote to him on the excellence of the Buddha, and sent him a copy of the system. This so moved him that he sought ordination under the Thera Kaccana the Great. In due course he acquired sixfold abhinna. Thereupon he had a mind to visit the Buddha, and taking leave of the Thera, came in course of time to the Middle Country, and had an interview with the Master. The latter asked him the question, 'How goes  it with you, bhikkhu? Are you prospering?' And he replied: 'Exalted One, from the time when I was admitted into your Rule, all sorrow and pain left me, all sense of peril was calmed.' And he declared anna in making that confession, uttering this verse:

The factors of my life well understood

Stand yet a little while with severed root. Sorrow is slain! that quest I've won, and won

Is purity from fourfold Venom's stain.

# CANTO II. PSALMS OF TWO VERSES

CXXI. Uttara

Reborn in this Buddha-age at Rajagaha as the son of an eminent brahmin and named Uttara, he graduated in brahmin lore, and became renowned for his breeding, beauty, wisdom and virtue. Vassakara, a leading minister of Magadha, seeing his attainments, was desirous of marrying him to his daughter. But he with heart set on release declined, and he attended the teaching of the General of the Norm. Winning faith, he entered the Order and fulfilled his novitiate, waiting upon Sariputta.

Now the Thera fell ill, and Uttara set out in the morning to seek a physician. On his round he set down his bowl on the banks of a lake and went to the water to wash out his mouth. Then a certain thief, pursued by the police, escaped from the town by the chief gate, and running by, dropped his stolen jewels into the novice's bowl, and fled. Then, as the latter came back to his bowl, the king's men passed in pursuit, and seeing the bowl, said: 'This is the thief! He has done the burglary!' And binding his arms behind, they brought him before Vassakara, the brahmin, and punished him.

Then the Exalted One, contemplating the ripeness of his insight, went thither, and placing a gentle hand, like dropping of crimson gold, on Uttara's head, spake thus: 'Uttara, this is the fruit of previous action. Come here to pass, it is to be accepted by thee through the power of reflection,' and so taught him the Norm according to his need. Uttara, thus ambrosially anointed by the touch of the Master's hand, was transported with joy and rapture, and through the ripeness of his insight and the charm of his Master's teaching, so cast off all impurity that he attained sixfold abhinna. Rising clear of the stake, he stood in the air, performing a miracle out of compassion for others. To the amazement of all, his wound was healed. When asked by the bhikkhus, 'Brother, how were you able, suffering such pain, to apply insight?' he said, 'Since I clearly saw, Brothers, the evil of rebirths and the nature of the conditioned, it was not the lesser evil of present pain that could hinder me from increasing insight, and achieving attainment':

There is no life that lasteth evermore,

Nor permanence in things from causes come.

They are reborn, the factors of our life,

Thereafter they dissolve and die away.

Since this the evil claiming all my thought,

Sooth am I one who doth not seek to be.

Detached from all that worldly aims commend,

Of th' intoxicants have I now made an end.

CXXII. Pindola-Bharadvaja

Reborn in this Buddha-age as the son of the chaplain to king Udena of Kosambi, he was named Bharadvaja. Having learnt the three Vedas, and teaching the hymns with great success to a school of brahmin youths, the work became distasteful. And leaving them, he went to Rajagaha Seeing there the gifts and favours bestowed on the Order of the Exalted One, he entered the same. He overcame intemperance in diet by the Teacher's methods, and acquired sixfold abhinna.

He thereupon announced before the Exalted One that he would answer the questions of any Brethren in doubt concerning path or fruit, thus uttering his 'lion's roar.' Wherefore the Exalted One said of him: 'The chief among my disciples who are lion-roarers is Pindola-Bharadvaja.' Now there came to him a former friend, a brahmin of a miserly nature. And the Thera persuaded him to make an offering, handing it over to the Order. And because the brahmin believed the Thera was greedy and self-seeking, the latter set himself to instruct him in the privileges of religious gifts, saying:

Not without rule and method must we live.

But food as such is never near my heart.

'By nutriment the body is sustained': This do I know, and hence my quest for alms.

'A [treacherous] bog' it is:— the wise know well:

These bows and gifts and treats from wealthy folk.

'Tis like steel splinter bedded in the flesh,

For foolish brethren hard to extricate.


CXXIII Valliya

Reborn in this Buddha-age at Savatthi as the son of an eminent brahmin, he was named Valliya. While adolescent and in the power of the senses, he formed virtuous friendships, whereby he came to the Exalted One, found faith and entered the Order, soon thereafter establishing insight and winning arahantship. Reflecting on the past with its worldly objects and desires, and on how, by the Ariyan Path, he now had turned from all that, he thus declared anna:

Within the little five-doored hut an ape Doth prowl, and round and round from door to door

He hies, rattling with blows again, again.

Halt, ape! run thou not forth! for thee

'Tis not herein as it was wont to be.

Reason doth hold thee captive. Never more

Shalt roam far hence [in freedom as of yore].


## CXXIV Gangatiriya

Reborn in this Buddha-age at Savatthi as a citizen's son, he was named Datta. And when, in his domestic  life, he transgressed through ignorance, then discovered his offence, anguish seized him so that he left the world. Distressed at his deeds, he adopted a course of austerity, and dwelt on the bank of the Ganges, making himself a tent of palm-leaves. Hence he became known as Ganga-tiriya (Ganges-sider). And he resolved to speak to no one. So he kept silence for a whole year. In the second year, a woman of the village where he sought alms, wishing to find out whether he was dumb, spilt milk as she filled his bowl. And he let fall the words: 'Enough, sister.' But in the third year, after strenuous effort, he won arahantship. Thereupon he declared anna by word of mouth, extolling his past procedure in these verses:

On Ganga's shore three palm-tree leaves I took

And made my hut; my bowl like funeral pot

Wherewith men sprinkle milk upon a corpse;

My cloak from refuse of the dust-heap culled.

Two years, from one rain-season till the next,

I [there abode], nor spake a word save once.

So till the third year passed-then the long night

Of gloom asunder burst [and broke in light].


## CXXV. Ajina

Reborn in this Buddha-age at Savatthi, in the family of a certain poor brahmin, he was wrapt at birth in an antelope's skin, and was hence named Antelope (Ajina). Growing up in poverty, he saw the Jeta Grove presented, and the power and majesty of the Buddha. And gaining faith he left the world, and not long after acquired supernormal thought. When he had moreover won arahantship, he, in consequence of past deeds, remained unhonoured and unknown. And some worldly novices among the bhikkhus despised him for this. Then the Thera agitated them with these verses:

E'en though a man have gained the Triple Lore,

Have vanquished death and purged th' intoxicants,

Yet, let him be to fame unknown, poor fools

May in their ignorance look down on him.

But let him get the good things of this world,

Then though he be of evil breed, natheless

Service and honour will they render him.


## CXXVI. Melajina

Reborn in this Buddha-age at Benares, in a nobleman's family, and named Melajina, he became distinguished for learning and accomplishments, and renowned in all the country. When the Exalted One stayed at Benares, in Isipatana, Melajina went to hear him preach the Norm; and gaining faith, he entered the Order and won arahantship.

And when the bhikkhus asked how far he had acquired supernormal qualities, he uttered a 'lion's roar':

When I had heard the Master preach the Norm,

No doubts my mind could thenceforth entertain

In him all-knowing and invincible.

Nor in a mighty hero like to him,

Lord of the caravan, driver of men,

Peerless and grand, nor in the Path, the Rule, Can ever want of faith disturb my soul.

## CXXVII. Radha

Reborn in the time of our Exalted One at Rajagaha, as a brahmin, he was in his old age unable to perform his various duties. Being passed over, he went to the Master and revealed his needs. The Master, contemplating his graduation in essential conditions, ordered Sariputta to admit him. Soon after that he won arahantship. And thereafter, keeping near the Master, he became pre-eminent among those who, deriving from the Master's teaching, could speak impromptu.

Now one day seeing how want of self-training occasioned governance by the passions, he exhorted thus:

E'en as into an ill-roofed house the rain

Doth pierce and penetrate continually,

So into mind by exercise untrained

Doth passion ever pierce and penetrate.

And as into a well-roofed house no rain

Doth pierce and penetrate continually.

So into mind by calm and insight trained

Doth passion never pierce and penetrate.


CXXVIII.  Suradha

Reborn in this Buddha-age as the younger brother of the aforesaid Radha, he followed his elder brother's example, and became an arahant also. To show the saving guidance of the Rule, he declared anna thus:

All coming back to birth is now destroyed.

The Conqueror's Rule hath guided all my ways. That which we call the Net have I put off; The lust that leads to life is rooted out.

And the great quest, for which I left the world,

Forsaking home a homeless life to lead,

Even that quest and high reward I've won,

For I am he whose bonds are riven in twain.


CXXIX.  Gotama

Reborn in this Buddha-age at Rajagaha, in a brahmin family, and named Gotama, he fell, when still a youth, into bad company, and gave all that he had to a courtesan. Repenting thereafter of his vicious ways, he beheld a vision of the Master seated— of Him who had discerned the progress of his mind and his attainment of the conditions. He with heart assured went to the Master, was taught, and believed. Entering the Order, he won arahantship, even as the razor touched his hair. And while he was pondering the bliss of jhana and of fruition, a lay-companion asked him concerning his property. He confessed how he had lived unchastely, and declaring anna by his present purity from passion, said:

At ease they sleep, the wise and pure, who ne'er

Are bound to womankind, for these must aye

Be kept 'neath watch and ward, and among them

'Tis ever hard to learn the truth of things.

War to the knife with thee, O lust, we've waged.

Now are we quit and free of debt to thee.

 Now fare we onward to that Going-out, Where at our journey's end we weep no more.


CXXX.  Vasabha

Reborn in this Buddha-age at Vesali, as the son of a Licchavi raja, he was won over by the majesty of the Buddha when the latter went to Vesali, and left the world. In due course he won arahantship, and thereafter, gracious to his patrons, he did not reject the necessaries they provided, but enjoyed what he received. The common-minded deemed him self-indulgent, but he continued taking no account of them.

But near him dwelt a fraudulent bhikkhu, who deceived the people by pretending to lead the simple life, content with little, and was honoured by them. Then Sakka, ruler of the devas, discerned this, and came to Vasabha Thera and asked: 'Your reverence, what is it that an impostor does?' The Thera, in rebuke to that evil-doer, replied:

He erst doth work destruction to himself;

Thereafter doth he ruin other men.

Most throughly works he mischief to himself,

E'en as decoy-bird by its own deceit.

No brahmin he, by outward colour judged.

By inner hue shall ye the brahmin know.

He in whom deeds show evil, even he

Is swarth of face, O consort of Suja.

# CANTO II. PSALMS OF TWO VERSES
## PART II

CXXXI Cunda the Great

Reborn in this Buddha-age in the kingdom of Magadha, at Naḷaka village, as the son of the brahminee Rupasari,  and younger brother of Sariputta, he followed the latter into the Order, and after arduous, strenuous effort won arahantship. And glorying in his attainment and in solitude of life, he uttered this psalm:

The will to learn maketh of learning growth;

Learning makes insight grow, and by insight

We know the Good; known Good brings bliss along.

Seek ye the lonely haunts remote from men. Practise the life of liberty from Bonds.

If there ye come not by your heart's desire,

Dwell with the Brethren, mindful and controlled.


CXXXII Jotidasa

Reborn in this Buddha-age as the son of a wealthy brahmin, in the Padiyattha country, he was named Jotidasa. When come of age he saw Kassapa the Great one day going his round for alms, and entertained him in his house, and heard him discourse. On the hill near the village he himself had a great vihara built for the Thera, and supplied him with the four requisites. Moved thereafter by the Thera's teaching he left the world, and not long after won the sixfold abhinna. After ten years, during which he learnt  the three Pitakas, with special proficiency in the Vinaya-Pitaka, and waited on the fraternity, he set out with many bhikkhus to salute the Exalted One at Savatthi. On the way he entered a theologian's park, and seeing a brahmin practising the fivefold austerity, he asked: 'Why, brahmin, do you not burn otherwise in a different heat?' The brahmin annoyed, answered: 'Master shaveling, what other heat is there?' The Thera replied:

Anger, and envy, and all cruel deeds,

And pride, and arrogance, and wanton strife,

Craving, and ignorance, and lust of life:

These burn away and let thy body be!

and therewith taught him the Norm. And all those theologians besought him for ordination.

On leaving Savatthi he went to his former home, and admonished his relatives in these verses:

They who in divers ways by deeds of force

And violence, rude and rough-mannered folk,

Do work their fellow-creatures injury,

Thereby they too themselves are overthrown, For never is th' effect of action lost.

The deed a man doth, be it good or ill,

To all his doing is he verily the heir.


CXXXIII Herannakani

Reborn in this Buddha-age as the son of one who was a tenant-in-chief of the King of Kosala, and in command of bandits, he succeeded to his father's position at the latter's death. Converted on seeing the Buddha accept the Jeta Grove, he put his younger brother in his place, left the world, and soon after won arahantship. He thereupon sought to turn his brother to a better life, and on seeing him attached to it, urged him in these verses:

The days, the nights flit by and pass away.

Life is arrested, and the span

To mortals given is consumed and fails,

Like water in the shallow mountain streams.

But evil actions still the fool commits,

Nor understands how dire the aftermath,

Till comes the bitter hour of action's fruit.

Hearing the Thera's homily, the brother besought the king's leave, and left the world, and not long after found salvation.


CXXXIV Somamitta

Reborn in this Buddha-age at Benares, in a brahmin's family and named Somamitta, he became an expert in the three Vedas, but was converted by the Thera Vimala and took orders. He dwelt near the Thera, fulfilling his duties. But the latter was given to sloth and torpor. And Somamitta, thinking 'Who can be virtuous near a sluggard?' went to Kassapa the Great, and attending his lectures, established insight, aud soon after attained arahantship. Thereupon he rebuked Vimala in these verses:

As one who, mounted on a puny plank,

Is in mid-ocean whelm'd beneath the waves,

So even he of blameless life doth sink,

When thrown together with the man of sloth;

Wherefore from such an one keep well apart

The sluggard and the poor in energy.

Dwell thou with them who live aloof,

With wise, with noble souls who have renounced,

Who in rapt contemplation ever strive.

Hearing him, Thera Vimala was deeply moved, and establishing insight, bestirred himself to win salvation, the which he will be seen hereafter to attain.


CXXXV Sabbamitta

Reborn in this Buddha-age in the family of a brahmin of Savatthi, and named Sabbamitta, he saw, at the presentation of the Jeta Grove, the wondrous power of the Buddha, and entering the Order he obtained a subject for exercise and dwelt in the forest. After the rains he went into Savatthi, to salute the Buddha, and on his way there lay a fawn caught in a trapper's net. The doe, though not in the net, kept near from love for her young, yet dared not come close to the snare. The fawn, turning hither and thither, bleated for pity. Then the Thera: 'Alas! the suffering that love brings to creatures!' Going further he saw many bandits wrapping a man they had captured alive in straw, and about to set fire to it. Hearing his cries, the Thera, out of his distress at both these things, uttered a verse within hearing of the bandits.

Folk are bound up with folk and cling to folk.

Folk suffer scathe from folk and wreak the same.

What boots thee then this folk, and brood of folk?

Let the folk go and get thee gone from them,

Who as they go injure so many folk.

So saying, he forced his way to insight, and won arahantship. But the brigands, listening to his teaching, were moved in heart and renounced the world, practising the Norm in principle and in detail.

## CXXXVI Mahakaḷa

Reborn in this Buddha-age at the town of Setavya, in the family of a merchant, he was named Mahakaḷa. When come of age and dwelling at home, he took five hundred carts of merchandise to trade with to Savatthi. While resting there with his men in the evening, he saw the laity going with perfumes and garlands to the Jeta Grove, and went with them. There he heard the Master preach the Norm, believed, and entered the Order. Deciding on cemetery-contemplation, he dwelt in the charnel-field. And one day a woman named Kaḷi, employed as crematrix, in order to give the Thera an object-study, cut off from a recently cremated body both thighs and both arms, and breaking the head into the semblance of a milk-bowl, arranged all the members together, placed them where the Thera studied for him to look at, and sat down at the side. The Thera seeing this exhorted himself in these verses:

Kaḷi, woman broad and swart of hue as blackbird,

Now hath broken off a thighbone, now another;

Now hath broken off an arm, and now another;

Now the skull hath broken off as 'twere a milk bowl,

Made them ready and is seated.

He who witless doth not understand, but maketh

Cause for life renewed, comes back again to sorrow.

Wherefore he who knows creates no more new causes.

May I ne'er so lie again with scattered members!

Thus wholly sell-mastered, the Thera brought forth insight and won arahantship.

## CXXXVII Tissa

Reborn in this Buddha-age at Rajagaha, in a brahmin's family, and named Tissa, he became an expert in the Vedas, teaching the mantras to five hundred brahmin boys, and winning the highest praise and renown. When the Master came to Rajagaha, Tissa saw the Buddha-majesty, and believed and entered the Order, thereafter winning arahantship through established insight. So also he won praise and renown.

Now certain worldly-minded bhikkhus noting the attention paid to the Thera were unable to endure it. The Thera knew this, and declared the evil in such attentions and his own detachment therefrom in these verses:

Many the foes he gets, the bhikkhu shorn,

Wrapt in his robe, to whom the world gives gifts

Of food and drink, raiment and where to lodge.

Let him then, knowing all the bane herefrom,

The fearsome peril in the world's regard,

Taking but little, free from lusting's taint,

Wary and mindful, hold his onward way.

Then those bhikkhus straightway sought the Thera's forgiveness.


## CXXXVIII Kimbila

His meeting with the Buddha, his emotion and his leaving the world are told in Canto I., the verse beginning, 'As bidden by some power.' Here the Thera tells how he dwelt  fraternally with his comrades, the venerable Anuruddha and the venerable Bhaddiya, Sakiyan rajas:

Where lies the Eastern Bamboo Grove we dwell,

Sons of the Sakiyans, comrades [all and true].

No little wealth have we renounced for this,

Contented with whatever fills our bowl.

Quickened and ardent is our energy,

Earnest and resolute [our heart's intent],

Ever we boldly press toward [our goal].

Love of the Norm our [sure and sole] delight,

All worldly loves by us forsworn outright.


## CXXXIX Nanda

Reborn in this Buddha-age at Kapilavatthu, as the son of Raja Suddhodana and of Great Pajapati, and a joy to his kin, on his naming day he was named Nanda.

When Nanda was of age, the Master, rolling the Wheel of the Norm, came out of compassion to Kapilavatthu. Making a shower of rain the occasion, he told the Vessantara Jataka. On the second day, by the verse 'Rise up,' he established his father as a Stream-winner; Pajapati also by the verse, 'Follow after a holy life,' and the raja further, as a Once-returner. On the third day, when seeking alms at the coronation-hall where congratulations were being offered to Prince Nanda on his wedding, the Master handed the prince his bowl and wished him luck. And he, taking the bowl, followed the Master to the Vihara, who there ordained him, though Nanda wished it not.

From that time, knowing that Nanda was oppressed by his distaste, the Master trained it away, so that Nanda, by thoroughgoing meditation, established insight and attained arahantship. Thereafter, enjoying the bliss of liberty, be said: 'O excellent method of the Master, whereby I was drawn out of the bog of rebirth and set on Nibbana's strand!' And joying in his reflections he uttered these verses:

Heedless and shallow once my thoughts were set

On all the bravery of outward show;

Fickle was I and frivolous; all my days

Were worn with wanton sensuality.

But by the Buddha's skilful art benign,

Who of sun's lineage cometh, was I brought

To live by deeper thought, whereby my heart

From (the great swamp of endless) life I drew.

And the Exalted One, discerning how eminently he was trained in self-control, declared him before the Order to be chief therein among his disciples, even therein conferring that distinction to which the Thera, in past ages, had once aspired.


CXL Sirimat

Reborn in this Buddha-age at Savatthi, in a burgess's family, he was named Sirimat (Faustus) because of his family's good fortune and constant success. His younger brother, as increaser of that good fortune, was named Sirivaḍḍha (growth of luck). They both saw the majesty of the Buddha when the Jeta Grove was presented, believed, and entered the Order. Sirivaḍḍha, though at first he won no abnormal powers, was honoured and fêted by laity and recluses. But Sirimat, through defective karma, was little honoured; nevertheless, exercising himself in calm and insight, he soon won the sixfold abhinna.

Now the ordinary bhikkhus and novices, not knowing Sirimat was an Ariyan, continued to disparage him and to honour his brother. Then the Thera, blaming their faulty judgment, said:

Others may laud and honour him

Whose self is uncontrolled.

Surely amiss their praise is given,

Since self is uncontrolled.

Others may chide and censure him

Whose self is well controlled.

Surely amiss their blame is given,

Since self is well controlled.

Then Sirivaḍḍha, hearing him, was agitated, and establishing insight, not long after he also completed his salvation. And they who had blamed the Thera sought his forgiveness.

# CANTO II. PSALMS OF TWO VERSES
# PART III

CXLI Uttara

Reborn in this Buddha-age at Saketa, in a brahmin's family, he was named Uttara. Convinced by the twin-miracle at the Gandamba tree at Savatthi, whither some business had taken him, he was induced to leave the world when the Master, at Saketa, preached the Kalaka Park discourse. Going with the Master to Rajagaha, he there developed insight and acquired sixfold abhinna. Returning again to Savatthi to wait on the Buddha, the bhikkhus asked him: 'What, Brother, have you already accomplished your religious duties?' He, declaring anna, replied in these verses:

Well do I understand the factors five,

And well is craving rooted out in me,

Developed are the seven wisdom-chords,

And all the poison-fumes are shrunk to nought.

And since the factors now are understood,

I—look you!—casting out the Huntress fell

[Who sets her netted snare for every thought], And cultivating wisdom's harmony, Sane and immune, in peace shall pass away.


CXLII Bhaddaji

Reborn in this Buddha-age at Bhaddiya, as the only child of a councillor whose fortune was worth eighty crores, he was named Bhaddaji, and was brought up in luxury, like that attending the Bodhisat in his last rebirth. ... (The Commentary then relates the story of his sudden realization of arahantship while listening for the first time to the Buddha, the latter having come from Savatthi purposely to seek him out; together with his following the Master and his company, the week after, to Kotigama, and retiring to the bank of the Ganges to become absorbed in jhana. Thence he emerges only when the Master came by, not heeding the preceding chief Theras. To vindicate his new supreme attainments, the Buddha invites him on to his own ferry-boat, and bids him work a wonder. Bhaddaji thereupon raises the submerged palace he dwelt in when he was King Panada, all being told in the 'Maha-panada-Jataka,' ii., No. 264.) Then the Thera described the golden mansion in which he had once lived, speaking of himself, that self having passed away, as of another:

Panada was that king by name

Whose palace was of gold;

Sixteen apartments deep it stood,

Aloft a thousandfold.

A thousand flights it rose on high,

Its walls with scroll-work dight,

With many a flaunting banner hung,

With emeralds glittering bright.

'Twas there they danced, Gandharvas danced,

Six thousand in seven bands.


CXLIII Sobhita

Reborn in this Buddha-age at Savatthi, in a brahmin's family, he was named
Sobhita. And after he had heard the Master teach, had left the world and acquired
sixfold abhinna, he practised recollecting his former lives with such success that
the Master ranked him foremost among those who could so remember. And he,
reflecting on his pre-eminence in attainment, was filled with joy, and breathed
forth this psalm:

A bhikkhu mindful, gifted with insight,

With strenuous effort strongly set to work,

Have I [the infinite past] recalled to mind:

Five hundred ages in a single night.

O let the Onsets Four of mindfulness My study be, the Seven, the (noble) Eight!
For I [the infinite past] have called to mind:

Five hundred ages in a single night.


CXLIV 'Valliya'

Reborn in this Buddha-age at Vesali, in a brahmin's family, he was named
Kanhamitta. Come of age, he saw the majesty of the Buddha when the latter came
to Vesali, and believing, he took orders under Maha-Kaccana. Dull of insight, and
beginning to make effort, he was so long dependent upon the wisdom of his co-
religionists that they called him Valliya (Creeperling), saying, 'Like ivy and such
plants, that cannot grow leaning on nothing, so he cannot get on without leaning
on someone who is wise.'

And it came to pass that he went to hear Thera Venudatta preach, and becoming thereby heedful and intelligent and ripe in knowledge, he asked that proficient teacher, saying:

All that by earnest work has to be done,

All that one fain to wake to truth must do.

All that shall be my work nor shall I fail.

O see my forward strides in energy!

And do thou show me how and where to go—

The Path that's founded on Ambrosia—So I in silent study pondering

Shall to the silence of the seers attain,

As glides great Ganga's river to the main.

Then Venudatta gave him an exercise for study, and he, working at it, not long after won arahantship. Declaring anna, he uttered those same verses.


CXLV Vitasoka

Reborn in this Buddha-age, in the two hundred and eighteenth year thereof, as the younger brother of King Dhammasoka, he was named Vitasoka. Come of age, he acquired the accomplishments befitting noble youths, and then as a lay-pupil of Thera Giridatta became highly proficient in the Sutta- and Abhidhamma-Pitakas.

Now one day when his hair was being dressed, he took the mirror from the barber's hand, and contemplating his body, saw some grey hairs. In agitation he sent down insight into his mind, and exerting himself to meditate, he became, as he there sat, a Stream-winner. Taking Orders under Giridatta, he not long after won arahantship. Thereupon he thus declared anna:

'Now let him shave me!'—so the barber came.

From him I took the mirror and, therein

Reflected, on myself I gazed arid thought:

'Futile for lasting is this body shown.'

[Thus thinking on the source that blinds our sight

My spirit's] darkness melted into light.

Stripped are the swathing vestments utterly! Now is there no more coming back to be?

CXLVI Punnamasa

Reborn in this Buddha-age at Savatthi in the family of a landed proprietor, he left
the world after the birth of his firstborn. And dwelling near a village, he strove and
worked till he acquired sixfold abhinna. Going thereupon to Savatthi and saluting
the Master, he dwelt in a charnel-field. Now his son died, and his wife, desirous
that their property, having no heirs, should not be taken over by the rajas, went
with a large following to greet her husband, and induce him to leave the religious
life. But the Thera, to show his passionless state and to vindicate his attainment,
stood in the air and said:

All the five Hindrances that bar the way Against the safe, sure peace I put aside.

The mirror of the holy Norm I grasped:— The knowing and the seeing what we
are—

So I reflected on this grouped frame Within and eke without, and I beheld

How, whether it was mine or not of me,

"The body empty [is and vanity]

.

CXLVII Nandaka

Reborn in this Buddha-age at Campa, in a burgess's family, he was named
Nandaka. He was the younger  brother of Bharata, whose story will next be told.
When both were come of age, they heard that Sona-Kolivisa had left the world.
And saying: 'Even Sona who is so delicate has gone forth; now what of us?' they,
too, left the world. Bharata soon acquired sixfold abhinna, but Nandaka, through
the strength of the corruptions, was not able to command insight, and could only
practise for it. Then Bharata, wishing to help him, made him his attendant, and
went forth from the vihara. Sitting down near the road he discoursed to him of
insight.

Now a caravan passing by, an ox, unable to pull his cart through a boggy place,
fell down. The leader had him released from the cart, and fed with grass and water.
His fatigue allayed, the ox, reharnessed and strengthened, pulled the cart out of
the bog. Then Bharata Baid: 'Did you see that business, brother Nandaka?' 'I did.'
'Consider its meaning.' And Nandaka said: 'Like the refreshed ox, I, too, must
draw forth myself out of the swamp of samsara.' And taking this as his subject
in practising, he won arahantship. Then to his brother he declared anna in these
verses:

E'en though he trip and fall, the mettled brute

Of noble breed will steadfast stand once more.

Incited yet again to effort new,

Foredone no longer, draws his load along.

So look on me as one who having learned

Of Him, the all-enlightened One, and gained

True insight, am become of noble breed,

And of the Very Buddha son indeed.


CXLVIII Bharata

Now when his younger brother Nandaka had confessed that he had gotten anna, Bharata conceived the idea: 'Let us both go forthwith to the Master, and tell him how we have carried out holiness of life.' And he said these verses to Nandaka:

Come, Nandaka, now go we unto Him

Whose blessed teaching taught us all we know;

And in the presence of the Wake, the Chief,

Let's roar the lion's paean of our hearts.

That quest for which the holy Sage in [love

And great compassion bade us both go forth—

That Good supreme both you and I have won,

And every bond that hindered us is gone.


CXLIX Bharadvaja

Reborn in this Buddha-age at Rajagaha in a brahmin's family, he came to be designated by his gens-name of Bharadvaja. Living the domestic life, a son was born to him, and he named him Kanhadinna. When the boy was of proper age, his father said, 'Come, dear boy, and study under such and such a teacher,' and sent him to Takkasila. On his way thither he made friends with a great Thera, a disciple of the Master, heard him teach the Norm, took orders, and after due training won arahantship.

Now his father Bharadvaja heard the Exalted One teach the Norm at the Bamboo Grove Vihara, and he, too, left the world and realized arahantship. But Kanhadinna came to salute the Master at Rajagaha, and with joy he saw his father seated near the latter. And he asked himself: 'My father, too, has gone forth. Has he, I wonder, attained the end of the religious life?' Then he discerned that his father was an arahant, and wishing to make him utter a lion-roar, asked him: 'Hast thou succeeded in attaining the end of that for which we leave the world?' Then Bharadvaja showed his attainment in these verses:

'Tis thus th' enlightened lift their triumph-song,

Like lions roaring in the hill-ravine, Heroes who in the holy war have won,

And conquered evil, Mara and his host.

The servant of the blessed Master I,

A votary of the Norm and Brotherhood;

And glad and gratified my heart to see

My son purged of the poisons, sane, immune.


CL Kanhadinna

Reborn in this Buddha-age at Rajagaha, in a brahmin's family, he was named Kanhadinna. Come of age, and impelled by the efficient cause culminating, he came to the General of the Norm, heard the Norm, believed, left the world, and developing insight, won arahantship. Thereupon he thus declared anna:

Waited have I on saintly men and heard

Full many times the saving truths [they taught].

Hearing I knew I should attain the road

That leads away from things that age and die.

And so in me all lust to live again

Thus being utterly cast out, since then

In me 'tis no more found, nor was't, nor will it e'er

Come back in me, nor at this hour doth rise in me.

# CANTO II. PSALMS OF TWO VERSES
## PART IV

CLI Migasira

Reborn in this Buddha-age in the family of a brahmin of Kosala, he was named
Migasira after the constellation under which he obtained birth. And having acquired
brahmin culture, he practised the skull-spell, so that, when he had muttered the
spell and tapped with his nail on the skull, he would declare, 'This person is
reborn in such a sphere,' even with respect to those who had been dead three
years. Disliking domestic life, he became a Wanderer, and through his art won
favour and respect. Coming to Savatthi and going before the Master, he declared
his power, saying: 'I, master Gotama, can tell the destiny of dead persons.' 'How
do you tell it?' He let a skull be brought, and, muttering his rune and tapping with
his nail, he asserted purgatory or some other sphere to be the place of rebirth.

Then the Exalted One had the skull of a bhikkhu brought, who had attained
complete outgoing (parinibbana), and said: 'Tell now his destiny to whom this
skull belonged!' Migasira muttered and tapped, but saw neither the beginning
nor the end. Then the Master said: 'Art not able, Wanderer?' He replied, 'I must
first make sure,' and turning the skull round never so much—for how should he
know the goings of an arahant?—stood ashamed,  perspiring, dumb. 'Art tired,
Wanderer?' 'Ay, I am tired; I cannot discern the destiny of this one. Do you make
it known?' 'I know it, and more besides. He is gone to Nibbana.' Then said the
Wanderer: 'Give me this hidden lore!' 'Then do you take orders.' So Migasira was
ordained, and was given exercises in calm. Well grounded in jhana and abhinna,
he practised insight, and not long after won arahantship. He then confessed anna
thus:

Since I went forth and entered on the Rule

Ordained by the Enlightened One Supreme,

Emancipated as I went, I rose

Transcending all these things of sense-desire.

While He, that Very Brahmin, looked on me,

O then my heart was set at liberty! Yea, since all bonds are broke for evermore,

For me Emancipation's fixed and sure!


CLII Sivaka

Reborn in this Buddha-age at Rajagaha in a brahmin's family, he was named
Sivaka. And when he had acquired a complete education, he followed his

inclination to leave the world. Coming as a Wanderer to hear the Master teach the Norm, he received faith, entered the Order, and eventually won arahantship. He then thus confessed anna:

Transient the little houses [of our life],

Built here, built there, again, ever again.

Hunting the house-builder [thus far I come];

Birth is but woe again, ever again.

 Thou'rt found, house-maker thou, thou'rt seen at last!

Never again shalt fashion house [for me]:

Broken are all thy walls, shattered thy roofs.

Stayed is the further rise of consciousness;

Blown 'twill be even here to nothingness.


CLIII Upavana

Reborn in this Buddha-age at Savatthi, in a brahmin's family, he was named Upavana. He saw at the Jeta Grove presentation the majesty of the Buddha, and entering the Order, practised for insight, and won sixfold abhinna.

Now Upavana. became attendant on the Exalted One. And at that time the Exalted One was attacked by cramp. And Devahita, a brahmin lay-friend of the Thera, living at Savatthi, was supplying him with the four necessaries. Seeing him come with bowl and robe, Devahita discerned that he needed something different and said: 'Let your reverence be supplied. What do you need?' And Upavana. answered:

The Arahant, the Well-Come of all men,

The Holy Sage, he suffereth sore with wind.

If there be any water heated here,

O give it to me, brahmin, for the Sage.

Revered by them to whom we reverence owe,

Cherished by them who claim our pious care,

Honoured by them to whom honour is due,

For Him I do beseech it may be brought.

Thereat the brahmin offered both hot water and suitable medicine. Thereby the Master's sickness was healed, and to him the Exalted One rendered thanks.


CLIV Isidinna

Reborn in this Buddha-age in the country of the Sunaparantas, in the family of a councillor, he was named Isidinna. Grown up, he saw the double miracle at the presentation of the Sandalwood Pavilion, and coming with a satisfied mind to the Master, he heard the Norm, and became a Stream-winner. While still living a domestic life, a compassionate spirit urged him, saying:

I mark the pious laity who treasure on their lips the Norm;

How you may often hear them say: 'Transient are all this world's desires!'

But in their hearts lies love of pelf, of precious stones and jewelled rings,

And that which fills their thought is care of sons and daughters and of wives.

Nay, verily, they do not know the inward meaning of the Norm;

E'en though you often hear them say: 'Transient are all this world's desires!'

To cut themselves from passions free, they lack the spiritual health,

And therefore cleaveth aye their heart to wife and children, and to wealth.

When the layman heard this, he was thrilled with emotion, and leaving the world, he not long after won arahantship. In confessing anna, he repeated these verses.


CLV Sambula-Kaccana

Reborn in this Buddha-age in the kingdom of Magadha, as the son of a burgess of the Kaccana's, he was named Sambula, but was known as Sambula-Kaccana. After he had heard the Master teach the Norm, and had entered the Order, he went to the neighbourhood of the Himalaya, and practised his insight exercises in a cave called Bhera-vayana ('dreadful-passage').

Now one day there arose a great storm-cloud out of season, towering high in the heavens, emitting roars of thunders, forked lightning, and rushing noise. And it began to rain, and thunderbolts burst. All creatures—bears, hyenas, buffaloes, elephants—cried out in fear and trembling. But the Thera had stirred up insight, and, careless as to body and life, heeded not the noise, but cooled by the storm so composed his mind, that he quickened insight, and won arahantship together with abhinna.

Thereupon reflecting on his achievement he was filled with joy, and in a psalm confessed anna:

God's rain pours down, ay, and god's rain roars down,

And I alone in fearsome hollow dwell.

Yet dwelling so in fearsome rocky dell

To me no fear comes nigh, no creeping dread,

No quailing [of my soul].

For such the law

Within the blessed Norm, that dwelling so

To me no fear comes nigh, no creeping dread,

No quailing [of my soul] to me, alone.


CLVI Khitaka

Reborn in this Buddha-age in the kingdom of Kosala as the son of a brahmin, and named Khitaka, he heard the Norm from the Master, and entering the Order, dwelt in a forest till he won arahantship. Thereupon continuing in the bliss of fruition, of Nibbana, a Thera enthusiastic for endeavour, he went to the bhikkhus dwelling in that forest to stir enthusiasm in them. First asking concerning their good, he spoke these verses, therein confessing anna:

Whose heart stands like a rock, and swayeth not,

Void of all lust for things that lust beget,

And all unshaken in a shifting world? To heart thus trained, whence shall come aught of ill?

My heart stands like a rock, and swayeth not,

Void of all lust for things that lust beget,

And all unshaken in a shifting world.

My heart thus trained-whence shall come ill to me?


CLVII Sona-Potiriyaputta

Reborn in this Buddha-age at Kapilavatthu, as the son of the zemindar Potiriya, he was named Sona. Come of age, he became chief captain of the forces of Bhaddiya, a Sakiyan raja. Now Bhaddiya having left the world, as will be described below, Sona thought: 'If even the raja has left the world, what have I to do with domestic life?' So he took orders, but remained sluggish, not given to meditative exercise. On him the Exalted One, dwelling in the Mango Grove at Anupiya, sent forth his glory, and arousing him to mindfulness uttered admonitory verses:

Nay, not for this that thou mayest slumber long,

Cometh the night in starry garlands wreathed.

For vigil by the wise this night is here.

Hearing him, Sona was exceedingly agitated, and keeping his shortcomings before the mind, adopted the open-air practice, exercising himself for insight. And he uttered this verse:

If in the fight my warrior-elephant

Advanced, 'twere better, fallen from his back, Dead on the field [and trampled I should lie],

Than beaten live a captive to the foe.

So saying, he stirred up insight and won arahantship, and thereupon repeated the Master's words and his own as his confession of anna.


CLVIII Nisabha

Reborn in this Buddha-age in the country of the Koḷiyans, in a clansman's family, he was named Nisabha. Come of age, he saw the Buddha's wisdom and power at the fight between the Sakiyans and Koḷiyans, and believing, entered the Order, anon winning arahantship.

Thereupon seeing a fellow-bhikkhu spending his time  carelessly, he admonished him, adding another verse to show he acted that which he preached:

Put them away, those fivefold things of sense,

Objects that charm and captivate the mind.

Thou who through faith didst give up home and world,

Become end-maker of its grief and pain.

With thought of death I dally not, nor yet

Delight in living. I await the hour

With mind discerning and with heedfulness.

CLIX Usabha

Reborn in this Buddha-age at Kapilavatthu in the family of a Sakiyan raja, he was named Usabha. And when the Master visited his own folk, Usabha saw his power and wisdom, believed in him, and entered the Order. From that time he fulfilled no religious duties, but passed all day in society and all night in sleep.

Now one day, muddled in mind and unheedingly dropping off to sleep, he dreamt that he shaved, put on a crimson cloak, and, sitting on an elephant, entered the town for alms. There, seeing the people gathered together, he dismounted full of shame. Thereupon he awoke thinking: 'Why, this was a dream! Muddled in head and thoughtless I saw myself in sleep.' And with anguish he established insight, and in due course won arahantship.

Thus having made the dream his goad, he celebrated it to confess anna, saying:

A cloak the hue of purple mango-buds

Draping about my shoulder, I bestrode

The back of elephant, and so to seek

Mine alms into the village street I rode.

Down from his back [in very shame] I slid—

[When lo! I woke and] anguish seized me then.

This arrogant self was then made meek and mild,

Purged were the poisons [that my mind defiled].


CLX Kappata-kura

Reborn in this Buddha-age at Savatthi in poor circumstances, the only way he knew of to support himself was to go about, clad in rags, pan in hand, seeking for rice-grains Hence he became known as Kappata-kura—'Rags-and-rice.' When grown up, he maintained himself by selling grass. Reaping this one day in the forest, he saw a Thera. Doing obeisance he sat down near him, and heard him teach the norm. Then be believed, and saying 'What to me is this wretched mode of life?' he entered the Order, bestowing his ragged cloth in a certain place. And when repugnance [to his new life] arose in him, he would go and look at the rags and feel unsettled. So doing, he seceded seven times from the Order. Then the bhikkhus told the Exalted One of this. And he one day, when Kappata-kura, as bhikkhu, sat in the preaching-hall at the edge of the congregation dozing, admonished him in these verses:

'These,' saith he, 'are the rags of Rags-and-Rice!

Too heavy is the gear I'm wearing now.'

Full measure of the Norm hath he in shower

Ambrosial; and yet no step he takes

To practise contemplative discipline.

O Kappata, thou shouldst not sway and nod,

Nor make me cuff the word into thine ear.

Never a whit thou, Kappata, hast learned,

Sleepily swaying 'midst the listeners here.

Thus the Exalted One upbraided him strongly, as if He had pierced his very bones, as if a fierce elephant had gone down into his path. And he, greatly disturbed, established insight, and soon won arahantship. Thereupon he repeated the verses which had been the goad that sent him to the goal, so that they became his confession of anna.

# CANTO II. PSALMS OF TWO VERSES
## PART V

CLXI Kumara-Kassapa

Reborn in this Buddha-age at Rajagaha, his mother was the daughter of a councillor. She having failed to gain her parents' consent to leave the world while yet a maiden, was married, and obtained her husband's consent to take Orders, not knowing at the time that she had conceived. When later the bhikkhunis saw her condition, they consulted Devadatta, who replied: 'She is no true nun!' They then consulted Him-of-the-Ten-Powers. He entrusted the matter to Thera Upali, who convened certain residents at Savatthi, including the lay-patroness Visakha, and in full  assembly, the king being present, pronounced the Sister to have been with child when she took orders. The Master approved his decision. So she brought forth her child at the Vihara, a boy like a golden statue, end the king reared him, and brought him later on to the Master to join the Order. Because he joined as a youth, and they would ask, when the Exalted One said, 'Send for Kassapa,' or 'Give this fruit or biscuit to Kassapa,' 'Which Kassapa?' and because of his royal rearing, he became known as Kumara-Kassapa, even after he was grown to manhood.

Now whire he exercised himself for insight and learnt the Buddha-word, he dwelt in Dark Wood. Then a deva, one who had with him done only the mountain-recluse's course, and having become a Non-Returner, had been reborn as a Great-Brahma in the Pure Abodes, determined to show Kumara-Kassapa a method for attaining the Paths and Fruits. And he came into the Dark Wood, and showed him fifteen questions which only the Master could answer. So he asked them before the Exalted One and learnt them; whereupon having conceived insight, he attained arahant-ship.

Thereupon, having been ranked by the Master foremost among those who had the gift of varied and versatile discourse, he reviewed his career, and under the aspect of  extolling the virtues of the Jewel-Trinity, confessed his anna:

All hail the Buddhas, and all hail the Norms. Hail the blest System by our Master wrought,

Wherein he that doth hear may [be enrolled

And] come to realize a Norm like ours.

Down countless ages have its members come,

Reborn now as this compound, now as that.

But this for them is now the very last,

The final confluence [of the factors five,']

In flux of rebirth and mortality.

Now come they never more again to be.


## CLXII Dhammapala

Reborn in this Buddha-age, when the Master had passed away, in the kingdom of Avanti, as a brahmin's son, he was named Dhammapala. As he was returning from Takkasila, his schooldays finished, he saw on his way a certain Thera in a single cell, and hearing from him the Norm, he believed, left the world, and acquired sixfold abhinna.

Now, as he was ruminating in the bliss of his achievement, two novices climbed a tree at the Vihara to pick blossoms, and a branch breaking, they were falling. Seeing them, the Thera caught them with his hand, and by his iddhi-power placed them unhurt upon the ground. And he taught them, saying:

The brother who while young hath given himself

Wholly to carry out the Buddha's plan,

Who keepeth vigil in a sleeping world,

Not vainly, not for naught he spends his days.

So let the wise man, so let him who aye

Remembereth that which Buddhas have enjoined,

Devote himself to faith and righteousness,

To know the blessedness They brought to us,

And the true vision of the holy Norm.


## CLXIII Brahmali

Reborn in this Buddha-age in the kingdom of Kosala, as a brahmin's son, he was named Brahmali. When grown up, being impelled by the fullness of conditions, distress arose in him because of the continual round, and, through associating with spiritually minded friends, he left the world, and took his exercise to a forest. From the maturity of his knowledge he soon developed insight, and acquired sixfold abhinna.

Dwelling thereafter in the bliss of the Paths, the Thera, so versed in compassing endeavour, uttered one day these verses, on behalf of the bhikkhus in that forest, concerning devotion to endeavour:

In whom the senses have been hushed to calm,

Like horses well tamed by the charioteer,

In whom no vain conceits are found, nor aught

Of poison-fumes survives, a man like this

May stir up envy e'en among the gods.

 In me the senses have been hushed to calm,

Like horses well tamed by the charioteer,

In me no vain conceits are found, nor aught

Of poison-fumes survives;—one such as I

May stir up envy e'en among the gods.


CLXIV Mogharajan

Reborn in this Buddha-age in a brahmin's family, and named Mogharajan, he studied under the brahmin Bavariya. Growing distressed, he became an ascetic. He was one of the sixteen, Ajita and others, who was sent by Bavariya to the Master to interview him. When Mogharajan had asked his question and been answered, he attained arahantship.

Thereafter he acquired distinction by wearing rough cloth which caravaners, tailors and dyers had thrown away. Wherefore the Master assigned him the first place among those who wore such rough clothing [he thereby realizing his aspiration made many ages ago].

At another time, from want of care and through former karma, pimples and the like broke out and increased on bis body. Judging that his lodging was infected, he spread out a couch of straw in the Magadha fields, and there, though it was winter, he lodged. Of him, waiting one day  upon the Master, and paying his respects, the latter of his courtesy inquired in the following verse:

Well, Mogharajan, thou skin-sufferer,

Thou blest of heart and constantly serene,

Cometh the time when winter nights are cold,

And thou a brother poor—how wilt thou fare?

Thus asked, the Thera explained the matter to the Master:

Rich are the cornfields of the Magadhese, And thriving, every one, I've heard it said.

My little straw-built canopy doth please

Better than others' way of finding ease.


CLXV Visakha the Pancali's Son

Reborn in this Buddha-age in the kingdom of Magadha, as the son of a district raja, he was named Visakha. But because he was the son of the daughter of the king of the Pancalas, he became known afterwards as the Pancali's son.

At his father's death he succeeded to his title, but when the Master came to his neighbourhood he went to hear him, and believed, and left the world. Following him to Savatthi, he established insight, and acquired sixfold abhinna.

Thereupon, in kindness to his own folk, he visited his native place. And as people kept coming to hear him, he was one day asked: 'How many qualities, your reverence, should a man acquire to be a preacher of the Norm?' The  Thera taught them the essential feature of such an one as follows:

Let him not be puffed up, nor other folk

Belittle, nor despise nor yet molest

The victor who hath overcome the world. Nor let him drag the praises of himself

Before the public; let him be sober, meek,

And moderate in speech and virtuous.

Is there a man who can the truth discern,

Tho' it be very subtle and refined?

Who skilled to measure spiritual growth,

Is yet of lowly, and of gentle mind.

Who shapes his life by rule of Them that Wake:

For him, Nibbana is not hard to find.


CLXVI Culaka

Reborn in this Buddha-age at Rajagaha, as a brahmin's son, he was named Culaka. When he saw the Master tame the elephant Dhanapala, he believed, and left the world. Working at his training, he dwelt in the Indra-sal-tree Cave. One day as he sat in the entrance of the cave, looking down over the Magadha 'field,' a great storm-cloud filled the sky with piled-up masses, and amid deep, lovely roars, the rain camo down. The flock of peacocks, hearing the thunder, joyously uttered their ké-ká cry, and danced around. The touch of the storm-breeze brought coolness and comfort to the Thera in his cavern-lodge, so that with a suitable temperature his mind became concentrated. He entered the avenue of his exercise, and, discerning that the favourable moment was come, he praised his practice, breaking out in these verses:

Hark! how the peacocks make the welkin ring,

Fair-crested, fine their plumes and azure throat,

Graceful in shape and pleasant in their cry.

And see how this broad landscape watered well

Lies verdure-clad beneath the dappled sky!

Healthy thy frame and fit and vigorous

To make good progress in the Buddha's rule.

Come then and grasp the rapt thought of the saint, And touch the crystal bright, the subtly deep,

The elusive mystery—even the Way

Where dying cometh not, ineffable.

And so the Thera, admonishing himself, attained under seasonable conditions to mental concentration, and evoking insight, won arahantship. Thereupon reviewing what he had wrought, with zest and joy he repeated those lines as the confession of anna.


CLXVII Anupama

Reborn in this Buddha-age in a wealthy family at Kosala, his beauty obtained him the name of Anupama—'Peerless.' Come of age, he felt the working of the efficient cause, forsook the world, and dwelt in the forest, practising for insight. But his mind hovered about external objects, revolving about his theme for meditation, so that he thus rebuked himself:

O heart! gone gadding after things that please,

O thou that shapest many a shaft of doom,

There and there only dost thou ever tend

Where block and stake rise at the bitter end.

I call thee, heart, the breaker of my luck!

I call thee, heart, despoiler of my lot!

Lo! He whom many an age thou couldst not find,

The Master now is come—suffer it not

That I to wreck and ruin be consigned.

Thus admonishing his own consciousness, the Thera developed insight, and won arahantship.


CLXVIII Vajjita

Reborn in this Buddha-age in a wealthy Kosalan family, after deceasing from the Brahma world, he ever wept in his mother's arms. And because he could not endure the touch of a woman, he came to be called Vajjita—'abstaining.' Come of age, he saw the Master work the twin-miracle, and believing, he entered the Order, and acquired sixfold abhinna. Thereupon remembering his former existence, he was stirred with holy emotion, and said:

A traveller I these long, long ages past,

And round about the realms of life I've whirled;

One of the many-folk and blind as they,

No Ariyan truths had I the power to see.

But earnestly I strove for light and calm;

And now all shattered lies the endless way.

All future bournes abolished utterly,

Now cometh never more rebirth for me.

And this became the Thera's confession of anna.


CLXIX Sandhita

Reborn in this Buddha-age in a wealthy family of Kosala and named Sandhita, he heard, when come of age, a sermon on impermanence, and this alarmed him so that he entered the Order. Through the maturity of his knowledge he established insight, and acquired sixfold abhinna. Recalling his own former life, how after the passing away of Sikhi Buddha he had worshipped at the Bo-tree and acquired discernment of impermanence, he declared his winning of the goal, by that efficient cause, in these verses:

Beneath the tree—the holy Bodhi-tree—

Clad in the glory of its vernal green,

To me musing and mindful came a thought—

A Buddha-burdened thought.

'Tis one and thirty aeons since it came.

Natheless so fruitful proved that thought in me,

By dint thereof o'er the intoxicants

The victory is wrought!

# CANTO III. PSALMS OF THREE VERSES

CLXX Anganika-Bharadvaja

Reborn in this Buddha-age near the Himalaya, at the city of Ukkattha, in the family of a very rich brahmin, he was named Anganika-Bharadvaja. And when he had learned all Vedic lore and art, his inclination for renunciation induced him to leave the world and carry on penance for salvation. Wandering here and there, he met the Buddha Supreme on a country tour, and with satisfied mind heard him teach. Leaving his false ascetics, he took orders, and practising for insight, in due course acquired sixfold abhinna.

Abiding thereafter in the bliss of liberty, he took compassion on his kinsfolk, and visited and taught them in the Refuges and the Precepts; then leaving them, he went to dwell in a forest near the village of Kuṇḍiya of the Kurus.

Going for some purpose to Uggayama, he was accosted by some brahmin acquaintances, who said: 'Master Bharadvaja, what have you seen that you have left the brahmin communion for this community?' And he, showing that outside the Buddha's church there was no pure rule, said:

Purity without principle my quest,

When in the grove I fostered sacred fire.

Painful the penances I wrought for heaven,

All ignorant of purity's true path.

This happiness by happy ways is won— O see the seemly order of the Norm! The threefold wisdom have I gotten now,

And all the Buddha's ordinance is done.

Once but a son of brahmins born was I; To-day I stand brahmin in very deed,

Versed in the triple lore and graduate, By sacramental bathing consecrate.

Then those brahmins hearing him, expressed enthusiastic appreciation of the Sasana.


CLXXI Paccaya

Reborn in this Buddha-age at the city of Rohi, in a nobleman's family, he was named Paccaya. Inheriting the estate at his father's death, he decreed to hold a great ceremonial oblation, and a great assembly foregathered.

At that congress, the Master, seated on a throne in a jewelled pavilion made by (his ancestor) Vessavana, taught the Norm, while all the people gazed at him.

Even the great multitude understood the doctrine, but raja Paccaya went further. For impelled by earlier causes, he renounced his estate and left the world. And even as he had vowed in Kassapa Buddha's time, so now, entering his cell, he vowed to attain before he left it again. And now at last, insight growing, and knowledge attaining full maturity, he attained arahantship.

Thereupon, celebrating his achievement, he thus confessed anna:

Five days have now gone by since I went forth,

A learner, and my mind not perfected. Then in the heart of me within my cell

Retired uprose unfaltering resolve:

I will not eat nor will I drink again,

Nor from this lodging let me issue forth,

Nor will I even lie upon my side,

While yet the dart of Craving lies undrawn.

Thus steadfast I abiding—O behold

And mark the forward stride of energy:

The Threefold Wisdom have I made my own,

And all the Buddha bids us do is done!


CLXXII Bakula

Born at Kosambi in a councillors family before our Exalted One appeared, he was being bathed for his health in the Great-Yamuna River, when a fish swallowed him  out of the nurse's hands. The fish was caught bv an angler and sold to the wife of a Benares councillor. When it was split open, the child through the might of his merit appeared unhurt. The wife cherished him as her son, and when she heard his story, asked him of his parents. The king decided they should have him in common, hence he was named Ba-kula ('two-families,' bi-kin).

After a prosperous life he heard the Master preach, and left the world at eighty years of age. For seven days he remained unenlightened, but as the eighth dawned he attained arahantship, together with thorough mastery of the letter and spirit of the doctrine.

One day the Master, when assigning manifold eminence to his disciples, ranked Bakula foremost for good health. Thereafter he, when about to pass away, confessed anna in the midst of the Brethren thus:

He who is fain to-morrow to perform

The things that he should yesterday have done,

Forfeit of happy opportunity,

He shall anon repent him fierily.

Let him but talk of that which should be done;

Let him not talk of what should not be done!

Of him who talketh much, but doeth not,

Wise men take stock, and rate him at his worth.

 O great, O wondrous is Nibbana's bliss,

Revealed by Him, the Utterly Awake!

There comes no grief, no passion, haven sure,

Where ill and ailing perish evermore!


CLXXIII Dhaniya

Reborn in this Buddha-age at Rajagaha in a potter's family and named Dhaniya,
he practised the potter's craft. It was at his house that the Master taught Pukkusati
the noble the Sutta of the System of Elements. Dhaniya, hearing of Pukkusati
dying as an arahant [that very night], thought: 'Mighty to guide verily is the
Buddha-sasana, wherein a single night suffices to release a man from the sorrows
of rebirth!' So he entered the Order. But he continued to occupy himself with
making tiles for roofs. Reproved for making a clay hut by the Exalted One, he took
up his abode in a bhikkhu's lodging, and there won arahantship.

Thereafter, on the occasion of admonishing bhikkhus who, as self-mortifying,
held themselves superior to others, he confessed anna thus:

If one in the recluse's discipline

Take thought how he may live in happy ease,

Let him not scorn the Order's uniform,

Nor hold in disrespect its food and drink.

If one in the recluse's discipline

Take thought how he may live in happy ease,

Let him frequent a shelter like the lair

Of watersnake or mouse [primitive, bare].

 If one in the recluse's discipline

Take thought how he may live in happy ease,

 Let him be glad whate'er the day may bring, And let him be intent on one main thing.


CLXXIV Matanga's Son

Reborn in this Buddha-age in Kosala as the son of Matanga a landowner, he came to be called after his father. He grew up idle in habits, and when his people rebuked him, he made acquaintance with the bhikkhus, noting how happily the Sakiya-son recluses lived. But when he heard the Master teach the Norm, he believed and took orders. Seeing the power of iddhi wielded by bhikkhus, he aspired to the same. And practising exercises, he won sixfold abhinna.

Thereupon he scourged slothfulness, extolling his own rush of energy in these verses:

Too cold! too hot! too late! such is the cry.

And so, past men who shake off work [that waits

Their hand], the fateful moments fly.

But he who reckons cold and heat as less

Than straws, doing his duties as a man,

He no defaulter proves to happiness.

 Dabba- and kusa-grass and pricking stems,

And all that hurts in brush and underwood.

Forth from my breast I'll push and thrust away,

And go where I the growth may cultivate

Of heart's detachment, lone and separate.


CLXXV Khujja-Sobhita

Reborn in this Buddha-age at Pataliputta, in a brahmin's family, he was named Sobhita. But being a little hunchbacked, he was called Crooked Sobhita. Come of age at the time of the Master's passing away, he was ordained by Ananda, and acquired sixfold abhinna.

Now, at the first Great Council in the Sattapanni Cave, he was bidden fetch Ananda Thera to the Assembly. Now at that time the company of devas sent an angel to stand at the entrance to the Cave to counteract the work of Mara. And Khujja-Sobhita announced his own coming to the angel in this verse:

One of the Brethren who in Patna dwell,

Learned and erudite, lo! at the door,

Advanced in years, stands Crooked Sobhita.

Then the angel informed the Saṅgha of the Thera'e advent:

One of the Brethren who in Patna dwell,

Learned and eloquent, lo! at the door,

Advanced in years, he stands borne by the winds.

Then the Saṅgha giving him opportunity, the Thera approached them and confessed anna:

Good fight he made, and made good sacrifice, And in the battle won:— now by such war,

The fervent following of the holy life,

In happiness he resteth [evermore].


CLXXVI Varana

Reborn in this Buddha-age in Kosala as a brahmin's son, he was named Varana. Come of age, he heard a Thera preach the Norm in a forest, and believing, entered the Order. One day going to wait upon the Buddha he saw, on the way, a family quarrel, through which some were slain. Distressed, he hastened to the Exalted One, and told him. And the latter, discerning the progress of his mind, exhorted him, saying:

Whoso here causeth fellow-creatures pain,

From this and from the other-world, from both

This man may forfeit all they yield of good.

Whoso with loving heart compassion takes

On every fellow-creature, such a man

Doth generate of merit ample store.

Train ye yourselves in pious utterance,

In waiting ever on the wise and good,

In haunting secret solitary seat,

And in the calm and concentrated mind.

When these verses were ended, Varana, developing insight, won arahantship.


CLXXVII Passika

Reborn in this Buddha-age in the family of a Kosalan brahmin, he saw the Master
work the twin miracle, and believed. Entering the Order he fell ill while performing
the studies of a recluse. His own people attended him and healed him. But he,
greatly stirred by his recovery, pressed forward his study, and acquired sixfold
abhinna. Thereupon he went through the air to his own people, and established
them in the Refuges and the Precepts. And some of his kin, so established, died
and were reborn in heaven. When Passika waited on the Master, the latter asked
after the health of his kin. And Passika thus made answer:

Though I alone, 'mong unbelieving kin,

Had faith and wit enough, discerned the Nonn

And clove to virtue, this was for their good.

For see! mine own folk, whom for pity's sake

I took to task, roused and rebuked by me,

Through their affection and their piety

Constrained, towards the Brethren wrought good work.

They who are now gone hence, ending this span,

They reap much happiness among the gods.

Brothers of mine are there, my mother too,

Fain for the pleasures that they now enjoy.


CLXXVIII Yasoja

Reborn in this Buddha-age at the gate of the city of Savatthi in a fisher's village,
as the son of the headman of the 500 fishermen's families, he was called Yasoja.
Come of age, he was one day fishing with the fishermen's sons in the River

Aciravati. And casting his net, he caught a great gold-coloured fish. They showed it to King Pasenadi, who said: 'The Exalted One will know the cause of the fish's colour.' And the Exalted One told them that the fish had, in Kassapa Buddha's time, been a wicked bhikkhu, who had since then suffered in purgatory; that his sisters were still there, but that his brother as Thera had perfected life; and then for their good he taught the Kappila Sutta.

Thereupon Yasoja in deep emotion renounced the world, and his companions with him. Of his going with them to wait on the Exalted One at the Jeta-Vana, and of their dismissal because of the noise they made on arriving, the record stands in the Udana. Dismissed, and dwelling on the banks of the River Vaggumuda, Yasoja, like a highbred horse, his mettle stirred, strove and toiled till he acquired sixfold abhinna. Thereafter the Exalted One sent for him. And he, from practising all the special austerities, was emaciated and uncomely. Then the Exalted One commended his self-denial in this verse:

Lo! here a man with frame so pale and worn;

Like knotted stems of cane his joints, and sharp

Th' emaciated network of his veins.

In food and drink austerely temperate,

His spirit neither crushed nor desolate.

And Yasoja so commended, extolled the love of solitude, and taught doctrine thus:

In the great forest, in the mighty woods,

Touched though I be by gadfly and by gnat,

I yet would roam, like warrior-elephant

In van of battle, mindful, vigilant.

Alone a man is even as Brahma.

And as the angels if he have one mate.

Like to a village is a group of three.

Like to a noisy crowd if more there be.

## CLXXIX Satimattiya

Reborn in this Buddha-age in the kingdom of Magadha as a brahmin's son, he having the essential conditions entered the Order among the forest bhikkhus, and through study and practice acquired sixfold abhinna. Thereupon he instructed bhikkhus, and preached to many folk on the Refuges and the Precepts. One family in particular he converted to faith and trust; and in that house he was greatly welcomed, the only daughter, a pretty, lovely girl, respectfully providing him with food.

One day Mara, plotting to disturb and disgrace him, took his shape, and going to the maiden, grasped her hand. But she, feeling that this was no human touch, loosed her hand. But the others in the house saw it and lost faith in the Thera. He, knowing nothing, perceived next day their changed manner. And discerning that Mara had been at work, he vowed to loose the dead dog from their neck, and made them tell him what had happened. And the housemaster, hearing his explanation, begged his forgiveness, and declared he himself would wait upon him. The Thera told the matter in these verses:

The trust thou once didst place in me,

To-day it lives no more. What's thine is thine;

But in this house no evil have I done.

Transient and wavering is the layman's faith:—

So have I marked. Folk love and then grow cold.

Why for that should a holy brother die?

Cooked stands the sage's food a little here,

A little there, in one clan or the next.

I will go round to seek my little alms;

My legs are strong enough forsooth for that.


## CLXXX Upali

Reborn in this Buddha-age in a barber's family, he was named Upali. Come of age he left the world, following Anuruddha and the other five nobles, when the Exalted One was staying at Anupiya Grove, as is recorded in the Pali. Now when he was taking a subject for exercise from the Master, he said: 'Send me not away, Lord, to dwell in the forest.' 'Bhikkhu, you dwelling in the forest, will develop one subject only; if you dwell with us, you will become proficient in both book-knowledge and insight.' The Thera, consenting to the Master's word, practised for insight, and in due time won arahantship.

Moreover, the Master himself taught him the whole Vinaya-Pitaka. And later, after Upali had won the Master's commendation of his decision in the three cases of Ajjuka, the Kurukacchaka bhikkhu and Kumara-Kassapa, he was ranked first among those who knew the Vinaya.

One feast-day, when he was reciting the Patimokkha, he thus admonished the brethren:

He who for faith's sake hath renounced the world,

And stands a novice in the Order new,

Friends let him choose of noble character,

Pure in their lives, of zeal unfaltering.

He who for faith's sake hath renounced the world,

And stands a novice in the Order new,

Among the Order let that bhikkhu dwell,

And wisely learn its code of discipline.

He who for faith's sake hath renounced the world,

And stands a novice in the Order new,

Skilled in what should be done, or left undone,

Let him uncompanied hold on his way.


CLXXXI Uttarapala

Reborn in this Buddha-age at Savatthi in a brahmin family, he was named Uttarapala. He saw the Twin Miracle, and believing, entered the Order, and pursued his studies. One day, amid desultory recollections, sensual desires beset him, but after a violent mental struggle, he arrested the corrupting moods (kilesa's), and in earnest meditation won arahantship.

Thereupon reflecting on his victory, he uttered a 'lion-roar':

Me seeming wise, forsooth, and spent enough

In pondering on the things that make for good,

Me overthrew fivefold desires of sense,

Bewilderers [of the reason] of the world.

Though lodged in Mara's reach, by mighty dart

Assailed, yet did my strength suffice to win

From snare set by the King of Death release.

Now are all sense-desires put far away!

Now are all rebirths shattered once for aye!

Destroyed is birth-and-death's eternity!

Now cometh nevermore rebirth for me!


## CLXXXII Abhibhuta

Reborn in this Buddha-age in a raja's family at the city of Vetthapura, he was named Abhibhuta, and succeeded to the estate at his father's death. Now when the Exalted One arrived at his city on tour, Abhibhuta went to hear him, and on the morrow offered him hospitality. The Exalted One expressed the thanks he felt, and thereupon taught him the Norm more in detail. Then the raja found faith, left his estate for the Order, and realized arahantship.

While he was dwelling in the bliss of emancipation, his kindred, councillors and retainers came to him lamenting that he had left them without a chief. And he, teaching them the Norm by way of extolling the reason of his renunciation, said:

Hear, O ye kinsmen, and give ear to me,

All and as many as are gathered here!

The Norm it is that ye shall learn from me:—

Painful is birth again and yet again!

Bestir yourselves, rise up, renounce and come,

And yield your hearts unto the Buddha's Rule.

Shake off the armies of the King of Death

As doth the elephant a hut of straw.

Whoso within this righteous discipline

Shall come with diligence to understand.

Rebirth's eternal round put far away.

All pain and suffering he shall end for aye.

CLXXXIII Gotama

Reborn in this Buddha-age in the Sakiyan clan, he came to be known only by his gens name. He found faith when the Master visited his kinsfolk, and entering the Order and studying for insight, acquired sixfold abhinna. Now, while  he was dwelling in the bliss of emancipation, his kinsfolk asked him one day why he had put them aside and gone forth. And he, to show both the ill he had suffered in Samsara and the happiness of Nibbana which he then had gotten, said:

Lo! as I fared through being, I came to the kingdom infernal,

So to the dolorous realm of the Petas, times without number.

Evil befell me again in manifold shapes of the beast-world.

Glad enough reborn as human, rarely I won to the heavens.

Yea, in the realms of vision, in realms where all sense was abolished

Have I been placed, and in realms 'twixt consciousness and the unconscious.

All this becoming lies clearly before me as void of real value,

Born of preceding conditions, unstable and constantly drifting.

So comprehending the coming to be of this self of me, heedful,

Came I at length to find Peace, yea, the Peace [wherein I am resting].


CLXXXIV Harita

Reborn in this Buddha-age at Savatthi in a brahmin family, he fell into the habit, from pride of birth, of calling other men low-born. Even after he had heard the Norm, and believed and entered the Order, he persisted from the  cumulative force of the habit. But one day, after hearing the Master preach, he reviewed his own mental procedure, and was distressed to mark the surrender to conceit and arrogance. Expelling it all, he conjured up insight and won arahantship. Thereafter, dwelling in the bliss of emancipation, he testified to anna in thus admonishing the bhikkhus:

He who is fain to-morrow to perform

The things that he should yesterday have done,

Forfeit of happy opportunity,

He shall anon repent him fierily.

Let him but talk of that which should be done;

Let him not talk of what should not be done!

Of him who talketh much but doeth not,

Wise men take stock, and rate him at his worth.

O great, O wondrous is Nibbana's bliss,

Revealed by Him, the Utterly Awake!

There comes no grief, no passion, haven sure,

Where ill and ailing perish evermore!


## CLXXXV Vimala (2)

Reborn in this Buddha-age at Benares in a brahmin family, he entered the Order under Thera Amitta, and through his instigation acquired insight and won arahantship. Thereupon he admonished a bhikkhu who was his comrade as follows:

From evil-minded friends keep far away,

And make thy choice among the best of men.

To his advice hold fast, and let thy heart

Aspire to happiness immutable.

As one who, mounted on a puny plank,

Is in mid-ocean whelmed beneath the waves,

So even he of blameless life doth sink,

When throw'n together with the man of sloth.

Wherefore from such an one keep well apart,

The sluggard and the poor in energy.

Dwell thou with them who live aloof,

With wise, with noble souls who have renounced,

Who in rapt contemplation ever strive.

Canto IV. Psalms of Four Verses

CLXXXVI Nagasamala

Reborn in this Buddha-age in a clan of Sakiyan rajas, he made the perishableness of life his principle, and, conjuring up insight, attained arahantship. He thereupon testified to anna, as occurring in his own experience, thus:

Bedecked with trinkets and with pretty frock,

Wreathed with flowers, raddled with sandal wood,

In the main street, before the multitude

A nautch girl danced to music's fivefold sound.

Into the city I had gone for alms,

And passing I beheld the dancer decked

In brave array, like snare of Mara laid.

Thereat arose in me the deeper thought: Attention to the fact and to the cause.

The misery of it all was manifest;

Distaste, indifference the mind possessed.

And so my heart was set at liberty.

O see the seemly order of the Norm!

The Threefold Wisdom have I made my own,

And all the Buddha bids me do is done.


CLXXXVII Bhagu

Reborn in this Buddha-age in a clan of Sakiyan rajas, he left the world, together with his clansmen, Anuruddha and Kimbila, and dwelt by the village of Balakalona. And one day, when he had left his cell to discipline his tendency to sloth and torpor, he fell as he was stepping up on to the terrace. Using this as his goad, he accomplished self-mastery, and developing insight, he won arahantship. Thereupon, as he was living in the bliss of fruition, the bliss of Nibbana, the Master, coming to congratulate him on his solitude, asked him: 'How now, bhikkhu, do you continue in earnest?' And he assenting, replied:

Foredone by drowth I gat me from my cell

For exercise, and climbed the terrace-steps,

And fell thereby all drowsy to the earth.

Chafing my limbs, once more I mounted up;

And while on terrace to and fro I went,

Within 'twas all alert, composed, intent.

Thereat arose in me the deeper thought:

Attention to the fact and to the cause.

 The misery of it all was manifest;

Distaste, indifference the mind possessed;

And so my heart was set at liberty.

O see the seemly order of the Norm!

The Threefold Wisdom have I made my own,

 And all the Buddha bids me do is done.

This was the Thera's confession of anna.


CLXXXVIII Sabhiya

In the time of our Exalted One he took rebirth as the son of a nobleman's daughter, whose parents had committed her to the charge of a Wanderer, that she might learn other doctrines and usages. Sabhiya, when grown up, also became a Wanderer, and learning various recitations, became a great dialectician, and found none to equal him. Making his hermitage by the city gate, he gave lessons to the children of noblemen and others, and devised twenty questions, which he asked recluses and brahmins. In the narrative to the Sabhiya-Sutta it is handed down, that a Brahma god from the Pure Abodes devised the questions. There, too, it is told how the Exalted One, when he came to Rajagaha, to the Bamboo Grove, so answered the questions, that Sabhiya believed on him, and entering the Order, established insight and won arahantship.

But after this it was in admonishing the bhikkhus who sided with the seceding Devadatta that he spoke these verses:

People can never really understand

That we are here but for a little spell.  But they who grasp this truth indeed,

Suffer all strife and quarrels to abate.

And whereas they who cannot understand.

Deport themselves as they immortals were.

They who can really understand the Norm

Are as the hale amid a world diseased.

All flaccid action, all corrupted rites,

Suspicious conduct in religious life:

On all such work follows no high reward.

He who among his fellow-brethren wins

No reverence is far from the good Norm,

As is the firmament far from the earth.


## CLXXXIX Nandaka

Reborn in the time of our Exalted One at Savatthi in a clansman's family, he was called Nandaka. He entered the Order after hearing the Master teach the Norm, and developing insight won arahantship. Thereafter, while dwelling in the bliss of emancipation, he gave a lesson by the Master's order one feast-day to the bhikkhunis, and caused 500 of them to attain arahantship. Wherefore the Exalted One ranked him foremost among the exhorters of the brethren and sisters.

Now, one day, while seeking alms in Savatthi, a woman, to whom he had been married, saw him and laughed with  sinful heart. The Thera, seeing her action, taught her the Norm under the aspect of emphasizing repugnance at the body,thus:

Fie on the fulsome thing malodorous!

A very tool of Mara, even this,

Thy body, whence exude those many streams,

In number nine, that never cease their flow.

Build no conceits from former passages.

Try not to allure the Elect-who-Thus-have-Come! The very heavens delight them not, how then

Should aught that's merely earthly ever please?

The fools who lack discretion, they whose mind

Is sullied, and their heart by dullness cloaked,

Such men in charms of body take delight,

For they are fast in bonds by Mara thrown.

To them who are untouched by lust, or hate,

Or ignorance, these things no pleasures be.

Cut are the cords; they from all bonds are free.


CXC Jambuka

Reborn in this Buddha-age in a very poor family, he inclined, as in a previous birth, to feeding on excremeut, and left the world to be a naked ascetic. Practising many austerities, and eating beans one by one on the point of a straw, he was fifty-five years old when the Exalted One, seeing the conditions of arahantship shining within his heart like a lamp in a jar, himself went to him, and teaching him the Norm, converted him. Then said he: 'Come, bhikkhu!' thereby ordaining him. And Jambuka thereupon conjuring up insight, the Master established him in arahantship. This is in outline, but a full account is given in the Commentary on the Dhammapada verse:

Bean after bean by point of straw. …

At the hour of his passing away he showed that, though once wrongly living, he, by leaning on the Buddha Supreme, had gotten where a disciple ought to get, thus:

For five and fifty years covered with dust

And dirt, eating a dinner once a month, And pulling out my hair from head and face,

On one leg would I stand, I used no couch,

Dry dung I ate, nor would accept when bid.

So wrought I actions leading to much woe

And ruin, swept along by mighty flood,

Till I a refuge in the Buddha found:—

O see how to that Refuge I am come!

O see the seemly order of the Norm!

The Threefold Wisdom have I made my own,

And all the Buddha bids me do is done.

CXCI Senaka

Reborn in this Buddha-age in a brahmin family, as the son of the sister of the Thera Kassapa of Uruvela, he was named Senaka. When he had learnt the brahmins' Vedic culture, he dwelt with his family. And at that time the people held a festival every year in the former half of March (Phagguna), and a baptizing at the landing-stage, the festival being called the Gaya-Lent.

Then the Exalted One, out of compassion for those who could be led, stayed near that riverside. And when the people assembled, Senaka came too, and hearing the Master teaching the Norm, was converted, entered the Order, and in due course won arahantship. Thereafter, reflecting on his victory, ho was filled with joy, and breathed forth this psalm:

O welcome was to me that day of spring,

When at Gaya, at Gaya's river-feast,

I saw the Buddha teach the Norm supreme,

Saw the great Light, Teacher of multitudes,

Him who hath won the highest, Guide of all,

The Conqueror of men and gods, unrivalled Seer.

Mighty magician, hero glorious,

Far-shining splendour, pure, immune of mind, The Master who hath slain all asavas,

And hath attained that where no fear can come.

Long lay I bound and harassed by the ties

Of sect and dogma—ah! but now 'tis He,

The Blessed Lord hath rescued Senaka

From every bond and set at liberty.


CXCII Sambhuta

Reborn in this Buddha-age in a clansman's family, he was converted, after the Exalted One had passed away, by the Treasurer of the Norm. And entering the Order, he developed insight and attained arahantship. So he lived in the bliss of emancipation till, a century after the Parinibbana of the Exalted One, the Vajjian brethren of Vesali put forward the ten theses, and were resisted by the Thera Niyasa and the Kakandakan brethren, and a recension of Norm and Vinaya was made by 700 arahants. Then the Thera, moved by righteous emotion at the proposed perversion of Dhamma and Vinaya, uttered these verses, testifying thereby to annna:

He who decides in season meet for pause,

And he who dallies when he should decide, This fool by want of plan and principle

Doth journey hence to suffer many ills.

Rewards that should be his do melt away,

As in the dark weeks melts the waning moon.

Dishonour he incurs, at variance with his friends.

He who is slow in season meet for pause,

Who crosses when 'twere wrong to hesitate,

This wise man by his plan and principle

Doth surely win his way to happiness.

The gains that shall be his wax ripe and full,

As in bright weeks doth wax the crescent moon.

Honour, renown he wins, at one with friends.


CXCIII Rahula

Reborn in this Buddha-age through our Bodhisat, as the son of Princess Yasodhara, he was reared with a great retinue of nobles. The circumstances of his entering the Order are recorded in the Khandhaka. And he, his knowledge ripened by gracious words in many Sutta passages, conjured up insight, and so won arahantship. Thereupon, reflecting on his victory, he confessed anna:

Twice blest of fortune am I whom my friends

Call 'Lucky Rahula.' For I am both

Child of the Buddha and a Seer of truths;

Yea, and intoxicants are purged from me;

Yea, and there's no more coming back to be.

Ar'hant am I, worthy men's offerings;

'Thrice skilled' my ken is of ambrosial things.

Blinded are beings by their sense-desires,

Spread o'er them like a net; covered are they

By cloak of craving; by their heedless ways

Caught as a fish in mouth of funnel-net,  But I, that call of sense abandoning,

Have cut and snapt the bonds of devil's lure.

Craving with craving's root abolishing;

Cool am I now; extinct is fever's fire.


CXCIV Candana

Reborn in this Buddha-age at Savatthi in a wealthy clan, and named Candana, he lived a domestic life till he  heard the Master preach the Norm; and became thereupon a Stream-winner. When a child was born to him, he left his home for the Order, and taking an insight exercise, dwelt in the forest. Coming into Savatthi to salute the Master, he stayed in a charnel-field. And his wife, hearing of his coming, adorned herself, and, taking her child and many attendants, approached him, judging that by her attractions she could induce him to secede from the Order. He, seeing her coming from afar, thought: 'Now will I get outside her reach!' And he so conjured up insight that he acquired sixfold abhinna. Thereupon he rose aloft, and so taught her the Norm, establishing her in the Refuges and the Precepts. Then he went back to his former haunts. And when his bhikkhu comrades asked him, saying, 'Serene are you looking, brother; what truths have you discerned?' he told of his achievement, and testified to anna in these verses:

In golden gear bedecked, a troop of maids

Attending in her train, bearing the babe

Upon her hip, my wife drew near to me.

I marked her coming, mother of my child,

In brave array like snare of Mara laid.

Thereat arose in me the deeper thought: Attention to the fact and to the cause.

The misery of it all was manifest;

Distaste, indifference the mind possessed;

And so my heart was set at liberty.

O see the seemly order of the Norm!

The Threefold Wisdom have I made my own,

And all the Buddha bids me do is done.


CXCV Dhammika

Reborn in this Buddha-age in a family of Kosalan brahmins, and named Dhammika, he won faith at the presentation of the Jeta Grove, and entered the Order. Becoming a resident at a village Vihara, he grew impatient and irritable over the duties of incoming bhikkhus, so that the latter abandoned the Vihara. Thus he became sole master of the Vihara. And a layman reported this to the Exalted One. The Master sent for Dhammika, and asked him to explain. Thereupon he said: 'Not only now are you impatient; you were so formerly also'; and at the bhikkhus' request he gave a 'tree-talk' on the Norm, with admonition over and above, as follows:

Well doth the Norm protect him in sooth who follows the Norm.

Happiness bringeth along in its train the Norm well practised.

This shall be his reward by whom the Norm is well practised:

Never goeth to misery he who doth follow the Norm.

For not of like result are right and wrong:

Wrong leads to baleful, right, to happy doom.

Wherefore let will be applied to [master] the things that we know.

So let him hail with delight so welcome a blessing as this.  Firm in the Welcome One's Norm the disciples fare onward,

Valiantly following Him, their sovereign Refuge.

Plucked out the root of all this cancerous lump, The net of craving wholly torn away,

The round of life renewed hath ceased,

And naught of clinging doth remain,

E'en as the moon on fifteenth day

Sails in clear sky without a stain.

When the Master had taught three of the verses, Dhammika, bearing them in mind, developed insight even as he sat, and won arahantship. And to show the transformation in himself to the Master, he declared anna by the last verse.

CXCVI Sabbaka

Reborn in this Buddha-age at Savatthi in a brahmin family and named Sabbaka, he heard the Exalted One teaching the Norm, and believing, entered the Order. Taking an exercise, he went to the Lonagiri Vihara on the banks of the river Ajakarani, and there in due time won arahantship. Going thereupon to salute the Master at Savatthi, he stayed a little while, entertained by his kinsfolk. And having confirmed them in the Refuges and the Precepts, he was anxious to return to his dwelling. They begged him to stay and be supported by them. But he, showing them why he had come, and declaring his love of retirement by praise of his dwelling-place, said:

Whene'er I see the crane, her clear bright wings

Outstretched in fear to flee the black stormcloud,

A shelter seeking, to safe shelter borne,

Then doth the river Ajakarani

Give joy to me.

Whene'er I see the crane, her plumage pale

And silver white outstretched in fear to flee

The black stormcloud, seeing no refuge nigh,

The refuge seeking of the rocky cave,

Then doth the river Ajakarani Give joy to me.

Who doth not love to see on either bank

Clustered rose-apple trees in fair array

Behind the great cave [of my hermitage]

Or hear the soft croak of the frogs, well rid

Of their undying mortal foes proclaim:

'Not from the mountain-streams is't time to-day

To flit. Safe is the Ajakarani.

She brings us luck. Here is it good to be.'

Then the relatives suffered him to depart. And because he showed herein his delight in empty places, this became the Thera's confession of anna.

## CXCVII Mudita

Reborn in this Buddha-age in the family of a Kosalan commoner, he was named Mudita. When he was come of age, his clan for some reason became objectionable to the king. Mudita, terrified of the king, ran away, and  entering the forest, approached the dwelling of an arahant Thera. The latter, seeing his terror, bade him fear not, and reassured him. 'How long, your reverence, will it take before I am free from danger?' 'When seven or eight months have passed.' 'I cannot wait so long; I will leave the world, your reverence; ordain me!' So he begged, to protect his life. The Thera ordained him. And he, coming to believe in the doctrine, lost his fears and exercised himself for insight. Failing to win arahantship, he vowed not to leave his retreat till he had, and thereupon succeeded. Thereafter experiencing the bliss of emancipation, he was asked as to his success by his fellow-bhikkhus. And he told them how he had succeeded, thus:

I left the world that I might save my life,

And, once ordained, I won back faith and hope;

Valiant in energy I onward pressed.

Now an it must be, let this body break

And waste and let its flesh consume,

My limbs let falter at the knee and fail;

I will not eat nor will I drink again,

Nor from this lodging let me issue forth,

Nor will I even lie upon my side,

While yet the dart of Craving lies undrawn!

Thus steadfast I abiding—O behold

And mark the forward stride of energy:

The Threefold Wisdom have I made my own,

And all the Buddha bids us do is done!

# CANTO V. PSALMS OF FIVE VERSES

CXCVIII Rajadatta

Reborn in this Buddha-age at Savatthi in a caravan-leaders' family, his parents called him Rajadatta ('given by the king'), because they had obtained him through praying to Vessavana, the great firmament deity. Come of age, he once took 500 carts of merchandise to Rajagaha. Now there he squandered all his money, spending a thousand a day on a beautiful courtesan, so that he was penniless and had not enough to eat, and wandered about in wretchedness. So he came with other laymen to the Bamboo Grove, where the Master sat teaching the Norm to a great congregation. And Rajadatta, seated at the fringe of the assembly, heard and believed, and entered the Order. Undertaking the Dhutangas, he dwelt in a charnel-field.

Now another caravan-leader also spent his thousand on the courtesan, and wore on his hand a ring of great value, which she coveted. She got men to steal it, but the owner's servants told the police, and they raided her house, slew her, and cast her body into the charnel-field.

The Thera Rajadatta, walking therein to find a foul object for meditation, noticed this corpse. For a while  he concentrated his attention, but the portions of her yet unmangled by dogs and jackals distracted him and all but overmastered him. Much distraught, he exhorted his heart, and went away for a brief space; then recommencing, he induced jhana, confirmed his insight, and so won arahantship.

Thereupon, reflecting on his success and filled with zest and joy, he said:

A bhikkhu to the charnel-field had gone,

And there he saw a woman's body cast

Untended 'mid the dead, the food of worms.

Most men had felt repugnance at the sight,

Seeing the corpse, the poor dead evil thing.

In me was sensual passion manifest,

And I became as blind and lost control.

But swifter from that place than seething rice

Could boiling overflow, I turned and fled; Aside elsewhere I took my seat cross-legged,

In heedful and discriminating mood.

Thereon arose in me the deeper thought: Attention to the fact and to the cause.

The misery of it all was manifest.

Distaste, indifference the mind possessed;

And so my heart was set at liberty.

O see the seemly order of the Norm!

The Threefold Wisdom have I made my own,

And all the Buddha bids us do is done.


CXCIX Subhuta

Reborn in this Buddha-age in the family of a commoner of Magadha, and named Subhuta, his disposition to seek  escape caused him to quit domestic life and to join sectarian ascetics. Finding among them nothing genuine, and seeing the happiness enjoyed by Upatissa, Kolita, Sela and others, after they had entered the Order, he believed in our doctrine and entered also. After winning the favour of his teachers and preceptors, he went into retreat with an exercise. And developing insight he won arahantship.

Thereupon he declared anna by reviewing the suffering he had endured by self-mortification, and his subsequent happiness in jhana, etc.:

A man who yokes himself to things unfit,

Desiring to accomplish work therein,

If seeking he doth not attain, his quest

Doth bear the intrinsic markings of mischance.

If he surrender but one [vantage-point]

Of misery['s source] drawn out and overcome,

Like luckless throw of dice his state may be.

But if he throw all [he hath gained] away,

No better is he than a blinded man,

Who sees not if the road be smooth or rough.

Of him who talketh much, but doeth not,

Wise men take stock, and rate him at his worth.

 Just as a beauteous flower of lovely hue

But lacking odour, so is uttered word

That barren proves, by action not made good.

Just as a beauteous flower of lovely hue

And fragrant odour, so is uttered word

That fruitful proves, in action holding good.


CC Girimananda

Reborn in this Buddha-age at Rajagaha as the son of King Bimbisara's chaplain, he was named Girimananda. He saw the power and majesty of a Buddha when the Master attended the meeting at Rajagaha, and he entered the Order. During his studies he stayed awhile at a village, then came back to the town to salute the Master. And Bimbisara the maharaja heard of his coming, and going to him, said: 'Do you dwell here, your reverence; I will supply your needs.' But from his much business he forgot, so that the Thera dwelt in the open. And the weather-gods held off the rain for fear of wetting the Thera. Then the king, noting the drought, built him a hermitage. And the Thera, sheltered in his hut, put forth all his efforts, and combining energy and calm, conjured up insight and won arahantship. Then, delighted at its advent, he confessed anna while the rain fell from above:

God rains as 'twere a melody most sweet.

Snug is my little hut, sheltered, well-roofed.

Therein I dwell, my heart serene and calm.

Now an it pleaseth thee to rain, god, rain!

God rains as 'twere a melody most sweet.

Snug is my little hut, sheltered, well-roofed.

Therein I dwell, and peace within my heart.

Now, etc.

Therein I dwell, all passion purged away.

………..

Therein I dwell, all hatred purged away.

………..

Therein I dwell, all error purged away.

Now an it pleaseth thee to rain, god, rain!

CCI Sumana

Reborn in this Buddha-age in the family of a commoner of Kosala, and named Sumana, he grew up in happy circumstances. His mother's brother became an arahant, dwelling in the forest, and when Sumana came of age, this uncle ordained him, giving him exercises on ethical conduct. Finally, when the four jhanas and fivefold abhinna were acquired, the Thera showed him the way of insight, so that he soon acquired arahantship. And when he went to his uncle and was asked concerning his success, he thus made confession:

That which my teacher wished that I should know

In doctrines good, and of his kindness taught

To me who longed for the Ambrosial:

That now, even the task prescribed, is done.

Yea, won and realized is the Norm

E'en for my own, not learnt 'as such and such:' Pure lore is mine, dispelled is every doubt.

Let me stand near to thee and testify:

I know the where and when of former lives,

And clearly shines the Eye Celestial;

The Good Supreme, Ar'hantship, have I won, And what the Buddha bids us do is done.

Well have I learnt, who used all diligence,

The method and the training in thy rule;

For all th' Intoxicants are purged away;

Now cometh never more the life renewed.

Noble thy cult and thou hast guided me.

Compassionate, 'tis thou hast favoured me.

Thine admonitions have not proved inept.

Once an apprentice, now am I adept.

CCII Vadda

Reborn in this Buddha-age at the city of Bharukaccha in a commoner's clan, and named Vaḍḍha, he grew up in due course. Now his mother, distressed at the continuity of rebirth and death, entrusted her son to her kinsfolk, and entered the Order among the bhikkhunis. She thereafter won arahantship. Her son, too, entered the Order under Thera Veḷudanta, and learning the Buddha-Word, became learned and eloquent in preaching. And one day, feeling the responsibility of office, he thought: 'I will go alone and see my mother, nor put on my cloak.' So he went to the  bikkhunis' quarters. His mother, seeing him, rebuked him: ' Why are you come here alone and without your cloak?' And he, convicted in doing that which was unfit, returned to his Vihara, and seated in the day-room, there attained arahantship, testifying to anna under the aspect of ascribing his achievement to his mother's admonition:

O well in sooth my mother used the goad!

I marked her word, and by my parent taught,

I stirred up effort, put forth all my strength,

And won the goal, th' enlightenment supreme.

Ar'hant am I, meet for men's offerings. Thrice wise, th' ambrosial vision I behold;

 Conquered is Namuci and all his host, And now I dwell henceforth sane and immune.

Yea, the intoxicants that once were there,

Within, without me, are extracted clean;

Nought doth remain nor may they re-appear.

Lo! wise and ripe in grace the Sister was,

Who spake this word of pregnant good to me:

For thee now even as for me, [my son,]

No jungle of the mind doth bar the way.

A final barrier is made to Ill.

Last mortal frame is this, to which belongs

The way world without end of birth and death,

Nor ever cometh more rebirth [for thee].

CCIII Kassapa of the River

Reborn in this Buddha-age in a clan of Magadha brahmins, as the brother of Uruveḷa-Kassapa, his religious inclination made him dislike domestic life, and he became an  ascetic. With 300 ascetics he carried on a hermit's life on the banks of the River Neranjara, and thus he became known, by his habit and the name of his gens, as Kassapa of the River. Now how the Exalted One ordained him and his company by the summons, 'Come, bhikkhu,' is recorded in the Khandaka. He was confirmed in arahantship by the Exalted One's sermon on Burning. Thereafter reflecting on his achievement, he confessed anna by way of extolling his rooting out of error:

O truly for my good it was that He,

The Buddha came to the Neranjara,

Whose doctrine hearing, I renounced wrong views.

The celebrant in many a sacrifice,

I fostered sacred fire, oblations made;

'These be the pure and holy rites!' methought—

O blind and average worldling that I was!

Errant in wilderness of heresies,

By their contagion dazed and led astray,

I deemed that pure religion which was false.

And blinded was I, shiftless, ignorant.

Now is all error put away for me;

Broken the line of comings back to be.

Worth every gift, the Fire I celebrate: I worship 'Him who on This Wise hath Come.'

Illusions all have I put far away.

Crushed is the thirst for going on to be,

And shattered is the endless round of life.

Now cometh nevermore rebirth for me!

CCIV Kassapa of Gaya

Reborn in this Buddha-age in a brahmin clan [his story resembles that of Kassapa of the River, save that his company numbered 200, and that he dwelt at Gaya]. He confessed anna by exalting the washing away of evil, thus:

At morn, at noonday, at the eventide

Thrice in the day I gat me at Gaya

Down in the water at Gaya's spring feast, For 'sins that I have done in other births,

In days gone by, those here and now hereby

I wash away':—thus did I once believe.

I heard a voice that uttered winning words,

Whereof the burden wedded Norm and Good.

And on their meaning, true and genuine,

I pondered much and reasoned earnestly.

Now from all evil am I truly bathed,

Cleansed from error, pure, immaculate.

In purity heir of the Purified,

His child, even the Buddha's very son.

For I have plunged into the Eightfold Stream,

And every evil thing I've washed away.

The Threefold Wisdom have I found and won,

And all the Buddha bids us do is done.


CCV Vakkali

Reborn in the time of our Master at Savatthi in a brahmin clan, they named him Vakkali. When he had grown wise and had learnt the three Vedas, and was  proficient in brahmin accomplishments, he saw the Master. Never sated by looking at the perfection of the Master's visible body, he went about with him. And when in his house he thought: 'I shall not [here] get a chance of seeing Him constantly'; so he entered the Order, and spent all his time, save at his meals and toilet, doing nothing else but contemplating the Exalted One. The Master, waiting for the maturity of his insight, for a long while made no comment; then one day he said: 'What is to thee, Vakkali, this foul body that thou seest? He who seeth the Norm, he it is that seeth me. For seeing the Norm he seeth me, and seeing me he seeth the Norm.' At the Master's words, Vakkali ceased to look, but he was unable to go away. Hence the Master thinking: 'This bhikkhu, if he get not deeply moved, will not awake," said on the last day of the rains: 'Depart, Vakkali!' Thus bidden, he could not stay; but thinking: 'What is life to me if I cannot see him?' climbed the Vulture's Peak to a place of precipices. The Master, knowing what Vakkali was about, thought: 'This bhikkhu, finding no comfort away from me, will destroy the conditions for winning the topmost fruits'; and revealing himself in a glory, spake thus:

Now let the bhikkhu with exceeding joy

Delighting in the Buddhas Way and Lore,

Go up on to the holy, happy Path,

Where things component ne'er excite him more.

And stretching forth his hand, he said: 'C'

The Thera, filled with mighty joy and rapture at the thought: 'I see Him-of-the-Ten-Powers, and mine is it to hear Him say: Come!' came to himself and realized what he was doing. Rising in the air, he stood on the nearest point of the hill while he pondered on the Master's verse;  then arresting his rapture, he realized arahantship, together with grasp of the form and meaning of the Norm. This is what is recorded both in the Aṅguttara Commentary and in that on the Dhammapada.

But here they say as follows: Admonished by the Master's 'What is to thee... ?' Vakkali dwelt on the Vulture's Peak, establishing himself in insight, and descending into the avenue thereof by the might of his faith. The Exalted One, knowing this, gave him a special exercise which he could not achieve, and 'from insufficient food he suffered from cramps. Knowing him thus suffering, the Exalted One went and asked him:

Thou who foredone with cramping pains,

Dwell'st in the jungle, in the woods,

Thy range confined, in hardship dire—

Tell me, bhikkhu, how wilt thou live?

And the Thera declaring his constant happiness through unworldly joys, replied:

With bliss and rapture's flooding wave

This mortal frame will I suffuse.

Though hard and rough what I endure,

Yet will I in the jungle dwell.

Herein myself I'll exercise:—

The Starting-points of Mindfulness,

The Powers five, the Forces too,

The Factors of Enlightenment—

So will I in the jungle dwell.

For I have seen [what friends have wrought]: Their striving roused, their straining mind,

Their staunch and ever onward stride,

In concord bound,—and having seen,

E'en in the jungle will I dwell,

 Remembering Him, the Very Wake,

Supremely tamed, intent, serene,—

With mind unwearied night and day,

Thus will I in the jungle dwell.

Thus saying, the Thera conjured up insight, and then it was that he won arahantship.


CCVI Vijitasena

Reborn in this Buddha-age in a Kosalan elephant-trainers' family, he was named Vijitasena. His maternal uncles, Sena and Upasena, had both entered the Order and become arahants, when Vijitasena, after learning the craft of his folk, saw the twin-miracle of the Master, believed, and being naturally of a religious disposition, entered the Order under his uncles. Training by their instructions he rose into the avenue of insight, but his mind remaining discursive through various external objects, he admonished it:

I will restrain thee, heart, as elephants

Are by the towngate's sallyport kept back.

I'll not abet thee in thy naughty ways,

Thou net of wishes, thou of body born.

Not thine 'twill be, thus checked, to go at large.

As elephant that wins not through the gate,

Struggle thy best, thou witch, again, again;

Thou shalt not roam, who art to sin so fain.

Even as one who firmly wields the hook

Doth turn th' unbroken, untamed elephant

Against its will, so will I turn thee back.

 As the good driver, in horsebreaking skilled,

Doth tame the mettle of the thoroughbred,

So will I bring thee too beneath control.

By virtue of the fivefold spiritual force.

Yea, by right heedfulness I'll bind thee fast,

Myself restrained, so will I master thee.

Curbed in the harness of right energy,

Thou shalt not, O my heart, go far from me.

Thus restraining his thoughts did the Thera expand insight and win arahantship.


CCVII Yasadatta

Reborn in this Buddha-age in a clan of Malla rajas, and named Yasadatta, he was educated at Takkasila. Thereafter making a tour with the Wanderer Sabhiya, they came to Savatthi, where Sabhiya put questions to the Exalted One. Yasadatta listened to the answers, thinking as he took his seat, eager to criticize: 'I will show the defects in the Samana Gotama's discourse.' Now the Exalted One knew what was in his mind, and at the end of the 'Sabhiya Sutta' admonished him in these verses:

Who witless and with captious mind

Doth hear the Conqueror's doctrine told,

Far, far from the true Norm is he,

As from the heaven is the earth.

Who witless and with captious mind

Doth hear the Conqueror's doctrine told.

From the true Norm he wanes away,

As in the month's dark half the moon.

 Who witless, etc. …

In the true Norm he withers up,

As fish where water runneth low.

Who witless, etc. …

In the true Norm he doth not thrive,

As rotten seed in furrow sown.

He who with glad contented mind

Doth hear the Conqueror's doctrine told,

He, casting out th' Intoxicants,

Doth realize the Influctuate, Doth win the Peace ineffable,

And is perfected, sane, immune.

Thus admonished by the Master, Yasadatta was filled with emotion, entered the Order, and, establishing insight, in due course won arahantship. And in confessing anna he uttered these very verses.


CCVIII Sona-Kutikanna

Reborn in this Buddha-age in the country of Avanti in the family of a very wealthy councillor, he was given the name of Sona. Wearing ear-jewelry worth a crore, he became known as Koti-, or Kuti-kanna (Crore-ears). Grown up, he became a landowner, and when the venerable Kaccana the Great stayed near his house, he ministered to his wants, learned the Norm, and finally growing disturbed, entered the Order through him. Collecting with  great difficulty a company of ten, he soon took leave of the Thera to go to Savatthi and salute the Master. Being admitted to pass the night in the Master's portion, and in the morning invited to recite, he was commended for the sixteen Atthakas. And when the verse—

'Seeing the evils of a worldly life,'

was finished, he developed insight and won arahantship.

And when he had obtained the Master's consent to the three matters which Kaccana the Great had commissioned him to ask, he returned to his own dwelling-place, and told the Thera his instructor. This is recorded more fully in the Udana and Anguttara Commentaries, but there it is said that he attained arahantship while studying under his teacher.

Anon, while dwelling in the bliss of emancipation, he reviewed his achievement, and full of joy he breathed out these verses:

Not only did I ordination win,

Emancipated am I, sane, immune;

Yea, him have I now seen, th' Exalted One, And where he dwelt, there with him did I lodge.

Far through the night he stayed beneath the sky,

Then, versed in everything's abiding-place,

The Master in his chamber went to rest.

His robe spread Gotama and laid him down,

Like unto lion in a rocky cave,

For whom all fear and dread have passed away.

Thereafter in the presence of the Chief,

The Wake, did Sona, framing goodly speech,

Disciple of the Buddha, speak the Norm.

Well doth he know the factors of this life,

Well doth he cultivate the [Ariyan] Way,

So, having won to that most perfect Peace,

Shall he complete becoming, sane, immune.


CCIX Kosiya

Reborn in this Buddha-age in a Magadhan brahmin's family, he was called by his family name: Kosiya. Come of age, he often went to hear the General of the Norm teaching, and thereby, believing in the doctrine, entered the Order, and in due course won arahantship. Thereupon reviewing his achievement, he extolled the venerableness and determining power for good of the wise in these verses:

He that is valiant and learn'd in the word of the masters,

Therein can rest and therefor can cherish affection,

Him ye may call devoted and wise: thus he may be

One that winneth distinction in knowledge of doctrines.

 Him, whose steadfast philosophy hardship unparalleled

Testing has no power to disturb or bewilder,

Him ye may call strong-willed and wise: thus he may be

One that winneth distinction in knowledge of doctrines.

He who abideth as ocean unyielding, unfathomed

As to his insight in problems subtle and delicate,

Him ye may call inexpugnable, wise: thus he may be

One that winneth distinction in knowledge of doctrines.

Erudite, one who beareth the Word in his memory,

Practiser he of all doctrine, greater and lesser,

Him ye may call all this and wise: thus he may be

One that winneth distinction in knowledge of doctrines.

He who knoweth the meaning of that which is spoken,

Knowing the meaning, shapeth his actions accordingly.

'Meaning-within-side' call him and wise: thus he may be

One that winneth distinction in knowledge of doctrines.

# CANTO VI. PSALMS OF SIX VERSES

CCX Kassapa of Uruvela

Reborn in the day of our Exalted One as the firstborn, of three brothers in a brahmin family, they were all called by their family name Kassapa, and they all learned the three Vedas. They had a following of five, three, and two hundred brahmin youths respectively. And finding no vital truth in their scriptures, but only subjects of worldly interest, they left the world and became ascetics. And they became named after the places where they dwelt as rishis, the eldest with his company going to dwell at Uruvela. Many days after this came the great renunciation of our Bodhisat, the starting of the Norm-Wheel, the arahantship of the five Theras, the conversion of the fifty-three associates headed by Yasa, the sending forth of the sixty arahants, 'Go ye, bhikkhus, and wander …, the conversion of the thirty wealthy friends, and the coming of the Master to Uruvela. When he had there wrought many wonders, beginning with the taming of the Naga, Kassapa was convinced and entered the Order, his brothers following his example. To them and their 1,000 followers, the Master, seated on the crest of a rock on Gaya Head, uttered the discourse on Burning, establishing them all as arahants.

But Uruvela-Kassapa reviewing his achievement, uttered lion-roar verses, attesting anna:

Beholding all the wondrous works achieved

By the high powers of glorious Gotama,

At first, natheless, myself I humbled not,

Being deceived by envy and by pride.

But He, Driver of men, who knew my thought

And my intent, took me at length to task.

Thereby anguish befell me, I was seized

By thrill mysterious, hair-raising dread.

And then the gifts that erst accrued to me As famed ascetic poor and worthless seemed.

All these I thereupon esteemed as nought,

And in the Conqueror's Order was enrolled.

Once well content with sacrifice, 'bove all

Concerned within these worlds once more to live

Now have I set myself to extirpate

All passion, all ill will, illusion too.

How erst I lived I know; the heavenly eye,

Purview celestial, have I clarified;

Power supernormal, reading others' thought,

Hearing ineffable, have I achieved.

And the great Quest for which I left the world,

Forsaking home, a homeless life to lead,

Even that quest, that high reward I've won,

For every fetter now is broken down.


CCXI Tekicchakari

Reborn in this Buddha-age as the son of a brahmin named Subuddha, he was safely brought into the world by the aid of physicians. Hence he was named Tekicchakari, 'doctor-made.' He grew up, learning the arts and learning of his clan. Now his father, by his wisdom and policy having incurred the jealousy and suspicion of the King of Benares (sic), was by King Candagutta thrown into prison. Then Tekicchakari, hearing of this, took fright and fled, taking sanctuary with the Thera dwelling at the Vihara Hall, and telling him the cause of his trouble. The Thera ordained him and gave him an exercise, whereupon he became an open-air sedent bhikkhu, heedless of heat or cold, and devoted especially to the cultivation of the Sublime Moods. Him Mara the Evil One saw, as one slipping out of his reach; and in the desire of unbalancing the Thera, he drew nigh in the guise of a field-herd, when the harvest was over, tempting him thus:

All harvested is now the rice, and threshed

The barley. Not a bite or sup I'll get!

What shall I do?

Then the Thera, thinking, 'This fellow tells me of his state. But it is myself that I ought to admonish. I have no business to be discoursing,' thus exhorted himself to meditate on the Three Bases:

Think on the Buddha! infinite the thought!

Thou thus in gladsome piety, thy frame

With rapture all suffused, shalt ever dwell

Upon the heights.

Think on the Dhamma! …

Think on the Order! infinite the thought! Thou thus in gladsome piety, thy frame

With rapture all suffused, shalt ever dwell

Upon the heights.

Then Mara again, wishing to dissuade him from solitude, pretended to be his well-wisher, saying:

Dost dwell beneath bare skies? Cold are these nights

And wintry now. See that thou perish not

With cold foredone. Get thee within thy lodge,

Thy door well barred!

Then the Thera, showing that in house-dwelling was a fetter, but that there he was at ease, said:

My heart transported shall reach out and touch

The Four Immeasurable Moods; thereby

Ever shall I in blissful ease abide.

Not mine foredone by cold to fail, who dwell

Unmoved and calm.

Thus saying, the Thera developed insight and realized arahantship.

And because this Thera lived in the time of King Bindusara, these verses must be understood as having been rehearsed as canonical at the Third Council.


## CCXII Maha-naga

Reborn in this Buddha-age at Saketa as the son of a brahmin named Madhu-Vasettha, he was given the name of Maha-naga. He saw the wonder wrought by Thera Gavampati, while the Exalted One was staying in the Anjana Wood, and receiving faith, he entered the Order under the Thera, winning arahantship through his counsels.

Now while he abode in the bliss of emancipation, the Thera Maha-naga saw how the six bhikkhus habitually failed to show respect to their co-religionists, and he admonished them in verses which became his confession of anna:

Who towards his fellows in the Rule

Showeth no reverence nor respect,

From the true Norm he wilts away,

Like fish where water runneth low.

Who towards his fellows in the Rule

Showeth no reverence nor respect,

In the true Norm he doth not thrive,

Like rotten seed in furrow sown.

Who towards, etc.

Far from Nibbana standeth he

Within the Norm-Lord's cult and school.

Who towards his fellows in the Rule

Showeth due reverence and respect,

From the true Norm falls not away,

Like fish where many waters be.

 Who towards his fellows in the Rule

Showeth due reverence and respect,

In the true Norm he thriveth well

As seed benign in furrow sown.

Who towards his fellows in the Rule

Showeth due reverence and respect,

He to Nibbana's very near,

Within the Norm-Lord's cult and school.


CCXIII Kulla

Reborn in this Buddha-age at Savatthi in the family of a landowner, and named
Kulla, he was converted by faith, and was ordained by the Master. But he was
often seized by fits of lustful passion. The Master, knowing his tendencies, gave
him the exercise on foul things, and bade him often meditate in the charnel-
field. And when even this sufficed not, he himself went with him and bade him

mark the process of putrefaction and dissolution. Then, as Kulla stood with heart disinfatuated, the Exalted One sent out a glory, producing in him such mindfulness that he discerned the lesson, attained first jhana, and on that basis developing insight, won arahantship.

Reviewing his experience, he breathed forth these verses, first speaking of himself (then repeating the Master's words and finally adding his own):

Kulla had gone to where the dead lie still

And there he saw a woman's body cast,

Untended in the field, the food of worms.

 Behold the foul compound, Kulla, diseased,

Impure, dripping, exuding, pride of fools.'

Grasping the mirror of the holy Norm,

To win the vision by its lore revealed,

I saw reflected there, without, within,

The nature of this empty fleeting frame.

As is this body, so that one was once,

And as that body, so will this one be. And as it is beneath, so is't above,

And as it is above, so is't beneath.

As in the daytime, so is it at night,

And as't was once, so will't hereafter be,

And as't will be, so was it—in the past.

Not music's fivefold wedded sounds can yield

Such charm as comes o'er him who with a heart

Intent and calm rightly beholds the Norm!

These verses were the Thera's confession of anna.

CCXIV Malunkya's Son

Reborn in this Buddha-age at Savatthi as the son of the King of Kosala's valuer, his mother was named Malunkya, and he became known by her name. When he was come of age his naturally religious disposition prevailed, and he left the world as a Wandering ascetic. Then, on hearing the Master teach, he entered the Order, and in due course won sixfold abhinna. Visiting his home out of compassion  for his kinsfolk, these entertained him with great display of hospitality, seeking to allure him back, and saying: 'With this wealth that belongs to you, you could support a family and do good works.'

But the Thera, unfolding his disposition, said:

Is there a man who careless, heedless dwells,

Craving in him will like a creeper grow.

He hurries hankering from birth to birth, In quest of fruit like ape in forest tree.

Whom she doth overcome,—the shameful jade,

Craving, the poisoner of all mankind, - Grow for him griefs as rank as jungle-grass.

But he who doth her down,—the shameful jade,

Hard to outwit,—from him griefs fall away

As from the lotus glides the drop of dew.

This word to you, as many as are here Together come: May all success be yours!

Dig up the root of craving, as ye were

Bent on the quest of sweet usira root.

Let it not be with you that, ye the reed,

Mara the stream, he break you o'er and o'er!

Bring ye the Buddha-Word to pass; let not

This moment of the ages pass you by!

That moment lost, men mourn in misery.

As dust [mixed and defiled], is carelessness;

And dust-defilement comes through carelessness.

By earnestness and by the Lore ye hear,

Let each man from his heart draw out the spear.

CCXV Sappadasa

Reborn in this Buddha-age at Kapilavatthu as the son of the King Suddhodana's chaplain, he was named Sappadasa. He received faith on the occasion of the Master's visit to his own people, and entered the Order. Overmastered by corrupt habits of mind and character (the kilesa's), he never got concentration and singleness of mind. This finally distressed him so much that he was about to commit suicide, when, the inward vision suddenly expanding, he attained arahantship. Confessing anna he said:

Full five and twenty years have passed since I

Had left the world and in the Order lived,

And yet not for one fingersnap of time

Had I found peace [and sanity] of mind.

Intent and single vision ne'er I won,

Distraught and harassed by desires of sense;

In tears, wringing my hands, I left the lodge.

Nay now I'll take a knife or else—For what

Is life to me? And how can such as I,

Who by my life the training have denied,

Do better than set term to it and die?

So then I came and with a razor sat me down

Upon my couch. And now the blade was drawn

Across my throat to cut the artery. ...

 When lo! in me arose the deeper thought:

Attention to the fact and to the cause.

The misery of it all was manifest;

Distaste, indifference the mind possessed,

And so my heart was set at liberty!

O see the seemly order of the Norm!

The Threefold Wisdom have I made my own,

And all the Buddha bids us do is done.

CCXVI Katiyana

He was reborn in this Buddha-age at Savatthi as the son of a brahmin of the Kosiya family, but was named Katiyana after the family of his mother. Seeing his friend Samannakani become a Thera, he, too, entered the Order. While at his studies he determined to discipline himself at night as to sleep. While pacing on the terrace he dozed, overcome by sleepiness, and fell right there to the ground. The Master, seeing what had happened, went himself, and standing above him, called him 'Katiyana!' He thereat rose up, saluted, and stood much agitated. Then the Master taught him the Norm thus:

Rise up, rouse thee, Katiyana, seat thee cross-legged. Be not filled with drowsiness. Watch and keep vigil.

Child of heedless race, let not the King of Mortals

By a simple trick o'ercome thee self-indulgent.

E'en as billow sweeping o'er the mighty ocean

So may round of birth and age o'erwhelm and drown thee.

See that thou dost make thyself an isle of safety, For nought else is there may serve thee as a refuge.

Lo! for thee the Master hath prepared this Right Way,

Past all bonds and past all fear of birth and dying.

Be thou diligent when night is young, and after;

Strive with all thy might, and strenuous make thy study.

Loose all earlier ties; live as befits a brother,

Robed in yellow cloak, by razor shaved, and alms fed.

Be not fain for pastimes, nor to lengthened slumbers Be addicted. Contemplate, O Katiyana!

Concentrate, conquer, O Katiyana! Make thee

Adept in the path to sure salvation leading.

Hast thou won the ultimate purification,

Thou shalt reach the Going-out, as flame in water.

Light of feeble ray is as a wind-torn creeper.

So do thou, clansman of Indra, clutching nothing,

Shake off Mara. Cleans'd of passion for sensations,

Wait thine hour, e'en here in holy coolness dwelling.

Thus aided by the Master's homily to win the Nibbana wherein is no residual base of rebirth, the Thera developed insight and attained arahantship. Thereafter he uttered the verses as taught by the Master in confessing anna.


## CCXVII Migajala

Reborn in this Buddha-age at Savatthi as a son of the great lay-lady Visakha, he would often go to the Vihara to hear the Norm. Finally he entered the Order, and in due course won arahantship. Confessing anna he said:

Well taught it is by Him who seeth all—

The Buddha, offspring of the sun's high race—

Through it all bonds are bygone things, through it

All constant rolling on is razed away;

It leadeth on and out, it beareth o'er,

Through it the root of craving withers up;

Cutting the poison-root, our tragic doom,

It bringeth us to evil's utter end;

By severing the root of ignorance,

It breaks in pieces Kamma's living car; It hurls the bolt of insight on the goods

That dower consciousnesses at rebirth;

The truth 'neath all our sentience laying bare,

And from all fevered grasping setting free,

Revealer 'tis to us, by knowledge given,

Of rebirth as a fiery pit of coals;

Of mighty properties, far-reaching, deep,

Averter of decay and death to come:—

Such is the A E P Assuager of all ill, auspicious, blest.

Action it knoweth,—what the act doth mean,—

And fruit of action as the fruit indeed.

Showing a vision by the light of truth

Of things as come to be by way of cause.

Yea, to the mighty Haven doth it wend;

High peace it brings and bliss lies at the end.

Thus the Thera, showing in manifold ways the Ariyan Norm, declared how he himself had followed it as confession of anna.


CCXVIII Jenta

The Chaplain's Son

Reborn in this Buddha-age at Savatthi as the son of the King of Kosala's chaplain, he was named Jenta. When grown up he became intoxicated with his advantages of birth, wealth, and position, despising where he should have honoured, and stiff with pride. One day he approached the Master, who was teaching in the midst of a great company, and be thought: 'If the Samana Gotama will first address me, I will also speak; I will not voluntarily address him.' Thus the Exalted One not addressing him, and he through pride not speaking either, he showed the motive for his coming as he stood there. Him the Exalted One then addressed in a verse:

To dwell on proud, vain fancies is not well.

Cultivate, brahmin, that which profiteth.

The good which thou dost seek in coming here—

That, and that only shouldst thou dwell upon.

Jenta thinking, 'He knows my thoughts!' was greatly drawn to him, and fell at his feet, paying the highest degree of homage. And he asked the Master, saying:

For whom is one to cultivate no pride?

Whom should one honour? Whom should one revere?

To whom if one show reverence is it well?

To him the Exalted One:

For mother and for father too, likewise

For eldest brother, for the teacher, for

The brahmin and for them of yellow robe:

For these is one to cultivate no pride,

These should one honour, these should one revere,

To these if one show reverence it is well.

The arahants cool, adept, sane, immune,

For whom pride perished as they crossed the goal, To them beyond all others homage pay.

Jenta by that teaching became a Stream-winner, entered the Order, and in due course won arahantship. Thereupon in celebrating his achievement he thus declared anna:

Infatuated with my birth, my wealth

And influence, with the beauty of my form

Intoxicated, thus I led my life.

O'ermuch I fancied none was like to me.

A poor young fool by overweening spoilt,

Stubborn with pride, posing and insolent.

Mother and father, ay, and others too

Claiming respect and honour, never one

Did I salute, discourteous, stiff with pride.

Then saw I Him the Guide, Leader Supreme,

The peerless Chief 'mong drivers of mankind,

In glory shining like the sun, with all

The company of brethren in his train.

Casting away conceit and wanton pride,

A pious gladness filling all my heart,

Lowly I rendered homage with the head

To Him among all creatures Best and Chief.

Well extirpated now and put away

Is both o'erweening and hypocrisy;

The what and that 'I am' is snapt in twain,

Yea, every form of self-conceit is slain.


CCXIX Sumana

Reborn in this Buddha-age he took birth in the family of a certain lay-disciple who had become the lay-attendant of the venerable Thera Anuruddha. Now that layman's children till then had died young. And the father said: 'If yet one more son is born to me, I will have him ordained by the Thera. After ten months a healthy boy was born to him, and accordingly, when the child was seven years old, he was ordained. And from the ripeness of his insight, it was not long before he acquired sixfold abhinna, waiting the while upon the Thera. Taking a jar to fetch him water, Sumana through iddhi-power came to the Anotatta Lake. And a wicked serpent-king, coiled about the lake, reared its great hood aloft and would not suffer him to get water. Then Sumana took the shape of a garuda-bird and  overcame the serpent, and flew back with the water to the Thera. And the Master, seated in Jeta Grove, saw him as he went, and called Sariputta to see, praising him in the four verses below.

Now Sumana, in testifying to anna, added those verses to his own as follows:

When newly made a brother seven years old,

By supernormal power I overcame

The wondrous potence of the serpent king,

Whenas I water for my teacher's use

From the great lake of Anotatta fetched.

Me coming thus the Master saw and spake:

See, Sariputta, how the little lad

Holding his jar of water comes along,

Rapt all his being, utterly intent.

Noble his carriage on his gracious quest,

And well-matured in supernormal power,

This novice of our Anuruddha's band.

By trainer of high breeding highly bred,

By the proficient made throughly expert,

By perfect competence made competent,

By Anuruddha taught and disciplined:

He having won the highest peace and good

And realized the influctuate, even he—

This novice Sumana—[would hide his power]

And thus: Let no man know me! doth desire.


CCXX Nhataka-muni

Reborn in this Buddha-age at Rajagaha in a brahmin clan, and well educated in Vedic lore, he became known by the mark and order of a graduate as Nhataka, the bath-graduate. Becoming an ascetic, he dwelt in a forest glade three leagues from Rajagaha, living on wild rice and worshipping fire.

Now the Master, seeing the conditions of arahantship shining within his heart like a lamp in a jar, came to his hermitage. He, filled with pleasure thereat, placed before him food prepared in his own way. The Exalted One ate it; and so three days went by. On the fourth day the Exalted One said: 'You who are of such extreme delicacy, how can you support life on this food ?' And thus commenting on saintly content, he taught him the Norm. And the ascetic thereupon from Stream-winner became arahant. The Exalted One confirmed him therein and went. But he, continuing to dwell there, fell ill of cramp. The Master went, and with kindness asked after his health:

Thou who foredone with cramping pains

Dwell'st in the jungle, in the woods,

Thy range confined, in hardship dire,

Tell me, bhikkhu, how wilt thou live?

Then the Thera:

With bliss and rapture's flooding wave

This mortal frame is all suffused.

Though hard and rough what I endure,

Yet will I in the jungle dwell.

Wisdom's seven branches practising,

The Powers five, the Forces too, Rapt to ethereal heights of thought,

So will I in the jungle dwell.

From all corrupting thoughts set free,

With heart all pure and undefiled,

Often to contemplation given,

So will I in the jungle dwell.

And all the intoxicants that once,

Within, without, beset my life,

Hewn and cast out are one and all,

Never to rise for me again.

The factors five are understood, Persisting yet with severed root.

The end of sorrow now is won,

And all rebirth for me is done.


CCXXI Brahmadatta

Reborn in this Buddha-age at Savatthi, as a son of the King of Kosala, and named Brahmadatta, he witnessed the majesty of the Buddha at the Jeta Grove inauguration, entered the Order because he believed, and in due course acquired sixfold abhinna, together with thorough grasp of the letter and meaning of the Norm.

One day as he went round for alms, a brahmin abused him. The Thera heard in silence and went on with his business. The brahmin again reviled him, and people commented on the Thera's silence. Whereupon Brahmadatta taught them, saying:

Whence rises wrath for him who void of wrath

Holds on 'the even tenor of his way,'

Self-tamed, serene, by highest insight free?

Worse of the two is he who, when reviled,

Reviles again. Who doth not, when reviled,

Revile again, a twofold victory wins.

Both of the other and himself he seeks

The good; for he the other's angry mood

Doth understand and soothe [checking himself].

Him who of both is the physician, since

Himself he healeth and the other too,

Folk deem a fool, they knowing not the Norm.

Then the reviling brahmin, hearing these words, was both distressed and glad of heart, and besought the Thera's forgiveness. Yea, he took Orders under him, and was taught the exercise of meditating on love towards others, the Thera thus arming him against obsession by anger:

If anger rise in thee, then think upon

The Figure of the Saw; and if arise

Craving t'indulge thyself, remember thou

The Parable of how they ate the Child.

If, lusting for new lives in heaven and earth,

Thy heart run wild, O check and curb it swift

By mindfulness, as 'twere the beast men find

In young corn grazing trespasser, and bind.


CCXXII Sirimanda

Reborn in this Buddha-age at Suṁsumaragira in a brahmin family, he entered the Order through faith got on hearing the Master teaching in the Bhesakala Wood. One feast-day, while he was seated where the Patimokkha was  to be recited at the end of the recitation of the introduction ...' for [a fault] when declared shall be light to him,' he pondered on the advantage gained by the confession of faults concealed, and thereupon exclaimed with eager interest and gladness: 'Oh, how utterly pure is the rule of the Master!' And so expanding insight he attained arahantship. Reviewing the course thereto with a glad heart, he admonished the brethren:

Heavily falls the rain of guilt on fault

Concealed; less heavy where the fault lies bare

By death the world is smitten sore; by age

And by decay 'tis shrouded and beset,

Pierced by the dart of craving evermore,

By itch of pestering desires assailed.

By death the world is held enslaved; by age

And by decay escorted, guarded sure, Without a refuge, everlastingly

Struck as by thief with bludgeon and with sword.

Like forest fires behold them drawing nigh:—

Death and disease, decay, dread trinity,

Whom to confront no strength sufficeth, yea,

No swiftness aught avails to flee away.

Make thou the day not futile, not in vain,

Whether it be by little or by much.

For every day and night that thou dost waste,

By so much less thy life remains to live.

Whether thou walk or stand or sit or lie,

For thee the final day of life draws nigh;

No time hast thou to dally heedlessly.


CCXXIII Sabbakama

Reborn in this Buddha-age, after the Exalted One had passed away, at Vesali in a noble clan, and named Sabbakama, he, when he was come of age, gave gifts and possessions to his kinsfolk, and following his religious inclination left the world, taking orders under the Treasurer of the Norm. In course of his studies he came back to Vesali with his instructor and visited his family. And his former wife, afflicted, lean, in sorry array and tears, greeted him and stood by. Seeing her thus, affection led by pity arose in him, and losing the deeper view in the present object, carnal feeling came over him. Then like a high-bred horse at the touch of the whip, anguish arose, and he departed to the charnel field to learn the lesson of Foul Things. Thereby jhana supervening, he expanded insight and won arahantship. Now his father-in-law brought his daughter decked out once more in finery to the Vihara, with a great retinue, seeking to make him secede, but the Thera declared to them how he had ejected all such desires as follows:

This twaybased thing, impure, malodorous,

Full of foul matter, ebbing thus and thus,

Is cherished as the chief of all our care.

Ah hidden deer by craft, as fish by hook,

As ape by pitch, so is the world ensnared.

Sights, sounds and tastes, odours and things to touch,

That please and charm, the fivefold way of sense:

All these are shown combined in woman's shape.

 The worldlings, who with heart inflamed pursue

And woo her, swell the dreadful field of death And make accumulation of rebirth.

But he who shuns it all, as with the foot

The serpent's head is shunned, he, vigilant,

Doth circumvent this poisoner of the world.

And I who evil saw in sense-desires

And in renunciation safety, lo!

Detached from all that worldly aims commend,

Of all th' intoxicants have made an end.

# CANTO VII. PSALMS OF SEVEN VERSES

CCXXIV Sundara-Samudda

Reborn in this Buddha-age at Rajagaha, as the son of a very wealthy councillor, he was named Samudda. And because of his beauty he became known as Sundara-Samudda. In the prime of his youth he saw the majesty of the Buddha at the festival of his coming to Rajagaha, and through faith and his native inclination he left the world for the Order. Entrusted with a message he went from Rajagaha, to Savatthi and there stayed with a virtuous friend, learning how to practise himself in insight. Now his mother at Rajagaha, seeing other councillors' sons and their wives dressed in their best enjoying themselves at a festival, thought of her son and wept. And a certain courtesan to comfort her offered to go and entice him back. The mother promised, if she would do so, and he were to marry her, to make her mistress of the family, and gave her many gifts. Well attended, she went to Savatthi, and stopping at a house where the Thera came day after day on his alms round, she caused him to be carefully attended to, showing herself decked and adorned and wearing golden slippers. And one day, slipping these off at the house door,  she saluted him with clasped hands as he passed and invited him in with seductive air. Then the Thera, a worldly thought fluttering, resolved then and there to make a supreme effort, and so standing, conjured up meditation and acquired sixfold abhinna. Concerning this it is said:

Adorned and clad to make a gallant show,

Crowned with a wreath and decked with many gems,

Her feet made red with lac, with slippers dight,

A woman of the town accosted me,

Doffing her slippers, greeting hands-to-head,

With soft, sweet tones and opening compliment:

'So young, so fair, and hast thou left the world—

Stay here within my Rule and Ordinance.

Take thou thy fill of human pleasures. See,

'Tis I will give thee all the means thereto.

Nay, 'tis the truth that I am telling thee.

Or if thou doubt, I'll bring thee fire and swear.

When thou and I are old, we both of us

Will take our staff to lean upon, and so

We both will leave the world and win both ways.'

Seeing that public woman making plea,

And proffering obeisance gaily decked

In brave array like snare of Mara laid,

Thereat arose in me the deeper view:

Attention to the fact and to the cause.

The misery of it all was manifest;

Distaste, indifference the mind possessed;

And so my heart was set at liberty.

O see the seemly Order of the Norm!

The Threefold Wisdom have I made my own,

And all the Buddha bids us do is done.


CCXXV Lakuntaka-Bhaddiya

Reborn in the time of our Master at Savatthi in a wealthy family, he was named Bhaddiya, but from his extreme shortness, he was known as Lakuntaka (Dwarf)-Bhaddiya. Hearing the Master preach, he entered the Order, and becoming learned and eloquent, he taught others their work with a sweet voice. Now on a festival-day, a certain woman of the town, driving with a brahmin in a chariot, saw the Thera and laughed, showing her teeth. The Thera, taking that row of teeth as an object-sign, evoked jhana, and on that basis established insight and became a Non-Returner. And after practising mindfulness regarding the body, admonished by the Captain of the Norm, he was established in arahantship. Later he thus confessed anna:

Beyond the gardens of Ambataka, In woodland wild, craving and craving's root

Withdrawn, and rapt in deepest reverie,

There happy sits fortunate Bhaddiya.

And some are charmed by cymbals, lutes and drums,

And I in leafy shadow of my trees

Do dwell entranced by the Buddha's Rule.

Let but the Buddha grant one boon to me,

And if that boon were mine, I'd choose for all

Perpetual study in control of self.

They who decry me for my shape, and they

Who listen spell-bound to my voice, such folk

In toils of lust and impulse know me not.

The fool hemmed in on every side knows not

The inner life, nor sees the things without,

And by a voice forsooth is led away.

And if the inner life he knoweth not,

Yet can discern the things that are without,

Watching alone the outer fruits that come,

He also by a voice is led away.

He, who both understands the inner life,

And doth discern the things that are without,

Clear-visioned, by no voice is led away.


CCXXVI Bhadda

He was reborn in this Buddha-age at Savatthi in a Councillor's family, as the child of hitherto childless parents, to  whom, after prayers to gods and the like, none had been born. They had gone to the Master saying, 'If, your reverence, we shall get a child we will offer him to you as your servant.' They named him Bhadda (Faustus), and when he was seven years old, they dressed him in his best, and led him to the Master, saying, 'This, your reverence, is the child we got after asking you; we deliver him to you.' The Master bade Ananda ordain him, and withdrew to the Fragrant Chamber. And Ananda instructed him, and so ripe was in him the efficient cause that, while studying, even as the sun rose, he conjured up contemplation, and acquired sixfold abhinna.

Now the Exalted One knew what had happened, and called, 'Come, Bhadda!' So he went, saluting the Master with clasped hands. This was his ordination. And this Buddha-ordination, the Thera, beginning with his birth, magnified when thus confessing anna:

An only child was I, to mother dear

And to my father dear. By many a rite

And much observance was I gotten, ay,

And many prayers. To do me kindness they,

My good desiring, and my happiness,

Conducted me—father and mother too—

Into the presence of the Buddha blest.

'Hardly hath he been gotten, this our child,

And he is delicate and softly reared.

Him do we give, O Lord, to thee, that he

May wait as servant on the Conqueror.'

The Master took me unto Him and thus

To Ananda did say: 'Quickly admit

This child, for he a thoroughbred shall be.'

And then, thus sanctioning my coming forth,

The Conqueror withdrew to spend the night.

And as the sun rose up out of the dawn

Lo! then my heart was set at liberty.

 Then to complete his work the Master, roused

From quietude: 'Come, Bhadda!' called to me;

Thereby to me was ordination given.

Seven were my years when I was thus ordained.

The Threefold Wisdom have I made my own.

Hail to the seemly order of the Norm!


CCXXVII Sopaka

Reborn in this Buddha-age to a pariah's wife, he was called, according to his birth, Sopaka (pariah). Some say he was born in a trader's family. This is contradicted by the Apadana text (paḷiya):

When to my last birth I had won,

 Into Sopaka-womb I came.

Four months after birth he lost his father, and was maintained by his uncle. The latter, when Sopaka was seven years old, was bidden by his own ill-tempered son to kill the child. So he took him to the charnel-field, bound his hands, and tied him by the neck to a corpse, thinking, 'Let the jackals and others devour him,' for he was not able himself to kill the child, who had come to his last rebirth. The jackals and other creatures came, and the child at midnight cried:

O what the fate in store for me,

 Or who to the orphan lone is kin!

In midst of dreadful deathfield bound,

 Whom shall I find to be my friend?

The Master, at that hour surveying what fellow-men were redeemable, saw the conditions of arahantship shining  within the child's heart, and drew his attention by emitting a glory, saying:

Come then, Sopaka, fear thou not;

Behold the Man-who-thus-hath-come!

I, even I, will bear thee o'er,

 As moon comes safe from Rahus jaws.

The boy by the Buddha's power broke his bonds, and at the end of the verse stood, a Stream-winner, before the Fragrant Chamber. Now his mother sought him, and the uncle telling her nothing, she went to the Exalted One, thinking 'the Buddhas know all, past, future, and present.' The Master, as she came, hid the boy by iddhi, and to her saying, 'Lord, I cannot find my son, nevertheless the Exalted One knows what he is doing?' he replied:

Sons are no shelter nor father, nor any kinsfolk.

 For one o'erta'en by death, bloodbond is no refuge, …

so teaching her the Norm. She, hearing, became a Stream-winner, but the boy an arahant. Then the Exalted One withdrew iddhi, and she, overjoyed, beheld her son. Hearing he was arahant, she suffered him to leave the world, and went her way.

Now he came and saluted the Master, as he was walking in the shade of the Fragrant Chamber, and followed him. And the Exalted One, desiring to grant him ordination, asked him the ten questions beginning: 'What is the one'?' He, grasping the Master's intention, supplied the answers, 'All beings are sustained by food,' etc., by his omniscience. Whence the name of the 'Boy-Questions' arose.

And the Master, satisfied in mind by his replies, ordained him. All this the Thera set forth in confessing añña thus:

In the shade upon the terrace walking, lo! the Chief of men.

Thither went I, in His presence worshipping the Man of men.

Draped my robe was on one shoulder, forth my clasped hands were stretched,

In the footsteps of the highest of all beings so I walked.

Then He asked me questions, He so skilled in questions and so wise.

And unwavering, unaffrighted answered there the Master I.

He The-thus-Come then commended how the questions answered were.

And the brethren-host surveying, to them made this matter known

'Fortunate are they of Anga, and of Magadha, from whom

Such as he procureth raiment, food and lodging, medicine

And the reverence that is seemly, yea, they're happy!' so He said.

'From to-day henceforth, Sopaka, come to see Me when thou wilt.

Our discourse alone, Sopaka, shall thine ordination be.'

Seven were my years when to me ordination thus was given.

Now I bear the final body. Hail! fair Order of the Norm.


CCXXVIII Sarabhanga

Reborn in this Buddha-age at Rajagaha, as the son of a certain brahmin, he was given a name according to or independent of family traditions, he having no distinctive marks [and that name is forgotten]. But he became, when of age, an ascetic, making a hut for himself out of reed-stalks, which he had broken off, and from that time he was known as Sara-bhanga—reed-plucker. Now the Exalted One, looking over the world with the Awakened Eye, discerned in him the conditions of arahantship, and going to him taught him the Norm. And he, convicted and becoming a member, in due course won arahantship, continuing to live in his hut. This became decayed and crumbling, and people noticing it, said: 'Why, your reverence, do you not repair it?' The Thera, saying: 'The hut was made when I was doing ascetic practices; now I cannot do the like,' set forth the whole matter thus:

Ay, reeds in handfuls once I plucked, and built

A hut wherein I sojourned; hence the name

'Reedpicker' given me by the common voice.

But not to me doth it belong to-day

To pluck the reeds in handfuls as of yore,

Because of what the training doth prescribe,

Revealed to us by glorious G.

How wholly and entirely he did ail:—

That had Reedpicker never seen before.

This sorely ailing state he came to see

Through word of Him who is beyond the gods.

The self-same Path by which V went,

The Path of S and of V Of K, KONAGAMANA,  And K, e'en by that very Road
Lo! now to us there cometh G.

 And all these seven Buddhas,—they for whom

Craving was dead, and nought was grasped, and who

Stood planted on Abolishing of Ill—

They taught this Norm, ay, even such as they,

Who were themselves the body of the Norm,

In great compassion for us all, e'en these

Four Ariyan Truths: the Truth of Ill; the Cause;

The Path; the End, th' abolishing, of Ill,

Whereby the endless tale of grief and pain

In life's great cycle cannot take its course; For when this body dies and life is
spent,

No other rebirth cometh more—yea, free

Am I from birth, from evil utterly!

# CANTO VIII. PSALMS OF EIGHT VERSES

CCXXIX Kacca[ya]na the Great

Reborn in this Buddha-age at Ujjeni, in the family of the chaplain of King Caṇḍapajjota, he learned the three Vedas as he grew, and succeeded, at his father's death, to the post of chaplain. And he was known by his gens name of Kaccana. Now the king heard of the Buddha's advert, and said: 'Teacher, do you go and bring the Master hither.' He, with a party of seven, went to the Master, who taught him the Norm with such effect that at the end of the lesson, he, with his seven attendants, were established in arahantship with thorough grasp of letter and meaning. Then the Master, saying, 'Come, bhikkhus!' stretched forth his hand, and they forthwith were as Theras of a century of rain-seasons, hair of two fingers' length cut off, and equipped with bowl and robes.

Then the Thera, having successfully accomplished his own salvation, invited the Master on the king's behalf:

'Lord, the King Pajjota desires to worship at your feet and hear the Norm.' The Master said: 'Do you, bhikkhu, go  yourself; by your mission, too, will the king be satisfied.' He, thus bidden, went with the seven, satisfied the king's desire, established him in the faith, and returned to the Master.

One day many bhikkhus, having put aside their duties, and finding pleasure in worldly activities and in society, were leading desultory lives. The Thera thereupon admonished them in two verses, and in the next six admonished the king:

Let not a brother occupy himself

With busy works, let him keep clear of folk,

Nor strive [to copy nor to emulate].

Who greedy seeks to taste life's feast entire,

Neglects the good that brings true happiness.

A treacherous bog it is, this patronage

Of bows and gifts and treats from wealthy folk.

'Tis like a fine dart bedded in the flesh,

For erring human hard to extricate.

(To the King.)

Not evil are the actions of a man

Because of what another [saith or doth];

'Tis of himself he must from wrong abstain,

Of their own acts the offspring mortals be.

No speech of others makes a man a thief,

No speech of others makes a man a sage;

And what we know at heart we really are,

That do the gods who know our hearts know too.

People can never really understand

That we are here but for a little spell.

But they who grasp this truth indeed,

Suffer all strife and quarrels to abate.

The wise man is alive, and he alone,

Although his wealth be utterly destroyed;

And if the man of wealth do wisdom lack,

For all his wealth he doth not truly live.

(To the King consulting him about a dream.)

Things of all sorts by way of ear we hear;

Things of all sorts by way of eye we see;

And for the wise and strong it is not fit

All to neglect as things unseen, unheard.

Let him as seeing be as he were blind,

Let him as hearing be as he were deaf,

Let him, in wisdom versed, be as one dumb,

And let the man of strength be as the weak;

But let the thing of genuine good arise:—

Be that for him the nesting-place of thought.

CCXXX Sirimitta

Reborn in this Buddha-age at Rajagaha as the son of a very wealthy landowner, he was named Sirimitta, his mother being sister to Sirigutta, whose story is included in the Dhammapada Commentary. Now he, Sirimitta, Sirigutta's nephew, found faith when the Master subdued the elephant Dhanapala. And he entered the Order, and in due course became arahant.

One day rising from his seat to recite the Patimokkha, he took a painted fan, and reseating himself, taught the Norm to the bhikkhus, and in so doing, distinguished the more eminent virtues thus:

From anger and from hatred free,

Clean of deceit, of slander bare,

Look you! a brother such as he,

When he goes hence, will weep no more.

From anger and from hatred free,

Clean of deceit, of slander bare,

Ever 'door-guarded' brother, he,

When be goes hence, will weep no more.

From anger, etc.

… of slander bare,

Brother of noble virtue, he,

When he goes hence, will weep ro more.

 From anger, etc.

Brother of virtuous comrades, he,

When he goes hence, will weep no more.

From anger, etc.

Brother of noble insight, he,

 When he goes hence, will weep no more.

Having discoursed against anger and so on, he then set forth the supreme career by verses describing the right attitude for individuals, testifying thereby to anna in himself:

Of him whose faith in the Tathagata

Is firmly planted and unwavering,

Whose virtues are commended by the good

And pleasing in the eyes of Ariyans,

Who dwells contented with the Brotherhood,

Who in his views is candid and sincere:

'No pauper he,' they say, with so much wealth,

Nor sterile and in vain the life of him.

So let the wise man, so let him who aye

Remembereth that which Buddhas have enjoined,

Devote himself to faith and righteousness,

To know the blessedness they brought to us

And the true vision of the holy Norm.


CCXXXI Panthaka Major

When our Master had gone to Rajagaha, rolling the excellent wheel of righteousness, Panthaka, the elder son  of a rich councillor's daughter and one of her father's servants, used to go with his grandfather to hear the Master, and so won faith with insight. Entering the Order, he became highly versed in the Buddha-Word, and in the four abstract jhanas, in due time becoming arahant. Dwelling in the bliss of jhana and of fruition, he was reviewing one day his achievement, and in great joy thereat burst into a 'lion's roar' thus:

When first I saw the blessed Master, Him

For whom no fear can anywhence arise,

A wave of deep emotion filled my soul

At sight of Him, the peerless man of men.

Had a man erst on hands and knees besought

Favour of Fortune's goddess hither come,

And won the grace of Master such as this,

Still might he fail to win [the thing he sought].

I for my part [all hindrance] cast away—

[The hope of] wife and children, coin and corn, And let my hair and beard be shorn, and forth

Into the homeless life I went from home.

The life and training practising, all faculties

Well held in hand, in loyalty to Him,

Buddha supreme, master of self I lived.

Then longing rose within my heart, I yearned

[To consummate]: 'Now will I no more sit,

Not even for a moment, while the dart

Of craving sticketh and is not outdrawn.

Of me thus aye abiding, O! behold And mark the onward stride of energy:

 The Threefold Wisdom have I made my own,

And all the Buddha bids us do is done.

I know the where and when of former lives,

And clearly shines the eye celestial.

Ar'hant am I, worthy men's offerings.

Released and without basis for rebirth.

For as the darkness melted into light,

And the day broke with rising of the sun,

From craving, stanched and dry, had come release,

And on my couch cross-legged I sat in peace.

# CANTO IX. PSALM OF NINE VERSES

CCXXXII Bhuta

Reborn in this Buddha-age in a suburb of the city of Saketa as the son of a wealthy councillor, he was the last and only surviving child, the others having been devoured by a hostile Yakkha. He was therefore well guarded, but the demon (bhuta) had meanwhile gone to wait on Vessavana and came back no more—On the child's naming day he was called Bhuta, for they said: 'May compassionate non-humans protect him!' He by virtue of his merit having grown up without accident, reared with three residences as was Yasa, went, when the Master came to Saketa, with other laymen to the Vihara and heard the Norm. Entering the Order, he went to dwell in a cave on the banks of the River Ajakarani. There he won arahantship. Thereafter, he visited his relatives out of kindness to them, staying himself in the Anjana Wood. When they besought him to stay, urging that this would result in mutual benefit, the Thera, declaring his love for and happiness in the monachistic life, spoke these lines before he left them:

When the wise man hath grasped, that age and death, yea, all

Whereto the undiscerning world-folk cling is Pain,

And Pain thus understanding, dwells with mind intent

And rapt in ecstasy of thought:— no higher bliss

Is given to men than this.

When the fell poisoner he hath banned who bringeth pain,—

Ay, even Craving, who doth sweep him towards the pain

Of being prisoned in the web of many things,

Obsessed,—and he delivered dwells with mind intent

And rapt in ecstasy of thought:— no higher bliss

Is given to men than this.

When by insight he sees the happy-omened Path,

Twice fourfold, ultimate, that purifies from all

That doth defile, and seeing, dwells with mind intent,

Rapt in an ecstasy of thought:— no higher bliss

Is given to men than this.

When work of thought makes real and true the way of peace,

From sorrow free, untarnished and uncorrelate, Cleansing from all that doth defile, and severing

From every bond and fetter, and the brother sits

Rapt in an ecstasy of thought:— no higher bliss

Is given to men than this.

When in the lowering sky thunders the storm-cloud's drum,

And all the pathways of the birds are thick with rain,

 The brother sits within the hollow of the hills,

Rapt in an ecstasy of thought:— no higher bliss

Is given to men than this.

Or when by rivers on whose banks together crowd

Garlands of woodland blossoms bright with many a hue,

With heart serene the brother sits upon the strand,

Rapt in an ecstasy of thought:— no higher bliss

Is given to men than this.

Or when at dead of night in lonely wood god rains,

And beasts of fang and tusk ravin and cry aloud,

The brother sits within the hollow of the hills,

Rapt in an ecstasy of thought:— no greater bliss

Is given to men than this.

 When he hath checked the mind's discursive restlessness, And to the mountain's bosom hies and in some cave

Sits sheltered, free from fear and from impediment,

Rapt in an ecstasy of thought:— no greater bliss

Is given to men than this.

 When he in healthful ease abides, abolisher

 Of stain and stumbling-stone and woe, open to peace [The portals of the mind], lust-free, immune from dart, Yea, all intoxicants become as nought, and thus

Rapt in an ecstasy of thought:— no greater bliss

Is given to men than this.

# CANTO X. PSALMS OF TEN VERSES

CCXXXIII Kaḷudayin

He going on in rebirth among gods and men, was born on the same day as our Bodhisat, in the family of one of the king's ministers at Kapilavatthu. Yea, on that one day were born these seven: the Bodhisat, the Bodhi-tree, the mother of Rahula, and the four treasures:— the riding-elephant, the horse Kanthaka, Channa, and Kaḷudayin. Now on his naming day, the child was called Udayin, and because he was dark of feature he became known as Kaḷ'-Udayin. He grew up as the play-fellow of the Bodhisat. But later, when the Lord of the World had gone forth in the Great Renunciation, had become omniscient, and was staying in the Bamboo Grove near Rajagaha, rolling on the excellent wheel of the Norm, King Suddhodana heard thereof, and sent a minister with a suite of a thousand, saying: 'Bring my son hither.' And that minister and suite, arriving when the Norm was being preached, heard, and all becoming arahants, the Master stretched forth his hand, saying: 'Come ye, bhikkhus!' … And they abiding among the Ariyas, did not deliver the king's message. And the like happened with other messengers. So the king sent Kaḷudayin, saying: 'This Udayin is of the same age as the Ten-powered, and is akin to me and affectionate; I will send him; go you, my dear, with a thousand men, and bring the Ten-powered One.' So he went, saying: 'If I, sire, may leave the world, then will I bring hither the Exalted One.' 'Whatever you do, show me my son,' was the reply. He, too, fared like the first minister and became arahant. Now he thought: 'Not yet is it time for Him to go to the city. When the rains have come, and the woods are in flower and the earth is covered with verdure, then 'twill be time.' And when the time was come, he spoke these verses to the Master, praising the beauty of the journey:

Now crimson glow the trees, dear Lord, and cast

Their ancient foliage in quest of fruit. Like crests of flame they shine irradiant,

And rich in hope, great Hero, is the hour.

Verdure and blossom-time in every tree,

Where'er we look delightful to the eye,

And every quarter breathing fragrant airs, While petals falling, yearning comes for fruit:—

'Tis time, O Hero, that we set out hence.

Not over hot, nor over cold, but sweet,

O Master, now the season of the year.

O let the Sakiyans and the Koḷiyans

Behold thee with thy face set toward the West,

Crossing the [border-river] Rohini.

 In hope the field is ploughed, in hope the seed is sown,

In hope of winning wealth merchants fare over sea.

The hope I cherish, may that hope be realized!

Again and yet again is seed in furrow sown.

Again and yet again the cloud-king sends down rain,

Again and yet again the ploughmen plough the field,

Again and yet again comes corn into the realm.

Again and yet again do beggars go their round;

Again and yet again the generous donors give;

Again and yet again when many gifts are given,

Again and yet again the donors find their heaven.

Surely a hero lifts to lustrous purity

Seven generations past wherever he be born.

And so methinks can He, the vastly wise, the god

Of gods. In Thee is born in very truth a Seer.

Suddhodana is named the mighty prophet's sire,

And mother of the Buddha was [our queen] Maya.

She, having borne the Wisdom being in her womb,

Found, when the body died, delight in Tusita.

She, Gotamid, dying on earth, deceasing hence,

Now lives in heavenly joys attended by those gods.

Now when the Exalted One, thus besought, discerned salvation coming for many by his going, he set out attended by 20,000 arahants, walking a yojana each day. And the Thera went by power of iddhi to Kapilavatthu, into the king's presence. 'Who are you?' he was asked; and he: 'If you know not the minister's son whom you sent to the Exalted One, know that I am he':

Son of the Buddha I, yea, e'en of such as He,

Th' Angirasa, to whom there lives not any peer,

Who that which is insuperable hath o'ercome.

And father of my Father art thou, Sakiyan,

To me thou, Gotamid, art grandsire in the Norm.


## CCXXXIV Ekavihariya

(Tissa-Kumara.)

He was reborn in this Buddha-age, after the Exalted One had passed away, as the youngest brother of the King Dhammasoka. And King Asoka, in the 218th year after that Passing Away, having united all India in one empire, and made his own younger brother Tissa viceregent, enlisted Tissa's friendship for the Sasana by a single stratagem.

Now the prince, while hunting, was so impressed at the sight of the Greek Thera, Maha Dhammarakkhita, seated under a tree, that he also longed to live so in the forest. When he had seen the Thera's supernormal powers, he  returned to the palace and told the king he wished to leave the world. Asoka could not in any way dissuade him. Longing for the happiness of the recluse, he uttered these verses:

If there be none in front, nor none behind

Be found, is one alone and in the woods

Exceeding pleasant doth his life become.

Come then! alone I'll get me hence and go

To lead the forest-life the Buddha praised, And taste the welfare which the brother knows,

Who dwells alone with concentrated mind.

Yea, swiftly and alone, bound to my quest, I'll to the jungle that I love, the haunt

Of wanton elephants, the source and means

Of thrilling zest to each ascetic soul.

In Cool Wood's flowery glades cool waters lie, Within the hollows of the hills; and there

I'll bathe my limbs when hot and tired, and there

At large in ample solitude I'll roam.

Lone and unmated in the lovely woods,

When shall I come to rest, work wrought, heart cleansed?

O that I might win through, who am so fain!

I only may achieve the task; herein

None for his fellow-man can aught avail.

I'll bind my spirit's armour on, and so

The jungle will I enter, that from thence

I'll not come forth until Nibbana's won.

I'll seat me on the mountain-top, the while

The wind blows cool and fragrant on my brow,

And burst the baffling mists of ignorance.

Then on the flower-carpet of the wood,

Anon in the cool cavern of the cliff,

Blest in the bliss of Liberty I'll take

Mine ease on thee, old Fastness o' the Crag.

Lo! I am he whose purpose is fulfilled.

And rounded as the moon on fifteenth day.

Destroyed all deadly canker, sane, immune,

I know rebirth comes ne'er again for me.


CCXXXV Kappina the Great

Reborn before our Master's birth in the border country at a town named Kukkuta (Cock), in a raja's family, he was named Kappina. At his father's death he succeeded, as raja Kappina the Great. He, to extend his knowledge, would send men of a morning out of the four gates to the cross-roads, bidding them arrest passing scholars and tell him. Now by that time our Master had come into the world, and was dwelling at Savatthi. And traders of that town brought goods to Kukkuta and disposed of them. Then saying, 'Let us see the king,' they took gifts and announced themselves. The king accepted their gifts, saluting them, and asked whence they came, and what their country and king were like, and what sort of religion (dhamma) was theirs? 'Sire,' they replied to the last question, 'we are not able to tell you with unwashen mouths.' The king sent for a gold ewer of water, and they, with cleansed mouths and hands at salute, said: 'Sire, in our country the Treasure of a Buddha has arisen.' At the one word 'Buddha,' rapture suffused the king's whole body. '"Buddha," say you, friends?' And he made them tell him thrice that infinite word, giving them 100,000 pieces. They told him also of the Treasure of the Norm and of the Order, and he trebled his gift, and forthwith renounced the world, his ministers doing likewise. Now they set forth [to find the Exalted One] and came to the Ganges. There they made a determination by the power of truth, saying: 'If [there be] a Master, a Buddha Supreme, let not even a hoof of these horses be wetted!' Then they crossed on the surface of the full river, and so crossed yet another river, coming thirdly to  the great river, Candabhaga, which they crossed in like manner.

The Master, too, who on that day had risen at dawn, and, filled with great compassion, surveyed the world, discerning that'to-day Kappina the Great has renounced his kingdom, and comes with a great following to enter the Order; 'tis fit I go far to meet him,' first went with a company of bhikkhus to Savatthi for alms, then went himself through the air to the banks of the Candabhaga, and sat down cross-legged under a great banyan facing the landing-stage of the ford, sending forth the Buddha-rays. Kappina and his men saw the rays darting to and fro, and said: 'We are come on account of the Master, and lo! here He is!' And they drew near, prostrating themselves. Then the Master taught them the Norm, so that they were all established in arahantship, and asked to become recluses. The Master said, 'Come, bhikkhus!' and this was their sanction and their ordination. Then he took them back with him through the air to the Jetavana.

One day the Exalted One asked whether Kappina taught the Norm to the bhikkhus? They said that he lived inactively, enjoying his happiness. Kappina, when sent for, admitted this was true, and was told: 'Brahmin! do not so; from to-day teach the Norm to them that have arrived.' Kappina assented, worshipping, and by his very first discourse established a thousand recluses in arahantship.

Wherefore the Master assigned him the foremost rank among those who taught the Brethren.

Now one day the Thera taught the Sisters as follows:

Can ye but see that which is coming ere it come, And mark such business as will benefit or harm,

Nor foes nor friends, howe'er they seek, will find a rift.

The man by whom the breathing exercise

With self-control is to perfection brought,

Practised with method as the Buddha taught,

He casts a radiant sheen about the world,

As doth the moon emerging free from cloud.

Lo! now the mind of me is white indeed, Expanded beyond measure, practised well,

Its nature understood, and strenuous;

Shedding a radiance on every side.

The wise man is alive and he alone,

Although his wealth be utterly destroyed;

And if the man of wealth do wisdom lack,

For all his wealth he doth not truly live.

Wisdom is arbiter of what is heard.

Wisdom doth nourish honourable fame.

With wisdom in his company a man

Even in pain and sorrow findeth joys.

Here is a fact that's not of yesterday;

Tis not abnormal nor anomalous:

'Where ye are being born, ye also die.'

What have we there save what is natural?

 For after being born we do but lead

A life that is a dying hour by hour.

Whoe'er are born in that same life they die—

Such is the nature of all living things.

That brings no good to the dead which is good for the living.

 Mourning the dead is no honour nor purification, Nor is it praised by the wise, by recluses and brahmins.

Mourning vexes the eye and the body, wasteth

Comeliness, strength [of body and mind] and intelligence.

If he be blithesome, all the four quarters become

Cordial well-wishers, e'en if his lot be not happy.

Wherefore let laymen desire to receive in their family

None but them that are wise and discreet and much learned.

They by the power of their wisdom accomplish their business,

E'en as a boat doth effect a crossing o'er the full river.

## CCXXXVI Cuḷa-Panthaka

(Roadling Minor)

His previous story is told in the Eighth Canto, in the chronicle of Roadling major.
The remainder is [told in the Commentary on the Cuḷasetthi-Jataka.]

He, on another occasion, uttered these verses:

Sluggish and halt the progress that I made,

And therefore was I held in small esteem.

My brother judged I should be turned away,

And bade me, saying: 'Now do thou go home.'

So I, dismissed and miserable, stood

Within the gateway of the Brethren's Park,

Longing at heart within the Rule to stay.

And there he came to me, the Exalted One,

And laid his hand upon my head; and took

My arm, and to the garden led me back.

To me the Master in his kindness gave

A napkin for the feet and bade me thus:

'Fix thou thy mind on this clean thing, the while

Well concentrated thou dost sit apart.'

And I who heard his blessed Word abode

Fain only and alway to keep his Rule, Achieving concentrated thought and will,

That I might win the crown of all my quest.

And now I know the where and how I lived,

And clearly shines the Eye Celestial; The Threefold Wisdom have I made my own,

And what the Buddha bids us do is done.

In thousand different shapes did Panthaka

Himself by power abnormal multiply;

And seated in the pleasant Mango-Grove, Waited until the hour should be revealed.

Then did the Master send a messenger,

Who came revealer of the hour to me,

And at th' appointed time I flew to Him.

Low at his feet I worshipped; then aside

I sat me down; and me so seated near

Whenas he had discerned, the Master then

Suffered that men should do him ministry.

High altar He where all the world may give,

Receiver of th' oblations of mankind,

Meadow of merit for the sons of men,

He did accept the gifts of piety.


## CCXXXVII Kappa

Reborn in this Buddha-age in the kingdom of Magadha, as the son of a provincial hereditary raja, he succeeded his father, but was addicted to self-indulgence and sensuality. Him the Master saw, as he roused himself from a reverie of great compassion and surveyed the world for treasure for his net of insight. And pondering, 'What now will he become?' he discerned that 'This one, hearing from me a discourse on foul things, will have his heart diverted from lusts, and will renounce the world and win arahantship.' Going to Kappa through the air, he addressed to him these verses:

Filled full with divers things impure,

Great congeries of excrement,

Like stale and stagnant pool of slime,

Like a great cancer, like a sore,

Filled full of serum and of blood,

As't were from dung-heap issuing,

Dropping with fluid-ever thus

The body leaks, a carrion thing.

By sixty tendons kept in place,

And smeared with plaster of the flesh,

By dermis armed and cuticle—

In carrion carcase lies small gain.

By bony framework rendered firm,

By sinew-threads together knit,

The which, as they in concert work,

Effect our postures manifold;

Faring world without end to death,

E'en to the King of Mortals' realm:—

If it be even here cast off,

A man may go where'er he will.

The body cloaked in ignorance,

Entrammelled by the fourfold tie,  The body flood-engulfed and drowned,

In net of latent bias caught,

To the five Hindrances a slave,

By restless play of mind obsessed,

By pregnant craving ever dogged,

In trammels of illusion swathed:—)

Lo! such a thing this body is,

Carried about on Karma's car,

To manifold becoming doomed,

Now to success, to failure then.

And they who say of it ''Tis mine!'—

Poor foolish blinded many-folk—

They swell the dreadful field of death, Grasping rebirth again, again.

They who this body seek to shun,

As they would serpent smeared with slime,

They, vomiting becoming's root,

Shall make an end, sane and immune.

Kappa, hearing the Master discourse in so many figures on the nature and destiny of the body-complex, in fear, and aversion at his own body, besought him in distress for ordination. The Master consigned him to a bhikkhu to be ordained. Kappa received five exercises, and forthwith attained arahantship as his hair was being shaved. He thereupon went to render homage to the Master, and seated at one side, confessed anna in those very verses. Hence they became Thera-verses.


## CCXXXVIII Upasena, Vanganta's son

Reborn in this Buddha-age at the village of Nalaka as the son of Rupasari, the brahminee, he was named Upasena.

 Having come of age and learnt the three Vedas, he renounced the world after hearing the Master teach the Norm. Ordained but one year, he thought, 'I will multiply the breed of the Ariyas,' and himself ordained another bhikkhu, and with him went to wait upon the Master. The latter, having heard of this, rebuked his hasty procedure. Then Upasena thought: 'If now, on account of having a following, I am blamed by the Master, on that same account will I earn his praise.' And studying for insight, he won in due course arahantship. Thereafter, himself adopting the austerer practices, he persuaded others to do likewise, and with such success that the Exalted One ranked him foremost among those who were generally popular.

At another time he was asked by that other bhikkhu, when at Kosambi, what was to be done during the dissensions and the schism there? Upasena taught him thus:

Lonely the spot and far away where noise

Scarce comes, the haunt of creatures of the wild:

'T is there the Brother should his couch prepare

For purposes of studious retreat.

From rubbish-pile, or from the charnel-field,

Or from the highways let him take and bring

Worn cloths and thence a cloak of patchwork make,

And in such rough apparel clothe himself.

In lowliness of mind from house to house,

In turn unbroken let the Brother fare

 Seeking his alms, sense guarded, well controlled;

With any fare content rough though it be,

Nor fain for other than he gets, or more,

For if he once indulge in greed for tastes,

Ne'er can his mind in jhana take delight.

In great content, with very sparse desires,

Remote, secluded: so the sage should live,

Detached from housefolk and the homeless, both.

Let him so show himself as he were dull

And dumb, nor let the wise man speech prolong

Unduly, when in midst of gathered folk.

Let him not any man upbraid; let him

Refrain from hurting; let him be in rule

And precept trained, and temperate in food.

Let him be one who concentrates upon

The symbol, skilled in genesis of thought.

To practise Calm let him devote himself,

And Intuition also in due time.

With energy and perseverance armed,

Let him be ever to his studies yoked;

Nor till he have attained the end of Ill,

Let the wise man go forth in confidence.

Thus if the Brother, fain for purity

[Of knowledge and of vision] shall abide,

The working of th' Intoxicants shall cease,

And he shall reach and find Nibbana's peace.

Now the Thera, in so admonishing that bhikkhu, showed his own attainment, and confessed anna.

CCXXXIX Gotama

Reborn before the manifestation of our Exalted One at Savatthi, in a brahmin family from Udicca, he grew up an expert in the Vedas and an unrivalled orator.

Now our Exalted One, having arisen and started the rolling of the wheel of the Norm, after converting Yasa and his friends, came on to Savatthi at the urgent request of Anathapiṇḍika. Gotama the brahmin saw and heard him, and asked for ordination. Ordained by a bhikkhu at the Master's bidding, he attained arahantship even as his hair was being shaved. After a long residence in the Kosala country, he returned to Savatthi. And many of his relations, eminent brahmins, waited upon him and asked him which, of the many gospels as guides to life that were current, he judged should be followed. He addressed them thus:

Let the recluse discern his own real good,

And let him well consider all the Word

He heareth preached, and what therein beseems

The holy life whereunto he hath come.

Religious friendships in the Rule, a course

Of ample training, and the wish to hear

Men fit to teach:— this the recluse beseems.

For Buddhas reverence; towards the Norm

Honour sincere; for the Fraternity

Care and esteem:— this the recluse beseems.

Of decorous habit and in living pure,

In conduct blameless, and the intelligence

 Adjusted well:— this the recluse beseems.

In what he does and what he leaves undone

Using deportment that doth favour find;

To higher training of the heart and mind

Fervently given:— this the recluse beseems.

Haunts of the forest, lone, remote, where sounds

May hardly come, 'mong these the earnest sage

Should make his choice:— this the recluse beseems.

And virtue, and much learning, and research

To know how in themselves things really are,

Grasp of the Truths:— this the recluse beseems.

To meditate upon the Impermanent,

And on the absence of all soul, and on

The foul, and in the world to find no charm

To bind the heart:— this the recluse beseems.

To meditate on Wisdom's seven arms,

On paths to mystic potency, on powers

And forces five, and on the eightfold Path,

The Ariyan:— this the recluse beseems.

Let the true sage put Craving far away;

Let him uproot and crush the Intoxicants;

Let him live Free:— this the recluse beseems.

Thus the Thera, in praising the course suitable to a recluse, magnified the efficiency of his Order, and contrariwise the ineffectualness of a recluse not of it. Then those brahmins, mightily approving of the Rule, were established in the precepts and so forth.

# CANTO XI. PSALM OF ELEVEN VERSES

CCXL Sankicca

Reborn in this Buddha-age at Savatthi in a family of very eminent brahmins, his mother died just prior to his birth, so that he was discovered unburnt upon the funeral pyre. For the life of a being in his last birth cannot perish ere he attain arahantship, even if he fell down Mount Sineru. At seven years of age, when he heard of his mother dying at his birth, he was thrilled, and said, 'I will leave the world.' So they brought him to Sariputta. And he won arahantship even as his hair was being cut off. How he offered his life to brigands to save 8,000 bhikkhus is told in the Dhammapada Commentary.

Now a certain layman, desiring to wait upon him, asked him to dwell in the neighbourhood, saying:

What is the gain for thee, dear lad, to dwell

During the rains within the distant woods,

Like Ujjuhana, marshy, jungle-crowned?

Sweeter for thee Verambha, Cave of Winds,

Since they who meditate must dwell apart.

Then the Thera, to show the charm of the forest and other things, replied:

E'en as the wind of the monsoon blows up

And all around the cloud-wrack, in the rains,

[So in the forest lone, remote, arise]

The thoughts that with detachment harmonize,

And all my spirit whelm and overspread.

'Twas the dun-feathered one, in charnel-field

Going his rounds, that made to rise in me

Clear thought about this body, passion-purged.

Moreover, he whom others need not guard,

He too who hath no others whom to guard:—

Even the bhikkhu, dwells in happy ease,

Regardless of what men desire and love.

Crags where clear waters lie, a rocky world,

Haunted by black-faced apes and timid deer,

Where 'neath bright blossoms run the silver streams:—

Those are the highlands of my heart's delight.

I've dwelt in forests and in mountain caves,

In rocky gorges and in haunts remote,

And where the creatures of the wild do roam;

But never mine the quest, with ill-will fraught,

Ungentle and ignoble .—'Let us hunt,

Let's slay these creatures, let us work them ill!'

 The Master hath my fealty and love,

And all the Buddha's bidding hath been done.

Low have I laid the heavy load I bore; Cause for rebirth is found in me no more.

The Good for which I bade the world farewell,

And left the home a homeless life to lead,

That highest Good have I accomplishèd,

And every bond and fetter is destroyed.'

With thought of death I dally not, nor yet

Delight in living. I await the hour,

Like any hireling who hath done his task.

With thought of death I dally not, nor yet

Delight in living. I await the hour

With mind discerning and with heedfulness.

# CANTO XII. POEMS OF TWELVE VERSES

CCXLI Silavat

Reborn in this Buddha-age at Rajagaha, as a son of King Bimbisara, he was named Silavat. When he was come of age, his brother Ajatasattu was king, and wished to put him to death, but was unable, because Silavat was in his last span of life, and had not won arahantship. Then the Exalted One, discerning what was going on, sent Moggallana the Great to fetch him. And Prince Silavat alighted from his elephant, and did obeisance to the Exalted One. Then the latter taught him, adapting the doctrine to his temperament, so that the youth won faith, entered the Order, and in due time became an arahant. He dwelt in Kosala, and when Ajatasattu sent men to murder him, he taught them and converted them, so that they, too, joined the Order. And he preached to them thus:

In morals 'tis that ye should train yourselves

Here on this earth, in morals practised well.

For moral culture well applied doth bring

Near to our reach success of every kind.

Let the wise man protect his morals well,

Who doth to threefold happiness aspire:

A good name and the gain of this world's goods

And, when this life is o'er, the joys of heaven.

The moral man, restrained, wins many friends;

Th'immoral, working mischief, loseth friends.

Dispraise and ill-fame wins th'immoral man;

Aye wins the good man fame, approval, praise.

Nothing there is of spiritual worth

But hath the moral habit as its base,

Its matrix and its vanguard and its source;

Make ye therefore your morals wholly pure.

Morals do give the tether and the term,

Light and delight affording to the heart; The strand whence all th'enlightened put
to sea; Make ye therefore your morals wholly pure.

No force is there like unto moral force;

Weapon supreme the moral habit is;

Chief decoration is the moral life;

Wondrous invulnerable coat of mail.

A mighty causeway is morality;

A peerless fragrance, sov'reign frankincense,

Wherewith we safely travel far and wide.

Good morals are the best viaticum, Sov'reign munitions [for life's pilgrimage],

Good morals are a peerless talisman,

Wherewith we safely travel far and wide.

The evil-minded man wins blame on earth,

And in the after-life a woeful doom;

A fool no matter where hath sorry cheer,

Not firmly planted on morality.

The man of virtuous mind wins fame on earth,

And in the after-life the radiant realms.

No matter where, the brave are of good cheer,

Their hearts well stablished in morality.

Chief here below is morals, but the man

Of wisdom is supreme; 'mong gods and men

He doth prevail who is both good and wise.

## CCXLII Sunita

Reborn in this Buddha-age as one of a family of flower-scavengers, he earned his living as a road-sweeper, not making enough to still his hunger. Now in the first watch of the night the Exalted One, attaining that mood of great pity so largely practised by Buddhas, surveyed the world. And he marked the conditions of arahantship in the heart of Sunita, shining like a lamp within a jar. And when the night paled into dawn he rose and dressed, and with bowl and robe, followed by his bhikkhu train, walked to Rajagaha for alms, and sought the street where Sunita was cleaning. Now Sunita was collecting scraps, rubbish, and so on into heaps, and filling therewith the baskets he carried on a yoke. And when he saw the Master and his train approaching, his heart was filled with joy and awe. Finding no place to hide in on the road, he placed his yoke in a bend of the wall, and stood as if stuck to the wall saluting with clasped hands. Then the Master, when he had come near, spoke to him in voice divinely sweet, saying: 'Sunita! what to you is that wretched mode of living? Can you endure to leave the world?' And Sunita, experiencing the rapture of one who has been sprinkled by ambrosia, said: 'If even such as I, Exalted One, may in this life take orders, why should I not? May the Exalted One suffer me to come forth.' Then the Master said: 'Come, bhikkhu!' And he, by that word receiving sanction and ordination, was by magic power invested with bowl and robes. The Master, leading him to the Vihara, taught him an exercise, and he won first the eight attainments and fivefold abhinna; then developing insight, the sixth. And Sakka and the Brahma gods came and did homage to him, as it is written:

Those deities seven hundred, glorious,

Brahmas and Indra's following drew nigh

And gladly paid Sunita homage due,

As high-bred victor over age and death.

The Exalted One saw him surrounded by gods, and smiled and commended him, teaching the Norm by the verse:

'By discipline of holy life! …

Now many bhikkhus, desirous of raising their 'lion's roar,' asked Sunita: 'From what family did you come forth? Or why did you leave the world? And how did you penetrate the truths?' Then Sunita told them the whole matter thus:

Humble the clan wherein I took my birth,

And poor was I and scanty was my lot;

Mean task was mine, a scavenger of flowers.

One for whom no man cared, despised, abused,

My mind I humbled and I bent the head

In deference to a goodly tale of folk.

And then I saw the All-Enlightened come,

Begirt and followed by his bhikkhu-train,

Great Champion ent'ring Magadha's chief town.

I laid aside my baskets and my yoke,

And came where I might due obeisance make,

And of his lovingkindness just for me,

The Chief of men halted upon his way.

Low at his feet I bent, then standing by,

I begged the Master's leave to join the Rule

And follow him, of every creature Chief.

Then he whose tender mercy watcheth all

The world, the Master pitiful and kind,

Gave me my answer: Come, bhikkhu! he said.

Thereby to me was ordination given.

Lo! I alone in forest depths abode,

With zeal unfaltering wrought the Master's word,

Even the counsels of the Conqueror.

While passed the first watch of the night there rose

Long memories of the bygone line of lives.

While passed the middle watch, the heav'nly eye,

Purview celestial, was clarified.

While passed the last watch of the night, I burst

Asunder all the gloom of ignorance.

 Then as the night wore down at dawn

And rose the sun, came Indra and Brahma,

Yielding me homage with their clasped hands:

Hail unto thee, thou nobly born of men!

Hail unto thee, thou highest among men!

Perished for thee are all th' intoxicants;

And thou art worthy, noble sir, of gifts.

The Master, seeing me by troop of gods

Begirt and followed, thereupon a smile

Revealing, by this utterance made response:

'By discipline of holy life, restraint

And mastery of self: hereby a man

Is holy; this is holiness supreme!'

# CANTO XIII. PSALM OF THIRTEEN VERSES

CCXLIII Sona-Koḷivisa

He got rebirth, in the lifetime of our Exalted One, at the city of Campa, in the family of a distinguished councillor. From the time when his birth was expected, his father's great wealth increased even more, and on his birthday the whole town kept festival. Now because of his generosity in a previous birth to a Silent Buddha, his body was as fine gold and most delicately soft, wherefore he was named Sona (golden). On the soles of his feet and the palms of bis hand grew fine down of golden colour, and he was reared in luxury, in three mansions suited to each of the three seasons.

Now when our Master had attained omniscience and begun rolling the wheel of the Norm, and was staying at Rajagaha, King Bimbisara sent for Sona. He, having arrived with a great company of fellow-townsmen, heard the Master teach the Norm, and, winning faith, obtained his parents' consent to enter the Order. He received a subject of study from the Master, but was unable to concentrate, owing to his maintaining intercourse with people while he stayed in Cool Wood. And he thought: 'My body is too delicately reared to arrive happily at happiness. A recluse's duties involve bodily fatigues.' So he disregarded the painful sores on his feet got from pacing up and down, and strove his utmost, but was unable to win. And he thought: 'I am not able to create either path or fruit. Of what use is the religious life to me? I will go back to lower things and work merit.' Then the Master discerned, and saved him by the lesson on the Parable of the Lute, showing him how to temper energy with calm. Thus corrected, he went to Vulture's Peak, and in due course won arahantship. Reflecting on his achievement, he thus declared his anna:

Who once in Anga's realm was passing rich,

A squire to Anga's king, lo! he to-day

Is of fair wealth in spiritual things.

Yea, past all ill hath Sona won his way.

Five cut thou off; Five leave behind, and Five beyond these cultivate!

He who the Fivefold Bond transcends—a Brother Flood-crossed is he called.

Seest thou a Brother with a rush-like mind,

[Stuck-up and empty], trifler, keen to taste

External things? Never will he attain

Fulness of growth within the moral code,

In mental training, or in insight's grasp.

 For such neglect that which they have to do,

But what should not be done they bring to pass.

In these conceited, desultory minds

Grow [the rank weeds of] the intoxicants.

In whom the constant governance of sense

Is well and earnestly begun, the things

That should be left undone they practise not;

Ever what should be done they bring to pass.

For them who live mindful and self-possessed,

The intoxicants wane utterly away.

In the straight Path, the Path that is declared,

See that ye walk, nor turn to right or left.

Let each himself admonish and incite;

Let each himself unto Nibbana bring!

When overtaxed and strained my energies,

The Master—can the world reveal his peer?—

Made me the parable about the lute,

And thus the Man who Sees taught me the Norm.

And I who heard his blessed word abide

Fain only and alway to do his will. Calm I evolved and practised, equipoise, That so to highest Good I might attain.

And now the Threefold Wisdom have I won,

And all the Buddha's ordinance is done.

He who hath compassed yielding up the world.

And hath attained detachment of the mind, Who hath achieved conquest of enmity,

And grasping rooted out that bringeth birth,

And death of craving hath attained and all

That doth bewilder and obscure the mind,

 And of sensations marked the genesis:—

His heart is set at perfect liberty.

For such a Brother rightly freed, whose heart

Hath peace, there is no mounting up of deeds,

Nor yet remaineth aught for him to do.

Like to a rock that is a monolith, And trembleth never in the windy blast,

So all the world of sights and tastes and sounds,

Odours and tangibles, yea, things desired,

And undesirable can ne'er excite

A man like him. His mind stands firm, detached.

And of all that he notes the passing hence.

# CANTO XIV. PSALMS OF FOURTEEN VERSES

CCXLIV Revata

This Thera's verse has already been recorded in the first Canto, where is incorporated the admonition to his sisters' sons to be mindful. Here are incorporated the verses he published during his life in the Order. This is the point of them: When he had won arahantship, he went from time to time with the great Theras, Sariputta and the rest, to visit the Master, and after staying for a while, returned to the Acacia Wood, dwelling in the bliss of fruition won and in the Sublime Moods. And thus he continued till he was an aged man. Going thus one day to visit the Buddha, he stayed not far from Savatthi in a forest. Now the police came round on the track of thieves. The thieves running by the Thera dropped their booty near him and ran. And the police, running up, arrested the Thera, dragged him before the king, and said: 'This, Sire, is the thief!' The king had him released, and asked him: 'Has your reverence committed this robbery or not?' Then the Thera, who had never from his birth done anything of the sort, taught the Norm, by way of showing his incapacity for such an act, in these verses:

Since I went forth from home to homeless life,

Ne'er have I harboured conscious wish or plan

Un-Ariyan or linked with enmity.

Ne'er mine the quest, all this long interval;—

'Let's smite our fellow-creatures, let us slay,

Let them be brought to pain and misery.'

Nay, love I do avow, made infinite,

Well trained, by orderly progression grown,

Even as by the Buddha it is taught.

With all am I a friend, comrade to all,

And to all creatures kind and merciful;

A heart of amity I cultivate,

And ever in good will is my delight.

A heart that cannot drift or fluctuate

I make my joy; the sentiments sublime

That evil men do shun I cultivate.

Whoso hath won to stage of ecstasy Beyond attention's range of flitting sense,

He, follower of the Enlightened One Supreme,

To Ariyan silence straightway doth attain.

E'en as a mountain crag unshaken stands

Sure-based, a Brother with illusions gone

Like very mountain stands unwavering.

The man of blameless life, who ever seeks

For what is pure, doth deem some trifling fault,

That is no heavier than the tip of hair,

Weighty as [burden of the gravid] cloud.

E'en as a border city guarded well

Within, without, so guard ye well yourselves.

See that the Moment pass not vainly by.

 With thought of death I dally not, nor yet

Delight in living. I await the hour

Like any hireling who hath done his task.

With thought of death I dally not, nor yet

Delight in living. I await the hour

With mind discerning and with heedfulness

The Master hath my fealty and love,

And all the Buddha's bidding hath been done.

Low have I laid the heavy load I bore,

Cause for rebirth is found in me no more.

The Good for which I bade the world farewell,

And left the home to lead the homeless life,

That highest Good have I accomplished,

And every bond and fetter is destroyed.

Work out your good with zeal and earnestness:

This is my [last] commandment unto you. For lo! now shall I wholly pass away,

To me comes absolute enfranchisement.


CCXLV Godatta

Reborn in this Buddha-age at Savatthi, in a family of caravan-leaders, he was named Godatta. After his father's death he arranged his estate, and taking 500 carts full of wares travelled about, maintaining himself by trading. One day an ox fell on the road while drawing its cart, and his men could not raise it, so he himself went and smote it severely. Then the ox, incensed at his ruthlessness, assumed a human voice and said: 'Godatta, this long time have I unreservedly given my strength to draw your burdens, but to-day when I was unable and fell, you hurt me badly. Well then! Wherever henceforth you are reborn, may I be there as your enemy able to hurt you!' Godatta was thrilled at hearing this, and thought: 'What do I in this way of life who have thus hurt living things?' And he divested himself of all his property, and took orders under a certain great Thera, in due course attaining arahantship.

Now one day as he was abiding in the bliss of fruition, he discoursed to Ariyan groups, both lay and religious, on worldly wisdom:

E'en as the mettled brute of noble breed,

Yoked to his load, drawing his load along,

Though worn by burden past his powers, [unfair],

Breaks not away, revolting from his bonds,

So they in whom, as water in the sea,

Wisdom abounds, despise not other men;

This among creatures is the Ariyan rule.

Living in time, come 'neath the power of time;

Subject to dread concerning future life, Men go their ways to pain and misery,

Yea, here below the sons of men do mourn.

Elated by some pleasant hap, by ill

Depressed, the fools are smitten to and fro, Who nothing as it really is can see.

But they who can escape the seamstress fell, 'Twixt pain and pleasure holding Middle Way,

They stand as any pillar at the gate.

Neither elated they, nor yet depressed.

For not to gain or loss, to honour, fame,

To praise or blame, to pleasure or to pain—

Where'er it be—do they take hold and cling,

No more than drop of dew to lotus-leaf.

Hale and serene are heroes everywhere,

And everywhere unconquered [bound to win].

Of him who rightly seeks and nought doth gain,

And him who gains but seeketh wrongfully,

Better is he who rightly sought and lost

Than he who gained by methods that were wrong.

Of them who have repute, but scanty dower

Of wit, and them who know, but lack repute,

Better the wise men who do lack repute

Than great repute and men of little wit.

Of praises by the unintelligent,

And blame and criticism by the wise,

Better the censure of th' intelligent

Than are the commendations of a fool.

The pleasure born of sensuous desire,

The pain that comes from life detached, austere,

Better the pain that comes from life austere

Than pleasure born of sensuous desire.

To live by wrong; for doing right to die,

Better 'twere thus to die than so to live.

They who have put off sense-desire and wrath,

Peace in their heart regarding life to come, They walk the world from lust and craving free;

Likes and dislikes are not for such as these.

The factors of enlightenment, the powers,

These have they studied and the forces too.

So winning perfect peace, as fires extinct,

They wholly pass away, sane and immune.

# CANTO XV. PSALMS OF SIXTEEN VERSES

CCXLVI Anna-Kondanna

Reborn before our Exalted One, in the village of Dona-vatthu, not far from Kapilavatthu, in a very wealthy brahmin family, he came to be called by his family name, Koṇḍanna. When grown up he knew the three Vedas, and excelled in runes concerning marks. Now when our Bodhisat was born, he was among the eight brahmins sent for to prognosticate. And though he was quite a novice, he saw the marks of the Great Man on the infant, and said: 'Verily this one will be a Buddha!' So he lived, awaiting the Great Being's renunciation. When this happened in the Bodhisat's twenty-ninth year, Koṇḍanna heard of it, and left the world with four other sons of mark-interpreting brahmins, Vappa and others, and for six years dwelt at Uruvela, near the Bodhisat, during the latter's great struggle. Then when the Bodhisat ceased to fast, they were disgusted, and went to Isipatana. There the Buddha followed them, and preached his Wheel sermon, whereby Koṇḍanna and myriads of Brahma angels won the fruition of the first path. And on the fifth day, through the sermon on 'No Sign of any Soul,' Koṇḍanna realized arahantship. Him the Master, later on, in conclave at the great Jeta Grove Vihara, ranked chief among those bhikkhus who were of long standing in the Order. And on one occasion Koṇḍanna's sermon on the Four Truths—a discourse bearing the impress of the three signs, dealing with non-substantiality, varied by divers methods, based on Nibbana, and delivered with the Buddha's own fluency—so impressed Sakka the god that he uttered this verse:

Hearing thy doctrine's mighty properties,

Lo! I thereby am more than satisfied.

Most passionless and pure the Norm thus taught,

From every form of grasping wholly free.

On another occasion the Thera, seeing how the minds of certain worldlings were mastered by wrong ideas, delivered himself on this wise:

Many the motley pictures in the world,

Enjoyed within this earth's circumference,

Inciting, I do note, man's purposes,

Fair-seeming hopes, and linked with fierce desire.

As dust by wind upchurned the rain-cloud lays,

So are those purposes composed and quenched,

When he by wisdom doth discern and see.

When he by wisdom doth discern and see:

'Impermanent is everything in life,'

Then he at all this suffering feels disgust.

Lo! herein lies the way to purity.

When he by wisdom doth discern and see,

That 'Everything in life is bound to Ill' Then he at all this suffering feels disgust.

Lo! herein lies the way to purity.

That 'Everything in life is Void of Soul,'

Then he at all this suffering feels disgust.

Lo! herein lies the way to purity.

Thereupon he showed that he had himself attained this insight, confessing anna, and saying:

Brother Koṇḍanna, wakened by the Wake:—

Lo! he hath passed with vigour out and on;

Sloughed off hath he the dyings and the births,

Wholly accomplishing the life sublime.

And be it 'flood' or 'snare' or 'stumbling-stone,'

Or be it 'mountain' hard to rive in twain, The net, the stumbling-stone I've hacked away,

And cloven is the rock so hard to break,

And crossed the flood. Rapt in ecstatic thought

I dwell, from bondage unto evil freed.

Now one day the Thera rebuked a bhikkhu, who had fallen into bad habits through unworthy friendships, and admonished him, saying:

A bhikkhu of distraught, unsteady mind,

Who doth associate with vicious friends,

In the great flood [of constant living] falls

Headlong and drowning sinks beneath its waves.

But who, with concentrated, steady mind,

Discreet and self-restrained in heart and sense,

Doth wisely join himself to virtuous friends,

His it may be to put an end to Ill.

Lo! here a man with worn and pallid frame;

Like knotted stems of cane his joints, and sharp

Th' emaciated network of his veins;

In food and drink austerely temperate,

His spirit neither crushed nor desolate.

In the great forest, in the mighty woods,

Touched though I be by gadfly and by gnat,

I yet would roam, like warrior-elephant,

In van of battle, mindful, vigilant.

With thought of death I dally not, nor yet

Delight in living. I await the hour

Like any hireling who hath done his task.

With thought of death I dally not, nor yet

Delight in living. I await the hour

With mind discerning and with heedfulness.

The Master hath my fealty and love,

And all the Buddha's bidding hath been done.

Low have I laid the heavy load I bore,

Cause for rebirth is found in me no more.

The Good for which I bade the world farewell,

And left the home to lead the homeless life,

That highest Good have I accomplished.

What need have I as cenobite to dwell?

CCXLVII Udayin

Reborn in this Buddha-age at Kapilavatthu in a brahmin family, he saw the power and majesty of the Buddha when  he visited his family, believed in him, entered the Order, and in due course became an arahant. Now there are these three Theras named Udayin: the minister's son, Kaḷudayin, recorded above, this brahmin, and Udayin the Great. This one, when the Sutta of the Elephant Parable had been taught on the occasion when Seta, King Pasenadi's elephant, was publicly admired, was stirred to enthusiasm at thought of the Buddha, and thinking: 'These people admire a mere animal. Come now, I will proclaim the virtues of that great and wondrous Elephant, the Buddha!' he uttered these verses:

Buddha the Wake, the son of man,

Self-tamed, by inward vision rapt,

Bearing himself by ways sublime,

Glad in tranquillity of heart;

To whom men honour pay as one

Who hath transcended all we know; To whom gods also honour yield:—

So I, an arahant, have heard—

From jungle to Nibbana come, With every fetter left behind,

Glad in renouncing worldly joys,

Extracted like fine gold from ore,

Like elephant superb is he,

On wooded heights in Himalay:—

Lo, him behold! Naga Superb-

 For, sure, of all we 'Naga' name,

(Serpent or elephant or man)

Supremely true that name for him—

This Naga will I praise to you,

For he 'no sin' —na agun— doth. Mercifulness, sobriety: These be two of the Naga's feet;

Intelligence and mindfulness:

Other two feet of this Elephant.

The Naga's trunk is confidence;

His white tusks, equanimity;

His throat awareness, and his head

Is insight; testing touch of trunk

Is weighing wisely good and bad;

Shrine of the Norm his viscera;

Detachment is the tail of him.

So musing rapt, and breathing bliss, Composed in body and in mind,

Composed, this Naga, when he walks,

Composed, this Naga, when he stands,

Composed, this Naga, lying down,

And eke composed while he sits;

Self-governed whatsoe'er he doth:

This is the Naga's perfect way.

Blameless in all that he enjoys,

Enjoying naught that calls for blame,

Hath he but gotten food and gear,

From store laid up he doth refrain.

 Whether the tie be coarse or fine,

Bonds of all kinds he knaps in twain;

He goeth wheresoe'er he will,

Nor careth wheresoe'er he goes.

As lotus born within a lake,

By water nowise is defiled,

But groweth fragrant, beautiful,

So is the Buddha in this world,

Born in the world and dwelling there,

But by the world nowise defiled,

E'en as the lily by the lake.

A mighty fire that's spent itself,

And hath no fuel dieth down,

And of the smouldering ashes men

Do say 'That fire is now extinct.'

Lo! here's a parable the wise

Have taught to make their meaning known.

Great Nagas, they will understand

The Naga, by that Naga taught:

With passion gone, and hatred gone,

And dullness gone, sane and immune,

This Naga, yielding up his life,

Will clean 'go out,' sane and immune.


(POEMS OF SIXTEEN, SEVENTEEN, EIGHTEEN, NINETEEN VERSES
DESUNT)

# CANTO XVI. PSALMS OF TWENTY VERSES

CCXLVIII Adhimutta

Reborn in this Buddha-age as the sister's son of the Thera Sankicca, he left the world under his uncle's tuition, and while only a novice, won arahantship. And dwelling in the bliss of fruition, he wished for full ordination, and went home to ask his mother's leave. Now as he went, he fell in with highwaymen on the look-out for an offering to their deity, and they seized on him as a suitable sacrifice. He, thus assailed, stood undaunted and without blenching. Then the robber-chief was amazed, and commended him, saying:

Of all the lot whom we, for god or pelf,

Have smitten in our time, there's not been one

But hath shown fear, trembled and clamoured sore.

But thou, who'rt not affrighted, nay, whose face

Shows brighter bloom, why dost thou not lament.

When such a fearsome peril threatens thee?


Adhimutta:

No misery of mind, O chief, is there

For him who hath no wants. All fear have I

Transcended, since the Fetters were destroyed.

By death of that which leadeth to rebirth, The truths are seen e'en as they really are,

And hence in death there lies no fear for me,

Tis as a laying down the load I bore.

Well have I lived the holy life, and well

Made progress in the Ariyan Path; no fear

There lies in death, who puts an end to ills.

Void of delight the forms of birth appear, Like drinking poison one has thrown away.

He who hath passed beyond, from grasping free,

Whose task is done, sane and immune, is glad,

Not sorry, when the term of lives is reached,

As one who from the slaughter-house escapes.

He who the ideal order hath attained,

All the world over seeking nought to own,

As one who from a burning house escapes,

When death is drawing nigh he grieveth not.

All things soever which have come to be,

And all rebirth wherever it is got,

Nowhere therein is personal design:— So hath the mighty Sage declared to us.

 And he who knows that things are even so,

As by the Buddha it is taught, no more

Would he take hold of any form of birth

Than he would grasp a red-hot iron ball.

Comes not to me the thought: ''Tis I have been,'

Nor comes the thought: 'What shall I next become?'

Thoughts, deeds and words are no persisting [soul],

Therefore what ground for lamentations here?

To him who seeth, as it really is,

The pure and simple causal rise of things,

The pure and simple sequence of our acts:—

To such an one can come no fear, O chief.

That all this world is like the forest grass

And brushwood [no man's property] when one

By wisdom seeth this, finds naught that's 'Mine,'

Thinking: ''tis not for me,' he grieveth not.

This body irketh me; no seeker I

To live. This mortal frame will broken be,

And ne'er another from it be reborn.

Your business with my body, come, that do

E'en as ye will; and not on that account

Will hatred or affection rise in me.

The young men marvelled at his words, and thrilled

With awe, casting away their knives they said:

What are your honour's practices, or who

Is teacher to you? Of whose Ordinance

A member, have you gained this grieflessness?

Adhimutta:

My teacher is the Conqueror knowing all

And seeing all, the Master infinite

In pity, all the world's Physician, He.

 And He it is by whom these, truths are taught,

Norm to Nibbana leading, unsurpassed.

Within His Rule I've won this grieflessness.

Now when the robbers heard the well-spoke utterance of the sage,

They laid aside their knives, their arms, and some forsook that trade,

And some besought that they might leave the world for holy life.

They leaving thus, within the Buddha's welcome Rule grew wise,

The seven Factors practising and eke the Forces five,

Trained in the Powers, with hearts elate, happy they reached the Goal.

CCXLIX Parapariya

Reborn in this Buddha-age at Savatthi as the son of a certain very eminent brahmin, he was called, when adult, after his family name Parapara, 'the Parapariya' (Paraparite). Well educated in brahmin lore and accomplishments, he went one day into the Jeta Grove Vihara, at the Master's preaching hour, and took his seat at the fringe of the assembly. The Master, contemplating his character, taught the Sutta, called 'Practice of Faculties,' whereupon Parapariya found faith and entered the Order. After learning the Sutta by heart, he pondered over the meaning, thinking: 'In verses the meaning would appear so and so.' Thus pondering on the subject of sense-perception he established insight, and in due time won arahantship. Later he expressed his meditations in verse as follows:

To a Brother came these musings,

To the bhikkhu Parapariya,

As he sat alone, secluded,

World-detached and meditating:

What is there of course or order,

What is there in rite, or conduct,

Which may make a man accomplish

That which to himself is owing,

Nor work harm on any other?

Lo! the parts and powers of humans

Make for welfare and for evil:

Powers unguarded make for evil,

Guarded powers make for welfare.

One who guardeth parts and powers,

One who tendeth parts and powers,

He may do to self his duty,

Nor work harm on any other.

If he go with unrestrained

Power of sight among sense-objects,  All the evil ne'er discerning,

He doth not escape from sorrow.

If he go with unrestrained

Power of hearing sounds about him,

All the evil ne'er discerning,

He doth not escape from sorrow.

If in divers kinds of odours

He indulge, voluptuously,

Way of refuge ne'er discerning, He doth not escape from sorrow.

Taste of sour and sweet and bitter

Relishing and pondering over,

Cleaving to desires of palate:

Ne'er his heart will be awakened.

Lovely, luring things of contact,

Touching, feeling, pondering over,

Lust-exciting, he impassioned

Findeth divers forms of sorrow.

Yea, who in these sense-impressions

Cannot guard the mind [recipient],

Sorrow thereby will pursue him,

E'en by way of all five senses.

Body full of blood and matter

And of plenteous other carrion,

So by human skill and wit is

Rendered fair like painted casket,

That the bitter suffering from it

Shows as sweetly satisfying,

Bound to what we hold beloved,

As a razor blade, that's hidden

'Neath thick crust of honey-syrup,

 Undiscerned [by the greedy].

He who dotes on form of woman,

Taste and touch and scent of woman,

Findeth divers shapes of sorrow.

All that emanates from woman Permeating [all men's senses,]—

This and that man's five gates [open,]—

'Gainst all these to make a barrier

If a man have grit and valiance,

He is wise and he is righteous,

He is clever and far-seeing;

For he may, at ease and cheerful,

Set himself to righteous duties.

When immersed in temporal profit, If he shun vain undertakings,

If he judge it right to shun them,

He is earnest and far-seeing.

Is a work with good connected,

Is his love set on th' Ideal, Let him take the work and do it;

Other loves that Love surpasseth.

Many, manifold the methods

Whereby man his fellows cheateth;

Smiting, slaying, sore afflicting

He with violence oppresses.

As a strong man plying woodcraft,

Useth nail to smite a nail out,

 So the wise and virtuous brethren

Use one power to smite out others:—

Faith and effort, concentration,

Mindfulness and wisdom plying,

Five by other Five outsmiting,

Goes the saint from flaws released.

He is wise and he is righteous;

He hath kept the Rule proclaimed

Wholly, fully by the Buddha.

He is happy, he doth prosper.


CCL Telakani

He was reborn in this Buddha-age, before the Master's birth, at Savatthi, in a brahmin family, and named Telakani. Matured as to antecedents, he wearied of worldly desires, and left the world as a wandering recluse. Seeking for emancipation of spirit, he toured about, thinking: 'Who is he in the world who has got beyond?' and asking questions of recluses and brahmins without receiving satisfaction. Meanwhile our Exalted One had arisen, and was rolling the Norm-Wheel, working the good of the world. Him one day Telakani heard, and found faith, was ordained, and not long after won arahantship.

Sitting one day with bhikkhus, and remembering his own toiling and winning, he declared it all to them thus:

Oh the long days I cast about in thought,

Ardent to find truth [that could set me free]! No peace of mind I won, [but up and down

I fared,] asking of brahmin and recluse:

'What man in all the world hath got beyond?

Who in the Ambrosial hath a foothold won? Whose doctrine can I to my bosom take,

Whereby the Highest I may come to know?'

Caught on a hook within, my spirit hung

E'en as a fish that swallows baited food.

Captured I lay, as Vepachitti once,

The Asura, in mighty Indra's toils.

I dragged my chains along, nor found release

From this [unending source of] grief and dole.

Is there no man on earth who can unloose

My bonds, and make me know Enlightenment?

What brahmin, what recluse can tell me how

To break them off? Whose Norm can I accept,

Able to bear away old age and death?

Behold this load! coil of perplexity

And doubt, the mortal force of it

Wearing the temper, stiffening the mind,

And lacerating with a vast desire,

Fell offshoot from the bow of craving, due

To [forms of false opinion,] twice fifteen—

Behold, I say, how mightily about

My breast this pressure crushes where it lies!

The ruck of vain opinions not put off

 But quickened by foud hopes and memories: By this transfixed I stagger to and
fro,

And quiver as a leaf blown by the wind.

'Tis from within me that hath sprung the dart, Whence swiftly is consumed this
self of me, Even this body with its sixfold field

Of contact, where it doth proceed alway.

I see him not, that surgeon skilled, who can

Extract the dart and purge me of my doubts

By subtle probe, and not by other knife.

Can any one, without or knife or wound,

Leaving the members of me all unscathed,

Draw out this shaft that's stuck within my heart?

Master of Dhamma, he, the Best,

Who can the venom's fever-scathe disperse,

Who, were I fallen in the deep, could show

A hand and point where shallows sloped to land.

Yea, in a pool it is that I am plunged,

A pit of dust and mire undrainable,

Extended wide with treacherous counterfeit,

Envy and overstrain, torpor and sloth.

 Thunder of thought distracted overhead,

And fettering wraiths of cloud about my path:—

The rush of lust-borne impulse and intent

Doth thither sweep me—to a sceptic's doom.

And everywhere the streams are flowing by,

And ever burgeoning the creeper stands—

Those streams whose strength avails to stop?

That creeper who can sever from its root?

Make thee a dyke, good sir, to dam the streams;

See that the mind's strong current ruthlessly

Dash thee not hence like any log away!

'Twas even so for me who sought in fear,

On this side for the distant shore, when He,

The Master, followed by his saintly throng,

He the true Refuge, and with insight armed,

Held out to me a stairway, strongly wrought,

And firm, made of the Norm's pure heart of oak, And to me toiling spake: 'Be not afraid!'

I climbed up to the terrace where the mind

Alert and vigilant applies itself, Thence I could contemplate the sons of men

Delighting in that sense of 'I' and 'mine,' Wherein I once was wont to nurse conceits.

And when I saw the Way, even the ship

On which to embark, and dwelt no more on Self,

'Twas then that I beheld Nibbana's shore.

The dart that sprang from self, offshoot of her

Who to becoming leads—to stop all that

The perfect Path [the Ariyan] he taught.

The knotted bonds long buried in my life,

Fixed up about me for so many years,

The Buddha loosed and cast them off from me,

And every poison canker purged away.


CCLI Ratthapala

He was reborn in this Buddha-age in the country of the Kurus, in the township of Thullakotthika, as the son of a councillor named Ratthapala,and was called by his family name. Brought up in a large establishment of retainers, he was united, when adolescent, to a suitable wife, and enjoyed a prosperity resembling that of the devas. Now the Exalted One, touring in the Kuru country, came to Thullakotthika, and Ratthapala went to hear him teach. Receiving faith, he with great difficulty obtained his parents' leave to renounce the world. Going to the Master, he received ordination from a bhikkhu at the Master's command, and studying diligently developed insight and won arahantship. Thereupon he obtained permission to visit his parents, and went to Thullakotthika, going from house to house for alms. At his father's house he obtained rancid gruel, but ate it as if it were ambrosia. Invited by his father, he went next day to his home. And  when the ladies in fine array asked him: 'What are the celestial nymphs like, my lord, for whose sake you live the holy life?' he taught them the Norm in connection with impermanence, etc., repulsing their insinuating conduct:

769. Behold the tricked-out puppet-shape, a mass

Of sores, a congeries diseased, and full

Of many purposes and plans, and yet

In whom there is no power to persist! (769)

770. Behold the tricked-out form, bejewelled, ringed,

Sheathèd in bones and skinny envelope,

By help of gear made fine and fair to see!

771. Feet dyed with lac, with rouge the lips besmeared:

All good enough for dull wit of a fool,

But not for him who seeketh the Beyond!

772. The locks in eightfold plait, eyes fringed with black:

All good enough for dull wit of a fool,

But not for him who seeketh the Beyond!

773. Like a collyrium-pot, brand new, embossed,

The body foul within is bravely decked:

All good enough for dull wit of a fool,

But not for him who seeketh the Beyond.

774. The trapper set his snare. The deer came not

Against the net. We've eaten of the bait—

Let's go! the while deer trappers make lament.

775. Snapt is the hunter's snare! The deer came not

Against the net. We've eaten of the bait—

Let's go; the while deer catchers weep and wail.

Ratthapala thereupon went through the air to the Antelope Park of King Koravya, and seated himself on a stone slab. Now the Thera's father had had bolts put on his seven doors, and had sent men to prevent him from getting out, and to take off his yellow robes and clothe him in white. Hence the Thera's going through the air. Then the king, hearing where he was seated, went to him, and with courteous greeting asked him thus: 'Master Ratthapala, in this world men renounce it for some kind of misfortune—illness, loss of king, wealth or family. But you who have suffered no such thing, why have you left the world?' Then the Thera replied: 'The world passes away, is transient; the world is without refuge or providence; the world has no stronghold; the world is wanting and destitute, dissatisfied, the slave of craving.' Thus showing his separate condition, he recited a parallel in verse :

776. Men of much wealth I see in the world:—

Riches acquiring they err in not giving.

Make out of greed a great hoard of their wealth,

Yea, hankering yet after ever more pleasures.

777. The king having forcibly conquered the earth,

To the shore of the ocean, holding the land

This side of the sea, may yet all unsatisfied

Hanker after the further side also.

778. See where both king and full many another man

Nursing their cravings come to their dying.

Paupers becoming, they put off this body,

For never content lies in pleasures of this world.

779. Kinsfolk bewail him with tresses dishevelled,

Crying: 'Alas! would our kin were immortal!' Him in his shroud envelopt they bear away;

Raising a pyre they forthwith cremate him.

780. He lies a-burning, by forks being prodded,

Clad in one garment, stripped of all riches.

Never to one who is dying are kinsfolk

Refuge, nor friends, nay, nor even neighbours.

781. His wealth is annexed by his heirs, but the being Goeth according to all his past actions.

Never doth wealth follow after the dying,

Nor children, nor wife, nor wealth, nor a kingdom.

782. Never is long life gotten through riches,

Nor is old age ever banished by property.

Brief is this life, all the sages have told us;

Transient it is, and essentially changing.

783. All feel the Touch, both the poor and the wealthy;

Touched is the wise man no less than the fool.

But the fool, smitten down by his folly, lies prostrate;

The wise man, when feeling the Touch, never trembles.

784. Wherefore far better than riches is wisdom,

Whereby we arrive even here at the terminus.

For from not reaching the goal the dull-minded

Work wicked deeds in delusion, reborn

In spheres whether high or whether of no account.

785. Cometh a man to the womb and in other worlds

Findeth rebirth, being caught in Saṁsara,

Round sempiternal of livings consecutive;

Him one of little wit follows believing,

Cometh to birth both here and in other worlds.

786. E'en as a thief who is taken in burglary,

By his own act is condemned as a criminal,  So is the race, after death, in another world,

By its own doing condemned as a criminal.

787. For by the charm, sweet and diverse, of sense-desire,

One way or other the mind is unbalanced;

And seeing the evil in sensuous pleasures,

Therefore, O King, have I gone all forsaking.

788. Fall as fruit from the tree all the sons of men,

Youthful and aged, when breaks down the body,

This too seeing, O King, have I gone forth.

Better the safe, sure life of religion.

789. Full of high confidence I left the world

And joined the Order of the Conqueror.

Blameless my going forth has been, and free

From debt I live on my allotted share.

790. Looking on sense-desires as fire alight.

On gold and silver as a [noxious] knife,

[On life] from entry in the womb as ill,

And on the fearsome peril of the hells:—

791. Seeing, I say, great evils everywhere,

Thereat was I with anguish sore beset.

Then to me, pierced and wounded as I was,

Came fourfold victory: o'er sense-desires,

O'er rebirth, error, ignorance, VICTORY!

792. The Master hath my fealty and love, And all the Buddha's bidding hath been done.

Low have I laid the heavy load I bore,

Cause for rebirth is found in me no more.

793. The Good for which I bade the world farewell,

And left the home to dwell where home was not,

That highest Good have I accomplishèd,

And every bond and fetter is destroyed.

Then the Thera, having thus taught the Norm to King Koravya, went back to the Master. And He thereafter, in the assembly of the Ariyans, declared Ratthapala foremost of those who had left the world through faith.


CCLII Malunkya's Son

The story of this venerable one is given in Canto VI. (CCXIV.), wherein the Thera, established in arahantship, uttered a psalm by way of teaching his kinsfolk about the Path. But in this poem the Thera, not yet an arahant, had asked the Master for doctrine in brief, and he received this response: 'What think you, Malunkya's son, things which you have never seen, heard, smelt, tasted, touched, or perceived, of which you have no present impression, nor of which you wish you might have sensations and perception:— do you feel desire, or longing, or fondness for them?' 'No, lord.' 'Here, then, Malunkya's son, when you do get any sensation or perception of things, you will have just the sensations or perceptions only. And inasmuch as this is so, and you will get no [greed, ill-will, or illusion] thereby, or therein, either here or elsewhere, or hereafter, this, even this, is the end of pain.

And Malunkya's son, showing how well he had learnt that doctrine so summarized, expressed it in these verses:

Sight of fair shape bewildering lucid thought, If one but heed the image sweet and dear,

The heart inflamed in feeling doth o'erflow,

And clinging stayeth. Thus in him do grow

Divers emotions rooted in the sight,

Greed and aversion, and the heart of him

Doth suffer grievously. Of him we say,

Thus heaping store of pain and suffering:

Far from Nibbana!

Sound, bewildering lucid thought,

If one but heed the image sweet and dear,

The heart inflamed in feeling doth o'erflow,

And clinging stayeth. Thus in him do grow

Divers emotions rooted in the sight,

Greed and aversion, and the heart of him

Doth suffer grievously. Of him we say,

Thus heaping store of pain and suffering:

Far from Nibbana!

Smell bewildering lucid thought,

If one but heed the image sweet and dear,

The heart inflamed in feeling doth o'erflow,

And clinging stayeth. Thus in him do grow

Divers emotions rooted in the sight,

Greed and aversion, and the heart of him

Doth suffer grievously. Of him we say,

Thus heaping store of pain and suffering:

Far from Nibbana!

Taste bewildering lucid thought,

If one but heed the image sweet and dear,

The heart inflamed in feeling doth o'erflow,

And clinging stayeth. Thus in him do grow

Divers emotions rooted in the sight,

Greed and aversion, and the heart of him

Doth suffer grievously. Of him we say,

Thus heaping store of pain and suffering:

Far from Nibbana!

Touch, bewildering lucid thought,

If one but heed the image sweet and dear,

The heart inflamed in feeling doth o'erflow,

And clinging stayeth. Thus in him do grow

Divers emotions rooted in the sight,

Greed and aversion, and the heart of him

Doth suffer grievously. Of him we say,

Thus heaping store of pain and suffering:

Far from Nibbana!

Object, idea, bewildering lucid thought,

If one but heed the image sweet and dear,

The heart inflamed in feeling doth o'erflow,

And clinging stayeth. Thus in him do grow

Divers emotions rooted in idea,

Greed and aversion; and the heart of him

Doth suffer grievously. Of him we say,—

Thus heaping store of pain and suffering:—

Far from Nibbana!

He who for things he sees no passion breeds,

But mindful, clear of head, can suffer sense,

With uninflamed heart, nor staying clings;

And as he sees, so normally he feels; For him no heaping up, but minishing:

Thus doth he heedfully pursue his way.

Of him, building no store of ill, we say:—

Near is Nibbana!

He who for things he hears no passion breeds,

But mindful, clear of head, can suffer sense,

With uninflamed heart, nor staying clings;

And as he hears, so normally he feels;

For him no heaping up, but minishing:

Thus doth he heedfully pursue his way.

Of him, building no store of ill, we say:—

Near is Nibbana!

He who for things he smells no passion breeds,

But mindful, clear of head, can suffer sense,

With uninflamed heart, nor staying clings;

And as he smells, so normally he feels;

For him no heaping up, but minishing:

Thus doth he heedfully pursue his way.

Of him, building no store of ill, we say:—

Near is Nibbana!

He who for things he tastes no passion breeds,

But mindful, clear of head, can suffer sense,

With uninflamed heart, nor staying clings;

And as he tastes, so normally he feels;

For him no heaping up, but minishing:

Thus doth he heedfully pursue his way.

Of him, building no store of ill, we say:—

Near is Nibbana!

He who for things things touched no passion breeds,

But mindful, clear of head, can suffer sense,

With uninflamed heart, nor staying clings;

And as he is touched, so normally he feels;

For him no heaping up, but minishing:

Thus doth he heedfully pursue his way.

Of him, building no store of ill, we say:—

Near is Nibbana!

He who for things things felt no passion breeds,

But mindful, clear of head, can suffer sense,

With uninflamed heart, nor staying clings;

And as he doth perceive, so normally he feels;

For him no heaping up, but minishing:

Thus doth he heedfully pursue his way.

Of him, building no store of ill, we say:—

Near is Nibbana!

Then the Thera rose, saluted the Master and departed, not long after so developing insight that he won arahantship.

CCLIII Sela

Reborn in this Buddha-age, in Aṅguttarapa, in a brahmin family, at the brahmin village of Apana, he was named Sela. And he dwelt there when adult, proficient in the three Vedas and in brahmin arts, teaching mantras to 300 brahmin youths. Now at that time the Master, leaving Savatthi, toured in Anguttarapa with 1,250 bhikkhus. And divining the maturity of insight in Sela and his pupils, he halted at a certain wood. Then Keniya, the ascetic, having invited the Master and his band for the following day, made preparation of much food. And Sela with his 300 visited the hermitage and asked: 'What now, Keniya, is a minister of the King expected?' and so on. Keniya replied: 'I have invited the Buddha, the Exalted One for to-morrow.' Now Sela, thrilled with joyful enthusiasm at the word 'Buddha,' sought out the Master straightway with his youths, and after exchange of courtesies seated himself at one side. Contemplating the Exalted One, he thought: 'He has all the marks of one who is either a world-emperor, or a Buddha rolling back the veil of the world; yet I know not whether this religious Brother be a Buddha or not. But I have heard that they who are Exalted Ones, Arahants, Buddhas supreme, reveal themselves when their praises are uttered; for one who is not such a Buddha, when some one in his presence praises the virtues of a Buddha, is irritated and dissatisfied, because he has not won the serene confidence of Buddhas, and cannot endure the allusions. What if I were now to praise the Samana Gotama to his face with suitable verses? So he began:

O thou of perfect form and beauty rare,

Of fairest parts and lovely to behold,

Exalted One! thy colour like fine gold,

Thou valiant spirit, with the dazzling teeth,

Whose body shows the features that betray

The man of perfectly adjusted parts,

Yea, all the traits that mark the Super-Man;

Thou with the eyes so clear, thy countenance

So fair, broad, straight, majestic, thou dost shine

As doth the sun, the centre thou of all

The chosen band of brethren gathered round.

Thou bhikkhu noble of aspect, whose skin

Resembleth gold, say, what is friar's life

To thee with presence so supremely fair?

A Prince thou dost deserve to be, a Bull

Drawing the chariot of the world's empire;

Lord of the earth from end to end foursquare,

A conqueror, of Jambudipa chief.

Nobles and wealthy lords thy vassals be,

Thou sovran lord of lords, thou king of men,

Take thou thy power, O Gotama, and reign!

Then the Exalted One, fulfilling Sela's wish, replied:

'A king, O Sela, verily am I;

King of the Norm, above me there is none.

 And by my doctrine do I turn the wheel

Of sovereignty, wheel irreversible.'

Then Sela to win confirmation spoke again:

Wholly enlightened thou dost own thyself:

'King of the Norm, above me there is none

And by my doctrine do I turn the wheel

Of sovereignty'—so sayst thou, Gotama.

Who is the general of my lord the King,

Disciple following in the Master's steps?

Who after his example turns the wheel?

Now the venerable Sariputta was Beated at the right of the Exalted One, his head shining in beauty like a pile of gold. And showing him the Exalted One said:

'The wheel I set a-going of the Norm,

Above which, Sela, there is none, that wheel

Doth Sariputta after my example turn,

Who hath become like Him-who-Thus-hath-Come.

All that which should be known is known by me,

All culture of the mind, that have I wrought,

Whate'er should be renounced I have renounced,

Hence, brahmin! am I Buddha—one Awake.

 Subdue thy doubts regarding me, brahmin!

Have faith in me. Hard, hard it is to win

Repeated seeing—[as thou mayest now]—

Of them who rise on earth Buddhas Supreme.

And 'tis of such whose advent in the world

Is difficult and rare, that I in sooth

Am one, O brahmin! yea, a Buddha I,

Surgeon and Healer, over whom there's none.

Supreme my place and past compare my work,

In crushing the assaults of Mara's hosts. All that is hostile lieth 'neath my sway,

And I rejoice for no whence cometh fear.'

Then Sela the brahmin, so convinced by the Exalted One as to wish to take orders, said:

'Now pay good heed, sirs, to the words that He

Who sees, Healer and Hero, speaks to us,

Impressive as a forest lion's roar.

Supreme in place and past compare in work,

Who crusheth the assaults of Mara's hosts:—

Who that hath seen him would not feel convinced,

And were he never so obscure of birth? He who is fain for me may follow me;

And whoso is not fain may go his way;

But I will in this Rule renounce the world,

'Neath him who is so noble and so wise.'

Then the brahmin youths also, because they had attained to the requisite conditions, replied:

'If to thy judgment, sir, this Rule of him.

The Supreme Buddha, doth commend itself,

We too will in that Rule renounce the world,

'Neath him who is so noble and so wise.'

Then Sela, delighted because those youths shared in his resolve, showed them to the Master and asked for ordination:

These thrice one hundred brahmins with clasped hands

Beseech thee, O Exalted One, that we

May lead the holy life beneath thine eye.

Then the Exalted One, inasmuch as in past ages Sela, as teacher of just those 300, had sown the root of merit, and now in the last life had produced both his own insight and their maturity, discerned that they were ripe for ordination and said:

'Well, Sela, is the holy life set forth,

Clear to be seen and heard; swift is the fruit, Wherein not futile is the coming forth

For one who earnestly doth train himself.'

Thereupon the Exalted One said: 'Come ye, bhikkhus!' And they, by his mystic power endued with the robes and bowl of bhikkhus of long-standing, did obeisance and began their studies for insight, attaining arahantship on the seventh day. Thereat they came to the Master and confessed anna thus, Sela speaking:

Lo! thou who seest all, 'tis eight days since

We came and refuge found. In one se'nnight,

Exalted One! we're trainèd in thy Rule.

Thou art Buddha! our Master thou! and thou

The mighty Seer who Mara didst o'erthrow.

Thou who all evil tendencies hast purged,

And crossed [the flood of life's eternal sea],

'Tis thou dost aid the sons of men to cross.

Thou hast transcended every cause of birth,

And shattered every poison-growth within,

Thou even as a lion, grasping nought,

Hast banished every source of fear and dread.

Three hundred bhikkhus lo! before thee stand,

With clasped hands outstretched to honour thee,

Stretch forth thy feet, O hero! suffer them,

Thine arahants, their Master to salute.


CCLIV Bhaddiya, son of Kaḷi of the Godhas

Reborn in this Buddha-age at Kapilavatthu in a clan of Sakiyan rajas, he was named Bhaddiya. And when adult, he left the world together with Anuruddha and the other four nobles, while the Master was staying at the Mango Grove of Anupiya. And entering the Order, he won arahantship. Him (as the result of a primeval vow and efforts on his part), the Master in conclave at Jeta Grove, ranked as the best among those bhikkhus who were of aristocratic birth. And he, dwelling in the bliss of fruition, in the bliss of Nibbana, while in the forest, beneath a tree, in any lonely spot, was ever breathing forth the exclamation: 'Ah, what happiness! ah, what happiness!' Now bhikkhus hearing him told the Master; to whom Bhaddiya, when summoned, admitted the habit, adding: 'Formerly, lord, when I was ruling my principality, I was well provided with protection, yet even so I was ever fearful, nervous, distrustful. But now that I have renounced all, I am no longer in that state.' And before the Master he uttered his 'lion's roar,' thus:

What delicate gear was mine to wear,

When riding on my elephants,

What dainty fare was mine to eat,

Prepared by art from rice and flesh!

To-day a happy winner, stanch,

Pleased with what scraps his bowl is filled,

In contemplation, grasping nought,

Lives Bhaddiya, the Godha's son.

In cast-off rags attired, and stanch,

Pleased with what scraps his bowl is filled,

In contemplation, grasping nought,

Lives Bhaddiya, the Godha's son.

Seeking his daily alms and stanch,

Pleased with what scraps his bowl is filled,

In contemplation, grasping nought,

Lives Bhaddiya, the Godha's son.

In triple robe, no more, and stanch,

Pleased with what scraps his bowl is filled,

In contemplation, grasping nought,

Lives Bhaddiya, the Godha's son.

Taking each house in turn, and stanch,

Pleased with what scraps his bowl is filled,

In contemplation, grasping nought,

Lives Bhaddiya, the Godha's son.

With one good meal a day, and stanch,

Pleased with what scraps his bowl is filled,

In contemplation, grasping nought,

Lives Bhaddiya, the Godha's son.

Eating from bowl alone and stanch,

Pleased with what scraps his bowl is filled,

In contemplation, grasping nought,

Lives Bhaddiya, the Godha's son.

Refusing aftermeals and stanch,

Pleased with what scraps his bowl is filled,

In contemplation, grasping nought,

Lives Bhaddiya, the Godha's son.

Haunting the lonely woods and stanch,

Pleased with what scraps his bowl is filled,

In contemplation, grasping nought,

Lives Bhaddiya, the Godha's son.

 Sheltered by shade of tree and stanch,

Pleased with what scraps his bowl is filled,

In contemplation, grasping nought,

Lives Bhaddiya, the Godha's son.

'Neath open sky, unsheltered, stanch,

Pleased with what scraps his bowl is filled,

In contemplation, grasping nought,

Lives Bhaddiya, the Godha's son.

Haunting the charnel-fields and stanch,

Pleased with what scraps his bowl is filled,

In contemplation, grasping nought,

Lives Bhaddiya, the Godha's son.

Seated no matter where and stanch,

Pleased with what scraps his bowl is filled,

In contemplation, grasping nought,

Lives Bhaddiya, the Godha's son.

Resting in sitting posture, stanch,

Pleased with what scraps his bowl is filled,

In contemplation, grasping nought,

Lives Bhaddiya, the Godha's son.

Simple and few his wants and stanch,

Pleased with what scraps his bowl is filled,

In contemplation, grasping nought,

Lives Bhaddiya, the Godha's son.

With mind content, serene, and stanch,

Pleased with what scraps his bowl is filled,

In contemplation, grasping nought,

Lives Bhaddiya, the Godha's son.

Secluded, much alone and stanch,

Pleased with what scraps his bowl is filled,

In contemplation, grasping nought,

Lives Bhaddiya, the Godha's son.

Detached, aloof [from men] and stanch,

Pleased with what scraps his bowl is filled,

In contemplation, grasping nought,

Lives Bhaddiya, the Godha's son.

With surging energy and stanch,

Pleased with what scraps his bowl is filled,

In contemplation, grasping nought,

Lives Bhaddiya, the Godha's son.

Renouncing costly vessels wrought

In gold and lac, this earthen bowl

I grasped, and thus the second time

Anointment's consecration won.

Guarded by lofty circling walls,

And mighty gates with watchtowers high

And men-at-arms with sword in hand,

So was I wont in dread to dwell.

 To-day a happy winner, see,

At ease, all fear and fright removed,

In forest meditation plunged

Dwells Bhaddiya the Godha's son.

Firm planted on the moral code,

In clarity and insight trained,

In due succession have I won Release with every fetter gone!


## CCLV Aṅgulimala

He was reborn in this Buddha-Age as the son of the brahmin, Bhaggava, who was chaplain to the King of Kosala. On the night of his birth all the armour in the town shone. The King's state armour too, so that he, seeing it as he lay in bed, could get no sleep, but was nervous and alarmed. The chaplain that night consulted the stars and concluded that his son was born in the conjunction of the thieves' constellation. At dawn he waited on the king and asked if he had slept well. 'How could I have slept well, teacher?' replied the King, 'my armour was lit up all night. Now what can that presage?' 'Fear not, your majesty, in my house a child is born. Through his influence the armour in the whole town was lit up.' 'What then will he become, teacher?' 'The child will become a thief.' 'Single-handed, or leader of a gang?' 'Single-handed, sire.' 'Had we not better kill him?' 'If single-handed, he can be held in check.'

Now because he was born vexing the King's mind he was named Hiṁsaka. But afterwards when what was seen was seen no more, he became known as Ahiṁsaka. Through former Karma he had the strength of seven elephants. And while he studied under the first teacher at Takkasila, he respectfully waited on the latter and his wife, so that he was frequently with them at meals and so forth. But the other brahmin youths could not endure him, and at length brought about discord between him and the brahmin teacher, persuading the latter against him. Because of his pupil's great strength, the brahmin devised a stratagem for his ruin, and said: 'Ahiṁsaka, you have now finished as my pupil: give me my honorarium.' 'Very good, teacher, how will you have it?' 'Bring me a thousand human right-hand fingers.' For he expected that Ahiṁsaka would for shame bring one only, and could then be punished. Thereat Ahiṁsaka's long heaped-up ruthlessness came to the front, and girding on armour, he went to the Jalini forest, in Kosala, and from a cliff near the high road watched the passers-by, and rushing down smote off their fingers and hung them on a tree, till the vultures and crows had stripped the bones of flesh. Then making a garland of the fingerbones, he hung it round his shoulders as if decked for sacrifice. From that time he was called Fingerwreathed (Angulimala). And when through his deeds the road became tabu, he entered the villages, and these became deserted. Then the King proclaimed: 'Let a strong force come that we may quickly take the bandit.' And Angulimala's mother, of the Mantani brahmins, said to her husband: 'Our son is a thief and committing this and that. Send for him, bid him to stop doing these things.' But he replied: 'I have nought to do with sons of that sort; let the King do as he will.' Then she in love, took provisions and set out, saying: 'I will bring my son and stop him.'

The Exalted One thought: 'If she comes to him, Angulimala will kill her to make up his thousand fingers. This is his last birth. If I do not go there might be great loss. I will speak to him.' So after his meal he travelled the thirty leagues along the road, and warning off cowherds and the like, approached the Jalini Wood. Now Angulimala had just seen his mother, and was reckoning on her finger to make up his number, when the Exalted One showed himself between them. Then said the son: 'Why should I kill my mother for a finger? Let my mother live! Let me rather go for that recluse's finger.' And drawing his sword he stalked the Exalted One. Then the Exalted One exerted such magic power that, even though he was walking at his usual pace, Angulimala could not, even running, overtake him, but panting, pouring sweat, unable to lift his feet, stood like a stake and cried: 'Stop, friar!' The Exalted One said: 'Tho' I walk, yet have I stopped, and do you, Angulimala, stop!' Then the thief thought: 'They speak the truth, these Sakiyan friars, yet he says he has stopped, whereas it is I who have stopped. What can he mean?' So he asked

Thou who art walking, friar, dost say:

'Lo! I have stopped!'

And me thou tellest, who have stopped,

I have not stopped!

I ask thee, friar, what is the meaning of thy words?

How sayest thou that thou hast stopped, but I have not?

Then the Exalted One replied:

Yea, I have stopped, Angulimala, evermore,

Towards all living things renouncing violence;

Thou holdest not thy hand against thy fellow-men,

Therefore 'tis I have stopped, but thou still goest on.

Thereat Angulimala, as the Exalted One stood there revealing his true virtue, remembered what he had heard rumoured about him and, his insight reaching maturity, rapture pervaded his being, like a sheet of water spreading over the whole earth. And saying to himself, 'Great is this lion's roar. This can be none other, methinks, than the Samana Gotama; to help me the Exalted One is come hither!' he said:—

O long is it since mighty sage by me revered,

A friar, to this forest great, hath found his way!

Lo! I will readily forego a thousand crimes,

Hearing the righteous doctrine in this verse of thine.

And so the bandit doffed his armour and his sword

And threw them down a cliff, into a pit, a chasm.

Before the Welcome One, low worshipping, the thief

Straightway besought the Buddha's leave to be enrolled.

Thereat the Buddha, mighty Sage most pitiful,

Master of all the world and eke of all the gods,

Spake then these words to him, saying: 'Yea, C, B'

And e'en thereby to him was bhikkhu—status given.

He who in former days a wastrel living,

In later day no more so spends his time,

He goeth o'er the world a radiance shedding,

As when the moon comes free in clouded sky.

To whomsoe'er the ill deeds he hath wrought,

 By a good life are closed up and sealed, He goeth o'er the world a radiance shedding

As when the moon comes free in clouded sky.

Surely a brother who in youth doth give

Himself to live within the Buddha's Rule,

He goeth o'er the world a radiance shedding

As when the moon comes free in cloudy sky.

Thus abiding in the joy and ease of emancipation, he went into the town for alms. And men threw, here a clod, and there a stick at him, hitting him on the head, so that he came back to the vihara with broken bowl and sought the Master. The latter admonished him saying: 'Suffer it, brahmin, you have to suffer it. The result of your actions, for which you might have been roasted for centuries in purgatory, you are feeling now in this life.' Then the Thera, summoning up a heart of love for all beings without distinction, said:

O let my foes but hear the Norm as told to me,

And hearing join with me to keep the Buddha's Rule!

O let my foes but minister to men of peace,

Who e'en have taken to their hearts that holy Norm!

O let my foes from time to time but hear that Norm

From them who tell of gentleness, and who commend

Affection, and to what they hear, their actions suit!

 For such a foe would verily not work me harm,

Nor any other creature wheresoever found.

He would himself attain the peace inffable,

And thus attaining cherish all both bad and good.

The conduit-makers lead the stream,

Fletchers coerce the arrow shaft,

The joiners mould the wooden plank,

The self 'tis that the pious tame.

Some creatures are subdued by force,

Some by the hook, and some by whips;

But I by such an One was tamed

Who needed neither staff nor sword.

Innocens! such the name I bear, While Noxious in the past was I;

To-day most truly am I named,

For now I hurt not any man.

 Once an obnoxious bandit I,

Known by my name of Finger-wreathed,

Till toiling mid the awful flood,

I refuge in the Buddha found.

Once were my hands imbrued with blood;

Known was my name as Finger-wreathed.

O see the Refuge I have found,

With every craving rooted out!

Me who had wrought such direful deeds,

Fast going to my place of doom,

Me all that doing's aftermath

Hath touched e'en here-and freed from debt

Now take I my allotted share.

'Tis a fool's part heedless to waste his life:—

Such are the folk who will not understand.

He who is wise doth foster earnestness

As he were watching o'er his chiefest wealth.

Give not yourselves to wastage in your lives,

Nor be familiar with delights of sense.

He who doth strenuously meditate,

His shall it be to win the bliss supreme.

O welcome this that came nor came amiss!

O goodly was the counsel given to me!

'Mong divers doctrines mooted among men,

Of all 'twas sure the Best I sought and found.

O welcome this that came nor came amiss!

O goodly was the counsel given to me!

The threefold wisdom have I made mine own,

And all the Buddha's ordinance is done.

Deep in the wild beneath some forest tree,

Or in the mountain cave, is't here, is't there,

So have I stood and let my throbbing heart

 Transported beat. Happy I seek my rest,

Happy I rise, happy I pass the day,

Escaped from snare of evil—ah! behold

The Master's sweet compassion shown to me!

A child born of good brahmin stock was I;

Of pure and high descent this side and that.

This day the Welcome One doth call me son, The Master, yea, the Sovereign of the Norm.

Gone is all craving, nowhere have I hold.

Guarded the gates, and well controlled the sense.

Of this world's misery spewing forth the root,

From every poison-taint am I immune.

The Master hath my fealty and love,

And all the Buddha's ordinance is done.

Low have I laid the heavy load I bore:

Cause for rebirth is found in me no more.


## CCLVI Anuruddha

Reborn in this Buddha-age at Kapilavatthu, in the house of Amitodana the Sakiyan, he was named Anuruddha. Thus his elder brother was Mahananama the Sakiyan, the son of the Master's paternal uncle. And he was reared most delicately and luxuriously, in a different house for each of the seasons, and was surrounded with dancers and mimes, enjoying a divinely good fortune. And when he was summoned with the Sakiyan rajas to form a guard for the Master, he went to him in the Mango Wood at Anupiya, took orders, and within the period of the rains, acquired celestial vision. Again, receiving an exercise under the tuition of the General of the Norm, he went into the East Bamboo Wood, and studying, mastered seven of the thoughts of a great man, but could not learn the eighth. The Master, discerning this, taught it to him, teaching him the great course of the lineage of the Ariyans. Remembering this lesson, Anuruddha developed insight and realized arahantship, accompanied by supernormal and analytic powers. Him the Master ranked foremost among those who had attained the celestial eye. And he, dwelling in the bliss of emancipation, reviewed one day his achievement. And thrilled with joy, he breathed forth this psalm:

Forsaking mother, father, all his kin,

Sister and brother, quitting joys of sense,

Sits Anuruddha rapt in reverie.

By dance and song attended, by the sound

Of cymbals in the morn awaked:— not so

Were pure religion to be reached, too fain

Was I in Mara's precincts to abide.

And now that ail those things are left behind,

Fain with full heart to keep the Buddha's Rule,

Yea, passing over all the mighty Flood,

Sits Anuruddha rapt in reverie.

 Sights, sounds and tastes, odours and things to touch,

That please and charm, leaving all these behind,

Sits Anuruddha rapt in reverie.

From quest of alms he cometh back alone,

An unencumbered silent sage; from heap

Of rubbish to renew what garb he hath

Doth Anuruddha seek, sane and immune.

He seeketh, taketh, washeth, dyeth, wears

The shabby gear, this sage deliberate:—

For such is Anuruddha, sane, immune.

He who is big with wants and discontent,

Is puffed up and cleaveth to his kind,

Displayeth qualities corrupt and vile.

 And is he mindful, having few desires,

Contentedly serene and ne'er upset,

Delighting in seclusion, blithe of heart,

Aye strenuous:— his qualities are good

And such as to enlightenment belong,

And he, sane and immune,—saith the Great Seer.

He knew my heart's intent, the Master, he

Whose peer the world hath not, he came to me

By mystic power with body wrought of mind.

 To me, when further truths I wished to learn,

The Wake, the Buddha [that last truth] revealed;

He who in freedom from obsessions joyed

That freedom from obsessions taught to me.

And I who heard the blessed Norm abode

Fain only and alway to keep his Rule;

The Threefold Wisdom have I made my own,

And all the Buddha's ordinance is done.

 Ne'er have I rested supine five and fifty years, 'Tis five and twenty years since sloth was overcome.

No heaving breath left as He lay;

The mind in Jhana's steadfast stay,

With thought from every craving free,

Fixed on the Peace incessantly:

So passed the Man Who Saw away.

With mind unshaken, as they came,

He suffered pangs of death in peace;

Stole o'er His heart the last release:

Nibbana of the unfed flame.

The last things these that now we see of Him,—

Touch and the other senses of the Sage—

No other conscious states shall come to be,

When one that's wholly Wake doth pass away.

Now, a spirit, who in a former birth had been his attendant, seeing the Thera old and feeble, came, out of her former love for him, and bade him aspire to rebirth among the gods. But he made answer:

Sojourn amid the company of gods

Never again, seducer, comes for me.

Destroyed is all renewal of rebirth.

Now is there no more coming back to be.

Then the other bhikkhus, not seeing the goddess, were wondering to whom the Thera was speaking. To show his mystic power to them he said this verse:

He who e'en in a moment by a thousand ways can take

Purview of all the world, he is for Brahma's heaven fit. But here's a brother versed in power of magic who doth see

What time [both men and gods], thou goddess, die and come to be.

He now unfolds his former Karma:—

Lo! I was Annabhara long ago,A poor man working for my daily bread,

Then I to Uparittha, the recluse

Of holy fame, made humble offering.

Then was I born within the Sakiyan clan,

As Anuruddha known; by dance and song

Attended, and by clang of cymbals waked.

But I beheld the Buddha, the Awake,

The Master, for whom no whence cometh fear.

In him my heart believed and was at rest,

And from the home I sought the homeless life.

I know my former lives, and where and how

I lived in years gone by; among the gods

Thirty and Three I stood of Sakka's rank.

Seven times a king of men I held my sway,

Lord of the earth from end to end foursquare,

A conqueror, of Jambudipa chief, Using no force or arms I ruled by right.

Thence seven, and other seven spans of life,

E'en fourteen former births I recognize,

E'en then when in the world of gods reborn.

In fivefold concentrated ecstasy, My heart goes up in peace and unity.

Serene composure have I made my own;

My vision as a god's is clarified.

I know the destinies of other lives:—

Whence beings come and whither they do go;

Life here below, or other-where of life—

Steadfast and rapt, in fivefold Jhana sunk.

The Master hath my fealty and love, And all the Buddha's ordinance is done.

 Low have I laid the heavy load I bore,

Cause for rebirth is found in me no more.

In Veluva, in Vajjian land 'twill be

That life shall reach its final term for me;

And I 'neath bamboo-thicket's shade that day,

Sane and immune, shall wholly pass away.


CCLVII Parapariya

His story has been recorded above Now those verses he spoke in the Master's lifetime, himself not yet arahant, touching the governance of the six powers (five senses and mind). But these verses he uttered after the Master had passed away, and when his own passing away was at hand. And in them he declared the future of bhikkhus under a perverted Norm.

Now the first stanza was placed by the Compilers.

These be the thoughts that came to a Brother,

Seated beneath the great forest's fair blossoms,

Lone and aloof, in deep contemplation:—

How is the conduct of the Brethren changed

Since when the Sovereign of the world, the Man

Supreme, was yet abiding on the earth!

Raiment to shield from chilly winds, to hide

What should be hid, enough, no more, they sought,

Enjoyed contentedly whatever came.

Whether the food was excellent or poor,

Whether 'twas much or little, they partook

To keep life going, free from greedy whims.

 The requisites for men as living things,

And medicine too as means to live:— for these

Not fervently they cared, as care they did

How to destroy the poisons of the mind.

In the deep forests 'neath the shade of trees,

In caverns, in the bosom of the rocks,

Detachment studying and developing:—

So lived they making that their instant quest.

Of lowly, humble soul and frugal ways,

Gentle of heart, pliant and apt in mind,

Of gracious manner, speech not scurrilous,

Intent on good [for others and for self].

Pleasant and lovely therefore in their lives:—

Their goings, their enjoyments, their pursuits,—

Like the smooth tenour of a stream of oil.

For them every intoxicant was dead,

Mighty in Jhana they, mighty for good:

Now are those Elders wholly passed away.

Few now-a-days there be like unto them.

From dearth of good conditions and insight,

The Conqueror's Rule, compact of all that's best

In plan and mode, crumbles and wears away.

Bad the conditions and corrupt the age,

Wherein e'en they, who for the life detached

Had made good start, and to the higher things

That yet remain [might follow on],—e'en they

From the swift growth of all that doth corrupt,

Do influence for evil many folk.

Methinks they juggle with [the consciences

Of] fools as devils sport with the insane.

By the corruptions overcome, such men,—

Pursuing here and there what doth corrupt,

As one who calleth loud what he hath got, -

 They quarrel 'mongst themselves, forsaking quite

The blessed Norm, and, after errors gone,

Do ween:— Lo! this is better, this is best.

They who have turned their back on wealth and wife

And child, and left their home, if they but get

Spoon-alms, will do things that beseem them not.

They eat until they are replete, then down

They lie supine, and when awake, discourse

Concerning matters which the Master blamed.

All arts and handicrafts they highly rate

And practise:— such are bhikkhus' duties deemed,

The while from inner conquest they abstain.

And clay and oil and powder for the bath,

Water and food and lodging they present

To laymen, in the hope of richer alms;

Yea, toothsticks also and kapittha fruit, Petals of flowers to chew, and curries choice,

Mangoes and cocoanut, myrobalan.

In drug-purveying they as doctors be, In business matters like the laity,

Like courtezans do they parade their gear,

And play the lord like any noble squire.

 Adulterators they, tricksters and cheats,

Unscrupulous, by many stratagems,

In things of this world freely they indulge,

Pursuing ways and methods fit for fraud,

Seeking a livelihood by cunning craft,

They draw together plenteous store of wealth.

To settle business is the Chapter called,

Not in the interests of the holy Norm.

And when they preach to others, 'tis but gain

That is their motive not the good of men.

Many there be without the Order's fold

Who brawl and quarrel o'er the Order's gains:

Insolent spirits they, all unashamed

To live on offerings to others given.

Some too there are who lacking piety,

Though with head shaved, and with the yellow robe,

Yearn all the while to be revered,

And hanker after favours, treats, and gifts.

Thus when so much as now is fallen away,

No easy thing it is, as it was then,

Either to touch and win the unattained,

Or to hold fast what hath been touched and won.

As one who shoeless walks in thorny brake,

Calling up heedfulness at every step,

So should the sage in township make his tour.

Remembering the saints of other days,

And recollecting how it was they lived,

E'en though to-day be but the after-time,

He may yet win the Ambrosial Way of Peace.

Thus in the sal-wood spake the good Friar,

Well-trained and practised as to his faculties.

Then to the Saint came the Peace of the Passing-

Came to the Seer for whom was no rebirth.

# CANTO XVII. PSALMS OF THIRTY VERSES

CCLVIII Phussa

Reborn in this Buddha-age as the son of the ruler of a province, he was named Phussa, and was trained in all the accomplishments of noble youths. But because of the conditions to which he had attained, his heart hung not upon worldly desires, so that when he heard a certain great Thera preach the Norm, he believed, and entered the Order. Practising himself in Jhana, he thereby established insight, and in due course acquired sixfold abhinna.

Now one day an ascetic named Paṇḍara-gotta heard him teach the Norm. And seeing around the Thera a company of bhikkhus all of virtuous conduct, trained and controlled in body and mind, that ascetic thought: 'Excellent i' faith is this system! Long may it prevail on earth!' And he asked the Thera: 'How will it be, your reverence, with the progress of bhikkhus in the future?'

To explain this situation the Compilers first placed this verse:

Paṇḍarasa-gotta, hermit,

Seeing such a goodly audience,

Modest, quiet, contemplative,

Questions asked, addressing Phussa:—

What in the days to come will be your aims,

And what will be your tendencies and what

Will be your customs and observances? To me who ask thee do thou this declare.

Phussa:

List to my words, Seer, Paṇḍarasa named,

And store them in thy mind attentively;

I will pronounce concerning things to come.

Hasty of temper and malign,

Arrogant, hypocritical,

Deceitful, envious, bickerers:

Thus many in those days shall be;

Deeming they know the depths of truth,

While standing at the water's edge.

Flighty, irreverent towards the Norm;

And mutually irreverent.

Yea, many evils on this earth

Shall in the future come to pass.

This Norm of ours so well set forth

The stupid-minded will corrupt.

When in the Conclave voice and vote

Are giv'n, men, tho' in virtue poor,

Will forward be, in backers strong, Scurrilous and unscholarly.

When in the Conclave voice and vote

Are given, they of virtuous mind

And honesty will weaklings be,

Of shamefaced mood and little zeal.

 Silver and gold, fields, sites and herds, Slaves, maids and men, in days to come

The undiscerning will accept.

And foolish ones in testy mood,

Lacking in ethical restraint,

Will truculently go about

Like wild things spoiling for a fight.

Sobriety they will not know:—

They will be draped in robe of blue, Hypocrites, stiff-necked, obstinate,

Chatterers, skilled diplomatists, Counterfeiting the saints of old.

Hair sleek with oil, and frivolous mien,

And eyelids with collyrium dyed,

And swathed in robe of ivory hue:

Thus will they go about the streets.

The yellow robe, that goodly dye,

That freed souls wear without disgust,

The Banner of the Arahant,

Creates in them but queasiness,

Who hanker after robes of white.

Greedy of gain they will become,

Sluggish and poor in energy;

Finding fatigue in woodland haunts,

Around the township will they bide.

And ever bent on wrongful ways,

Without restraint, as pupils apt,

They'll follow those who get most gifts.

But they to whom no gifts are given,

Will find nor honour nor regard;

Though they be men of worth and charm,

No following will be theirs that day.

 Scorning their own, the yellow gear,

Some will wear red of foreign dye, And others will be found to wear

White robes of some sectarian flag.

Dishonour toward the yellow robe

They in those days will show; bhikkhus

Will not consider what it means.

Want of discernment such as this

Was tragedy unthinkable

To that wise beast who lay o'ercome

By pain, wounded, in dire distress.

For the Six-tusker then beheld

The well-dyed flag of arahants,

And thereanent the elephant,

Pointing the moral, verses spake:

'Who suffers vice, yet dons the saffron robe,

Keeping apart from self-control and truth,

Unworthy he to wear the saffron hue.

Who vice rejects, steadfast in virtuous ways,

And yokes himself to self-control and truth,

Worthy is he to wear the saffron hue'

Immoral, stupid and perverse,

A wanton doer, one whose heart

Wavers, whose mind is overcast:

Unworthy he of saffron robe.

 He who with virtue blest, is freed

From passion, is intent in heart,

Whose hopes and purposes are white Worthy is he of saffron robe.

A fool with mind puffed up, distraught,

For whom no moral code exists:

Gear white of hue doth he deserve.

For saffron robe what use hath he?

Brethren and Sisters, in that day,

With hearts corrupt, and impious,

Will bully and humiliate

Such as have trained their hearts in love.

And fools e'en by their Elders taught

Rightly to wear and use the robe,

For want of wit will listen not,

Perverse and wanton doers all.

And so the fools, instructed thus,

Lacking in mutual respect,

Will not their tutors' word obey,

No more than vicious hack its groom.

Thus in the age that is to come

Will be the course and tendencies

Of bhikkhus and of bhikkhunis,

When the last time shall be at hand.

Until this time of mighty dread

That now is not shall come to pass,

Be ye of gentle, docile hearts,

Filled with a mutual regard.

Be loving and be pitiful

And well controlled in virtue's ways,

 Strenuous, bent upon the goal,

And onward ever bravely press.

That danger doth in dalliance lie:—

That earnestness is sure and safe:—

This when ye see, then cultivate

The Eightfold Path, so shall ye touch,

So make your own, the Deathless Way.

Thus spake the Thera to his congregation. Now just these verses were his confession of aññā.


CCLIX Sariputta

His story and that of Moggallana the Great are taken together. Æons ago, in the days of the Buddha Anomadassi, they were playmates, named Sarada and

Sirivaddha, sons, the one of an eminent brahmin, the other of a great landowner. Sarada succeeded to his father's estate, but oppressed with the general doom of all creatures, he left the world to seek a path of release, inviting Sirivaddha to do likewise. 'I cannot,' answered Sirivaddha, but he yielded when Sarada, as a Rishi, had been visited by the Buddha. Now all Sarada's followers became arahants after hearing Anoma, the chief disciple, preach the Norm. But Sarada himself, being pre-occupied in mind, was unable to penetrate to the Paths and the Fruits. Thereupon both Sarada and Sirivaddha aspired, in presence of the Buddha, to occupy, like Anoma, the post of chief disciples to a Buddha in the future. This the Buddha promised should come to pass in the days of Gotama Buddha. There is no record of their subsequent kamma, but before our Exalted One arose, Sarada was reborn not far from Rajagaha, at the township  of the Upatissas, of Rupasari the brahminee, and on the same day Sirivaddha was born, not far from Rajagaha, at the township of the Kolitas, of Moggali the brahminee. And because each was the son of the head of his family, the one was named Upatissa, the other Kolita. Both boys were reared in luxury, and excelled in all accomplishments. But seeing the crowds one day assembled for the hill-top fair at Rajagaha, they both, because their insight had attained maturity, beheld how, within a century, all that folk would fall into the jaws of death, and with agitation they decided to seek a doctrine of release. And they left the world in the school of the Wanderer Sanjaya, agreeing each to tell the other if he first arrived at Amata.

In Sanjaya's teaching they found nothing genuine, and pursued their quest, asking recluses and brahmins, till through Assaji the bhikkhu, they found the Exalted One, and were by him ordained with the laying on of the hand and the words: Come, bhikkhus. Made Stream-winners by Assaji's summary of the Norm, they had no need to study, for each of the other three Paths. Why? Because of their consummate knowledge even as disciples. Thereby the Venerable Moggallana, on the seventh day, at the village of Kallavala in Magadha, overcame sloth and torpor by the Master's injunction, and listening to an exercise on elements, won the topmost point, while the Venerable Sariputta, half a month after his ordination, won it while dwelling with the Master in the Sukarakhata Cave at Rajagaha; while  Dighanakha, the Wanderer, his sister's son, was being taught the 'Vedanapariggaha' Suttanta. Thereafter the Master, in conclave at Jetavana, ranked Sariputta chief among his disciples in wisdom and insight.

And he, established in the position of General of the Norm, working for the good of beings, one day thus declared his anna before his fellow-disciples:

Whoso according to his powers

Is virtuous, saintly, clear in mind,

Earnest his purpose to perform,

Who loveth introspective work, Well concentrated and intent,

Lone and detached, blissful, serene:

This man is rightly Bhikkhu named.

When he of food or moist or dry partakes, Let him not fully satiated be.

Lean in the stomach, temperate at meals,

And watchful let the bhikkhu wend his way.

Hath he but eaten mouthfuls four or five,

Let him drink water: — here is sure enough

Refreshment for a bhikkhu filled with zeal.

Things that are seemly let him get and take:—

Raiment that's worn for this specific end:—

Comfort enough for bhikkhu filled with zeal.

 And when he sitteth cross-legged on his couch,

If but his knees be screened from falling rain, 'Tis ease enough for bhikkhu filled with zeal.

Whoso hath looked on pleasure as but pain;

Who hath discerned in pain the piercing dart;

 Saw no abiding self betwixt the two:— What world will hold, what fate detain that man?

Ne'er give me one with evil in his heart,

Inert, inactive, and intractable,

Knowing but little of the holy Norm.

What world will hold, what fate detain that man?

He who is learned in the holy Norm,

Can understand, is thoroughly intent

On moral base, and knit to inward calm:—

Let him for me the head and foremost stand.

Whose heart is to obsessions given o'er—

A deer seduced by fascination's snare—

He from Nibbana goeth far astray,

To utmost haven fails to find the course.

But he who from obsessions clears the heart,

Delighting in that path where these are not,

He to Nibbana surely finds the way,

To utmost haven safely steers his course.

Now one day the Thera, seeing where his younger brother Revata was dwelling—a waterless jungle of thorn and acacia trees—commended him, saying:

In village or the wild, in vale, on hill,

Where'er the men of worth, the arahants,

Their dwelling make, delightful is that spot.

Delightful are the forests, where no crowd

Doth come to take its pleasure; there will they

Who are released from passions find their joy.

Not seekers they for sense-satiety.

Again, the Thera showing kindness to an unfortunate brahmin named Radha, caused him to leave tho world and enter the Order. Afterwards, while on tour, he admonished Radha, pleased with his gentle behaviour:

As one who shows where treasures hidden lie,

So is the man of wisdom who discerns

What to avoid, and utters sage rebuke:—

If such an able guide ye see and heed,

For you who follow, better 'tis, not worse.

Now one day, the Master not going himself to suppress the corrupt settlement of the Assaji-Punabbasu bhikkhus on Kita Hill, Sariputta went instead with Moggallana and their followers. And when Sariputta's admonition was disregarded, he spake thus:

One should exhort, one should instruct, forbid,

Hinder that which is mischievous and wrong.

So acting, by the good is one beloved;

'Tis only evil-doers who take dislike.

When the brethren were saying that he whom the Master was teaching—namely,

Dighanakha the Wanderer—was fully prepared by his antecedents, Sariputta interposed, saying: That was not so:

Another was't to whom He taught the Norm—

The Exalted One, the Buddha, He who Sees—

For while the Norm was being taught I heard,

Seeking for good with hearing all attent.

And not in vain, I trow, my listening,

For I have won release, am sane, immune.

Nor to attain the vision of my past,

Nor for the means to see—the eye divine—

The mystic power to read the thoughts of men,

Discern decease, rebirth in earth and heaven,

Nor for the ear celestially attuned

Had I to pitch and to adjust the mind.

The next three stanzas were spoken of him, when, dwelling at the Dove's Cave Vihara, he took no injury from the Yakkha's blow:

Seated at foot of tree, with shaven head,

Wrapped in his cloak, in wisdom ranked supreme,

The Thera Upatissa musing deep,

His thought transcending acts percipient, Disciple of the supreme Buddha, he

Thus far in Ariyan silence was immersed.

E'en as a mountain-crag unshaken stands,

Sure-based, a Brother with illusions gone,

Like to that mountain stands unwavering.

Now one day, through the Thera's absence of mind, the lap of his robe hong down. And a novice said: 'Your reverence, it should be draped around you.' Then Sariputta, nodding, said: 'Good, you have done well to say so!' And going a little way, he draped his robe round him. And showing that for such as he that was a fault, he said:

The man of blameless life, who ever seeks

For what is pure, doth deem some trifling fault,

That is no heavier than the tip of any hair,

Weighty as [burden of the gravid] cloud.

Again he showed the equanimity of his mind in respect to living or dying with the verse:

Not fain am I to die nor yet to live.

I shall lay down this mortal frame anon

With mind alert, with consciousness controlled.

With thought of death I dally not, nor yet

Delight in living. I await the hour

Like any hireling who hath done his task.

Again, in teaching the Norm, he uttered these verses:

On both sides [of the scene we look,] and lo!

Tis dying, not the dearth of death [we see],  Be it the backward or the forward view. Fulfil ye then your course, lest ye be lost!

See that this moment pass not by for nought!

E'en as a border city guarded well

Within, without, so guard ye well yourselves!

See that the moment pass not and be lost,

For many mourn in woe that moment past.

Now one day, seeing the venerable Kotthita the Great, he spoke three stanzas proclaiming his excellence:

Whoso serene and calm, dead to the world,

Can utter wisdom's runes with wit unswelled,

Unruffled, he doth shake off naughty things,

As they were forest-leaves by wind-god blown.

Whoso serene and calm, dead to the world,

Can utter wisdom's runes with wit unswelled,

Unruffled, he doth strip off naughty things,

As they were forest-leaves by wind-god blown.

Calm and serene, by vice unharassed; free

From all that hinders clarity of mind,

Lovely in virtue, of discerning wit,

He should End-maker be of suffering.

The following was said concerning the Vajjians who believed in Devadatta, and approved of his doctrine:

Some souls there be on whom none should rely,

Be they housefolk, or e'en among recluses.

 Such as have once been good and turned to bad,

And then from bad have veered to good again.

Desires of sense, ill-will, torpor and sloth

In the bhikkhu, distraction of the mind,

And doubt:— five cankers of the heart are these.

Whoso can suffer both extremes of fate:

The favour and disfavour of the world,

The while he bides in sober earnestness,

Unwavering his concentrated mind:—

Him, musing ardent and unweariedly,

With intuition fine and delicate,

Zealous to slay the tendency to grasp:—

Him 'a good man' indeed should others call.

To draw yet other distinctions, instancing the Master and himself, he uttered these verses:

The mighty ocean, the extended earth,

The mountains, yea, the firmament afford

No picture meet to show how excellent

Th' emancipation of our Master's mind.

The Elder Brother, very wise, intent,

Who after His example turns the Wheel,

Is like to earth, to water, and to fire,

In that he feels no fondness nor disgust.

He hath the topmost place for wisdom now,

Mighty in intellect, a mighty sage;

Not dull is he though he seem dull of wit; Ever in blissful cool he wends his way.

To show the completion of his life's task, he said:

The Master hath my fealty and love,

And all the Buddha's ordinance is done.

Low have I laid the heavy load I bore;

Cause for rebirth is found in me no more.

And when he came to his utter passing away, he thus admonished the brethren assembled around him:

Press on with earnestness and win the goal!

This the commandment that I give to you.

Lo! now my going-out complete will be.

From all am I released and utterly.


CCLX Ananda

Deceased from the Tusita heaven, together with our Bodhisat, he took birth in the family of Amitodana the Sakiyan. And because the kinsfolk said, 'He is born bringing you happiness' (ananda), so they named him. When he was grown up, and the Renunciation, Supreme Enlightenment and Wheel-rolling had taken place, and the Exalted One had finished his visit to Kapilavatthu, Ananda renounced the world with Bhaddiya and the others, and was ordained by the Exalted One. Not long after he heard a discourse by Punna of the Mantanis, and completed the First Path.

Now during the first twenty years of the Exalted One's Buddhahood, his personal attendants were not permanently such. One day it was Nagasamala, who, taking bowl and cloak, walked [after him]; another day Nagita, another day, Upavana, Sunakkhatta, Cunda the novice, Sagata, Meghiya. Usually the Master did not favour one more than the others. But one day the Master, seated in the Buddha's seat of supremacy, in the cell of the Fragrant Chamber, surrounded by the brethren, addressed them thus: 'I, bhikkhus, am now advanced in years; and some bhikkhus, when they have been told, "Let us go this way," take another way, and some drop my bowl and cloak on the ground. Do ye know of a bhikkhu to be my permanent body-servant?' Then a righteous thrill went through the brethren, and the venerable Sariputta arose, and, bowing to the Exalted One, said: 'I, lord, will wait upon you.' Him the Exalted One rejected, and Moggallana the Great also. And all the great disciples said, 'We will wait upon you,' save only Ananda. But he just sat in silence. Then they said to him: 'Brother, do you, too, ask the Master for the post of attendant?' 'If I did ask, what sort of post-gaining would that be? He himself will say of whom he approves.' Then the Exalted One said: 'Ananda, bhikkhus, is not to be urged by others; if he knows it of himself, he will wait upon me.' Then the brethren said again: 'Get up, brother Ananda, ask the Master for the post.'

Then Ananda stood up and said: 'If, lord, the Exalted One will refuse me four things and grant me four things, then will I wait upon the Exalted One. Will he never give me any choice garment or food gotten by him, nor a separate "fragrant cell," nor go if he has received an invitation? For if he do not deny me these things, some will say: "Where is the burden [of such service]? Ananda serves that he may get clothes, good fare and lodging, and be included in the invitations." And further, will the Exalted One go when I have received invitations? Will he suffer me to bring those to him who have come from afar and around to see him? Will he, when I am perplexed, suffer me to come to him? Will he repeat to me doctrines he has taught while I was present? [sic. absent, not present] For if he do not grant me these things, some will say: "Where is the advantage [in such service]?" If when I am asked to bring the Exalted One to a meal next day he will not come, or if he will not consent to see whom I would bring, people will put no trust in me, and will say he shows me no attention. And if he do not explain the doctrine and its divisions, they will say: "Friend, do you not know, however much you follow him like his shadow?" If, then, the Exalted One will grant me these eight boons, I will wait upon him.' And the Exalted One granted them.

So from that day thenceforth Ananda waited upon him of the Ten Powers, bringing him water and toothpick, washing his feet, accompanying him, sweeping his cell, and so forth. During the day he kept at hand to mark the Master's: 'This should be procured,' 'That should be done.' And at night, taking a stout staff and lantern, he would go nine times round the 'fragrant cell,' making response if the Master called that he might not succumb to drowsiness.

Then the Master, in Ariyan conclave at the Jeta Grove, ranked him the foremost bhikkhu in five respects: erudition, mental vigilance, power of walking, steadfastness, ministering care. ... And so this great Brother, remaining yet a student after the Master had passed away, when admonished by the bhikkhus and alarmed by a fairy—as has been related above-thought, 'To-morrow the Council will take place, but it is not suitable that I, who am doing a student's work, should go to the assembly to recite the Doctrine with the Masters, the Elders.' Then zeal awoke in him, and far through the night he practised insight on the Terrace. His efforts yet unrewarded, he entered the Vihara, and seated on his couch, and desirous to lie down, he inclined his body. His head had not touched the pillow, nor his feet left the ground, when in that interval his heart was freed from the intoxicants without any grasping whatever, and he won Sixfold abhinna. Therefore he entered the Council Hall.

Now the verses he had uttered from time to time were collected, and included in the Brethren's Psalms at the recital of the Khuddaka-Nikaya.

The first stanzas were delivered in admonition to those bhikkhus whom he saw consorting with Devadatta's partisans:

With slanderer and man of wrath,

With the mean-hearted and malign No commerce should the wise man hold.

Evil is concourse with the bad.

With the believer and the wise,

The gentle and the learned man Communion should the wise man hold.

For blest is concourse with the good.

The following verse was uttered, when the lay-follower Uttara was suffering her own beauty to dispose her to sensuality, and in order to make her understand the frailty of the body. Some say it was spoken in admonition of those who lost their heads at sight of Ambapali:

Behold the tricked-out puppet shape, a mass

Of sores, a congeries diseased, teeming

With many purposes and plans, and yet

In whom there is no power to persist.

Behold the tricked-out form, bejewelled, ringed,

All sheathed in bones and skinny envelope,

By help of gear made fine and fair to see.

The next two verses were a psalm uttered by the Thera when he had won arahantship that night on his couch:

Much learn'd in holy lore and eloquent,

The leal henchman of the Buddha he;

Now hath the burden fallen from his back. Released, the Gotaimid lies down to rest.

For him the deadly cankers live no more;

Gone are the chains, the barriers all behind;

In blissful cool he bears his final frame,

For ever past the power of birth and death.

Wherein are founded and set up the truths

Taught by the Buddha of the Sun's great line:—

The Path that to Nibbana straight doth lead—

There, too, stands Ananda the Gotamid.

Now one day Moggallana the brahmin cattle-herd asked the Thera: 'You are very learned in the Buddha's Rule. How many of the doctrines your Master taught do you keep in your mind?' The Thera replied:

Eighty-two thousand from the Buddha's self

I've learned, from brethren yet two thousand more:

Hence four and eighty thousand texts in all

The number that for me have currency.

One day the Thera showed a man of desultory life the danger of no culture thus:

Whoso but little knowledge hath,

That man grows old as doth an ox. His fleshly bulk is multiplied,

But understanding groweth not.

The following verses he said concerning a bhikkhu who despised another as less learned than himself:

The learned man who doth despise,

For knowledge, him who little knows,

Is as a blind man who doth bear

A lamp:— so 'tis borne in on me.

Wait on the men of learning; look

That learning nowise injured be;

For 'tis the root of holy life; Hence bear the Doctrine in your hearts.

Knowing the sequence of the text, And versed in what the text doth mean,

Apt to interpret and explain: This scholar grasps the Norm aright,

And well its sense doth ascertain.

By patience eager purpose grows, Up surges effort; then he weighs;

Thus timely exercising will, Within he grows composed, intent.

Who in the Norm is widely versed

And bears its doctrines in his heart,

Disciple of the Buddha, wise,

Eager to understand the Norm: Such as he is, him follow ye.

Who in the Norm is widely versed

And bears its doctrines in his heart,

Of the great Master's treasure Ward, An eye is he for all the world,

Whom all should honour and revere.

Who in the Norm is widely versed

Who in the Norm takes his delight, Doth love and con it over well,

And lets it live in memory,

That brother from the holy Norm

Will ne'er secede nor fall away.

One day he stirred up a listless, slothful bhikkhu thus:

Art thou so heavy, loth to act?

Life hourly ebbing, canst not rise?

To give thy body pleasures gross

So greedy? Whence should come to thee

The happy ease of holy friar?

The following verse the Thera uttered on hearing of the passing away of the General of the Norm:

The firmament on every hand

Grows dim, yea, all confused stand

The truths I seemed to understand. Gone is the noble friend we love,

And dark is earth and heaven above.

And is the comrade passed away,

And is the Master gone from hence?

No better friend is left, methinks,

Than to mount guard o'er deed and sense.

They of the older time are gone;

The new men suit me not at all.

Alone to-day this child doth brood,

Like nesting-bird when rain doth fall.

The next stanza was spoken by the Master, and the next by the Thera, delighting to do his will:

Full many folk from divers regions come

To see. Forbid them not as hearers of the Norm;

Suffer them to behold me, 'tis the hour.

 Full many folk from divers regions come

To see. The Master opportunity

Doth give. The Man who Sees forbiddeth none.

The next five stanzas were spoken to show his position as chief attendant:

For five-and-twenty years a learner I;

No sensual consciousness arose in me.

O see the seemly order of the Norm!

For five-and-twenty years a learner I;

No hostile consciousness arose in me.

O see the seemly order of the Norm!

For five-and-twenty years on the Exalted One

I waited, serving him by loving deeds,

And like his shadow followed after him.

For five-and-twenty years on the Exalted One

I waited, serving him with loving speech,

And like his shadow followed after him.

For five-and-twenty years on the Exalted One

I Waited, serving him with loving thoughts,

And like his shadow followed after him.

When pacing up and down, the Buddha walked,

Behind his back I kept the pace alway;

And when the Norm was being taught, in me

Knowledge and understanding of it grew.

But I am one who yet has work to do,

A learner with a mind not yet matured;

And now the Master hence hath passed away,

Who e'er to me such sweet compassion showed!

O! then was terror, then was mighty dread,

Then stiffened hair and quivered creeping nerve,

 When he, endowed with every crowning grace

The All-Enlightened Buddha passed away.

The three following stanzas were added by the members of the Council in praise
of the Thera:

Who in the Norm is widely versed,

And bears its doctrines in his heart—

Of the great Master's treasure Ward—

An eye was he for all the world,

Ananda, who is passed away.

Who in the Norm is widely versed,

And bears its doctrines in his heart—

Of the great Master's treasure Ward—

An eye was he for all the world,

Dispelling gloom in darkest place.

Sage of the tireless ministry,

Foremost in mindful vigilance,

Foremost in steadfast fortitude, Upholder of the holy Norm,

Of all its jewels living mine:—

Our Elder Brother, Ananda.

And this verse he said as he lay a-dying his last death:

The Master hath my fealty and love,

And all the Buddha's ordinance is done.

Low have I laid the heavy load I bore,

Cause for rebirth is found in me no more.

# CANTO XVIII. PSALMS OF FOURTY VERSES

CCLXI Kassapa the Great

Our Master had already arisen, and was turning the Wheel of the Norm, and staying at Rajagaha, when at the brahmin village of Maha-tittha in Magadha, this Thera was reborn as Pippali-manava, the son of the chief wife of Kapila the brahmin. Four years later Bhadda Kapilani was reborn of the chief wife of the Kosiya-gotta brahmin at Sagala in the kingdom of Madda. Now Pippali-manava, refused to marry. 'While you live,' he told his parents, 'I will take care of you: afterwards I shall leave the world.' But to appease his mother he had a statue made of a beautiful maiden, dressed in crimson and ornaments, and showed it her saying: 'Mother, if I find anyone like this, I will lead the domestic life.' His mother was a clever lady, and sent brahmins forth, with the statue, on that quest. They came to Sagala, and setting the statue by the river's edge, sat down apart. Now Bhadda's nurse, who had bathed her charge, and gone down again for her own bath, saw the statue, and thinking: 'What! is my young lady so ill bred?' slapped it on the cheek, and discovered it was not Bhadda, but a gold statue. The brahmins accosted her, inquiring about her mistress, and she brought them to the house of Kosiyagotta, where they were made welcome. And they sent word to Kapila:

'We have got the maiden; do you act accordingly.' But Pippali-manava and Bhadda, being both unwilling to marry, wrote secretly each to the other, thus— He: 'Bhadda!' and she: 'Sir!' 'May you obtain a ménage suitable to your birth and fortune. I shall leave the world. Do not act so as to regret hereafter.' Now the two letter-bearers met, questioned each other, read the letters, and said: 'Look at the work of these children!' Throwing away the letters in the forest, they wrote others and took them. So the marriage was celebrated. But the wedded pair spent the night separated by a chain of flowers. And when Pippali-manava's parents died, he and Bhadda decided one day, after they had dined and talked together, to renounce the world.

And they got out yellow raiment from their wardrobes, and cut off each other's hair, slung bowls from their shoulder, passed out through their weeping servants, to all of whom they gave their freedom, and departed together, Pippali-manava walking in front.

And looking back, he thought: 'Here is Bhadda Kapilani, a woman worth the whole of India, walking at my heels. Someone seeing us will think: "These have renounced the world, but cannot do without each other." So, falsely accusing us, they may incur danger of purgatory.' And he told Bhadda this, and she agreed that a woman must needs be a hindrance to the male recluse. So they settled, at the cross roads, that he should go right and she left. Then the earth, though it could bear all Sineru, trembled at the weight of such virtue. And the supreme Buddha, seated in the fragrant chamber of the great vihara in the Bamboo Wood, knew what the earthquake signified, and gathering eighty chief Theras together, he walked three leagues on the road, and seated himself at the foot of the Bahuputtaka

Banyan, between Rajagaha and Nalanda. And though he was clad in a ragged robe, the Buddha-rays shone forth from him and darted to and fro, and the tree took on different colours. Then Kassapa the Great perceived: 'This will be our Master, through whom I have left the world.' And bending low, he said: 'The lord, the Exalted One, is my Master! I am his disciple.' And the Exalted One said: 'Sit, Kassapa, and I will show thee thine inheritance.' And in three homilies he gave him ordination. So they returned to Rajagaha, Kassapa exchanging his new robe for the Master's old one, and with humility and zeal determining to practise the thirteen dhutangas. And on the eighth day thereafter he won arahantship with thorough grasp of the spirit and letter of the Norm. Him the Master pronounced chief among those who undertook the extra austerities. And he, by way of showing the charm of detachment, told his experiences, in admonishing the brethren, thus:

I.

On seeing bhikkhus mingling with crowds, and frequenting laymen's houses:

Walk not where many folk would make thee chief.

Dizzy the mind becomes, and hard to win

Is concentrated thought. And he who knows:

'Ill bodes the company of many folk,'

Will keep himself aloof from haunt of crowds.

 Go not, O sage, to hearths of citizens.

Who greedy seeks to taste life's feast entire,

Neglects the good that brings true happiness.

A treacherous bog it is, this patronage

Of bows and gifts and treats from wealthy folk.

'Tis like a fine dart, bedded in the flesh,

For erring human hard to extricate.

II. An exhortation to bhikkhus to practice content respecting the four necessaries of life:

Down from my mountain-lodge I came one day

And made my round for alms about the streets.

A leper there I saw eating his meal,

[And as was meet, that he might have a chance,]

In [silent] courtesy I halted at his side.

He with his hand all leprous and diseased

Put in my bowl a morsel; as he threw,

A finger, mortifying, broke and fell.

Leaning against a wall I ate my share,

Nor at the time nor after felt disgust.

For only he who taketh as they come

 The scraps of food, medicine from excrement, The couch beneath the tree, the patchwork robe,

Stands as a man in north, south, east, or west.

III. When he was asked, in his latter years: 'How is your reverence able at your time of life day after day to climb the hills?

Where some do perish as they climb the rocks,

Heir of the Buddha, mindful, self-possessed,

 By forces of the spirit fortified,

Doth Kassapa ascend the mountain brow.

Returning from the daily round for alms,

Kassapa mounts some craggy coign and sits

In meditation rapt, nor clutching aught,

For far from him hath he put fear and dread.

Returning from the daily round for alms,

Kassapa mounts some craggy coign and sits

In meditation rapt, nor clutching aught,

For he 'mong those that burn is cool and still.

Returning from the daily round for alms,

Kassapa mounts some craggy coign and sits

In meditation rapt, nor clutching aught,

His task is done, and he is sane, immune.

IV. On being asked further: 'But why does your reverence at your time of life dwell in the mountain-jungle? Is not the Bamboo Grove, or others like it pleasant to you? he replied:

Those upland glades delightful to the soul,

Where the kareri spreads its wildering wreaths, Where sound the trumpet-calls of elephants:

Those are the braes wherein my soul delights.

Those rocky heights with hue of dark blue clouds,

Where lies embosomed many a shining tarn

Of crystal-clear, cool waters, and whose slopes

The 'herds of Indra' cover and bedeck:

Those are the braes wherein my soul delights.

Like serried battlements of blue-black cloud,

Like pinnacles on stately castle built,

Re-echoing to the cries of jungle folk:

Those are the braes wherein my soul delights.

Fair uplands rain-refreshed, and resonant

With crested creatures' cries antiphonal,

Lone heights where silent Rishis oft resort:

Those are the braes wherein my soul delights.

Here is enough for me who fain would dwell

In meditation rapt, mindful and tense.

Here is enough for me, who fain would seek

The highest good, a brother filled with zeal.

Here is enough for me, who fain would dwell

In happy ease, a brother filled with zeal.

Here is enough for me who give myself

To studious toil, so am I filled with zeal.

Clad with the azure bloom of flax, blue-flecked

As sky in autumn; quick with crowds

Of all their varied winged populace:

Such are the braes wherein my soul delights.

Free from the crowds of citizens below,

But thronged with flocks of many winged things,

The home of herding creatures of the wild:

Such are the braes wherein my soul delights.

Crags where clear waters lie, a rocky world,

Haunted by black-faced apes and timid deer,

Where 'neath bright blossoms run the silver streams:

Such are the braes wherein my soul delights.

 For that which brings me exquisite delight

Is not the strains of string and pipe and drum, But when, with intellect well poised, intent,

I gain the perfect vision of the Norm.

V.

When admonishing bhikkhus delighting in secular activities and greedy as to gifts of things needful for life, he said:

Let not a brother occupy himself

With busy works; let him keep clear of folk,

Nor strive [to copy nor to emulate].

Who greedy seeks to taste life's feast entire,

Neglects the good that brings true happiness.

Let not a brother occupy himself

With busy works; let him keep clear of this

That nowise tendeth to his real good;

The body toils and suffers weariness,

And thus afflicted he attains no calm.

VI. The following verses were spoken to admonish on certain occasions:

By mere repeating with a muttering lip, We see not e'en ourselves for what we are;

And so, stiff-necked, we go about and deem:

'A better man am I than he, than they!'

No better, truly, is the fool, and yet

He deems himself to be the better man.

But him, poor creature of a stiff-necked mind,

Commend not they who truly understand.

Who is not exercised about himself,

In this way or in that:—'the better man

Am I'; 'no better, I'; or 'I am worse,'

Or yet again 'I am as good as he'—

He who doth really know, and speaketh truth, Whose heart in righteousness is well composed,

And holdeth fast the saint's serenity, Him do they praise, who truly understand.

He who among his fellow-brethren wins

No reverence, is far from the good Norm

As is the firmament far from the earth.

But they who well have planted modesty

And eke discretion alway in their heart,

They in the holy life do richly thrive;

For them rebirths are ever at an end.

A brother who, though clad in patchwork robe,

Is of a puffed-up and unsteady mind,

As 'twere a monkey in a lion's hide,

No glory from his gear august doth gain.

But who, with uninflated, steadfast mind,

Is prudent, with his senses well controlled,

He shineth glorious in a patchwork robe,

As lion in the sombre mountain cave.

VII. On witnessing the gods of the Brahma world doing obeisance to the Venerable Sariputta, and marking how the Venerable Kappina smiled:

See how they stand, those thronging deities Of mystic potency and glorious,

Ten times a thousand, all of Brahma's heaven,

 Around our valiant Captain of the Norm,

Great son of Sari, calm and rapt in thought,

Acclaiming him with clasped hands upraised:—

'Hail thou, humanity's aristocrat!

Glory to thee, O thou supremest man!

Lo! past our thinking are thy ranging thoughts;

 O wondrous are th' Enlightened of the world! Their intuition, how profoundly deep,

Beyond the powers to which we testify,

Though we be skilled as archer splitting hairs!'

Then, seeing Sariputta thus adored

By hosts divine, saint most adorable,

A smile stole o'er the face of Kappina.

VIII. The Thera's 'lion's roar' concerning himself:

In the whole field of Buddha's following,

Saving alone the mighty Master's self,

I stand the foremost in ascetic ways;

No man doth practise them so far as I.

The Master hath my fealty and love, And all the Buddha's ordinance is done.

Low have I laid the heavy load I bore,

Cause for rebirth is found in me no more.

For never thought for raiment, nor for food,

Nor where to rest doth the great mind affect,

Immeasurable, of our Gotama,

 No more than spotless lotus-blossom takes

A mark from water; to self-sacrifice Continually prone, he from the sphere

Threefold of new becoming is detached.

The neck of him is like the fourfold tower

Of mindfulness set up; yea, the great Seer

Hath faith and confidence for hands; above,

The brow of him is insight; nobly wise,

He ever walketh in cool blessedness.

# CANTO XIX. PSALMS OF FIFTY VERSES

CCLXII Talaputa

Reborn in this Buddha-age at Rajagaha in an actor's family, he acquired proficiency at theatres suited to clansmen, and became well known all over India as leader of a company of actors. With a company of five hundred women and with great dramatic splendour he attended festivals in village, township and royal residence, and won much fame and favour. Now when he had been giving performances at Rajagaha with his usual success, his ripening insight prompted him to visit the Master. And seated at one side, he said: 'I have heard it said, your reverence, by teachers and their teachers, when speaking of actors, that the actor who, on the stage, counterfeiting truth, amuses and delights his audience, will be reborn after death among the gods of laughter. What does the Exalted One say on this point?' Thrice the Exalted One rejected the question, saying: 'Ask me not of this, director.' But when asked the fourth time, ho said: 'Director, those persons who induce sensual, misanthropic, or mentally confused states in others and cause them to lose earnestness, will after death be reborn in purgatory. But if he thinks as you have heard, then his opinion is wrong. And the fate of one who thus holds wrong opinions is to be reborn either in purgatory, or as an animal.' Thereupon Talaputa wept. 'Said I not to you, director, "Ask me not concerning this?"' 'Not for this reason, your reverence, do I weep, that the Exalted One has thus spoken concerning the future state, but because older actors have deceived me, saying that an actor holding a public performance is reborn in a happy life.'

Then Talaputa listened to the Master's teaching, and receiving faith, was ordained, and after due study won arahantship. Thereafter, showing in varied detail how he had restrained and chastened his heart to deeper understanding, he uttered these verses:

I.

When shall I come to dwell in mountain caves,

Now here, now there, unmated [with desire],

And with the vision gained

Into impermanence

Of all that into being doth become—

Yea, this for me, e'en this, when shall it come to be?

O when shall I, who wear the patchwork cloak,

Be a true saint of yellow robe,

Without a thought of what is 'mine';

And from all cravings purified,

With lust and hate, yea, and illusions slain,

So to the wild woods gone, in bliss abide?

O when shall I, who see and know that this

My person, nest of dying and disease,

Oppressed by age and death,

Is all impermanent,

Dwell free from fear lonely within the woods—

Yea, when shall these things be?

O when shall I with insight's whetted sword

Have cut it down, this creeper of Desire, With all its tendrils twining far and strong,

Breeder of many fears,

Bearer of pain and woe—

Yea, even this! when shall it come to be?

O when shall I have power to draw the blade

Of insight, fiery splendour of the Saints,

And swiftly shatter Mara and his host,

While in the victor's posture seated still - Yea, when shall these things come to be?

O when may I in pious companies

Be seen among all such as hold the Norm

In reverence, given to noble toil

With them who see the heart of things,

With masters over sense—

Yea, when shall these things come to be?

O when will slackness, hunger, thirst,

No more distress me, nor the wind, the heat,

Insects and creeping things wreak scathe on him.

Who on the Fastness of the Crag Doth mind his own high needs—

Yea, when shall this thing come to be?

O when shall I with thought composed, intent,

And clarity of insight come to touch

That which the mighty Seer understood—

The Four, the Ariyan Truths,

So passing difficult to see—

Yea, even this, when shall this come to be?

 O when shall I, yoked to the avenues of calm.

With deeper vision see the things of sense

Innumerable—sights and sounds,

Odours and tastes and tangibles,

And all the inner objects of the mind

As things ablaze and burning - Yea, when cometh this for me?

O when shall I abide [unmoved]—

Because of speech abusive not downcast,

Nor when, again, my praise is sung,

Be fillèd with complacency— When cometh this for me?

O when as so much firewood, bindweed, straw,

 Shall I esteem the factors of my life, With all the countless, objects known by sense, Internal or without,

Judging them all alike—

[Hollow, impermanent]—yea, this for me, O when?

O when will [break above my head]

The purple storm-cloud of the rains,

And with fresh torrents drench my raiment in the woods,

Wherein I wend my way

Along the Path the Seers have trod before—

Yea, when shall this thing come to be?

 O when shall I, hearing the call adown the woods

Of crested, twice-born peacock [as I lie

At rest] within the bosom of the hill,

Arise and summon thought and will

To win th' Ambrosial—

Yea, when shall this come to be?

O when shall I, by spiritual powers upborne,

Cross over Ganga, Yamuna, Saraswati

Unsinking, yea, float o'er the awful mouth

Of hell-flung ocean waters—

Yea, when shall this come to be?

O when, like elephant in battle charging,

Shall I break through desire for joys of sense,

And to rapt contemplation given,

Shun all the marks of outward loveliness—

Yea, when shall these things come to be?

O when, like some insolvent pauper pressed

By many a dun discovering hidden store,

Shall I be filled with joy,

In that I have attained

The [refuge of] the mighty Master's Rule?

Yea, when shall this thing come to be?

II. Tis many years since thou, my heart, didst urge:

'Come now, enough of this house-life for thee!'

See then! I've left the world. Wherefore, O heart,

Dost lack devotion to thy task?

 Have I not, O my heart, been urged by thee:

'On Fastness of the Crag

Bright-plumaged passengers of air,

Greeting great Indra's thunder with their cries,

Do give him joy who ponders in the wood.

In social circle friends beloved and kin,

The joys of games, of art, delights of sense

All have I put away to come to this.

Well then, O heart, art thou not pleased with me?

'Twas only for myself I acted thus,

For no one else [made I this sacrifice].

Why then lament when comes the time to arm?

This life is all a-quake!—so I beheld. And I renounced the world and chose the Ambrosial Way.

Hath he not said—who sayeth all things well,

The best of beings, great Physician,

Tamer and driver of the sons of men—

Unsteady is the heart like [jigging] ape, So hardly may that heart,

With passions not o'ercome, be held in check.

For varied, sweet, entrancing are desires of sense,

Wherein the ignorant majority

Entangled lie. They do but wish for ill

Who seek to live again,

Led by their heart to perish in the Pit.

 'There in the jungle ringing with the cries

Of peacock and of heron wilt thou dwell,

By panthers and by tigers owned as chief. And for thy body cast off care;

Miss not thine hour, thine aim!' So wast thou wont, my heart, to urge on me.

'Create, develop thou the Ecstasies,

The fivefold moral Forces and the Powers,

The seven Wings of Wisdom

And the four Grades of concentrated will; Touch thou the Triple Lore

Within the Buddha's Rule':—

So wast thou wont, my heart, to urge on me.

'Create, develop in thy life the Path

Whereby thou mayest win Ambrosia—

The way of progress and egress,

Founded upon the ending of all Ill,

Eightfold, purging from all that doth defile':—

So wast thou wont, my heart, to urge on me.

'This mind and body shouldst thou scrutinize

And hold as "ill"; and all the source of ill

Do thou put far from thee;

Yea, here and now make thou an end of ill!—

So wast thou wont, my heart, to urge on me.

'And understand that transiency is ill,

Is empty, without soul, is bane and bale;

Restrain thy mind's discursive vagrancies':—

So wast thou wont, my heart, to urge on me.

'Shaven, unsightly, and apostrophized When come for alms, with skull-like bowl in hand Among the citizens,

Do thou now give thyself

Wholly to carry out the Master's Word, the Seer's—

So wast thou wont, my heart, to urge on me.

'Walk thou well-disciplined within the streets,

With mind unfettered by the sense-desires

Of them that live therein.

Be like the moon a fortnight old in cloudless sky:'—

So wast thou wont, my heart, to urge on me.

'He who in forest dwells and lives by alms,

Who haunts the field of death, wears patchwork robe,

Refrains from lying down, He ever finds the true ascetic joy':—

So wast thou wont, my heart to urge on me.

'As one who, having planted trees, seeks fruit,

Dost thou now, finding none, desire to cut

Thy tree down at the root?'—

Such was the parable thou mad'st, my heart,

When thou the unstable and th' impermanent

Didst urge on me.

Thou unseen thing that knowest from afar, Rising in single file, no more thy word

Will I obey. For thy sense-born desires

Lead but to woe, to bitter fruit, to brooding fear.

Henceforth toward Nibbana's peace alone

I'll set my face and walk.

 I did not leave the world when out of luck,

Nor as a shameless joke, nor from a whim,

Nor was I banished in disgrace,

Nor seeking livelihood,

When I did give consent, my heart, to thee.

'Good men do praise small needs and much content,

Yea, and renouncing of hypocrisy,

And the assuaging of all pain':—

Thus didst thou, O my heart, exhort me then.

Now go'st thou back to all thy former loves.

Craving and ignorance and loves and hates,

And things of beauty, all the pleasant thrills

And charm of sensuous joys:— these have I vomited,

Nor may I strive to come once more to things thus spurned.

Where'er my life has fallen, O my heart,

Thy word have I obeyed.

In many births thou'st not been vexed with me.

And this is all thy gratitude:—

This individual compound self,

With all the suffering wrought by thee

A-down the long, long æons of my life.

Tis thou, O heart, dost make us what we are.

Thou makest, we become. A brahmin now,

Then are we nobles, yea, a king, a seer, Burgess one day, and serf the next are we,

Or e'en a deity—and all

In virtue of thine agency alone;

Through thee alone have we been Asuras,

Thou working, have we been through hellish doom;

Again, one day, in realm of beasts reborn,

Or Petas, by thine agency alone.

Nay now, thou shalt not dupe me as of old

Time after time, again, ever again,

Like mountebank showing his little masque; Thou playest guileful tricks with me,

As with a lunatic. Tell me, my heart, wherein am I at fault?

Once roamed this heart a-field, a wanderer,

Wherever will or whim or pleasure led.

To-day that heart I'll hold in thorough check,

As trainer's hook the savage elephant.

To me the Master did insist:— this world

Was transient, temporal, without a soul.

Now, heart, leap forward in the Conqueror's Rule,

And bear me o'er the great forbidding floods.

For thee, O heart, things are not as of yore. 'Twill not suffice that I within thy power

Fall back to live once more.

Gone forth am I 'neath the Great Master's Rule.

Men such as I now am no forfeit will endure.

Mountains and seas, the rivers, earth itself,

The quarters four, the intervening points,

The nadir, yea, and all the heavens above:—

Three planes of being each impermanent

And all of them forlorn—

Where canst thou then, my heart, find ease and rest?

Since I've the goal so firm, so sure, O heart, What wilt thou do [to make me turn]?

No more be't mine, my heart, to follow thee.

None, in good sooth, would touch a bag

That opened at both ends. Fie! then,

On that full thing flowing with issues nine.

O [thou wilt love the life], be't on the crest

Of caverned cliffs, where herd boar and gazelle,

Or in fair open glade, or in the depths

Of forest freshened by new rain—'tis there

Lies joy for thee to cavern-cottage gone.

Fair-plumed, fair-crested passengers of air

With deep blue throats and many-hued of wing,

Give greeting to the muttering thundercloud

With cries melodious, manifold; 'tis they

Will give thee joy whiles thou art musing there.

And when the god rains on the four-inch grass, And on the cloud-like crests of budding woods,

Within the mountain's heart I'll seated be

Immobile as a lopped-off bough, and soft

As cotton down my rocky couch shall seem.

Thus will I do e'en as a master should.

Whate'er is got, be it enough for me.

And like a tireless tanner dressing hides, I'll make thee soft as catskin finely dressed.

Thus will I do e'en as a master should.

Whate'er is got, be it enough for me.

I'll lead thee in my power by force of will, Like a fierce elephant by skilled mahout.

With thee at length well tamed and steadfast grown,

Like trainer with a steed well purged of vice,

Then can I tread the Path of happy fate,

Haunted by them whose hearts are guarded well.

And to the object thou shouldst think upon

I'll bind thee by the power that training gives,

As elephant by strong cord bound to post.

So when I have thee guarded well, and trained

By clarity of thought, thou shalt become

Unleaning on all forms of future life.

When by the aid of insight thou hast dammed

Thine errant course, by study hast restrained,

   Turned it along the avenue [of truth], So thou canst see how all things do become:—

Rise into being and are then dispersed—

Then shalt thou be the [child and] heir of Him:

Knower and Teacher of the Things Supreme.

 On the fourfold hallucination set, As village lout didst drive me, O my heart. Come now and follow him, the Merciful,

Great Seer for whom all bonds and chains are broke.

Like creature of the wild roaming at large

In the fair flowering jungle, so thou too

Hast gone up on the lovely cloud-wreathed crest.

There on the mountain, where no crowd can come,

Shalt find thy joy, O heart, for never doubt

But thou shalt surely win to the Beyond.

They who remain subservient to thy will,

Male or female, enjoy what thou dost give,

Delight in ever coming back to be:—

Unknowing, in the wake of Mara's power,

These all, O heart, retainers are of thee.

# CANTO XX. POEM OF SIXTY VERSES

CCLXIII Maha Moggallana

His story is told in that of the venerable Sariputta. After he had been ordained a week, and while he was occupied with his duties near the hamlet of Kallavala in Magadha, torpor and sleepiness assailed him, so that the Master aroused him with the words: 'Moggallana, idleness is not the same as Ariyan silence.' Conquering his weakness by merely hearing an exercise on Elements given him by the Master, he attained the highest insight that a Buddha's disciple can reach. At another time the Master, in conclave at the Jeta Grove, pronounced him foremost in supernormal power of will (iddhi). And the verses which he spoke while thus gifted were collected in a series by the compilers of the Doctrine at the time of the Council:

I.

When exhorting the bhikkhus:

We forest-dwellers, beggars all,

Pleased with the scraps placed in our bowl.

The hosts of Mara we can smash If we have well learned self-control.

We forest-dwellers, beggars all,

Pleased with the scraps by which we're fed,

Mara and hosts let's sweep away,

As elephant a rush-built shed.

We who at root of shady tree

Work at our task persistently,

Pleased with the scraps placed in our bowl,

The hosts of Mara we can smash

If we have well learned self control.

We who at root of shady tree

Work at our task persistently,

Pleased with the scraps by which we're fed,

Mara and hosts let's sweep away,

As elephant a rush-built shed.

II. To a courtesan who sought to allure him:

Thou with that little hut of framework bony

And flesh encased by sinewy stitchery:—

Fie on thee, fie! thou full of smells unseemly,

Finding thyself in limbs that are not 'thou.'

O bag of muck enwrapped in skin! O witch

With ulcered breast! nine are the streams

That on thy body trickle night and day;

Thy body nine-streamed and malodorous,

Maker of bonds:—that let a bhikkhu shun

As one would ordure, would he fain be clean.

 Did but folk know thee as thou art, as I

Do know thee, they would shun thee from afar

As they would shun a cesspool in the rains.

Then that woman felt ashamed and bowed before the Thera saying:

Yea, O great hero, even so it is

As thou, O holy friar, hast pronounced.

And herein many miserably fail

And faint, as in a swamp an aged ox.

The Thera:

He who would fancy he can paint the sky

With yellow, or maybe some other hue,

Is to defeat foredoomed, and only that.

My heart is like that sky, beyond thy reach,

For it is well controlled within and calm. Wherefore bring not thine evil thoughts
to me,

As bird that flies bewildered into flame.

Behold the tricked-out puppet-shape, a mass

Of sores, a congeries diseased, teeming

With many purposes and plans, and yet

In whom there is no power to persist.

III. Concerning the passing away of Sariputta Thera:

O! then was terror, then was mighty dread,

Then stiffened hair and quivered creeping nerve,

When he, endowed with every crowning grace, The venerable Sariputta passed away.

O transient are our life's experiences!

Their nature tis to rise and pass away.

They happen in our ken, they cease to be.

O well for us when they are sunk to rest!

They who our fivefold organism see

As something 'other,' not the self, not soul, They penetrate the delicate things [of truth]

As arrow-point doth pierce a tip of hair.

They who behold our life's experience

As something 'other,' not the self, not soul,

They've pierced the subtle [mysteries of truth]

As arrow-point doth pierc e a tip of hair.

IV Spoken concerning Tissa Thera:

As one down-smitten by impending sword,

As one whose hair and turban are aflame,

So let the brother, mindful and alert,

Go forth, all worldly passions left behind.

Spoken concerning Yaddhamana Thera:

As one down-smitten by impending sword,

As one whose hair and turban are aflame,

So let the brother, mindful and alert,

Go forth, all lust of living left behind.


V

Spoken in connection with the 'Act of the Terrace' Dialogue:

By Him advised, who, perfectly evolved, For the last time a mortal body bore,

My foot uplifting with my toe I shook

The Terrace by Migara's Mother built.

VI Spoken concerning a certain bhikkhu:

Nothing hath this to do with tepid slackness,

Not by a little toil canst gain Nibbana,

Deliverance from every tie and chain.

See this young brother, this among you peerless!

Mara and all his host hath he defeated,

And [therefore] weareth he his final frame.

VII Concerning his own detached life:

The lightnings flash e'en in the rocky cave,

Smiting Vebhara's crest and Paṇḍava,

And in the mountain-bosom hid, a child

Of the incomparable Master sits,

Ardent in contemplative ecstasy.


VIII Entering Rajagaha for alms, he admonishes a nephew of Sariputta Thera, a brahmin of wrong opinions, who on seeing Kassapa the Great felt repugnance, as if he had seen the goddess of ill-luck herself:

The seer calm and serene, dead to the world,

Whose dwelling is remote, aloof from men, The heir of Buddha, Wake and Chief of all,

Greeted with honour by great Brahma's self;

Behold him, calm, serene, dead to the world,

The sage who dwells remote, aloof from men,

The heir of Buddha, Wake and Chief of all:—

Brahmin, give greeting low to Kassapa!

He who a hundred generations back

Can trace descent, all brahmin ancestors,

Himself as graduate and Veda-wise,

Again, again among mankind reborn,

Though he as teacher in the Vedas three

Past-master rank, wouldst honour him for that,

To him thy homage were not worth a straw.

He who before he breaks his fast can touch

Mental emancipation's eight degrees,

In grade ascending and so back again:— Then, only, cometh forth to seek for alms:—

Assault thou not a bhikkhu such as this.

Refrain from digging up thyself, [thy good]! Appease, brahmin, and gratify thy mind

In [contemplating] such an arahant.

 Swiftly lift up thy hands and greeting give.

Set not that head of thine in jeopardy.

IX When admonishing a bhikkhu named Potthila:

He doth not yet behold the blessed

Norm Who hath eternal living in his train;

From course precinct he wandereth afar,

Straying in error's devious dangerous ways.

Like to a worm obscene besmeared with dung,

He walloweth in the tainted things of life, Plunged in pursuit of favours and of gain,

Bare [of true profit] goeth Potthila.

X

In praise of the venerable Sariputta:

Yonder behold where Sariputta goes

So nobly fair! Emancipated he

By contemplation rapt, and purity, And all his inner self is well composed.

Exempt from moral scathe, all fetters broke,

In higher Vedas versed, slayer of Death,

Worthy that men should bring him offerings;

Incomparable field for great reward.

XI Spoken by the venerable Sariputta in praise of Moggallana the Great Thera:

See how they stand, those thronging deities Of mystic potency and glorious,

Ten times a thousand, Brahma's ministers,

Acclaiming Moggallana reverently:—

'Hail thou, humanity's aristocrat!

Glory to thee, thou highest among men!

Perished for thee are the intoxicants,

And thou, O lord, most worthy art of gifts!

In honour held by men and gods alike, Uprisen as the conqueror of death,

As lotus from the water takes no smear,

So thou in changing world dost not adhere.'

He who e'en in a moment by a thousand ways can take

Purview of all the world, as were he Brahma's very self. Yea, here's a brother versed in power of magic who doth see

What time doth suit [for gods and men] to die and come to be.


XII Moggallana the Great speaks, affirming his own gifts:

Now Sari's son by wisdom, virtue, self-control

Excelleth all; here let this brother stand supreme.

But I can instantly innumerable times

Create a living shape; skilled to transform myself

As other, yea, all magic power have I at will.

He of the Moggallanas, in the Rule of Him

Who stands alone, hath perfected his powers; In contemplative ecstasy and higher lore

Expert, valiant and self-controlled hath burst his bonds,

As doth the elephant a rotten fibre rope.

The Master hath my fealty and love,  And all the Buddha's ordinance is done.

Low have I laid the heavy load I bore;

Cause for rebirth is found in me no more.

The Good for which I bade the world farewell, And left the home to dwell where is no home,

That highest good have I attained and won,

And all that bound and fettered me is gone.


XIII In reproof of Mara who, had entered and then left the Thera's bowels:

What sort of hell was it where Dussi cooked

In anguish, when he injured Vidhura,

Disciple, holy Kakusandha too?

'Twas the infernal realm of iron spikes,

A hundred points, each dealing bitter pain.

This sort of hell it was where Dussi cooked

In anguish, when he injured Vidhura,

Disciple, holy Kakusandha too.

If thou a brother who can tell thus much—

Disciple of the Buddha-dost assail,

Black-hearted sprite! to misery thou must go.

Far in the midst of ocean, palaces

Have stood an aeon, exquisite, with hue

Of beryl-stones, flashing like crests of flame.

There dance full many nymphs in divers hues:—

If thou a brother who can tell thus much—

Disciple of the Buddha-dost assail,

Black-hearted sprite! to misery thou must go.

Incited by the Buddha's self I wrought,

With all the Bhikkhu-Order looking on,

 My foot uplifting, with my toe I shook

The Terrace by Migara's Mother built.

If thou a brother who can tell thus much—

Disciple of the Buddha-dost assail,

Black-hearted sprite! to misery thou must go.

I who my foot uplifting, with my toe

Caused Vejayanta's terraced fane to shake,

Rigid as iron by my magic power,

And thro'the deities sent thrill of dread:—

If thou a brother who can tell thus much—

Disciple of the Buddha-dost assail,

Black-hearted sprite! to misery thou must go.

He who in Vejayanta's terraced fane

Did take Sakka the deity to task:— 'Come, friend, and didst thou really understand

Release through end of craving [taught to thee]?'

To whom Sakka made answer truthfully—

If thou a brother who can tell thus much—

Disciple of the Buddha—dost assail,

Black-hearted sprite! to misery thou must go.

Who catechized great Brahma's very self,

Seated in conclave in Sudhamma's hall:— 'Come tell me, friend, hast thou to-day the views

Which in the days gone by were views of thine?

Or seest thou now the glory of thy heaven,

How age by age it all is passing by?'

To whom Brahma made answer truthfully:—

'My lord, no longer do I hold the views,

Which in the days gone by were views of mine.

I do behold the glory of my heaven,

How age by age it all is passing by.

To-day I hold it false what once I said:—

"I am eternal; permanent am I!"'

If thou a brother who can tell thus much—

Disciple of the Buddha—dost assail,

Black-hearted sprite! to misery thou must go.

Who in emancipation['s ecstasy] Hath touched great Neru's topmost pinnacle, Pubbavideha's forest world hath seen, And men that live on that remotest plain:—

If thou a brother who can tell thus much—

Disciple of the Buddha—dost assail,

Black-hearted sprite! to misery thou must go.

Fire doth not think: 'Lo! I will burn the fool!'

But if the fool lay hands on blazing fire,

The fire must burn and he must needs be burned.

Thus, Mara, thou on One who Thus hath Come Hast made attack, but 'tis to thine own hurt,

As when a foolish child doth touch the fire.

Demerit hath the Evil One begot,

Who made attack on One who Thus hath Come.

What? dost imagine, O thou Evil One,

That evil brings thee not its sure reward?

For this that thou hast done, long will it be,

Before that evil dieth out, O Death.  Aroint thee, Mara, from the awakened mind! Against the brethren cease thy wicked plots.

Thus in the forest of Bhesakaḷa Did Mara by a Brother censured stand.

Thereat the rated imp, dejected sore,

E'en where he stood, did vanish quite away.

Thus verily did the venerable Moggallana the Great utter his verses.

# CANTO XXI. POEMS OF SEVENTY-ONE VERSES

Called also

'The Great Nipata'

CCLXIV Vaṅgisa


Reborn in this Buddha-age at Savatthi in a brahmin family, he was named Vaṅgisa, and was taught the three Vedas. And he won favour as a teacher by tapping on skulls with his finger-nail, and discovering thereby where their former occupants were reborn. The brahmins saw in this a means of gain, and taking Vaṅgisa, toured about in villages, townships and royal residences. And for three years Vaṅgisa, had skulls brought to him and divined. Persuading the people to believe in him, he won fees of 100 and even 1000 (? kahapanas). And the brahmins took him about wherever they chose to go. Now he heard of the Master's virtues, and wished to visit him, but the brahmins objected, saying: 'Gotama the recluse will pervert you by his craftiness.' But Vaṅgisa heeded them not and went, seating himself at one side. The Master seeing him asked: 'Vaṅgisa, do you know any art or craft?' 'Yes, Master Gotama, I know the skull-spell. By that, tapping on a skull with my finger-nail, have I, for three years past ascertained where rebirth has taken place.' The Master let him be shown the skulls of individuals reborn in purgatory, as man, as god, and of one who had passed utterly away. Divining concerning all but the last, of that he could make nothing. Then the Master: 'Art not able, Vaṅgisa?' 'Let me make quite sure, said Vaṅgisa, and he turned it round again and again till the sweat stood on his brow—for how will he know the going of the arahant? And he stood there silent and shamed. 'Art tired, Vaṅgisa?' 'Ay, Master Gotama, I cannot find out where this one has been reborn. If you know, tell it.' 'Vaṅgisa, both this I know, and I know more than this:

He who of every creature knoweth well

 Whence they decease and where they come to be,

 Enlightened, well come, freed from every tie:

—Him call I brahmin.

 Whose destiny nor angel, god, nor man

 Doth know, the arahant, sane and immune:

—Him call I brahmin.'

Then said Vaṅgisa: 'Well then, Master Gotama, give me this hidden lore.' And doing obeisance, he seated himself as the Master's pupil. But the Master said: 'Let us give you the marks of a recluse.' Then Vaṅgisa thought: 'I must at all costs learn this spell.' And he said to his fellow-brahmins: 'Do not think it amiss if I take orders. When I have learned this spell, I shall be first in all India, and that will bring you good fortune.' So he asked for ordination, and the Exalted One commanded Nigrodhakappa Thera, who stood near, to ordain Vaṅgisa. The Thera did so, and then saying: 'You must first learn the accessories of the spell,' gave him the exercise of the thirty-two constituents of the body, and one on insight. Rehearsing the former, he established the latter faculty. And when brahmins came to ask whether he had acquired  the art, he replied: 'What art-acquiring? Go ye hence; I have no more to do with you.' The brahmins said: 'There! he too has got into the power of Gotama the recluse, perverted by craftiness. What have we to do with you as teacher?' And they went away. But Vaṅgisa realized arahantship.

As arahant, he went to the Master's presence and magnified him in scores of verses, comparing him to the moon, the sun, space, ocean, mountains, the lion, the elephant. Him the Master, seated in conclave, pronounced foremost in facility of speech. But what he said in verse, both before and after he became arahant, was collected and recorded by Ananda and the other Theras at the Council as follows:

I.

Spoken when a novice, after having been affected by the sight of many gaily dressed women, who had approached the Vihara, a feeling which he suppressed:

Alas! that now when I am gone from home

Into the homeless life, these graceless thoughts

Sprung from the Dark should flit about iny mind.

Were highborn warriors, mighty archers, trained

In champion bow-craft, such as never flee,

To scatter thousand arrows round about. …

But women! Well, far more than those may come,

Yet shall they never wreck my peace of mind,

Firmly established in the truths I stand.

 For even in his presence have I heard

The Buddha of the Sun's high lineage tell About the Path that to Nibbana goes;

And there the love of all my heart is given.

Now that I alway in such mood abide,

Dost think, vile one, thou canst draw nigh to me?

Then will I do the like, O Death, and thou

Wilt ne'er discover which the way I take.

II. Spoken when suppressing his own feelings, aversion, and so forth:

I who have given up dislikes and dotings

In all that stirs the lay imagination,

May not make anywhere a haunt for lusting.

He who from jungly vice hath gained the open,

From lusting free, 'tis he is truly Bhikkhu.

All things of visible shape here on earth dwelling,

Or in the upper air that's based on earth, Transient is all, and all away is wearing:—

Thus understanding they who think do walk.

In all that makes for life the folk cleave ever To what is seen and heard and touched and thought.

Who here, desires suppressing, unaffected,

Adhereth nowhere, him [the wise] call Saint.

Who cleave to views mistaken eight and sixty, Their nature of the common average sort,

They're fixed in courses evil and unrighteous. But whoso to no sect whate'er doth go,

Nor clutcheth at blown straws [of vain opinion], A genuine bhikkhu he all men may know.

Fully endowed, long since of self the master,

Candid yet wise, and free from craving's power,

A Saint, the way of peace he hath attained;

Serene and cool, awaits his final hour.

III Spoken when suppressing his own behaviour in connection with his facility of speech:

Renounce conceit, thou, Gotama's disciple! Wholly from path of pride remove thy foot.

Since with that path some time infatuated,

Long ere to-day thou truly didst repent.

By self-deceit deceived this generation,

Destroyed by vanity, is doomed to woe.

For many an age reborn in purgatory

Will folk destroyed by pride lament their doom.

He weepeth not at any time, the Brother:

Path-victor who the Highest hath achieved.

Both fame and happy conscience he enjoyeth.

'Norm-seer' say, and rightly say the wise.

Hence in this life, sober and unimpeded,

Dispelled all hindering clouds, and clear in mind,

Renouncing pride and vain conceits entirely,

Let me be found End-maker and serene.

IV One day as a novice he attended the venerable Ananda, whom one of the King's ministers had bidden to visit him. There they were surrounded by women highly adorned, who, saluting the Thera and asking questions, heard him preach the Norm. But Vaṅgisa was excited and moved with desire. Then he, being a well-bred man of faith and integrity, thought: 'This my emotion growing is unsuitable for my present and future good.' And seated as he was, he confessed his state to the Thera, saying:

My sense with passion burns, my mind's aflame.

Take thou compassion on me, Gotamid!

O tell me truly of a putting out!

And the venerable Ananda replied:

Because thy judgment is upset, perverse,

Therefore thy mind's aflame. Thou shouldst avoid The seeing lovely objects passion-linked.

Compel thy steeled and well-composèd mind

To contemplate what is not fair to view,

Let there be heedfulness concerning sense.

And be thou fillèd with a sane distaste.

Study the absence of the Threefold Sign; Cast out the baneful bias of conceit.

Hath the mind mastered vain imaginings,

Then mayst thou go thy ways, calm and serene.

V

Spoken after the Exalted One had taught the Sutta on 'Things Well-spoken' in praise of the Master:

Whoso can speak a word whereby

He works no torment to himself,

Nor causeth harm to fellow men—

That word is spoken well.

Pleasant the word that one should speak.

Speech that is grateful to the ear,

That lays not hold of others' faults:

Sweet is that word to hear.

Truth is the word that dieth not.

This is the old primeval Norm. On Truth and Good and Norm, 'tis said,

The saints do firmly stand.

That which th' Awakened speaks, the sure

Safe guide to make Nibbana ours,

To put a lasting end to Ill—

That is the Word Supreme.

VI Spoken in praise of Sariputta:

With insight into mysteries deep,

And richly dowered with learned lore,

Expert in paths both true and false,

The son of Sari, greatly wise,

Teacheth the bhikkhus in the Norm.

He teaches first in outline brief,

And then expounds in full detail.

And like the myna-bird's sweet song, His exposition poureth forth.

And while he teaches, they who hear

His honeyed speech, in tones they love

Of voice enchanting, musical,

With ravished ears, transported hearts,

Delighted list his every word.

VII Spoken after the Exalted One had discoursed in the Pavarana (Valediction or Dismissal) Suttanta:

To-day, at full moon, for full purity

Five hundred brethren are together come.

They all have cut their fetters and their bonds;

Seers who are free from rebirth and from ill.

And as a king who ruleth all the world,

Surrounded by his councillors of state,

Toureth around his empire everywhere,

Driving throughout the lands that end in sea,

 So him, who is our victor in the fight,

The peerless Master of our caravan,

We followers attend and wait upon,

Who hold the triple lore, slayers of Death.

All we are sons of the Exalted One.

No sterile babbler is among us found.

I worship him who strikes down craving's darts.

I greet the offspring of the Sun's great line.

VIII Spoken in praise of the Exalted One, who had been delivering a religious discourse to the brethren bearing upon Nibbana:

A thousand brethren, yea, and more than these

Attend around the Well-Come One, who here

Doth teach the Norm, the Pure, the Passionless, Even Nibbana, where can come no fear.

They hearken to the Norm's abundant flow,

Imparted by the Very Buddha blest,

O wondrous fair the All-Enlightened shines,

With all the Band of Brethren seated round.

Mysterious spirit thou, Exalted One!

The seventh in the lineage of the Seers, Like a great storm-cloud in the summer sky,

Thou on thy followers pourest precious rain.

And one of these, from meditation come,

Full fain his gracious Master to behold—

Thy true disciple, mighty Hero, see!

Low at thy feet Vaṅgisa worships thee.

Then the Exalted One asked: 'How now, Vaṅgisa, have you composed these verses beforehand, or did they occur to you just on the present occasion?' 'They occurred to me just now,' replied Vaṅgisa. ['Well then, let some more such verses occur to you.' 'Even so, lord'—and Vaṅgisa spoke further his praises:]

O'er Mara's devious ways he fares triumphant,

And every obstacle he breaketh down.

Behold him from all bondage our Deliverer;

Himself full fraught, he portions out the Norm.

For he hath shown a Way by many methods

For crossing o'er the [fearsome fourfold] Flood; And we to whom he hath declared Ambrosia, Stand as Norm-seers inexpugnable.

Light-bringer, he hath pierced beyond, beholding

Past all those stations where the mind doth halt. The topmost heights knowing and realizing,

To us he maketh known the path of sight.

Lo! now in truths so well revealed, for trifling

What place is there 'mong them who learn his Lore?

Hence zealously within that Master's System

Let each man train, and while he trains adore.

IX Spoken in praise of the venerable Thera Anna-Kondanna:

Who next to our Great Waked One was awoke,

Brother Kondanna, strong in energy,

Who oft enjoyeth hours of blissful ease—

[The harvest] of complete detachment won -

All that the Master's follower can win,

If he fulfil the training of the Rule—

All this Kondanna step by step hath won

By study strenuous and diligent.

Sublime in power and versed in triple lore,

Expert the thoughts of others to descry, Kondanna of the Buddha rightful heir,

Low at the Master's feet behold him lie.

X

Spoken in praise of the venerable Moggallana the Great, before the Exalted One, when the former discerned that the hearts of the 500 arahants, gathered together at Black Rock on Rishis' Hill at Rajagaha, were emancipated and free from the conditions for rebirth:

High on the hilly slopes disciples sit,

Holding the triple lore, slayers of Death,

Upon the pleasure of the seated Saint,

Who hath transcended all the power of ill.

And Moggallana great in mystic power

Doth scrutinize in thought the hearts of all,

And thus examining he finds them freed,

And having nought wherefrom to be reborn.

So do they wait upon that perfect Saint,

Who hath transcended all the power of ill,

And perfected on every hand his work—

So wait upon and honour Gotama.

XI Spoken in praise of the Exalted One, luminous by his own beauty and glory, when surrounded by the Order and the laity at the Gaggara Lotus-lake, at Campa:

As when th' obscuring clouds have drifted from the sky,

The moon shines splendid even as a sun,

So thou, Angirasa, most mighty Seer,

Dost with thy glory all the world illume.

XII Spoken when reflecting, as a new-made arahant, on his experiences and on the Master:

Drunk with divining art, of old we roamed

From town and village on to town again.

Then we beheld the All-Enlightened, Him

Who hath transcended all that we can know.

 He in the Norm instructed me—the Seer,

Who hath transcended all the power of ill.

And when we heard that Norm our heart was glad,

And faith and trust therein rose up in us.

Hearing his Word concerning body, mind,

Sensations, objects of the same, and all

The data of our knowledge—grasping these,

I left the world to lead the homeless life.

O surely for the weal of many folk

The advent is of Them-who-Thus-are-Come!—

Of women and of men who keep their Rule.

Yea, surely, and for highest good of those—

The Brethren and the Sisters, they who see

The order of what is, what may become—

For them the Seer did win Enlightenment.

By Him-who-Sees, the Buddha, Kin o' th' Sun, Well taught in kindness to all things that breathe

Are the Four Ariyan, Four Noble Truths;

Even the What and Why of Ill, and how

Ill comes, and how Ill may be overpassed,

E'en by the Ariyan, the Eightfold Path,

That leads to the abating of all Ill.

Such were the doctrines uttered thus, and I,

I saw them e'en as they were shown to me;

And now salvation have I surely won,

And all the Buddha's ordinance is done.

O welcome tidings! welcome time to me

To live and study near the Master's feet;

'Mong divers doctrines mooted among men

Of all 'twas sure the best I sought and found.

To heights of intuition have I won, From sense of hearing is the dullness swept;

The triple lore have I and magic power;

In knowing others' thought am I adept.

XIII When inquiring as to whether his tutor had passed wholly away at death:

I ask the Master—boundless is his wisdom—

Who as to this life severs every doubt:—

Here at Aggaḷava hath died a Brother,

Well-known and famous, cool and calm [his heart];

Nigrodha-Kappa, so thyself didst call him,

 Such was this good man's name, Exalted One. Revering thee he lived, his gaze
on Freedom,

And, Seer of what is stable, well he strove.

Of this disciple, Sakyan, all desirous

Are we to know the fate, thou Seer of all;

Attent the ear of everyone to hear it:—

Thou art our Master and thou art supreme.

 Do thou but sever from us all our doubting,

Tell thou me, amplest Wisdom, make it known:

Hath he indeed his life's long round completed?

Speak to us in our midst, O Seer of all,

As Sakka thousand-eyed in heavenly hall.

Bonds that here bind us, pathways of illusion,

Factors of ignorance, stations of doubt:—

Whate'er they be, confronted by the Master,

By Him-who-Thus hath-Come, they cease to be,

For among men the Eye Supreme is he.

For if, i' faith, some Man the world's corruptions

Sweep not away, as wind the lowering clouds,

The world were shrouded wholly in thick darkness,

And e'en the brighter minds would lose their light.

Light-bringers [to us all] are men of wisdom;

And thou, O Sage, methinks art even such.

 We have drawn nigh to one who seeth, knoweth; Reveal to us assembled Kappa['s
fate]!

Swiftly send forth thy voice in all its beauty,

O thou most beauteous; even as the swan,

With rich and mellow tones well modulated,

Lifts up its neck in measured trumpeting,

And we will hearken all, our hearts sincere.

Gone from his ways all future birth and dying; And him who shook them off without remainder,

Him now constraining will I cause to speak.

For average folk fail to fulfil their wishes,

But saints perform whatever they devise.

Well have we learnt how thou canst answer,

Whose insight straight to heart of things dost go,

Not vainly do we stand, once more saluting.

O baffle not, thou infinite in wisdom,

Who [Kappa's destiny] dost surely know.

The Ariyan Norm thou know'st in all its bearings, Knowing and strong to work, O baffle not!

As for cool waters when by heat we suffer,

Thy word we wait for:— rain that we may hear!

That holy life which, for the goal desirous,

He of the Kappas led, was't not in vain?

Passed he away fraught with the seed of rebirth, Or as one wholly free?—that would we hear.

[The Exalted One.]

All craving as to life of mind and body

He severed here below, and crossed the stream

Of craving flowing long deep-bedded in him,

Passed utterly beyond both birth and death.

(Thus spake the Exalted One, best in the Five.)

[Vaṅgisa]

Pleased is my heart to hear thy word,

O seventh of mighty Rishis thou! Not vain, in sooth, was my request,

Thou'st not deceived me, Holy One!

As Kappa spoke, so Kappa wrought,

Disciple of the Buddha he, For he hath cut the netted snare

By crafty Death outstretched and strong.

He of the Kappas saw the source

Of grasping, O Exalted One!

Ah! truly he hath passed beyond

The realm of Death so hard to cross.

Thee greater than the gods I greet,

With thee thy son, O best of men, A mighty hero like thee grown,

Of wondrous Being, very son.

Thus verily did the venerable Brother Vaṅgisa utter his psalm.

# ENVOI

Singing the pæan of their 'lion's' roar,

These children of the Buddha, sane, immune,

Winning the safe sure haven of their quest,

Dwelt in blest cool like flame of fire extinct.

# THERIGATHA

# VERSES OF THE ELDER NUNS

# THE BOOK OF THE ONES

1.1 An Unnamed Nun (1st)

Homage to that Blessed One, the perfected one, the fully awakened Buddha!

Sleep softly, little nun,

wrapped in the cloth you sewed yourself;

for your desire has been quelled,

like vegetables boiled dry in a pot.

It was thus that this verse was recited by a certain unnamed nun.

1.2 Mutta (1st)

Mutta, be released from your bonds,

like the moon released from Rahu's grip, the eclipse.

When your mind is released,

enjoy your alms free of debt.

It was thus that the Buddha regularly advised the trainee nun Mutta with these verses.

1.3 Punna

Punna, be filled with good qualities,

like the moon on the fifteenth day.

When your wisdom is full,

shatter the mass of darkness.

It was thus that this verse was recited by the senior nun Punna.

1.4 Tissa

Tissa, train in the trainings—

don't let the practice pass you by.

Detached from all attachments,

live in the world free of defilements.

1.5 Another Tissa

Tissa, apply yourself to good qualities—

don't let the moment pass you by.

For if you miss your moment,

you'll grieve when you're sent to hell.

1.6 Dhira

Dhira, touch cessation,

the blissful stilling of perception.

Win extinguishment,

the supreme sanctuary.

1.7 Vira

She's known as Vira because of her heroic qualities,

a nun with faculties developed.

She bears her final body,

having vanquished Mara and his mount.

1.8 Mitta (1st)

Having gone forth out of faith,

appreciate your spiritual friends, Mitta.

Develop skillful qualities

for the sake of finding sanctuary.

1.9 Bhadra

Having gone forth out of faith,

appreciate your blessings, Bhadra.

Develop skillful qualities

for the sake of the supreme sanctuary.

1.10 Upasama

Upasama, cross the flood,

Death's domain so hard to pass.

When you have vanquished Mara and his mount,

bear your final body.

1.11 Mutta (2nd)

I'm well freed, so very well freed,

freed from the three things that bent me over:

the mortar, the pestle,

and my humpbacked husband.

I'm freed from birth and death;

the attachment to rebirth is eradicated.

1.12 Dhammadinna

One who is eager and determined

would be filled with awareness.

One whose mind is not tied up with sensual pleasures

is said to be heading upstream.

1.13 Visakha

Fulfill the Buddha's instructions,

after which you'll not regret.

Having quickly washed your feet,

sit in a discreet place to meditate.

1.14 Sumana

Having seen the elements as suffering,

don't get reborn again.

When you've discarded desire for rebirth,

you will live at peace.

1.15 Uttara (1st)

I was restrained

in body, speech, and mind.

Having plucked out craving root and all,

I'm cooled and quenched.

1.16 Sumana, Who Went Forth Late in Life

Sleep softly, old lady,

wrapped in the cloth you sewed yourself;

for your desire has been quelled,

you're cooled and quenched.

1.17 Dhamma

I wandered for alms

though feeble, leaning on a staff.

My limbs wobbled

and I fell to the ground right there.

Seeing the danger of the body,

my mind was freed.

1.18 Saṃgha

Having given up my home, my child, my cattle,

and all that I love, I went forth.

Having given up desire and hate,

having dispelled ignorance,

and having plucked out craving, root and all,

I'm quenched and at peace.

The Book of the Ones is finished.

# THE BOOK OF THE TWOS

2.1 Abhirupananda

Nanda, see this bag of bones as

diseased, filthy, and rotten.

With mind unified and serene,

meditate on the ugly aspects of the body.

Meditate on the signless,

give up the underlying tendency to conceit;

and when you comprehend conceit,

you will live at peace.

It was thus that the Buddha regularly advised the senior nun Nanda with these verses.

2.2 Jenta

Of the seven awakening factors,

the path for attaining extinguishment,

I have developed them all,

just as the Buddha taught.

For I have seen the Blessed One,

and this bag of bones is my last.

Transmigration through births is finished,

now there are no more future lives.

It was thus that these verses were recited by the senior nun Jenta.

2.3 Sumaṅgala's Mother

I'm well freed, well freed,

so very well freed!

My pestle's shameless wind was wafting;

my little pot wafted like an eel.

Now, as for greed and hate:

I sear them and sizzle them up.

Having gone to the root of a tree,

I meditate happily, thinking, "Oh, what bliss!"

2.4 Addhakasi

The price for my services

amounted to the nation of Kasi.

By setting that price,

the townsfolk made me priceless.

Then, growing disillusioned with my form,

I became dispassionate.

Don't journey on and on,

transmigrating through rebirths!

I've realized the three knowledges,

and fulfilled the Buddha's instructions.

2.5 Citta

Though I'm skinny,

sick, and very feeble,

I climb the mountain,

leaning on a staff.

Having laid down my outer robe,

and overturned my bowl,

propping myself against a rock,

I shattered the mass of darkness.

2.6 Mettika

Though in pain,

feeble, my youth long gone,

I climb the mountain,

leaning on a staff.

Having laid down my outer robe

and overturned my bowl,

sitting on a rock,

my mind was freed.

I've attained the three knowledges,

and fulfilled the Buddha's instructions.

2.7 Mitta (2nd)

I rejoice in the host of gods,

having observed the sabbath

complete in all eight factors,

on the fourteenth and the fifteenth days,

and the eighth day of the fortnight,

as well as on the fortnightly special displays.

Today I eat just once a day,

my head is shaven, I wear the outer robe.

I don't long for the host of gods,

for stress has been removed from my heart.

2.8 Abhaya's Mother

My dear mother, I examined this body,

up from the soles of the feet,

and down from the tips of the hairs,

so impure and foul-smelling.

Meditating like this,

all my lust is eradicated.

The fever of passion is cut off,

I'm cooled and quenched.

2.9 Abhaya

Abhaya, the body is fragile,

yet ordinary people are attached to it.

I'll lay down the body,

aware and mindful.

Though subject to so many painful things,

I have, through my love of diligence,

reached the ending of craving,

and fulfilled the Buddha's instructions.

2.10 Sama

Four or five times

I left my dwelling.

I had failed to find peace of heart,

or any control over my mind.

Now it is the eighth night

since craving was eradicated.

Though subject to so many painful things,

I have, through my love of diligence,

reached the ending of craving,

and fulfilled the Buddha's instructions.

The Book of the Twos is finished.

# THE BOOK OF THE THREES

3.1 Another Sama

In the twenty-five years

since I went forth,

I don't know that I had ever found

serenity in my mind.

I had failed to find peace of heart,

or any control over my mind.

When I remembered the victor's instructions,

I was struck with a sense of urgency.

Though subject to so many painful things,

I have, through my love of diligence,

reached the ending of craving,

and fulfilled the Buddha's instructions.

This is the seventh day

since my craving dried up.

3.2 Uttama

Four or five times

I left my dwelling.

I had failed to find peace of heart,

or any control over my mind.

I approached a nun

in whom I had faith.

She taught me the Dhamma:

the aggregates, sense fields, and elements.

When I had heard her teaching,

in accordance with her instructions,

I sat for seven days in the same posture,

given over to rapture and bliss.

On the eighth day I stretched out my feet,

having shattered the mass of darkness.

3.3 Another Uttama

Of the seven awakening factors,

the path for attaining extinguishment,

I have developed them all,

just as the Buddha taught.

I attain the meditations on emptiness

and signlessness whenever I want.

I am the Buddha's rightful daughter,

always delighting in quenching.

All sensual pleasures are cut off,

whether human or divine.

Transmigration through births is finished,

now there are no more future lives.

3.4 Dantika

Leaving my day's meditation

on Vulture's Peak Mountain,

I saw an elephant on the riverbank

having just come up from his bath.

A man, taking a pole with a hook,

asked the elephant, "Give me your foot."

The elephant presented his foot,

and the man mounted him.

Seeing a wild beast so tamed,

submitting to human control,

my mind became serene:

*that* is why I've gone to the forest!

3.5 Ubbiri

"You cry 'Please be living!' in the forest.

Ubbiri, get a hold of yourself!

Eighty-four thousand people,

all named 'living being',

have been burnt in this funeral ground:

which one do you grieve for?"

"Oh! For you have plucked the dart from me,

so hard to see, hidden in the heart.

You've swept away the grief for my daughter

in which I once was mired.

Today I've plucked the dart,

I'm hungerless, extinguished.

I go for refuge to that sage, the Buddha,

to his teaching, and to the Sangha."

3.6 Sukka

"What's up with these people in Rajagaha?

They sprawl like they've been drinking mead!

They don't attend on Sukka

as she teaches the Buddha's instructions.

But the wise—

it's as if they drink it up,

so irresistible, delicious and nutritious,

like travelers enjoying a cool cloud."

"She's known as Sukka because of her bright qualities,

free of greed, serene.

She bears her final body,

having vanquished Mara and his mount."

3.7 Sela

"There's no escape in the world,

so what will seclusion do for you?

Enjoy the delights of sensual pleasure;

don't regret it later."

"Sensual pleasures are like swords and stakes

the aggregates are their chopping block.

What you call sensual delight

is now no delight for me.

Relishing is destroyed in every respect,

and the mass of darkness is shattered.

So know this, Wicked One:

you're beaten, terminator!"

3.8 Soma

"That state's very challenging;

it's for the sages to attain.

It's not possible for a woman,

with her two-fingered wisdom."

"What difference does womanhood make

when the mind is serene,

and knowledge is present

as you rightly discern the Dhamma.

Relishing is destroyed in every respect,

and the mass of darkness is shattered.

So know this, Wicked One:

you're beaten, terminator!"

The Book of the Threes is finished.

# THE BOOK OF THE FOURS

4.1 Bhadda Kapilani

Kassapa is the son and heir of the Buddha,

whose mind is immersed in samadhi.

He knows his past lives,

he sees heaven and places of loss,

and has attained the end of rebirth:

that sage has perfect insight.

It's because of these three knowledges

that the brahmin is a master of the three knowledges.

In exactly the same way, Bhadda Kapilani

is master of the three knowledges, destroyer of death.

She bears her final body,

having vanquished Mara and his mount.

Seeing the danger of the world,

both of us went forth.

Now we are tamed, our defilements have ended;

we've become cooled and quenched.

The Book of the Fours is finished.

# THE BOOK OF THE FIVES

5.1 An Unnamed Nun (2nd)

In the twenty-five years

since I went forth

I have not found peace of mind,

even for as long as a finger-snap.

Failing to find peace of heart,

corrupted by sensual desire,

I cried with flailing arms

as I entered a dwelling.

I approached a nun

in whom I had faith.

She taught me the Dhamma:

the aggregates, sense fields, and elements.

When I heard her teaching,

I retired to a discreet place.

I know my past lives;

my clairvoyance is purified;

I comprehend the minds of others;

my clairaudience is purified;

I've realized the psychic powers,

and attained the ending of defilements.

I have realized the six kinds of direct knowledge,

and fulfilled the Buddha's instructions.

5.2 Vimala, the Former Courtesan

Intoxicated by my appearance,

my figure, my beauty, my fame,

and owing to my youth,

I despised other women.

I adorned this body,

so fancy, cooed over by fools,

and stood at the brothel door,

like a hunter laying a snare.

I stripped for them,

revealing my many hidden treasures.

Creating an intricate illusion,

I laughed, teasing those men.

Today, having wandered for alms,

my head shaven, wearing the outer robe,

I sat at the root of a tree to meditate;

I've gained freedom from thought.

All bonds are cut off,

both human and divine.

Having wiped out all defilements,

I have become cooled and quenched.

5.3 Siha

Due to improper attention,

I was racked by desire for pleasures of the senses.

I was restless in the past,

lacking control over my mind.

Overcome by corruptions,

pursuing perceptions of the beautiful,

I gained no peace of mind.

Under the sway of lustful thoughts,

thin, pale, and wan,

for seven years I wandered,

full of pain,

finding no happiness by day or night.

Taking a rope

I entered deep into the forest, thinking:

"It's better that I hang myself

than I return to a lesser life."

I made a strong noose

and tied it to the branch of a tree.

Casting it round my neck,

my mind was freed.

5.4 Sundarinanda

"Nanda, see this bag of bones as

diseased, filthy, and rotten.

With mind unified and serene,

meditate on the ugly aspects of the body:

as this is, so is that,

as that is, so is this.

A foul stink wafts from it,

it is the fools' delight."

Reviewing my body in such a way,

tireless all day and night,

having broken through

with my own wisdom, I saw.

Being diligent,

properly investigating,

I truly saw the body

both inside and out.

Then, growing disillusioned with my body,

I became dispassionate within.

Diligent, detached,

I'm quenched and at peace.

5.5 Nanduttara

In the past I worshiped the sacred flame,

the moon, the sun, and the gods.

Having gone to a river ford,

I plunged into the water.

Undertaking many vows,

I shaved half my head.

Preparing a bed on the ground,

I ate no food at night.

I loved my ornaments and decorations;

and with baths and oil-massages,

I pandered to this body,

racked by desire for pleasures of the senses.

But then I gained faith,

and went forth to homelessness.

Truly seeing the body,

desire for sensual pleasure is eradicated.

All rebirths are cut off,

wishes and aspirations too.

Detached from all attachments,

I've attained peace of heart.

5.6 Mittakaḷi

Having gone forth out of faith

from the lay life to homelessness,

I wandered here and there,

jealous of possessions and honors.

Neglecting the highest goal,

I pursued the lowest.

Under the sway of corruptions,

I never knew the goal of the ascetic life.

I was struck with a sense of urgency

as I was sitting in my hut:

"I'm walking the wrong path,

under the sway of craving.

My life is short,

trampled by old age and sickness.

Before this body breaks apart,

there is no time for me to be careless."

I examined in line with reality

the rise and fall of the aggregates.

I stood up with mind liberated,

having fulfilled the Buddha's instructions.

5.7 Sakula

While staying at home

I heard the teaching from a mendicant.

I saw the stainless Dhamma,

extinguishment, the imperishable state.

Leaving behind my son and my daughter,

my riches and my grain,

I had my hair cut off,

and went forth to homelessness.

As a trainee nun,

I developed the direct path.

I gave up greed and hate,

along with associated defilements.

When I was fully ordained as a nun,

I recollected my past lives,

and purified my clairvoyance,

immaculate and fully developed.

Conditions are born of causes, crumbling;

having seen them as other,

I gave up all defilements,

I'm cooled and quenched.

5.8 Sona

I gave birth to ten sons

in this form, this bag of bones.

Then, when feeble and old,

I approached a nun.

She taught me the Dhamma:

the aggregates, sense fields, and elements.

When I heard her teaching,

I cut off my hair and went forth.

When I was a trainee nun,

my clairvoyance was clarified,

and I knew my past lives,

the places I used to live.

I meditate on the signless,

my mind unified and serene.

I achieved the immediate liberation,

extinguished by not grasping.

The five aggregates are fully understood;

they remain, but their root is cut.

Curse you, wretched old age!

Now there are no more future lives.

5.9 Bhadda Kundalakesa

My hair mown off, covered in mud,

I used to wander wearing just one robe.

I saw fault where there was none,

and no fault where there was.

Leaving my day's meditation

on Vulture's Peak Mountain,

I saw the stainless Buddha

at the fore of the mendicant Saṅgha.

I bent my knee and bowed,

and in his presence raised my joined palms.

"Come Bhadda," he said;

that was my ordination.

"I've wandered among the Aṅgans and Magadhans,

the Vajjis, Kasis, and Kosalans.

I have eaten the alms-food of the nations

free of debt for fifty years."

"O! He has made so much merit!

That lay follower is so very wise.

He gave a robe to Bhadda,

who is released from all ties."

5.10 Patacara

Plowing the fields,

sowing seeds in the ground,

supporting partners and children,

young men acquire wealth.

I am accomplished in ethics,

and I do the Teacher's bidding,

being neither lazy nor restless—

why then do I not achieve quenching?

Having washed my feet,

I took note of the water,

seeing the foot-washing water

flowing from high ground to low.

My mind became serene,

like a fine thoroughbred steed.

Then, taking a lamp,

I entered my dwelling,

inspected the bed,

and sat on my cot.

Then, grabbing the pin,

I drew out the wick.

The liberation of my heart

was like the quenching of the lamp.

5.11 Thirty Nuns

"Taking a pestle,

young men pound corn.

Supporting partners and children,

young men acquire wealth.

Do the Buddha's bidding,

after which you'll not regret.

Having quickly washed your feet,

sit in a discreet place to meditate.

Devoted to serenity of heart,

do the Buddha's bidding."

After hearing her words,

the instructions of Patacara,

they washed their feet

and retired to a discreet place.

Devoted to serenity of heart,

they did the Buddha's bidding.

In the first watch of the night,

they recollected their past lives.

In the middle watch of the night,

they purified their clairvoyance.

In the last watch of the night,

they shattered the mass of darkness.

They rose and paid homage at her feet:

"We have done your bidding;

we shall abide honoring you,

as the thirty gods honor Indra,

undefeated in battle.

Masters of the three knowledges, we are free of defilements."

It was thus that thirty senior nuns declared their enlightenment in the presence of Patacara.

5.12 Canda

I used to be in a sorry state.

As a childless widow,

bereft of friends or relatives,

I got neither food nor clothes.

I took a bowl and a staff

and went begging from family to family.

For seven years I wandered,

burned by heat and cold.

Then I saw a nun

receiving food and drink.

Approaching her, I said:

"Send me forth to homelessness."

Out of compassion for me,

Patacara gave me the going forth.

Then, having advised me,

she urged me on to the ultimate goal.

After hearing her words,

I did her bidding.

The lady's advice was not in vain:

master of the three knowledges, I am free of defilements.

The Book of the Fives is finished.

# THE BOOK OF THE SIXES

6.1 Patacara, Who Had a Following of Five Hundred

"He whose path you do not know,

not whence he came nor where he went;

though he came from who knows where,

you mourn that being, crying, 'Oh my son!'

But one whose path you do know,

whence they came or where they went;

that one you do not lament—

such is the nature of living creatures.

Unasked he came,

he left without leave.

He must have come from somewhere,

and stayed who knows how many days.

He left from here by one road,

he will go from there by another.

Departing with the form of a human,

he will go on transmigrating.

As he came, so he went:

why cry over that?"

"Oh! For you have plucked the dart from me,

so hard to see, hidden in the heart.

You've swept away the grief for my son,

in which I once was mired.

Today I've plucked the dart,

I'm hungerless, extinguished.

I go for refuge to that sage, the Buddha,

to his teaching, and to the Sangha."

It was thus that Patacara, who had a following of five hundred, declared her enlightenment.

6.2 Vasetthi

Struck down with grief for my son,

deranged, out of my mind,

naked, my hair flying,

I wandered here and there.

I lived on rubbish heaps,

in cemeteries and highways.

For three years I wandered,

stricken by hunger and thirst.

Then I saw the Holy One,

who had gone to the city of Mithila.

Tamer of the untamed,

the Awakened One fears nothing from any quarter.

Regaining my mind,

I paid homage and sat down.

Out of compassion

Gotama taught me the Dhamma.

After hearing his teaching,

I went forth to homelessness.

Applying myself to the Teacher's words,

I realized the state of grace.

All sorrows are cut off,

given up, they end here.

I've fully understood the basis

from which grief comes to be.

6.3 Khema

"You're so young and beautiful!

I too am young, just a youth.

Come, Khema, let us enjoy

the music of a five-piece band."

"This body is rotting,

ailing and fragile,

I'm horrified and repelled by it,

and I've eradicated sensual craving.

Sensual pleasures are like swords and stakes;

the aggregates are their chopping block.

What you call sensual delight

is now no delight for me.

Relishing is destroyed in every respect,

and the mass of darkness is shattered.

So know this, Wicked One:

you're beaten, terminator!"

"Worshiping the stars,

serving the sacred flame in a grove;

failing to grasp the true nature of things,

foolish me, I thought this was purity.

But now I worship the Awakened One,

supreme among men.

Doing the teacher's bidding,

I am released from all suffering."

6.4 Sujata

I was adorned with jewelry and all dressed up,

with garlands, and sandalwood makeup piled on,

all covered over with decorations,

and surrounded by my maids.

Taking food and drink,

staples and dainties in no small amount,

I left my house

and betook myself to the park.

I enjoyed myself there and played about,

and then, returning to my own home,

I saw a monastic dwelling,

and so I entered the Anjana grove at Saketa.

Seeing the light of the world,

I paid homage and sat down.

Out of compassion

the seer taught me the Dhamma.

When I heard the great hermit,

I penetrated the truth.

Right there I encountered the Dhamma,

the stainless, deathless state.

Then, having understood the true teaching,

I went forth to homelessness.

I've attained the three knowledges;

the Buddha's bidding was not in vain.

6.5 Anopama

I was born into an eminent family,

affluent and wealthy,

endowed with a beautiful complexion and figure;

Majjha's true-born daughter.

I was sought by princes,

coveted by sons of the wealthy.

One sent a messenger to my father:

"Give me Anopama!

However much your daughter

Anopama weighs,

I'll give you eight times that

in gold and gems."

When I saw the Awakened One,

the world's Elder, unsurpassed,

I paid homage at his feet,

then sat down to one side.

Out of compassion,

Gotama taught me the Dhamma.

While sitting in that seat,

I realized the third fruit.

Then, having cut off my hair,

I went forth to homelessness.

This is the seventh day

since my craving dried up.

6.6 Mahapajapati Gotami

Oh Buddha, my hero: homage to you!

Supreme among all beings,

who released me from suffering,

and many other beings as well.

All suffering is fully understood;

craving—its cause—is dried up;

the eightfold path has been developed;

and cessation has been realized by me.

Previously I was a mother, a son,

a father, a brother, and a grandmother.

Failing to grasp the true nature of things,

I've transmigrated without reward.

Since I have seen the Blessed One,

this bag of bones is my last.

Transmigration through births is finished,

now there are no more future lives.

I see the disciples in harmony,

energetic and resolute,

always staunchly vigorous—

this is homage to the Buddhas!

It was truly for the benefit of many

that Maya gave birth to Gotama.

He swept away the mass of suffering

for those stricken by sickness and death.

6.7 Gutta

Gutta, you have given up your child,

your wealth, and all that you love.

Foster the goal for which you went forth;

do not fall under the mind's control.

Beings deceived by the mind,

playing in Mara's domain,

ignorant, they journey on,

transmigrating through countless rebirths.

Sensual desire and ill will,

and identity view;

misapprehension of precepts and observances,

and doubt as the fifth.

O nun, when you have given up

these lower fetters,

you won't come back

to this world again.

And when you're rid of greed,

conceit, ignorance, and restlessness,

having cut the fetters,

you'll make an end to suffering.

Having wiped out transmigration,

and fully understood rebirth,

hungerless in this very life,

you will live at peace.

6.8 Vijaya

Four or five times

I left my dwelling;

I had failed to find peace of heart,

or any control over my mind.

I approached a nun

and politely questioned her.

She taught me the Dhamma:

the elements and sense fields,

the four noble truths,

the faculties and the powers,

the awakening factors, and the eightfold path

for the attainment of the highest goal.

After hearing her words,

I did her bidding.

In the first watch of the night,

I recollected my past lives.

In the middle watch of the night,

I purified my clairvoyance.

In the last watch of the night,

I shattered the mass of darkness.

I then meditated pervading my body

with rapture and bliss.

On the seventh day I stretched out my feet,

having shattered the mass of darkness.

The Book of the Sixes is finished.

# THE BOOK OF THE SEVENS

7.1 Uttara (2nd)

"Taking a pestle,

young men pound corn.

Supporting partners and children,

young men acquire wealth.

Work at the Buddha's bidding,

after which you'll not regret.

Having quickly washed your feet,

sit in a discreet place to meditate.

Establish the mind,

unified and serene.

Examine conditions

as other, not as self."

"After hearing her words,

the instructions of Patacara,

I washed my feet

and retired to a discreet place.

In the first watch of the night,

I recollected my past lives.

In the middle watch of the night,

I purified my clairvoyance.

In the last watch of the night,

I shattered the mass of darkness.

I rose up master of the three knowledges:

your bidding has been done.

I shall abide honoring you

as the thirty gods honor Sakka,

undefeated in battle.

Master of the three knowledges, I am free of defilements."

7.2 Cala

"As a nun with developed faculties,

having established mindfulness,

I penetrated that peaceful state,

the blissful stilling of conditions."

"In whose name did you shave your head?

You look like an ascetic,

but you don't believe in any creed.

Why do you live as if lost?"

"Followers of other creeds

rely on their views.

They don't understand the Dhamma,

for they're no experts in the Dhamma.

But there is one born in the Sakyan clan,

the unrivaled Buddha;

he taught me the Dhamma

for going beyond views.

Suffering, suffering's origin,

suffering's transcendence,

and the noble eightfold path

that leads to the stilling of suffering.

After hearing his words,

I happily did his bidding.

I've attained the three knowledges

and fulfilled the Buddha's instructions.

Relishing is destroyed in every respect,

and the mass of darkness is shattered.

So know this, Wicked One:

you're beaten, terminator!"

7.3 Upacala

"A nun with faculties developed,

mindful, seeing clearly,

I penetrated that peaceful state,

which sinners do not cultivate."

"Why don't you approve of rebirth?

When you're born, you get to enjoy sensual pleasures.

Enjoy the delights of sensual pleasure;

don't regret it later."

"Death comes to those who are born;

and when born they fall into suffering:

the chopping off of hands and feet,

killing, caging, misery.

But there is one born in the Sakyan clan,

an awakened champion.

He taught me the Dhamma

for passing beyond rebirth:

suffering, suffering's origin,

suffering's transcendence,

and the noble eightfold path

that leads to the stilling of suffering.

After hearing his words,

I happily did his bidding.

I've attained the three knowledges

and fulfilled the Buddha's instructions.

Relishing is destroyed in every respect,

and the mass of darkness is shattered.

So know this, Wicked One:

you're beaten, terminator!"

The Book of the Sevens is finished.

# THE BOOK OF THE EIGHTS

8.1 Sisupacala

"A nun accomplished in ethics,

her sense faculties well-restrained,

would realize the peaceful state,

so irresistible, delicious and nutritious."

"There are the Gods of the Thirty-Three, and those of Yama;

also the Joyful Deities,

the Gods Who Love to Create,

and the Gods Who Control the Creations of Others.

Set your heart on such places,

where you used to live."

"The Gods of the Thirty-Three, and those of Yama;

also the Joyful Deities,

the Gods Who Love to Create,

and the Gods Who Control the Creations of Others—

time after time, life after life,

they make identity their priority.

They haven't transcended identity,

those who transmigrate through birth and death.

All the world is on fire,

all the world is alight,

all the world is ablaze,

all the world is rocking.

The Buddha taught me the Dhamma,

unshakable, incomparable,

not frequented by ordinary people;

my mind adores that place.

After hearing his words,

I happily did his bidding.

I've attained the three knowledges,

and fulfilled the Buddha's instructions.

Relishing is destroyed in every respect,

and the mass of darkness is shattered.

So know this, Wicked One:

you're beaten, terminator!"

The Book of the Eights is finished.

# THE BOOK OF THE NINES

9.1 Vaddha's Mother

"Vaḍḍha, please never ever

get entangled in the world.

My child, do not partake

in suffering again and again.

For happy dwell the sages, Vaḍḍha,

unstirred, their doubts cut off,

cooled and tamed,

and free of defilements.

Vaḍḍha, foster the path

that the hermits have walked,

for the attainment of vision,

and for making an end of suffering."

"Mother, you speak with such assurance

to me on this matter.

My dear mom, I can't help thinking

that no entanglements are found in you."

"Vaḍḍha, not a jot or a skerrick

of entanglement is found in me

for any conditions at all,

whether low, high, or middling.

All defilements are ended for me,

meditating and diligent.

I've attained the three knowledges

and fulfilled the Buddha's instructions."

"Truly excellent was the goad

with which my mother urged me on!

Owing to her compassion, she spoke

verses on the ultimate goal.

After hearing her words,

being instructed by my mother,

I was struck with righteous urgency

for finding sanctuary.

Striving, resolute,

tireless all day and night,

spurred on by my mother,

I realized supreme peace."

The Book of the Nines is finished.

# THE BOOK OF THE ELEVENS

10.1 Kisagotami

"Pointing out how the world works,

the sages have praised good friendship.

Associating with good friends,

even a fool becomes astute.

Associate with good people,

for that is how wisdom grows.

Should you associate with good people,

you would be freed from all suffering.

And you would understand suffering,

its origin and cessation,

the eightfold path,

and so the four noble truths."

"'A woman's life is painful,'

explained the Buddha, guide for those who wish to train,

'and for a co-wife it's especially so.

After giving birth just once,

some women even cut their own throat,

while refined ladies take poison.

Being guilty of killing a person,

they undergo ruin both here and beyond.'"

"I was on the road and nearing childbirth,

when I saw my husband dead.

I gave birth there on the road

before I'd reached my own home.

My two children have died,

and on the road my husband lies dead—oh woe is me!

Mother, father, and brother

all burning up on the same pyre."

"Oh woe is you whose family is lost,

your suffering has no measure;

you have been shedding tears

for many thousands of lives."

"While staying in the charnel ground,

I saw my son's flesh being eaten.

With my family destroyed, condemned by all,

and my husband dead, I realized the deathless.

I've developed the noble eightfold path

leading to the deathless.

I've realized quenching,

as seen in the mirror of the Dhamma.

I've plucked out the dart,

laid down the burden, and done what needed to be done."

The senior nun Kisagotami,

her mind released, said this.

The Book of the Elevens is finished.

# THE BOOK OF THE TWELVES

11.1 Uppalavanna

"The two of us were co-wives,

though we were mother and daughter.

I was struck with a sense of urgency,

so astonishing and hair-raising!

Curse those filthy sensual pleasures,

so nasty and thorny,

where we, both mother and daughter,

had to be co-wives together.

Seeing the danger in sensual pleasures,

seeing renunciation as a sanctuary,

I went forth in Rajagaha

from the lay life to homelessness.

I know my past lives;

my clairvoyance is clarified;

I comprehend the minds of others;

my clairaudience is purified;

I've realized the psychic powers,

and attained the ending of defilements.

I've realized the six kinds of direct knowledge,

and fulfilled the Buddha's instructions.

I created a four-horsed chariot

using my psychic powers.

Then I bowed at the feet of the Buddha,

the glorious protector of the world."

"You've come to this sal tree all crowned with flowers,

and stand at its root all alone.

But you have no companion with you,

silly girl, aren't you afraid of rascals?"

"Even if 100,000 rascals like this

were to gang up,

I'd stir not a hair nor tremble.

What could you do to me all alone, Mara?

I'll vanish,

or I'll enter your belly;

I could stand between your eyebrows

and you still wouldn't see me.

I'm the master of my own mind,

I've developed the bases of psychic power well.

I've realized the six kinds of direct knowledge,

and fulfilled the Buddha's instructions.

Sensual pleasures are like swords and stakes;

the aggregates are their chopping block.

What you call sensual delight

is now no delight for me.

Relishing is destroyed in every respect,

and the mass of darkness is shattered.

So know this, Wicked One:

you're beaten, terminator!"

The Book of the Twelves is finished.

# THE BOOK OF THE SIXTEENS

12.1 Punnika

"I'm a water-carrier. Even when it's cold,

I must always plunge into the water;

I fear I'll get the stick from noble ladies,

harassed by fear of abuse and anger.

Brahmin, what are you afraid of,

that you always plunge into the water,

your limbs trembling

in the freezing cold?"

"Oh, but you already know,

Madam Punnika, when you ask me:

I am doing good deeds,

to block off the wickedness I have done.

Whosoever young or old

performs a wicked deed,

by ablution in water they are

released from their wicked deed."

"Who on earth told you this,

one fool to another:

'Actually, by ablution in water one is

released from a wicked deed.'

Would not they all go to heaven, then:

all the frogs and the turtles,

gharials, crocodiles,

and other water-dwellers too?

Butchers of sheep and pigs,

fishermen, animal trappers,

bandits, executioners,

and others of evil deeds:

by ablution in water they too would be

released from their wicked deeds.

If these rivers washed away

the bad deeds of the past,

then they'd also wash off goodness,

and thereby you would be excluded.

Brahmin, the thing that you are afraid of,

when you always plunge into the water,

do not do that very thing,

don't let the cold harm your skin."

"I have been on the wrong path,

and you've guided me to the noble path.

Madam, I give to you

this ablution cloth."

"Keep the cloth for yourself,

I do not want it.

If you fear suffering,

if you don't like suffering,

then don't do bad deeds

either openly or in secret.

If you should do a bad deed,

or you're doing one now,

you won't be freed from suffering,

though you fly away and flee.

If you fear suffering,

if you don't like suffering,

go for refuge to the Buddha, the poised,

to his teaching and to the Sangha.

Undertake the precepts,

that will be good for you."

"I go for refuge to the Buddha, the poised,

to his teaching and to the Sangha.

I undertake the precepts,

that will be good for me.

In the past I was related to Brahma,

today I truly am a brahmin!

I am master of the three knowledges, accomplished in wisdom,

I'm a scholar and a bathed initiate."

The Book of the Sixteens is finished.

# THE BOOK OF THE TWENTIES

13.1 Ambapali

My hair was as black as bees,

graced with curly tips;

now old, it has become like hemp bark—

the word of the truthful one is confirmed.

Crowned with flowers,

my head was as fragrant as a perfume box;

now old, it smells like dog fur—

the word of the truthful one is confirmed.

My hair was as thick as a well-planted forest,

it shone, parted with brush and pins;

now old, it's patchy and sparse—

the word of the truthful one is confirmed.

With plaits of black and ribbons of gold,

it was so pretty, adorned with braids;

now old, my head's gone bald—

the word of the truthful one is confirmed.

My eyebrows used to look so nice,

like crescents painted by an artist;

now old, they droop with wrinkles—

the word of the truthful one is confirmed.

My eyes shone brilliant as gems,

wide and deepest blue;

ruined by age, they shine no more—

the word of the truthful one is confirmed.

My nose was like a perfect peak,

lovely in my bloom of youth;

now old, it's shriveled like a pepper;

the word of the truthful one is confirmed.

My ear-lobes were so pretty,

like lovingly crafted bracelets;

now old, they droop with wrinkles—

the word of the truthful one is confirmed.

My teeth used to be so pretty,

bright as a jasmine flower;

now old, they're broken and yellow—

the word of the truthful one is confirmed.

My singing was sweet as a cuckoo

wandering in the forest groves;

now old, it's patchy and croaking—

the word of the truthful one is confirmed.

My neck used to be so pretty,

like a polished shell of conch;

now old, it's bowed and bent—

the word of the truthful one is confirmed.

My arms used to be so pretty,

like rounded cross-bars;

now old, they droop like a trumpet-flower tree—

the word of the truthful one is confirmed.

My hands used to be so pretty,

adorned with lovely golden rings;

now old, they're like red radishes—

the word of the truthful one is confirmed.

My breasts used to be so pretty,

swelling, round, close, and high;

now they droop like water bags—

the word of the truthful one is confirmed.

My body used to be so pretty,

like a polished slab of gold;

now it's covered with fine wrinkles—

the word of the truthful one is confirmed.

Both my thighs used to be so pretty,

like an elephant's trunk;

now old, they're like bamboo—

the word of the truthful one is confirmed.

My calves used to be so pretty,

adorned with cute golden anklets;

now old, they're like sesame sticks—

the word of the truthful one is confirmed.

Both my feet used to be so pretty,

plump as if with cotton-wool;

now old, they're cracked and wrinkly—

the word of the truthful one is confirmed.

This bag of bones once was such,

but now it's withered, home to so much pain;

like a house in decay with plaster crumbling—

the word of the truthful one is confirmed.

13.2 Rohini

"You fell asleep saying 'ascetics';

you woke up saying 'ascetics';

you only praise ascetics, madam—

surely you'll be an ascetic.

You provide ascetics

with abundant food and drink.

I ask you now, Rohini:

why do you like ascetics?

They don't like to work, they're lazy,

they survive on charity;

always on the lookout, greedy for sweets—

so why do you like ascetics?"

"Dad, for a long time now

you've questioned me about ascetics.

I shall extol for you

their wisdom, ethics, and vigor.

They like to work, they're not lazy;

by giving up greed and hate,

they do the best kind of work—

that's why I like ascetics.

As for the three roots of evil,

by pure deeds they shake them off.

They have given up all wickedness—

that's why I like ascetics.

Their bodily actions are pure;

their actions of speech likewise;

their actions of mind are pure—

that's why I like ascetics.

Immaculate as a conch-shell,

they're pure inside and out,

full of bright qualities—

that's why I like ascetics.

They're learned and memorize the teaching,

noble, living properly,

teaching the text and its meaning:

that's why I like ascetics.

They're learned and memorize the teaching,

noble, living properly,

unified in mind, and mindful—

that's why I like ascetics.

Traveling afar, and mindful,

thoughtful in counsel, and stable,

they understand the end of suffering—

that's why I like ascetics.

When they leave a village,

they don't look back with longing,

but proceed without concern—

that's why I like ascetics.

They hoard no goods in storerooms,

nor in pots or baskets.

They seek food prepared by others—

that's why I like ascetics.

They don't receive silver,

or gold whether coined or uncoined;

feeding on whatever comes that day,

that's why I like ascetics.

They have gone forth from different families,

even different countries,

and yet they all love one another—

that's why I like ascetics."

"Dear Rohini, it was truly for our benefit

that you were born in our family!

You have faith and such keen respect

for the Buddha, his teaching, and the Sangha.

For you understand this

supreme field of merit.

These ascetics will henceforth

receive our religious donation, too.

For there we will place our sacrifice,

and it shall be abundant."

"If you fear suffering,

if you don't like suffering,

go for refuge to the Buddha, the poised,

to his teaching and to the Sangha.

Undertake the precepts,

that will be good for you."

"I go for refuge to the Buddha, the poised,

to his teaching and to the Sangha.

I undertake the precepts,

that will be good for me.

In the past I was related to Brahma,

now I genuinely am a brahmin.

Possessing the three knowledges, I'm a genuine scholar,

I'm a knowledge-master, a bathed initiate."

13.3 Capa

"Once I carried a hermit's staff,

but these days I hunt deer.

My desires have made me unable to cross

from the awful marsh to the far shore.

Thinking me so in love with her,

Capa kept our son happy.

Having cut Capa's bond,

I'll go forth once again."

"Don't be mad at me, great hero!

Don't be mad at me, great sage!

If you're mired in anger you can't stay pure,

let alone practice austerities."

"I'm going to leave Nala!

For who'd stay here at Nala!

With their figures, the women trap

ascetics who live righteously."

"Please, Kaḷa, come back to me.

Enjoy pleasures like you did before.

I'll be under your control,

along with any relatives I have."

"Capa, if even a quarter

of what you say were true,

it would be a splendid thing

for a man in love with you!"

"Kaḷa, I am like a sprouting iris

flowering on a mountain top,

like a blossoming pomegranate,

like a trumpet-flower tree on an isle;

my limbs are anointed with yellow sandalwood,

and I wear the finest Kasi cloth:

when I am so very beautiful,

how can you abandon me and leave?"

"You're like a fowler

who wants to catch a bird;

but you won't trap me

with your captivating form."

"But this child, my fruit,

was begotten by you, Kaḷa.

When I have this child,

how can you abandon me and leave?"

"The wise give up

children, family, and wealth.

Great heroes go forth

like elephants breaking their bonds."

"Now, this son of yours:

I'll strike him to the ground right here,

with a stick or with a knife!

Grieving your son, you will not leave."

"Even if you feed our son

to jackals and dogs,

I'd never return again, you bitch,

not even for the child's sake."

"Well then, sir, tell me,

where will you go, Kaḷa?

To what village or town,

city or capital?"

"Last time we had followers,

we weren't ascetics, we just thought we were.

We wandered from village to village,

to cities and capitals.

But now the Blessed One, the Buddha,

on the bank of the Neranjara River,

teaches the Dhamma so that living creatures

may abandon all suffering.

I shall go to his presence,

he shall be my Teacher."

"Now please convey my respects

to the supreme protector of the world.

Circling him to your right,

dedicate my religious donation."

"This is the proper thing to do,

just as you have said to me.

I'll convey your respects

to the supreme protector of the world.

Circling him to my right,

I'll dedicate your religious donation."

Then Kaḷa set out

to the bank of the Neranjara River.

He saw the Awakened One

teaching the deathless state:

suffering, suffering's origin,

suffering's transcendence,

and the noble eightfold path

that leads to the stilling of suffering.

He paid homage at his feet,

circling him to his right,

and conveyed Capa's dedication;

then he went forth to homelessness.

He attained the three knowledges,

and fulfilled the Buddha's instructions.

13.4 Sundari

"Before, when your children passed away,

you would expose them to be eaten.

All day and all night

you'd be racked with despair.

Today, brahmin lady, you have exposed

seven children in all to be eaten;

Vasetthi, what is the reason why

you're not so filled with despair?"

"Many hundreds of sons,

hundreds of family circles,

both mine and yours, brahmin,

have been eaten in the past.

Having known the escape

from rebirth and death

I neither grieve nor lament,

nor do I despair."

"Wow, Vasetthi, the words you speak

really are amazing!

Whose teaching did you understand

that you say these things?"

"Brahmin, the Awakened One

at the city of Mithila,

teaches the Dhamma so that living creatures

may abandon all suffering.

After hearing the perfected one's teaching,

brahmin, which is free of all attachments,

having understood the true teaching there,

I've swept away grief for children."

"I too shall go

to the city of Mithila.

Hopefully the Buddha may release me

from all suffering."

The brahmin saw the Buddha,

liberated, without attachments.

He taught him the Dhamma,

the sage gone beyond suffering:

suffering, suffering's origin,

suffering's transcendence,

and the noble eightfold path

that leads to the stilling of suffering.

Having understood the true teaching there,

he agreed to go forth.

Three days later

Sujata realized the three knowledges.

"Please, charioteer, go;

take back this carriage.

Bidding my brahmin lady good health, say:

'The brahmin has now gone forth.

After three days,

Sujata realized the three knowledges.'"

Then taking the carriage,

along with a thousand coins, the charioteer

bade the brahmin lady good health, and said:

"The brahmin has now gone forth.

After three days,

Sujata realized the three knowledges."

Hearing that the brahmin had the three knowledges, the lady replied:

"I present to you this horse and carriage,

O charioteer, along with 1000 coins,

and a full bowl as a gift."

"Keep the horse and carriage, lady,

along with the thousand coins.

I too shall go forth in the presence of him,

this man of such splendid wisdom."

"Elephants, cattle, jewels and earrings,

such opulent domestic wealth:

having given it up, your father went forth,

enjoy these riches Sundari,

you are the family heir."

"Elephants, cattle, jewels and earrings,

such delightful domestic wealth:

having given it up, my father went forth,

racked by grief for his son.

I too shall go forth,

racked by grief for my brother."

"Sundari, may the wish you desire

come true.

Leftovers as gleanings,

and cast-off rags as robes—

make do with these,

free of defilements regarding the next life."

"Ma'am, while I am still a trainee nun,

my clairvoyance is clarified;

I know my past lives,

the places I used to live.

Relying on a fine lady like you,

a senior nun who beautifies the Sangha,

I've attained the three knowledges,

and fulfilled the Buddha's instructions.

Give me permission ma'am,

I wish to go to Savatthi,

where I shall roar my lion's roar

before the best of Buddhas."

"Sundari, see the Teacher!

Golden colored, golden skinned,

tamer of the untamed,

the Awakened One who fears nothing from any quarter."

"See Sundari coming,

liberated, without attachments;

desireless, detached,

her task completed, without defilements."

"Having set forth from Baranasi

and come to your presence, great hero,

your disciple Sundari

bows at your feet.

You are the Buddha, you are the Teacher,

I am your rightful daughter, brahmin,

born of your mouth.

I've completed the task and am free of defilements."

"Then welcome, good lady,

you're by no means unwelcome.

For this is how the tamed come

bowing at the Teacher's feet;

desireless, detached,

the task completed, without defilements."

13.5 Subha, the Smith's Daughter

"I was so young, my clothes so fresh,

at that time I heard the teaching.

Being diligent,

I comprehended the truth;

and then I became profoundly dispassionate

towards all sensual pleasures.

Seeing fear in identity,

I longed for renunciation.

Giving up my family circle,

bonded servants and workers,

and my flourishing villages and lands,

so delightful and pleasant,

I went forth;

all that is no small wealth.

Now that I've gone forth in faith like this,

in the true teaching so well proclaimed,

since I desire to have nothing,

it would not be appropriate

to take back gold and money,

having already got rid of them.

Money or gold

doesn't lead to peace and awakening.

It doesn't befit an ascetic,

it's not the wealth of the noble ones;

it's just greed and intoxication,

confusion and growing decadence,

dubious, troublesome—

there is nothing lasting there.

Depraved and heedless,

unenlightened folk, their hearts corrupt,

oppose each other,

creating disputes.

Killing, caging, misery,

loss, grief, and lamentation;

those sunk in sensual pleasures

see many disastrous things.

My family, why do you urge me on

to pleasures, as if you were my enemies?

You know I've gone forth,

seeing fear in sensual pleasures.

It's not due to gold, coined or uncoined,

that defilements come to an end.

Sensual pleasures are enemies and murderers,

hostile forces that bind you to thorns.

My family, why do you urge me on

to pleasures, as if you were my enemies?

You know I've gone forth,

shaven, wrapped in my outer robe.

Leftovers as gleanings,

and cast-off rags as robes—

that's what's fitting for me,

the essentials of the homeless life.

Great hermits expel sensual pleasures,

both human and divine.

Safe in their sanctuary, they are freed,

having found unshakable happiness.

May I not encounter sensual pleasures,

for no shelter is found in them.

Sensual pleasures are enemies and murderers,

as painful as a bonfire.

Greed is an obstacle, a threat,

full of anguish and thorns;

it is out of balance,

a great gateway to confusion.

Hazardous and terrifying,

sensual pleasures are like a snake's head,

where fools delight,

ordinary folk trapped in darkness.

Stuck in the mud of sensual pleasures,

there are so many ignorant in the world.

They know nothing of the end

of rebirth and death.

Because of sensual pleasures,

people jump right on to the path that goes to a bad place.

So many walk the path

that brings disease onto themselves.

That's how sensual pleasures create enemies;

they are so tormenting, so corrupting,

trapping beings with the world's material delights,

they are nothing less than the bonds of death.

Maddening, enticing,

sensual pleasures derange the mind.

They're a snare laid by Mara

for the corruption of beings.

Sensual pleasures are infinitely dangerous,

they're full of suffering, a terrible poison;

offering little gratification, they're makers of strife,

withering bright qualities away.

Since I've created so much ruination

because of sensual pleasures,

I will not relapse to them again,

but will always delight in quenching.

Fighting against sensual pleasures,

longing for that cool state,

I shall meditate diligently

for the ending of all fetters.

Sorrowless, stainless, secure:

I'll follow that path,

the straight noble eightfold way

by which the hermits have crossed over."

"Look at this: Subha the smith's daughter,

standing firm in the teaching.

She has entered the imperturbable state,

meditating at the root of a tree.

It's just eight days since she went forth,

full of faith in the beautiful teaching.

Guided by Uppalavanna,

she is master of the three knowledges, destroyer of death.

This one is freed from slavery and debt,

a nun with faculties developed.

Detached from all attachments,

she has completed the task and is free of defilements."

Thus did Sakka, lord of all creatures,

along with a host of gods,

having come by their psychic powers,

honor Subha, the smith's daughter.

The Book of the Twenties is finished.

# THE BOOK OF THE THIRTIES

14.1 Subha of Jivaka's Mango Grove

Going to the lovely mango grove

of Jivaka, the nun Subha

was held up by a rascal.

Subha said this to him:

"What harm have I done to you,

that you stand in my way?

Sir, it's not proper that a man

should touch a woman gone forth.

This training was taught by the Holy One,

it is a serious matter in my teacher's instructions.

I am pure and rid of blemishes,

so why do you stand in my way?

One whose mind is sullied against one unsullied;

one who is lustful against one free of lust;

unblemished, my mind is freed in every respect,

so why do you stand in my way?"

"You're young and flawless—

what will going-forth do for you?

Throw away the yellow robe,

come and play in the blossom grove.

Everywhere, the scent of pollen wafts sweet,

born of the flowering woods.

The start of spring is a happy time—

come and play in the blossom grove.

And trees crested with flowers

cry out, as it were, in the breeze.

But what kind of fun will you have

if you plunge into the woods all alone?

Frequented by packs of predators,

and she-elephants aroused by rutting bulls;

you wish to go without a friend

to the deserted, awe-inspiring forest.

Like a shining doll of gold,

like a nymph wandering in a park of colorful vines,

your matchless beauty will shine

in lovely clothes of exquisite muslin.

I'll be at your beck and call,

if we are to stay in the forest.

I love no creature more than you,

O pixie with such bashful eyes.

Were you to take up my invitation—

'Come, be happy, and live in a house'—

you'll stay in a longhouse sheltered from wind;

let the ladies look to your needs.

Dressed in exquisite muslin,

put on your garlands and your cosmetics.

I'll make all sorts of adornments for you,

of gold and gems and pearls.

Climb onto a costly bed,

its coverlet so clean and nice,

with a new woolen mattress,

so fragrant, sprinkled with sandalwood.

As a blue lily risen from the water

remains untouched by men,

so too, O chaste and holy lady,

your limbs grow old unshared."

"This carcass is full of carrion, it swells

the charnel ground, for its nature is to fall apart.

What do you think is so essential in it

that you stare at me so crazily?"

"Your eyes are like those of a doe,

or a pixie in the mountains;

seeing them,

my sensual desire grows all the more.

Set in your flawless face of golden sheen,

your eyes compare to a blue lily's bud;

seeing them,

my sensual excitement grows all the more.

Though you may wander far, I'll still think of you,

with your lashes so long, and your vision so clear.

I love no eyes more than yours,

O pixie with such bashful eyes."

"You're setting out on the wrong road!

You're looking to take the moon for your toy!

You're trying to leap over Mount Meru!

You, who are hunting a child of the Buddha!

For in this world with all its gods,

there will be no more lust anywhere in me.

I don't even know what kind it could be,

it's been smashed root and all by the path.

Cast out like sparks from fiery coals,

it's worth no more than a bowl of poison.

I don't even see what kind it could be,

it's been smashed root and all by the path.

Well may you try to seduce the type of lady

who has not reflected on these things,

or who has never attended the Teacher:

but *this* is a lady who knows—now you're in trouble!

No matter if I am abused or praised,

or feel pleasure or pain: I stay mindful.

Knowing that conditions are ugly,

my mind clings to nothing.

I am a disciple of the Holy One,

riding in the carriage of the eightfold path.

The dart pulled out, free of defilements,

I'm happy to have reached an empty place.

I've seen brightly painted

dolls and wooden puppets,

tied to sticks and strings,

and made to dance in many ways.

But when the sticks and strings are taken off—

loosed, disassembled, dismantled,

irrecoverable, stripped to parts—

on what could the mind be fixed?

That's what my body is really like,

without those things it can't go on.

This being so,

on what could the mind be fixed?

It's like when you see a mural on a wall,

painted with orpiment,

and your vision gets confused,

falsely perceiving that it is a person.

Though it's as worthless as a magic trick,

or a golden tree seen in a dream,

you blindly chase what is hollow,

like a puppet show among the people.

An eye is just a ball in a socket,

with a pupil in the middle, and tears,

and mucus comes from there as well,

and so different eye-parts are lumped all together."

The pretty lady ripped out her eye.

With no attachment in her mind at all, she said:

"Come now, take this eye,"

and gave it to the man right then.

And at that moment he lost his lust,

and asked for her forgiveness:

"May you be well, O chaste and holy lady;

such a thing will not happen again.

Attacking a person such as this

is like holding on to a blazing fire,

or grabbing a deadly viper!

May you be well, please forgive me."

When that nun was released

she went to the presence of the excellent Buddha.

Seeing the one with excellent marks of merit,

her eye became just as it was before.

The Book of the Thirties is finished.

# THE BOOK OF THE FORTIES

15.1 Isidasi

In Pataliputta, the cream of the world,

the city named for a flower,

there were two nuns from the Sakyan clan,

both of them ladies of quality.

One was named Isidasi, the second Bodhi.

They both were accomplished in ethics,

lovers of meditation and chanting,

learned, crushing corruptions.

They wandered for alms and had their meal.

When they had washed their bowls,

they sat happily in a private place

and started a conversation.

"You're so lovely, Venerable Isidasi,

your youth has not yet faded.

What problem did you see that made you

dedicate your life to renunciation?"

Being pressed like this in private,

Isidasi, skilled in teaching Dhamma,

voiced the following words.

"Bodhi, hear how I went forth.

In the fine town of Ujjeni,

my father was a financier, a good and moral man.

I was his only daughter,

dear, beloved, and cherished.

Then some suitors came for me

from the top family of Saketa.

They were sent by a financier abounding in wealth,

to whom my father then gave me as daughter-in-law.

Come morning and come night,

I bowed with my head to the feet

of my father and mother-in-law,

just as I had been told.

Whenever I saw my husband's sisters,

his brothers, his servants,

or even he, my one and only,

I nervously gave them a seat.

Whatever they wanted—food and drink,

treats, or whatever was in the cupboard—

I brought out and offered to them,

ensuring each got what was fitting.

Having risen bright and early,

I approached the main house,

washed my hands and feet,

and went to my husband with joined palms.

Taking a comb, adornments,

eyeshadow, and a mirror,

I myself did the makeup for my husband,

as if I were his beautician.

I myself cooked the rice;

I myself washed the pots.

I looked after my husband

like a mother her only child.

Thus I showed my devotion to him,

a loving, virtuous, and humble servant,

getting up early, and working tirelessly:

yet still my husband did me wrong.

He said to his mother and father:

"I'll take my leave and go,

I can't stand to live together with Isidasi

staying in the same house."

"Son, don't speak like this!

Isidasi is astute and competent,

she gets up early and works tirelessly,

son, why doesn't she please you?"

"She hasn't done anything to hurt me,

but I just can't stand to live with her.

As far as I'm concerned, she's just horrible.

I've had enough, I'll take my leave and go."

When they heard his words,

my father-in-law and mother-in-law asked me:

"What did you do wrong?

Tell us honestly, have no fear."

"I've done nothing wrong,

I haven't hurt him, or said anything bad.

What can I possibly do,

when my husband finds me so hateful?"

They led me back to my father's home,

distraught, overcome with suffering, and said:

"By caring for our son,

we've lost her, so lovely and lucky!"

Next my dad gave me to the household

of a second wealthy family-man.

For this he got half the bride-price

of that which the financier paid.

In his house I also lived a month,

before he too wanted me gone;

though I served him like a slave,

virtuous and doing no wrong.

My father then spoke to a beggar for alms,

a tamer of others and of himself:

"Be my son-in-law;

set aside your rags and bowl."

He stayed a fortnight before he said to my dad:

"Give me back my rag robes,

my bowl, and my cup—

I'll wander begging for alms again."

So then my mum and my dad

and my whole group of relatives said:

"What has not been done for you here?

Quickly, tell us what we can do for you!"

When they spoke to him like this he said,

"Even if you worship me, I've had enough.

I can't stand to live together with Isidasi

staying in the same house."

Released, he left.

But I sat by myself contemplating:

"Having taken my leave, I'll go,

either to die or to go forth."

But then the venerable lady Jinadatta,

learned and virtuous,

who had memorized the texts on monastic training,

came to my dad's house in search of alms.

When I saw her,

I got up from my seat and prepared it for her.

When she had taken her seat,

I honored her feet and offered her a meal,

satisfying her with food and drink,

treats, or whatever was in the cupboard.

Then I said:

"Ma'am, I wish to go forth!"

But my dad said to me:

"Child, practice Dhamma right here!

Satisfy ascetics and twice-born brahmins

with food and drink."

Then I said to my dad,

crying, my joined palms raised to him:

"I've done bad things in the past;

I shall wear that bad deed away."

And my dad said to me:

"May you attain awakening, the highest state,

and may you find the extinguishment

that was realized by the best of men!"

I bowed down to my mother and father,

and my whole group of relatives;

and then, seven days after going forth,

I realized the three knowledges.

I know my last seven lives;

I shall relate to you the deeds

of which this life is the fruit and result:

focus your whole mind on that.

In the city of Erakacca

I was a goldsmith with lots of money.

Drunk on the pride of youth,

I had sex with someone else's wife.

Having passed away from there,

I burned in hell for a long time.

Rising up from there

I was conceived in a monkey's womb.

When I was only seven days old,

I was castrated by the monkey chief.

This was the fruit of that deed,

because of adultery with another's wife.

Having passed away from there,

passing away in Sindhava grove,

I was conceived in the womb

of a lame, one-eyed she-goat.

I carried children on my back for twelve years,

and all the while I was castrated,

worm-eaten, and tail-less,

because of adultery with another's wife.

Having passed away from there,

I was reborn in a cow

owned by a cattle merchant.

A red calf, castrated, for twelve months

I drew a big plow.

I shouldered a cart,

blind, tail-less, feeble,

because of adultery with another's wife.

Having passed away from there,

I was born of a prostitute in the street,

neither woman nor man,

because of adultery with another's wife.

I died at thirty years of age,

and was reborn as a girl in a carter's family.

We were poor, of little wealth,

greatly oppressed by creditors.

Because of the huge interest we owed,

I was dragged away screaming,

taken by force from the family home

by a caravan leader.

When I was sixteen years old,

his son named Giridasa,

seeing that I was a girl of marriageable age,

took me as his wife.

He also had another wife,

a virtuous and well-known lady of quality,

faithful to her husband;

yet I stirred up resentment in her.

As the fruit of that deed,

they abandoned me and left,

though I served them like a slave.

Now I've made an end to this as well."

The Book of the Forties is finished.

# THE GREAT BOOK

16.1 Sumedha

In Mantavati city, Sumedha,

the daughter of King Konca's chief queen,

was converted by those

who practice the Buddha's teaching.

She was virtuous, a brilliant speaker,

learned, and trained in the Buddha's instructions.

She went up to her mother and father and said:

"Pay heed, both of you!

I delight in extinguishment!

No life is eternal, not even that of the gods;

what then of sensual pleasures, so hollow,

offering little gratification and much anguish.

Sensual pleasures are bitter as the venom of a snake,

yet fools are infatuated by them.

Sent to hell for a very long time,

they are beaten and tortured.

Those who grow in wickedness

always sorrow in the underworld due to their own bad deeds.

They're fools, unrestrained in body,

mind, and speech.

Those witless, senseless fools,

obstructed by the origin of suffering,

are ignorant, not understanding the noble truths

when they are being taught.

Most people, mum, ignorant of the truths

taught by the excellent Buddha,

look forward to the next life,

longing for rebirth among the gods.

Yet even rebirth among the gods

in an impermanent state is not eternal.

But fools are not scared

of being reborn time and again.

Four lower realms and two other realms

may be gained somehow or other.

But for those who end up in a lower realm,

there is no way to go forth in the hells.

May you both grant me permission to go forth

in the dispensation of him of the ten powers.

Living at ease, I shall apply myself

to giving up rebirth and death.

What's the point in hope, in a new life,

in this useless, hollow body?

Grant me permission, I shall go forth

to make an end of craving for a new life.

A Buddha has arisen, the time has come,

the unlucky moment has passed.

As long as I live I'll never betray

my ethical precepts or my celibate path."

Then Sumedha said to her parents:

"So long as I remain a lay person,

I'll refuse to eat any food,

until I've fallen under the sway of death."

Upset, her mother burst into tears,

while her father, though grieved,

tried his best to persuade her

as she lay collapsed on the longhouse roof.

"Get up child, why do you grieve so?

You're already betrothed to be married!

King Anikaratta the handsome

is in Varanavati: he is your betrothed.

You shall be the chief queen,

wife of King Anikaratta.

Ethical precepts, the celibate path—

going forth is hard to do, my child.

As a royal there is command, wealth, authority,

and the happiness of possessions.

Enjoy sensual pleasures while you're still young!

Let your wedding take place, my child!"

Then Sumedha said to him:

"Let this not come to pass! Existence is hollow!

I shall either go forth or die,

but I shall never marry.

Why cling to this rotting body so foul,

stinking of fluids,

a horrifying water-bag of corpses,

always oozing, full of filth?

Knowing it like I do, what's the point?

A carcass is vile, smeared with flesh and blood,

food for birds and swarms of worms—

why have we been given it?

Before long the body, bereft of consciousness,

is carried out to the charnel ground,

to be tossed aside like an old log

by relatives in disgust.

When they've tossed it away in the charnel ground,

to be eaten by others, your own parents

bathe themselves, disgusted;

what then of people at large?

They're attached to this hollow carcass,

this mass of sinews and bone;

this rotting body

full of saliva, tears, feces, and pus.

If anyone were to dissect it,

turning it inside out,

the intolerable stench

would disgust even their own mother.

Properly examining

the aggregates, elements, and sense fields

as conditioned, rooted in birth, suffering—

why would I wish for marriage?

Let three hundred sharp swords

fall on my body everyday!

Even if the slaughter lasted 100 years

it'd be worth it if it led to the end of suffering.

One who understands the Teacher's words

would put up with this slaughter:

'Long for you is transmigration

being killed time and time again.'

Among gods and humans,

in the realm of animals or that of demons,

among the ghosts or in the hells,

endless killings are seen.

The hells are full of killing,

for the corrupt who have fallen to the underworld.

Even among the gods there is no shelter,

for no happiness excels extinguishment.

Those who are committed to the dispensation

of him of the ten powers attain extinguishment.

Living at ease, they apply themselves

to giving up rebirth and death.

On this very day, dad, I shall renounce:

what's to enjoy in hollow riches?

I'm disillusioned with sensual pleasures,

they're like vomit, made like a palm stump."

As she spoke thus to her father,

Anikaratta, to whom she was betrothed,

approached from Varanavati

at the time appointed for the marriage.

Then Sumedha took up a knife,

and cut off her hair, so black, thick, and soft.

Shutting herself in the longhouse,

she entered the first absorption.

And as she entered it there,

Anikaratta arrived at the city.

Then in the longhouse, Sumedha

well developed the perception of impermanence.

As she investigated in meditation,

Anikaratta quickly climbed the stairs.

His limbs adorned with gems and gold,

he begged Sumedha with joined palms:

"As a royal there is command, wealth, authority,

and the happiness of possessions.

Enjoy sensual pleasures while you're still young!

Sensual pleasures are hard to find in the world!

I've handed royalty to you—

enjoy riches, give gifts!

Don't be sad;

your parents are upset."

Sumedha, having no use for sensual pleasures,

and having done away with delusion, spoke right back:

"Do not take pleasure in sensuality!

See the danger in sensual pleasures!

Mandhata, king of four continents,

foremost in enjoying sensual pleasures,

died unsated,

his desires unfulfilled.

Were the seven jewels to rain from the sky

all over the ten directions,

there would be no sating of sensual pleasures:

people die insatiable.

Like a butcher's knife and chopping block,

sensual pleasures are like a snake's head.

They burn like a fire-brand,

they resemble a skeleton.

Sensual pleasures are impermanent and unstable,

they're full of suffering, a terrible poison;

like a hot iron ball,

the root of misery, their fruit is pain.

Sensual pleasures are like fruits of a tree,

like lumps of meat, painful,

they trick you like a dream;

sensual pleasures are like borrowed goods.

Sensual pleasures are like swords and stakes;

a disease, a boil, misery and trouble.

Like a pit of glowing coals,

the root of misery, fear and slaughter.

Thus sensual pleasures have been explained

to be obstructions, so full of suffering.

Please leave! As for me,

I have no trust in a new life.

What can someone else do for me

when their own head is burning?

When stalked by old age and death,

you should strive to destroy them."

She opened the door

and saw her parents with Anikaratta,

sitting crying on the floor.

And so she said this:

"Transmigration is long for fools,

crying again and again at that with no known beginning—

the death of a father,

the killing of a brother or of themselves.

Remember the ocean of tears, of milk, of blood,

transmigration with no known beginning.

Remember the bones piled up

by beings transmigrating.

Remember the four oceans

compared with tears, milk, and blood;

Remember bones piled up high as Mount Vipula

in the course of a single eon.

Transmigration with no known beginning

is compared to this broad land of India;

if divided into lumps the size of jujube seeds,

they'd still be fewer than his mother's mothers.

Remember the grass, sticks, and leaves,

compare that with no known beginning:

if split into pieces four inches in size,

they'd still be fewer than his father's fathers.

Remember the one-eyed turtle and the yoke with a hole

blown in the ocean from east to west—

sticking the head in the hole

is a metaphor for gaining a human birth.

Remember the form of this unlucky body,

insubstantial as a lump of foam.

See the aggregates as impermanent,

remember the hells so full of anguish.

Remember those swelling the charnel grounds

again and again in life after life.

Remember the threat of the crocodile!

Remember the four truths!

When the deathless is there to be found,

why would you drink the five bitter poisons?

For every enjoyment of sensual pleasures

is so much more bitter than them.

When the deathless is there to be found,

why would you burn for sensual pleasures?

For every enjoyment of sensual pleasures

is burning, boiling, bubbling, seething.

When there is freedom from enmity,

why would you want your enemy, sensual pleasures?

Like kings, fire, robbers, flood, and people you dislike,

sensual pleasures are very much your enemy.

When liberation is there to be found,

what good are sensual pleasures that kill and bind?

For though unwilling, when sensual pleasures are there,

they are subject to the pain of killing and binding.

As a blazing grass torch

burns one who grasps it without letting go,

sensual pleasures are like a grass torch,

burning those who do not let go.

Don't give up abundant happiness

for the trivial joys of sensual pleasure.

Don't suffer hardship later,

like a catfish on a hook.

Deliberately control yourself among sensual pleasures!

You're like a dog fixed to a chain:

sensual pleasures will surely devour you

as hungry outcasts would a dog.

Harnessed to sensual pleasure,

you undergo endless pain,

along with much mental anguish:

relinquish sensual pleasures, they don't last!

When the unaging is there to be found,

what good are sensual pleasures in which is old age?

All rebirths everywhere

are bonded to death and sickness.

This is the ageless, this is the deathless!

This is the ageless and deathless, the sorrowless state!

Free of enmity, unconstricted,

faultless, fearless, without tribulations.

This deathless has been realized by many;

even today it can be obtained

by those who properly apply themselves;

but it's impossible if you don't try."

So said Sumedha,

lacking delight in conditioned things.

Soothing Anikaratta,

Sumedha cast her hair on the ground.

Standing up, Anikaratta

raised his joined palms to her father and begged:

"Let go of Sumedha, so that she may go forth!

She will see the truth of liberation."

Released by her mother and father,

she went forth, afraid of grief and fear.

While still a trainee nun she realized the six direct knowledges,

along with the highest fruit.

The extinguishment of the princess

was incredible and amazing;

on her deathbed, she declared

her several past lives.

"In the time of the Buddha Konagamana,

we three friends gave the gift

of a newly-built dwelling

in the Saṅgha's monastery.

Ten times, a hundred times,

a thousand times, ten thousand times,

we were reborn among the gods,

let alone among humans.

We were mighty among the gods,

let alone among humans!

I was queen to a king with the seven treasures—

I was the treasure of a wife.

That was the cause, that the origin, that the root,

that was the acceptance of the dispensation;

that first meeting culminated in extinguishment

for one delighting in the teaching.

So say those who have faith in the words

of the one unrivaled in wisdom.

They're disillusioned with being reborn,

and being disillusioned they become dispassionate."

It was thus that these verses were recited by the senior nun Sumedha.


The Verses of the Senior Nuns are finished.

# DIGHA NIKAYA

## SANGITI SUTTA – RECITING IN CONCERT

So I have heard. At one time the Buddha was wandering in the land of the Mallas together with a large Sangha of five hundred mendicants when he arrived at a Mallian town named Pava. There he stayed in Cunda the smith's mango grove.

Now at that time a new town hall named Ubbhataka had recently been constructed for the Mallas of Pava. It had not yet been occupied by an ascetic or brahmin or any person at all. The Mallas of Pava also heard that the Buddha had arrived and was staying in Cunda's mango grove. Then they went up to the Buddha, bowed, sat down to one side, and said to him: "Sir, a new town hall named Ubbhataka has recently been constructed for the Mallas of Pava. It has not yet been occupied by an ascetic or brahmin or any person at all. May the Buddha be the first to use it, and only then will the Mallas of Pava use it. That would be for the lasting welfare and happiness of the Mallas of Pava." The Buddha consented in silence.

Then, knowing that the Buddha had consented, the Mallas got up from their seat, bowed, and respectfully circled the Buddha, keeping him on their right. Then they went to the new town hall, where they spread carpets all over, prepared seats, set up a water jar, and placed a lamp. Then they went back to the Buddha, bowed, stood to one side, and told him of their preparations, saying: "Please, sir, come at your convenience."

Then the Buddha put on his outer robe and, taking his bowl and robe, went to the new town hall together with the Sangha of mendicants. Having washed his feet he entered the town hall and sat against the central column facing east. The Sangha of mendicants also washed their feet, entered the town hall, and sat against the west wall facing east, with the Buddha right in front of them. The Mallas of Pava also washed their feet, entered the town hall, and sat against the east wall facing west, with the Buddha right in front of them.

The Buddha spent most of the night educating, encouraging, firing up, and inspiring the Mallas with a Dhamma talk. Then he dismissed them: "The night is getting late, Vasetthas. Please go at your convenience."

"Yes, sir," replied the Mallas. They got up from their seat, bowed, and respectfully circled the Buddha, keeping him on their right, before leaving.

Soon after they left, the Buddha looked around the Sangha of monks, who were so very silent. He addressed Venerable Sariputta: "Sariputta, the Sangha of mendicants is rid of dullness and drowsiness. Give them some Dhamma talk as you feel inspired. My back is sore, I'll stretch it."

"Yes, sir," Sariputta replied.

And then the Buddha spread out his outer robe folded in four and laid down in the lion's posture — on the right side, placing one foot on top of the other — mindful and aware, and focused on the time of getting up.

Now at that time the Nigantha Nataputta had recently passed away at Pava. With his passing the Jain ascetics split, dividing into two factions, arguing, quarreling, and fighting, continually wounding each other with barbed words: "You don't understand this teaching and training. I understand this teaching and training. What, you understand this teaching and training? You're practicing wrong. I'm practicing right. I stay on topic, you don't. You said last what you should have said first. You said first what you should have said last. What you've thought so much about has been disproved. Your doctrine is refuted. Go on, save your doctrine! You're trapped; get yourself out of this — if you can!"

You'd think there was nothing but slaughter going on among the Jain ascetics. And the Nigantha Nataputta's white-clothed lay disciples were disillusioned, dismayed, and disappointed in the Jain ascetics. They were equally disappointed with a teaching and training so poorly explained and poorly propounded, not emancipating, not leading to peace, proclaimed by someone who is not a fully awakened Buddha, with broken monument and without a refuge.

Then Sariputta told the mendicants about these things. He went on to say: "That's what happens, reverends, when a teaching and training is poorly explained and poorly propounded, not emancipating, not leading to peace, proclaimed by someone who is not a fully awakened Buddha. But this teaching is well explained and well propounded to us by the Blessed One, emancipating, leading to peace, proclaimed by someone who is a fully awakened Buddha. You should all recite this in concert, without disputing, so that this spiritual path may last for a long time. That would be for the welfare and happiness of the people, for the benefit, welfare, and happiness of gods and humans.

And what is that teaching?

Ones

There are teachings grouped by one that have been rightly explained by the Blessed One, who knows and sees, the perfected one, the fully awakened Buddha. You should all recite these in concert, without disputing, so that this spiritual path may last for a long time. That would be for the welfare and happiness of the people, for the benefit, welfare, and happiness of gods and humans. What are the teachings grouped by one?

'All sentient beings are sustained by food.'

'All sentient beings are sustained by conditions.'

These are the teachings grouped by one that have been rightly explained by the Blessed One, who knows and sees, the perfected one, the fully awakened Buddha.

You should all recite these in concert, without disputing, so that this spiritual path may last for a long time. That would be for the welfare and happiness of the people, for the benefit, welfare, and happiness of gods and humans.

Twos

There are teachings grouped by two that have been rightly explained by the Buddha. You should all recite these in concert. What are the teachings grouped by two?

Name and form.

Ignorance and craving for continued existence.

Views favoring continued existence and views favoring ending existence.

Lack of conscience and prudence.

Conscience and prudence.

Being hard to admonish and having bad friends.

Being easy to admonish and having good friends.

Skill in offenses and skill in rehabilitation from offenses.

Skill in meditative attainments and skill in emerging from those attainments.

Skill in the elements and skill in attention.

Skill in the sense fields and skill in dependent origination.

Skill in what is possible and skill in what is impossible.

Integrity and scrupulousness.

Patience and gentleness.

Friendliness and hospitality.

Harmlessness and purity.

Lack of mindfulness and lack of situational awareness.

Mindfulness and situational awareness.

Not guarding the sense doors and eating too much.

Guarding the sense doors and moderation in eating.

The power of reflection and the power of development.

The power of mindfulness and the power of immersion.

Serenity and discernment.

The foundation of serenity and the foundation of exertion.

Exertion, and not being distracted.

Failure in ethics and failure in view.

Accomplishment in ethics and accomplishment in view.

Purification of ethics and purification of view.

Purification of view and making an effort in line with that view.

Inspiration, and making a suitable effort when inspired by inspiring places.

To never be content with skillful qualities, and to never stop trying.

Knowledge and freedom.

Knowledge of ending and knowledge of non-arising.

These are the teachings grouped by two that have been rightly explained by the Buddha. You should all recite these in concert.

Threes

There are teachings grouped by three that have been rightly explained by the Buddha. You should all recite these in concert. What are the teachings grouped by three?

Three unskillful roots: greed, hate, and delusion.

Three skillful roots: non-greed, non-hate, and non-delusion.

Three ways of performing bad conduct: by body, speech, and mind.

Three ways of performing good conduct: by body, speech, and mind.

Three unskillful thoughts: sensuality, malice, and cruelty.

Three skillful thoughts: renunciation, good will, and harmlessness.

Three unskillful intentions: sensuality, malice, and cruelty.

Three skillful intentions: renunciation, good will, and harmlessness.

Three unskillful perceptions: sensuality, malice, and cruelty.

Three skillful perceptions: renunciation, good will, and harmlessness.

Three unskillful elements: sensuality, malice, and cruelty.

Three skillful elements: renunciation, good will, and harmlessness.

Another three elements: sensuality, form, and formlessness.

Another three elements: form, formlessness, and cessation.

Another three elements: lower, middle, and higher.

Three cravings: for sensual pleasures, to continue existence, and to end existence.

Another three cravings: sensuality, form, and formlessness.

Another three cravings: form, formlessness, and cessation.

Three fetters: identity view, doubt, and misapprehension of precepts and observances.

Three defilements: sensuality, desire for continued existence, and ignorance.

Three realms of existence: sensual, form, and formless.

Three searches: for sensual pleasures, for continued existence, and for a spiritual path.

Three kinds of discrimination: 'I'm better', 'I'm equal', and 'I'm worse'.

Three periods: past, future, and present.

Three extremes: identity, the origin of identity, and the cessation of identity.

Three feelings: pleasure, pain, and neutral.

Three forms of suffering: the suffering inherent in painful feeling, the suffering inherent in conditions, and the suffering inherent in perishing.

Three heaps: inevitability regarding the wrong way, inevitability regarding the right way, and lack of inevitability.

Three darknesses: one is doubtful, uncertain, undecided, and lacking confidence about the past, future, and present.

Three things a Realized One need not hide. The Realized One's behavior by way of body, speech, and mind is pure. He has no misconduct in these three ways that need be hidden, thinking: 'May others not know this of me.'

Three possessions: greed, hate, and delusion.

Three fires: greed, hate, and delusion.

Another three fires: a fire for those worthy of offerings dedicated to the gods, a fire for householders, and a fire for those worthy of a religious donation.

A threefold classification of the physical: visible and resistant, invisible and resistant, and invisible and non-resistant.

Three choices: good choices, bad choices, and imperturbable choices.

Three individuals: a trainee, an adept, and one who is neither a trainee nor an adept.

Three seniors: a senior by birth, a senior in the teaching, and a senior by convention.

Three grounds for making merit: giving, ethical conduct, and meditation.

Three grounds for accusations: what is seen, heard, and suspected.

Three kinds of sensual rebirth. There are sentient beings who desire what is present. They fall under the sway of presently arisen sensual pleasures. Namely, humans, some gods, and some beings in the underworld. This is the first kind of sensual rebirth. There are sentient beings who desire to create. Having repeatedly created, they fall under the sway of sensual pleasures. Namely, the Gods Who Love to Create. This is the second kind of sensual rebirth. There are sentient beings who desire what is created by others. They fall under the sway of sensual pleasures created by others. Namely, the Gods Who Control the Creations of Others. This is the third kind of sensual rebirth.

Three kinds of pleasant rebirth. There are sentient beings who, having repeatedly given rise to it, dwell in pleasure. Namely, the gods of Brahma's Host. This is the first pleasant rebirth. There are sentient beings who are drenched, steeped, filled, and soaked with pleasure. Every so often they feel inspired to exclaim: 'Oh, what bliss! Oh, what bliss!' Namely, the gods of streaming radiance. This is the second pleasant rebirth. There are sentient beings who are drenched, steeped, filled, and soaked with pleasure. Since they're truly content, they experience pleasure. Namely, the gods replete with glory. This is the third pleasant rebirth.

Three kinds of wisdom: the wisdom of a trainee, the wisdom of an adept, and the wisdom of one who is neither a trainee nor an adept.

Another three kinds of wisdom: wisdom produced by thought, learning, and meditation.

Three weapons: learning, seclusion, and wisdom.

Three faculties: the faculty of understanding that one's enlightenment is imminent, the faculty of enlightenment, and the faculty of one who is enlightened.

Three eyes: the eye of the flesh, the eye of clairvoyance, and the eye of wisdom.

Three trainings: in higher ethics, higher mind, and higher wisdom.

Three kinds of development: the development of physical endurance, the development of the mind, and the development of wisdom.

Three unsurpassable things: unsurpassable seeing, practice, and freedom.

Three kinds of immersion. Immersion with placing the mind and keeping it connected. Immersion without placing the mind, but just keeping it connected. Immersion without placing the mind or keeping it connected.

Another three kinds of immersion: emptiness, signless, and undirected.

Three purities: purity of body, speech, and mind.

Three kinds of sagacity: sagacity of body, speech, and mind.

Three skills: skill in progress, skill in regress, and skill in means.

Three vanities: the vanity of health, the vanity of youth, and the vanity of life.

Three ways of putting something in charge: putting oneself, the world, or the teaching in charge.

Three topics of discussion. You might discuss the past: 'That is how it was in the past.' You might discuss the future: 'That is how it will be in the future.' Or you might discuss the present: 'This is how it is at present.'

Three knowledges: recollection of past lives, knowledge of the death and rebirth of sentient beings, and knowledge of the ending of defilements.

Three meditative abidings: the meditation of the gods, the meditation of Brahma, and the meditation of the noble ones.

Three demonstrations: a demonstration of psychic power, a demonstration of revealing, and an instructional demonstration.

These are the teachings grouped by three that have been rightly explained by the Buddha. You should all recite these in concert.

Fours

There are teachings grouped by four that have been rightly explained by the Buddha. You should all recite these in concert. What are the teachings grouped by four?

Four kinds of mindfulness meditation. It's when a mendicant meditates by observing an aspect of the body — keen, aware, and mindful, rid of desire and aversion for the world. They meditate observing an aspect of feelings … mind … principles — keen, aware, and mindful, rid of desire and aversion for the world.

Four right efforts. A mendicant generates enthusiasm, tries, makes an effort, exerts the mind, and strives so that bad, unskillful qualities don't arise. They generate enthusiasm, try, make an effort, exert the mind, and strive so that bad, unskillful qualities that have arisen are given up. They generate enthusiasm, try, make an effort, exert the mind, and strive so that skillful qualities arise. They generate enthusiasm, try, make an effort, exert the mind, and strive so that skillful qualities that have arisen remain, are not lost, but increase, mature, and are completed by development.

Four bases of psychic power. A mendicant develops the basis of psychic power that has immersion due to enthusiasm, and active effort. They develop the basis of psychic power that has immersion due to mental development, and active effort. They develop the basis of psychic power that has immersion due to energy, and active effort. They develop the basis of psychic power that has immersion due to inquiry, and active effort.

Four absorptions. A mendicant, quite secluded from sensual pleasures, secluded from unskillful qualities, enters and remains in the first absorption, which has the rapture and bliss born of seclusion, while placing the mind and keeping it connected. As the placing of the mind and keeping it connected are stilled, they enter and remain in the second absorption, which has the rapture and bliss born of immersion, with internal clarity and confidence, and unified mind, without placing the mind and keeping it connected. And with the fading away of rapture, they enter and remain in the third absorption, where they meditate with equanimity, mindful and aware, personally experiencing the bliss of which the noble ones declare, 'Equanimous and mindful, one meditates in bliss.' Giving up pleasure and pain, and ending former happiness and sadness, they enter and remain in the fourth absorption, without pleasure or pain, with pure equanimity and mindfulness.

Four ways of developing immersion further. There is a way of developing immersion further that leads to blissful meditation in the present life. There is a way of developing immersion further that leads to gaining knowledge and vision. There is a way of developing immersion further that leads to mindfulness and awareness. There is a way of developing immersion further that leads to the ending of defilements.

And what is the way of developing immersion further that leads to blissful meditation in the present life? It's when a mendicant, quite secluded from sensual pleasures, secluded from unskillful qualities, enters and remains in the first absorption ... second absorption ... fourth absorption. This is the way of developing immersion further that leads to blissful meditation in the present life.

And what is the way of developing immersion further that leads to gaining knowledge and vision? A mendicant focuses on the perception of light, concentrating on the perception of day regardless of whether it is night or day. And so, with an open and unenveloped heart, they develop a mind that's full of radiance. This is the way of developing immersion further that leads to gaining knowledge and vision.

And what is the way of developing immersion further that leads to mindfulness and awareness? A mendicant knows feelings as they arise, as they remain, and as they go away. They know perceptions as they arise, as they remain, and as they go away. They know thoughts as they arise, as they remain, and as they go away. This is the way of developing immersion further that leads to mindfulness and awareness.

And what is the way of developing immersion further that leads to the ending of defilements? A mendicant meditates observing rise and fall in the five grasping aggregates. 'Such is form, such is the origin of form, such is the ending of form. Such are feelings … perceptions … choices … consciousness, such is the origin of consciousness, such is the ending of consciousness.' This is the way of developing immersion further that leads to the ending of defilements.

Four immeasurables. A mendicant meditates spreading a heart full of love to one direction, and to the second, and to the third, and to the fourth. In the same way above, below, across, everywhere, all around, they spread a heart full of love to the whole world — abundant, expansive, limitless, free of enmity and ill will. They meditate spreading a heart full of compassion … rejoicing … equanimity to one direction, and to the second, and to the third, and to the fourth. In the same way above, below, across, everywhere, all around, they spread a heart full of equanimity to the whole world — abundant, expansive, limitless, free of enmity and ill will.

Four formless states. A mendicant, going totally beyond perceptions of form, with the ending of perceptions of impingement, not focusing on perceptions of diversity, aware that 'space is infinite', enters and remains in the dimension of infinite space. Going totally beyond the dimension of infinite space, aware that 'consciousness is infinite', they enter and remain in the dimension of infinite consciousness. Going totally beyond the dimension of infinite consciousness, aware that 'there is nothing at all', they enter and remain in the dimension of nothingness. Going totally beyond the dimension of nothingness, they enter and remain in the dimension of neither perception nor non-perception.

Four supports. After reflection, a mendicant uses some things, endures some things, avoids some things, and gets rid of some things.

Four noble traditions. A mendicant is content with any kind of robe, and praises such contentment. They don't try to get hold of a robe in an improper way. They don't get upset if they don't get a robe. And if they do get a robe, they use it untied, uninfatuated, unattached, seeing the drawback, and understanding the escape. And on account of that they don't glorify themselves or put others down. A mendicant who is deft, tireless, aware, and mindful in this is said to stand in the ancient, original noble tradition.

Furthermore, a mendicant is content with any kind of alms-food …

Furthermore, a mendicant is content with any kind of lodgings …

Furthermore, a mendicant enjoys giving up and loves to give up. They enjoy meditation and love to meditate. But they don't glorify themselves or put down others on account of their love for giving up and meditation. A mendicant who is deft, tireless, aware, and mindful in this is said to stand in the ancient, original noble tradition.

Four efforts. The efforts to restrain, to give up, to develop, and to preserve. And what is the effort to restrain?

When a mendicant sees a sight with their eyes, they don't get caught up in the features and details. If the faculty of sight were left unrestrained, bad unskillful qualities of desire and aversion would become overwhelming. For this reason, they practice restraint, protecting the faculty of sight, and achieving its restraint. When they hear a sound with their ears … When they smell an odor with their nose … When they taste a flavor with their tongue … When they feel a touch with their body … When they know a thought with their mind, they don't get caught up in the features and details. If the faculty of mind were left unrestrained, bad unskillful qualities of desire and aversion would become overwhelming. For this reason, they practice restraint, protecting the faculty of mind, and achieving its restraint. This is called the effort to restrain.

And what is the effort to give up? It's when a mendicant doesn't tolerate a sensual, malicious, or cruel thought that has arisen, but gives it up, gets rid of it, eliminates it, and exterminates it. They don't tolerate any bad, unskillful qualities that have arisen, but give them up, get rid of them, eliminate them, and obliterate them. This is called the effort to give up.

And what is the effort to develop? It's when a mendicant develops the awakening factors of mindfulness, investigation of principles, energy, rapture, tranquility, immersion, and equanimity, which rely on seclusion, fading away, and cessation, and ripen as letting go. This is called the effort to develop.

And what is the effort to preserve? It's when a mendicant preserves a meditation subject that's a fine foundation of immersion: the perception of a skeleton, a worm-infested corpse, a livid corpse, a split open corpse, or a bloated corpse. This is called the effort to preserve.

Four knowledges: knowledge of the present phenomena, inferential knowledge, knowledge of others' minds, and conventional knowledge.

Another four knowledges: knowing about suffering, the origin of suffering, the cessation of suffering, and the practice that leads to the cessation of suffering.

Four factors of stream-entry: associating with good people, listening to the true teaching, proper attention, and practicing in line with the teaching.

Four factors of a stream-enterer. A noble disciple has experiential confidence in the Buddha: 'That Blessed One is perfected, a fully awakened Buddha, accomplished in knowledge and conduct, holy, knower of the world, supreme guide for those who wish to train, teacher of gods and humans, awakened, blessed.' They have experiential confidence in the teaching: 'The teaching is well explained by the Buddha — visible in this very life, immediately effective, inviting inspection, relevant, so that sensible people can know it for themselves.' They have experiential confidence in the Sangha: 'The Sangha of the Buddha's disciples is practicing the way that's good, straightforward, methodical, and proper. It consists of the four pairs, the eight individuals. This is the Sangha of the Buddha's disciples that is worthy of offerings dedicated to the gods, worthy of hospitality, worthy of a religious donation, worthy of greeting with joined palms, and is the supreme field of merit for the world.' And a noble disciple's ethical conduct is loved by the noble ones, unbroken, impeccable, spotless, and unmarred, liberating, praised by sensible people, not mistaken, and leading to immersion.

Four fruits of the ascetic life: stream-entry, once-return, non-return, and perfection.

Four elements: earth, water, fire, and air.

Four foods: solid food, whether coarse or fine; contact is the second, mental intention the third, and consciousness the fourth.

Four bases for consciousness to remain. As long as consciousness remains, it remains involved with form, supported by form, founded on form. And with a sprinkle of relishing, it grows, increases, and matures. Or consciousness remains involved with feeling … Or consciousness remains involved with perception … Or as long as consciousness remains, it remains involved with choices, supported by choices, grounded on choices. And with a sprinkle of relishing, it grows, increases, and matures.

Four prejudices: making decisions prejudiced by favoritism, hostility, stupidity, and cowardice.

Four things that give rise to craving. Craving arises in a mendicant for the sake of robes, alms-food, lodgings, or rebirth in this or that state.

Four ways of practice: painful practice with slow insight, painful practice with swift insight, pleasant practice with slow insight, and pleasant practice with swift insight.

Another four ways of practice: impatient practice, patient practice, taming practice, and calming practice.

Four basic principles: contentment, good will, right mindfulness, and right immersion.

Four ways of taking up practices. There is a way of taking up practices that is painful now and results in future pain. There is a way of taking up practices that is painful now but results in future pleasure. There is a way of taking up practices that is pleasant now but results in future pain. There is a way of taking up practices that is pleasant now and results in future pleasure.

Four spectrums of the teaching: ethics, immersion, wisdom, and freedom.

Four powers: energy, mindfulness, immersion, and wisdom.

Four foundations: the foundations of wisdom, truth, generosity, and peace.

Four ways of answering questions. There is a question that should be answered definitively. There is a question that should be answered analytically. There is a question that should be answered with a counter-question. There is a question that should be set aside.

Four deeds. There are deeds that are dark with dark result. There are deeds that are bright with bright result. There are deeds that are dark and bright with dark and bright result. There are neither dark nor bright deeds with neither dark nor bright results, which lead to the end of deeds.

Four things to be realized. Past lives are to be realized through recollection. The passing away and rebirth of sentient beings is to be realized through vision. The eight liberations are to be realized through direct meditative experience. The ending of defilements is to be realized through wisdom.

Four floods: sensuality, desire for rebirth, views, and ignorance.

Four bonds: sensuality, desire for rebirth, views, and ignorance.

Four detachments: detachment from the bonds of sensuality, desire for rebirth, views, and ignorance.

Four ties: the personal ties to covetousness, ill will, misapprehension of precepts and observances, and the insistence that this is the only truth.

Four kinds of grasping: grasping at sensual pleasures, views, precepts and observances, and theories of a self.

Four kinds of reproduction: reproduction for creatures born from an egg, from a womb, from moisture, or spontaneously.

Four kinds of conception. Someone is unaware when conceived in their mother's womb, unaware as they remain there, and unaware as they emerge. This is the first kind of conception. Furthermore, someone is aware when conceived in their mother's womb, but unaware as they remain there, and unaware as they emerge. This is the second kind of conception. Furthermore, someone is aware when conceived in their mother's womb, aware as they remain there, but unaware as they emerge. This is the third kind of conception. Furthermore, someone is aware when conceived in their mother's womb, aware as they remain there, and aware as they emerge. This is the fourth kind of conception.

Four kinds of reincarnation. There is a reincarnation where only one's own intention is effective, not that of others. There is a reincarnation where only the intention of others is effective, not one's own. There is a reincarnation where both one's own and others' intentions are effective. There is a reincarnation where neither one's own nor others' intentions are effective.

Four ways of purifying a religious donation. There's a religious donation that's purified by the giver, not the recipient. There's a religious donation that's purified by the recipient, not the giver. There's a religious donation that's purified by neither the giver nor the recipient. There's a religious donation that's purified by both the giver and the recipient.

Four ways of being inclusive: giving, kindly words, taking care, and equality.

Four ignoble expressions: speech that's false, divisive, harsh, or nonsensical.

Four noble expressions: refraining from speech that's false, divisive, harsh, or nonsensical.

Another four ignoble expressions: saying you've seen, heard, thought, or known something, but you haven't.

Another four noble expressions: saying you haven't seen, heard, thought, or known something, and you haven't.

Another four ignoble expressions: saying you haven't seen, heard, thought, or known something, and you have.

Another four noble expressions: saying you've seen, heard, thought, or known something, and you have.

Four persons. One person mortifies themselves, committed to the practice of mortifying themselves. One person mortifies others, committed to the practice of mortifying others. One person mortifies themselves and others, committed to the practice of mortifying themselves and others. One person doesn't mortify either themselves or others, committed to the practice of not mortifying themselves or others. They live without wishes in the present life, extinguished, cooled, experiencing bliss, having become holy in themselves.

Another four persons. One person practices to benefit themselves, but not others. One person practices to benefit others, but not themselves. One person practices to benefit neither themselves nor others. One person practices to benefit both themselves and others.

Another four persons: the dark bound for darkness, the dark bound for light, the light bound for darkness, and the light bound for light.

Another four persons: the confirmed ascetic, the white lotus ascetic, the pink lotus ascetic, and the exquisite ascetic of ascetics.

These are the teachings grouped by four that have been rightly explained by the Buddha. You should all recite these in concert.

The first recitation section is finished.

Fives

There are teachings grouped by five that have been rightly explained by the Buddha. You should all recite these in concert. What are the teachings grouped by five?

Five aggregates: form, feeling, perception, choices, and consciousness.

Five grasping aggregates: form, feeling, perception, choices, and consciousness.

Five kinds of sensual stimulation. Sights known by the eye that are likable, desirable, agreeable, pleasant, sensual, and arousing. Sounds known by the ear

… Smells known by the nose … Tastes known by the tongue … Touches known by the body that are likable, desirable, agreeable, pleasant, sensual, and arousing.

Five destinations: hell, the animal realm, the ghost realm, humanity, and the gods.

Five kinds of stinginess: stinginess with dwellings, families, material possessions, praise, and the teachings.

Five hindrances: sensual desire, ill will, dullness and drowsiness, restlessness and remorse, and doubt.

Five lower fetters: identity view, doubt, misapprehension of precepts and observances, sensual desire, and ill will.

Five higher fetters: desire for rebirth in the realm of luminous form, desire for rebirth in the formless realm, conceit, restlessness, and ignorance.

Five precepts: refraining from killing living creatures, stealing, sexual misconduct, lying, and drinking alcohol, which is a basis for negligence.

Five things that can't be done. A mendicant with defilements ended can't deliberately take the life of a living creature, take something with the intention to steal, have sex, tell a deliberate lie, or store up goods for their own enjoyment like they did as a lay person.

Five losses: loss of relatives, wealth, health, ethics, and view. It is not because of loss of relatives, wealth, or health that sentient beings, when their body breaks up, after death, are reborn in a place of loss, a bad place, the underworld, hell. It is because of loss of ethics or view that sentient beings, when their body breaks up, after death, are reborn in a place of loss, a bad place, the underworld, hell.

Five endowments: endowment with relatives, wealth, health, ethics, and view. It is not because of endowment with family, wealth, or health that sentient beings, when their body breaks up, after death, are reborn in a good place, a heavenly realm. It is because of endowment with ethics or view that sentient beings, when their body breaks up, after death, are reborn in a good place, a heavenly realm.

Five drawbacks for an unethical person because of their failure in ethics. Firstly, an unethical person loses substantial wealth on account of negligence. This is the first drawback. Furthermore, an unethical person gets a bad reputation. This is the second drawback. Furthermore, an unethical person enters any kind of assembly timid and embarrassed, whether it's an assembly of aristocrats, brahmins, householders, or ascetics. This is the third drawback. Furthermore, an unethical person dies feeling lost. This is the fourth drawback. Furthermore, an unethical person, when their body breaks up, after death, is reborn in a place of loss, a bad place, the underworld, hell. This is the fifth drawback.

Five benefits for an ethical person because of their accomplishment in ethics. Firstly, an ethical person gains substantial wealth on account of diligence. This is the first benefit. Furthermore, an ethical person gets a good reputation. This is the second benefit. Furthermore, an ethical person enters any kind of assembly bold and self-assured, whether it's an assembly of aristocrats, brahmins, householders, or ascetics. This is the third benefit. Furthermore, an ethical person dies not feeling lost. This is the fourth benefit. Furthermore, when an ethical person's body breaks up, after death, they're reborn in a good place, a heavenly realm. This is the fifth benefit.

A mendicant who wants to accuse another should first establish five things in themselves. I will speak at the right time, not at the wrong time. I will speak truthfully, not falsely. I will speak gently, not harshly. I will speak beneficially, not harmfully. I will speak lovingly, not from secret hate. A mendicant who wants to accuse another should first establish these five things in themselves.

Five factors that support meditation. A mendicant has faith in the Realized One's awakening: 'That Blessed One is perfected, a fully awakened Buddha, accomplished in knowledge and conduct, holy, knower of the world, supreme guide for those who wish to train, teacher of gods and humans, awakened, blessed.'

They are rarely ill or unwell. Their stomach digests well, being neither too hot nor too cold, but just right, and fit for meditation.

They're not devious or deceitful. They reveal themselves honestly to the Teacher or sensible spiritual companions.

They live with energy roused up for giving up unskillful qualities and embracing skillful qualities. They're strong, staunchly vigorous, not slacking off when it comes to developing skillful qualities.

They're wise. They have the wisdom of arising and passing away which is noble, penetrative, and leads to the complete ending of suffering.

Five pure abodes: Aviha, Atappa, the Gods Fair to See, the Fair Seeing Gods, and Akanittha.

Five non-returners: one who is extinguished between one life and the next, one who is extinguished upon landing, one who is extinguished without extra effort, one who is extinguished with extra effort, and one who heads upstream, going to the Akanittha realm.

Five kinds of emotional barrenness. Firstly, a mendicant has doubts about the Teacher. They're uncertain, undecided, and lacking confidence. This being so, their mind doesn't incline toward keenness, commitment, persistence, and striving. This is the first kind of emotional barrenness. Furthermore, a mendicant has doubts about the teaching ... the Sangha ... the training ... A mendicant is angry and upset with their spiritual companions, resentful and closed off. This being so, their mind doesn't incline toward keenness, commitment, persistence, and striving. This is the fifth kind of emotional barrenness.

Five emotional shackles. Firstly, a mendicant isn't free of greed, desire, fondness, thirst, passion, and craving for sensual pleasures. This being so, their mind doesn't incline toward keenness, commitment, persistence, and striving. This is the first emotional shackle. Furthermore, a mendicant isn't free of greed for the body ... They're not free of greed for form ... They eat as much as they like until their bellies are full, then indulge in the pleasures of sleeping, lying, and drowsing ... They live the spiritual life hoping to be reborn in one of the orders of gods, thinking: 'By this precept or observance or mortification or spiritual life, may I become one of the gods!' This being so, their mind doesn't incline toward keenness, commitment, persistence, and striving. This is the fifth emotional shackle.

Five faculties: eye, ear, nose, tongue, and body.

Another five faculties: pleasure, pain, happiness, sadness, and equanimity.

Another five faculties: faith, energy, mindfulness, immersion, and wisdom.

Five elements of escape. Take a case where a mendicant focuses on sensual pleasures, but their mind isn't eager, confident, settled, and decided about them. But when they focus on renunciation, their mind is eager, confident, settled, and decided about it. Their mind is in a good state, well developed, well risen, well freed, and well detached from sensual pleasures. They're freed from the distressing and feverish defilements that arise because of sensual pleasures, so they don't experience that kind of feeling. This is how the escape from sensual pleasures is explained.

Take another case where a mendicant focuses on ill will, but their mind isn't eager ... But when they focus on good will, their mind is eager ... Their mind is in a good state ... well detached from ill will. They're freed from the distressing and feverish defilements that arise because of ill will, so they don't experience that kind of feeling. This is how the escape from ill will is explained.

Take another case where a mendicant focuses on harming, but their mind isn't eager ... But when they focus on compassion, their mind is eager ... Their mind is in a good state ... well detached from harming. They're freed from the distressing and feverish defilements that arise because of harming, so they don't experience that kind of feeling. This is how the escape from harming is explained.

Take another case where a mendicant focuses on form, but their mind isn't eager ... But when they focus on the formless, their mind is eager ... Their mind is in a good state ... well detached from forms. They're freed from the distressing and feverish defilements that arise because of form, so they don't experience that kind of feeling. This is how the escape from forms is explained.

Take a case where a mendicant focuses on identity, but their mind isn't eager, confident, settled, and decided about it. But when they focus on the ending of identity, their mind is eager, confident, settled, and decided about it. Their mind is in a good state, well developed, well risen, well freed, and well detached from identity. They're freed from the distressing and feverish defilements that arise because of identity, so they don't experience that kind of feeling. This is how the escape from identity is explained.

Five opportunities for freedom. Firstly, the Teacher or a respected spiritual companion teaches Dhamma to a mendicant. That mendicant feels inspired by the meaning and the teaching in that Dhamma, no matter how the Teacher or a respected spiritual companion teaches it. Feeling inspired, joy springs up. Being joyful, rapture springs up. When the mind is full of rapture, the body becomes tranquil. When the body is tranquil, one feels bliss. And when blissful, the mind becomes immersed. This is the first opportunity for freedom.

Furthermore, it may be that neither the Teacher nor a respected spiritual companion teaches Dhamma to a mendicant. But the mendicant teaches Dhamma in detail to others as they learned and memorized it. … Or the mendicant recites the teaching in detail as they learned and memorized it. … Or the mendicant thinks about and considers the teaching in their heart, examining it with the mind as they learned and memorized it. … Or a meditation subject as a foundation of immersion is properly grasped, attended, borne in mind, and comprehended with wisdom. That mendicant feels inspired by the meaning and the teaching in that Dhamma, no matter how a meditation subject as a foundation of immersion is properly grasped, attended, borne in mind, and comprehended with wisdom. Feeling inspired, joy springs up. Being joyful, rapture springs up. When the mind is full of rapture, the body becomes tranquil. When the body is tranquil, one feels bliss. And when blissful, the mind becomes immersed. This is the fifth opportunity for freedom.

Five perceptions that ripen in freedom: the perception of impermanence, the perception of suffering in impermanence, the perception of not-self in suffering, the perception of giving up, and the perception of fading away.

These are the teachings grouped by five that have been rightly explained by the Buddha. You should all recite these in concert.

Sixes

There are teachings grouped by six that have been rightly explained by the Buddha. You should all recite these in concert. What are the teachings grouped by six?

Six interior sense fields: eye, ear, nose, tongue, body, and mind.

Six exterior sense fields: sights, sounds, smells, tastes, touches, and thoughts.

Six classes of consciousness: eye, ear, nose, tongue, body, and mind consciousness.

Six classes of contact: contact through the eye, ear, nose, tongue, body, and mind.

Six classes of feeling: feeling born of contact through the eye, ear, nose, tongue, body, and mind.

Six classes of perception: perceptions of sights, sounds, smells, tastes, touches, and thoughts.

Six bodies of intention: intention regarding sights, sounds, smells, tastes, touches, and thoughts.

Six classes of craving: craving for sights, sounds, smells, tastes, touches, and thoughts.

Six kinds of disrespect. A mendicant lacks respect and reverence for the Teacher, the teaching, and the Sangha, the training, diligence, and hospitality.

Six kinds of respect. A mendicant has respect and reverence for the Teacher, the teaching, and the Sangha, the training, diligence, and hospitality.

Six preoccupations with happiness. Seeing a sight with the eye, one is preoccupied with a sight that's a basis for happiness. Hearing a sound with the ear … Smelling an odor with the nose … Tasting a flavor with the tongue … Feeling a touch with the body … Knowing a thought with the mind, one is preoccupied with a thought that's a basis for happiness.

Six preoccupations with sadness. Seeing a sight with the eye, one is preoccupied with a sight that's a basis for sadness. … Knowing a thought with the mind, one is preoccupied with a thought that's a basis for sadness.

Six preoccupations with equanimity. Seeing a sight with the eye, one is preoccupied with a sight that's a basis for equanimity. … Knowing a thought with the mind, one is preoccupied with a thought that's a basis for equanimity.

Six warm-hearted qualities. Firstly, a mendicant consistently treats their spiritual companions with bodily kindness, both in public and in private. This warm-hearted quality makes for fondness and respect, conducing to inclusion, harmony, and unity, without quarreling.

Furthermore, a mendicant consistently treats their spiritual companions with verbal kindness, both in public and in private. This too is a warm-hearted quality.

Furthermore, a mendicant consistently treats their spiritual companions with mental kindness, both in public and in private. This too is a warm-hearted quality.

Furthermore, a mendicant shares without reservation any material possessions they have gained by legitimate means, even the food placed in the alms-bowl, using them in common with their ethical spiritual companions. This too is a warm-hearted quality.

Furthermore, a mendicant lives according to the precepts shared with their spiritual companions, both in public and in private. Those precepts are unbroken, impeccable, spotless, and unmarred, liberating, praised by sensible people, not mistaken, and leading to immersion. This too is a warm-hearted quality.

They live according to the view shared with their spiritual companions, both in public and in private. That view is noble and emancipating, and brings one who practices it to the complete ending of suffering. This warm-hearted quality too makes for fondness and respect, conducing to inclusion, harmony, and unity, without quarreling.

Six roots of quarrels. Firstly, a mendicant is irritable and hostile. Such a mendicant lacks respect and reverence for the Teacher, the teaching, and the Sangha, and they don't fulfill the training. They create a dispute in the Sangha, which is for the hurt and unhappiness of the people, for the harm, hurt, and suffering of gods and humans. If you see such a root of quarrels in yourselves or others, you should try to give up this bad thing. If you don't see it, you should practice so that it doesn't come up in the future. That's how to give up this bad root of quarrels, so it doesn't come up in the future.

Furthermore, a mendicant is offensive and contemptuous … They're jealous and stingy … They're devious and deceitful … They have wicked desires and wrong view … They're attached to their own views, holding them tight, and refusing to let go. If you see such a root of quarrels in yourselves or others, you should try to give up this bad thing. If you don't see it, you should practice so that it doesn't come up in the future. That's how to give up this bad root of quarrels, so it doesn't come up in the future.

Six elements: earth, water, fire, air, space, and consciousness.

Six elements of escape. Take a mendicant who says: 'I've developed the heart's release by love. I've cultivated it, made it my vehicle and my basis, kept it up, consolidated it, and properly implemented it. Yet somehow ill will still occupies my mind.' They should be told, 'Not so, venerable! Don't say that. Don't misrepresent the Buddha, for misrepresentation of the Buddha is not good. And the Buddha would not say that. It's impossible, reverend, it cannot happen that the heart's release by love has been developed and properly implemented, yet somehow ill will still occupies the mind. For it is the heart's release by love that is the escape from ill will.'

Take another mendicant who says: 'I've developed the heart's release by compassion. I've cultivated it, made it my vehicle and my basis, kept it up, consolidated it, and properly implemented it. Yet somehow the thought of harming still occupies my mind.' They should be told, 'Not so, venerable! … For it is the heart's release by compassion that is the escape from thoughts of harming.'

Take another mendicant who says: 'I've developed the heart's release by rejoicing. I've cultivated it, made it my vehicle and my basis, kept it up, consolidated it, and properly implemented it. Yet somehow negativity still occupies my mind.' They should be told, 'Not so, venerable! … For it is the heart's release by rejoicing that is the escape from negativity.'

Take another mendicant who says: 'I've developed the heart's release by equanimity. I've cultivated it, made it my vehicle and my basis, kept it up, consolidated it, and properly implemented it. Yet somehow desire still occupies my mind.' They should be told, 'Not so, venerable! … For it is the heart's release by equanimity that is the escape from desire.'

Take another mendicant who says: 'I've developed the signless release of the heart. I've cultivated it, made it my vehicle and my basis, kept it up, consolidated it, and properly implemented it. Yet somehow my consciousness still follows after signs.' They should be told, 'Not so, venerable! … For it is the signless release of the heart that is the escape from all signs.'

Take another mendicant who says: 'I'm rid of the conceit "I am". And I don't regard anything as "I am this". Yet somehow the dart of doubt and indecision still occupies my mind.' They should be told, 'Not so, venerable! Don't say that. Don't misrepresent the Buddha, for misrepresentation of the Buddha is not good. And the Buddha would not say that. It's impossible, reverend, it cannot happen that the conceit "I am" has been done away with, and nothing is regarded as "I am this", yet somehow the dart of doubt and indecision still occupy the mind. For it is the uprooting of the conceit "I am" that is the escape from the dart of doubt and indecision.'

Six unsurpassable things: the unsurpassable seeing, listening, acquisition, training, service, and recollection.

Six recollections: the recollection of the Buddha, the teaching, the Sangha, ethics, generosity, and the deities.

Six consistent responses. A mendicant, seeing a sight with their eyes, is neither happy nor sad. They remain equanimous, mindful and aware. Hearing a sound with their ears … Smelling an odor with their nose … Tasting a flavor with their tongue … Feeling a touch with their body … Knowing a thought with their mind, they're neither happy nor sad. They remain equanimous, mindful and aware.

Six classes of rebirth. Someone born into a dark class gives rise to a dark result. Someone born into a dark class gives rise to a bright result. Someone born into a dark class gives rise to extinguishment, which is neither dark nor bright. Someone born into a bright class gives rise to a bright result. Someone born into a bright class gives rise to a dark result. Someone born into a bright class gives rise to extinguishment, which is neither dark nor bright.

Six perceptions that help penetration: the perception of impermanence, the perception of suffering in impermanence, the perception of not-self in suffering, the perception of giving up, the perception of fading away, and the perception of cessation.

These are the teachings grouped by six that have been rightly explained by the Buddha. You should all recite these in concert.

Sevens

There are teachings grouped by seven that have been rightly explained by the Buddha. You should all recite these in concert. What are the teachings grouped by seven?

Seven kinds of noble wealth: the wealth of faith, ethical conduct, conscience, prudence, learning, generosity, and wisdom.

Seven awakening factors: mindfulness, investigation of principles, energy, rapture, tranquility, immersion, and equanimity.

Seven prerequisites for immersion: right view, right thought, right speech, right action, right livelihood, right effort, and right mindfulness.

Seven bad qualities: a mendicant is faithless, shameless, imprudent, uneducated, lazy, unmindful, and witless.

Seven good qualities: a mendicant is faithful, conscientious, prudent, learned, energetic, mindful, and wise.

Seven aspects of the teachings of the good persons: a mendicant knows the teachings, knows the meaning, knows themselves, knows moderation, knows the right time, knows assemblies, and knows people.

Seven qualifications for graduation. A mendicant has a keen enthusiasm to undertake the training … to examine the teachings … to get rid of desires … for retreat … to rouse up energy … for mindfulness and alertness … to penetrate theoretically. And they don't lose these desires in the future.

Seven perceptions: the perception of impermanence, the perception of not-self, the perception of ugliness, the perception of drawbacks, the perception of giving up, the perception of fading away, and the perception of cessation.

Seven powers: faith, energy, conscience, prudence, mindfulness, immersion, and wisdom.

Seven planes of consciousness. There are sentient beings that are diverse in body and diverse in perception, such as human beings, some gods, and some beings in the underworld. This is the first plane of consciousness.

There are sentient beings that are diverse in body and unified in perception, such as the gods reborn in Brahma's Host through the first absorption. This is the second plane of consciousness.

There are sentient beings that are unified in body and diverse in perception, such as the gods of streaming radiance. This is the third plane of consciousness.

There are sentient beings that are unified in body and unified in perception, such as the gods replete with glory. This is the fourth plane of consciousness.

There are sentient beings that have gone totally beyond perceptions of form. With the ending of perceptions of impingement, not focusing on perceptions of diversity, aware that 'space is infinite', they have been reborn in the dimension of infinite space. This is the fifth plane of consciousness.

There are sentient beings that have gone totally beyond the dimension of infinite space. Aware that 'consciousness is infinite', they have been reborn in the dimension of infinite consciousness. This is the sixth plane of consciousness.

There are sentient beings that have gone totally beyond the dimension of infinite consciousness. Aware that 'there is nothing at all', they have been reborn in the dimension of nothingness. This is the seventh plane of consciousness.

Seven persons worthy of a religious donation: one freed both ways, one freed by wisdom, a personal witness, one attained to view, one freed by faith, a follower of the teachings, and a follower by faith.

Seven underlying tendencies: sensual desire, repulsion, views, doubt, conceit, desire to be reborn, and ignorance.

Seven fetters: attraction, repulsion, views, doubt, conceit, desire to be reborn, and ignorance.

Seven principles for the settlement of any disciplinary issues that might arise. Removal in the presence of those concerned is applicable. Removal by accurate recollection is applicable. Removal due to recovery from madness is applicable. The acknowledgement of the offense is applicable. The decision of a majority is applicable. A verdict of aggravated misconduct is applicable. Covering over with grass is applicable.

These are the teachings grouped by seven that have been rightly explained by the Buddha. You should all recite these in concert.

The second recitation section is finished.

Eights

There are teachings grouped by eight that have been rightly explained by the Buddha. You should all recite these in concert. What are the teachings grouped by eight?

Eight wrong ways: wrong view, wrong thought, wrong speech, wrong action, wrong livelihood, wrong effort, wrong mindfulness, and wrong immersion.

Eight right ways: right view, right thought, right speech, right action, right livelihood, right effort, right mindfulness, and right immersion.

Eight persons worthy of a religious donation. The stream-enterer and the one practicing to realize the fruit of stream-entry. The once-returner and the one practicing to realize the fruit of once-return. The non-returner and the one practicing to realize the fruit of non-return. The perfected one, and the one practicing for perfection.

Eight grounds for laziness. Firstly, a mendicant has some work to do. They think: 'I have some work to do. But while doing it my body will get tired. I'd better have a lie down.' They lie down, and don't rouse energy for attaining the unattained, achieving the unachieved, and realizing the unrealized. This is the first ground for laziness.

Furthermore, a mendicant has done some work. They think: 'I've done some work. But while working my body got tired. I'd better have a lie down.' They lie down, and don't rouse energy... This is the second ground for laziness.

Furthermore, a mendicant has to go on a journey. They think: 'I have to go on a journey. But while walking my body will get tired. I'd better have a lie down.' They lie down, and don't rouse energy... This is the third ground for laziness.

Furthermore, a mendicant has gone on a journey. They think: 'I've gone on a journey. But while walking my body got tired. I'd better have a lie down.' They lie down, and don't rouse energy... This is the fourth ground for laziness.

Furthermore, a mendicant has wandered for alms, but they didn't get to fill up on as much food as they like, coarse or fine. They think: 'I've wandered for alms, but I didn't get to fill up on as much food as I like, coarse or fine. My body is tired and unfit for work. I'd better have a lie down.' They lie down, and don't rouse energy... This is the fifth ground for laziness.

Furthermore, a mendicant has wandered for alms, and they got to fill up on as much food as they like, coarse or fine. They think: 'I've wandered for alms, and I got to fill up on as much food as I like, coarse or fine. My body is heavy and unfit for work, like I've just eaten a load of beans. I'd better have a lie down.' They lie down, and don't rouse energy... This is the sixth ground for laziness.

Furthermore, a mendicant feels a little sick. They think: 'I feel a little sick. Lying down would be good for me. I'd better have a lie down.' They lie down, and don't rouse energy... This is the seventh ground for laziness.

Furthermore, a mendicant has recently recovered from illness. They think: 'I've recently recovered from illness. My body is weak and unfit for work. I'd better have a lie down.' They lie down, and don't rouse energy for attaining the unattained, achieving the unachieved, and realizing the unrealized. This is the eighth ground for laziness.

Eight grounds for arousing energy. Firstly, a mendicant has some work to do. They think: 'I have some work to do. While working it's not easy to focus on the instructions of the Buddhas. I'd better preemptively rouse up energy for attaining the unattained, achieving the unachieved, and realizing the unrealized.' They rouse energy for attaining the unattained, achieving the unachieved, and realizing the unrealized. This is the first ground for arousing energy.

Furthermore, a mendicant has done some work. They think: 'I've done some work. While I was working I wasn't able to focus on the instructions of the Buddhas. I'd better preemptively rouse up energy.' They rouse up energy... This is the second ground for arousing energy.

Furthermore, a mendicant has to go on a journey. They think: 'I have to go on a journey. While walking it's not easy to focus on the instructions of the Buddhas. I'd better preemptively rouse up energy.' They rouse up energy... This is the third ground for arousing energy.

Furthermore, a mendicant has gone on a journey. They think: 'I've gone on a journey. While I was walking I wasn't able to focus on the instructions of the Buddhas. I'd better preemptively rouse up energy.' They rouse up energy... This is the fourth ground for arousing energy.

Furthermore, a mendicant has wandered for alms, but they didn't get to fill up on as much food as they like, coarse or fine. They think: 'I've wandered for alms, but I didn't get to fill up on as much food as I like, coarse or fine. My body is light and fit for work. I'd better preemptively rouse up energy.' They rouse up energy... This is the fifth ground for arousing energy.

Furthermore, a mendicant has wandered for alms, and they got to fill up on as much food as they like, coarse or fine. They think: 'I've wandered for alms, and I got to fill up on as much food as I like, coarse or fine. My body is strong and fit for work. I'd better preemptively rouse up energy.' They rouse up energy... This is the sixth ground for arousing energy.

Furthermore, a mendicant feels a little sick. They think: 'I feel a little sick. It's possible this illness will worsen. I'd better preemptively rouse up energy.' They rouse up energy... This is the seventh ground for arousing energy.

Furthermore, a mendicant has recently recovered from illness. They think: 'I've recently recovered from illness. It's possible the illness will come back. I'd better preemptively rouse up energy for attaining the unattained, achieving the unachieved, and realizing the unrealized.' They rouse energy for attaining the unattained, achieving the unachieved, and realizing the unrealized. This is the eighth ground for arousing energy.

Eight reasons to give. A person might give a gift after insulting the recipient. Or they give out of fear. Or they give thinking, 'They gave to me.' Or they give thinking, 'They'll give to me.' Or they give thinking, 'It's good to give.' Or they give thinking, 'I cook, they don't. It wouldn't be right for me to not give to them.' Or they give thinking, 'By giving this gift I'll get a good reputation.' Or they give thinking, 'This is an adornment and requisite for the mind.'

Eight rebirths by giving. First, someone gives to ascetics or brahmins such things as food, drink, clothing, vehicles; garlands, fragrance, and makeup; and bed, house, and lighting. Whatever they give, they expect something back. They see an affluent aristocrat or brahmin or householder amusing themselves, supplied and provided with the five kinds of sensual stimulation. They think: 'If only, when my body breaks up, after death, I would be reborn in the company of well-to-do aristocrats or brahmins or householders!' They settle on that thought, concentrate on it and develop it. As they've settled for less and not developed further, their thought leads to rebirth there. But I say that this is only for those of ethical conduct, not for the unethical. The heart's wish of an ethical person succeeds because of their purity.

Next, someone gives to ascetics or brahmins. Whatever they give, they expect something back. And they've heard: 'The Gods of the Four Great Kings are long-lived, beautiful, and very happy.' They think: 'If only, when my body breaks up, after death, I would be reborn in the company of the Gods of the Four Great Kings!' They settle on that thought, concentrate on it and develop it. As they've settled for less and not developed further, their thought leads to rebirth there. But I say that this is only for those of ethical conduct, not for the unethical. The heart's wish of an ethical person succeeds because of their purity.

Next, someone gives to ascetics or brahmins. Whatever they give, they expect something back. And they've heard: 'The Gods of the Thirty-Three ... the Gods of Yama ... the Joyful Gods ... the Gods Who Love to Create ... the Gods Who Control the Creations of Others are long-lived, beautiful, and very happy.' They think: 'If only, when my body breaks up, after death, I would be reborn in the company of the Gods Who Control the Creations of Others!' They settle on that thought, concentrate on it and develop it. As they've settled for less and not developed further, their thought leads to rebirth there. But I say that this is only for those of ethical conduct, not for the unethical. The heart's wish of an ethical person succeeds because of their purity.

Next, someone gives to ascetics or brahmins such things as food, drink, clothing, vehicles; garlands, fragrance, and makeup; and bed, house, and lighting. Whatever they give, they expect something back. And they've heard: 'The Gods of Brahma's Host are long-lived, beautiful, and very happy.' They think: 'If only, when my body breaks up, after death, I would be reborn in the company of the Gods of Brahma's Host!' They settle on that thought, concentrate on it and develop it. As they've settled for less and not developed further, their thought leads to rebirth there. But I say that this is only for those of ethical conduct, not for the unethical. And for those free of desire, not those with desire. The heart's wish of an ethical person succeeds because of their freedom from desire.

Eight assemblies: the assemblies of aristocrats, brahmins, householders, and ascetics. An assembly of the gods under the Four Great Kings. An assembly of the gods under the Thirty-Three. An assembly of Maras. An assembly of Brahmas.

Eight worldly conditions: gain and loss, fame and disgrace, praise and blame, pleasure and pain.

Eight dimensions of mastery. Perceiving form internally, someone sees visions externally, limited, both pretty and ugly. Mastering them, they perceive: 'I know and see.' This is the first dimension of mastery.

Perceiving form internally, someone sees visions externally, limitless, both pretty and ugly. Mastering them, they perceive: 'I know and see.' This is the second dimension of mastery.

Not perceiving form internally, someone sees visions externally, limited, both pretty and ugly. Mastering them, they perceive: 'I know and see.' This is the third dimension of mastery.

Not perceiving form internally, someone sees visions externally, limitless, both pretty and ugly. Mastering them, they perceive: 'I know and see.' This is the fourth dimension of mastery.

Not perceiving form internally, someone sees visions externally that are blue, with blue color, blue hue, and blue tint. They're like a flax flower that's blue, with blue color, blue hue, and blue tint. Or a cloth from Baranasi that's smoothed on both sides, blue, with blue color, blue hue, and blue tint. Mastering them, they perceive: 'I know and see.' This is the fifth dimension of mastery.

Not perceiving form internally, someone sees visions externally that are yellow, with yellow color, yellow hue, and yellow tint. They're like a champak flower that's yellow, with yellow color, yellow hue, and yellow tint. Or a cloth from Baranasi that's smoothed on both sides, yellow, with yellow color, yellow hue, and yellow tint. Mastering them, they perceive: 'I know and see.' This is the sixth dimension of mastery.

Not perceiving form internally, someone sees visions externally that are red, with red color, red hue, and red tint. They're like a scarlet mallow flower that's red, with red color, red hue, and red tint. Or a cloth from Baranasi that's smoothed on both sides, red, with red color, red hue, and red tint. Mastering them, they perceive: 'I know and see.' This is the seventh dimension of mastery.

Not perceiving form internally, someone sees visions externally that are white, with white color, white hue, and white tint. They're like the morning star that's white, with white color, white hue, and white tint. Or a cloth from Baranasi that's smoothed on both sides, white, with white color, white hue, and white tint. Mastering them, they perceive: 'I know and see.' This is the eighth dimension of mastery.

Eight liberations. Having physical form, they see visions. This is the first liberation.

Not perceiving physical form internally, they see visions externally. This is the second liberation.

They're focused only on beauty. This is the third liberation.

Going totally beyond perceptions of form, with the ending of perceptions of impingement, not focusing on perceptions of diversity, aware that 'space is infinite', they enter and remain in the dimension of infinite space. This is the fourth liberation.

Going totally beyond the dimension of infinite space, aware that 'consciousness is infinite', they enter and remain in the dimension of infinite consciousness. This is the fifth liberation.

Going totally beyond the dimension of infinite consciousness, aware that 'there is nothing at all', they enter and remain in the dimension of nothingness. This is the sixth liberation.

Going totally beyond the dimension of nothingness, they enter and remain in the dimension of neither perception nor non-perception. This is the seventh liberation.

Going totally beyond the dimension of neither perception nor non-perception, they enter and remain in the cessation of perception and feeling. This is the eighth liberation.

These are the teachings grouped by eight that have been rightly explained by the

Buddha. You should all recite these in concert.

Nines

There are teachings grouped by nine that have been rightly explained by the Buddha. You should all recite these in concert. What are the teachings grouped by nine?

Nine grounds for resentment. Thinking: 'They did wrong to me,' you harbor resentment. Thinking: 'They are doing wrong to me' … 'They will do wrong to me' … 'They did wrong by someone I love' … 'They are doing wrong by someone I love' … 'They will do wrong by someone I love' … 'They helped someone I dislike' … 'They are helping someone I dislike' … Thinking: 'They will help someone I dislike,' you harbor resentment.

Nine methods to get rid of resentment. Thinking: 'They did wrong to me, but what can I possibly do?' you get rid of resentment. Thinking: 'They are doing wrong to me …' … 'They will do wrong to me …' … 'They did wrong by someone I love …' … 'They are doing wrong by someone I love …' … 'They will do wrong by someone I love …' … 'They helped someone I dislike …' … 'They are helping someone I dislike …' … Thinking: 'They will help someone I dislike, but what can I possibly do?' you get rid of resentment.

Nine abodes of sentient beings. There are sentient beings that are diverse in body and diverse in perception, such as human beings, some gods, and some beings in the underworld. This is the first abode of sentient beings.

There are sentient beings that are diverse in body and unified in perception, such as the gods reborn in Brahma's Host through the first absorption. This is the second abode of sentient beings.

There are sentient beings that are unified in body and diverse in perception, such as the gods of streaming radiance. This is the third abode of sentient beings.

There are sentient beings that are unified in body and unified in perception, such as the gods replete with glory. This is the fourth abode of sentient beings.

There are sentient beings that are non-percipient and do not experience anything, such as the gods who are non-percipient beings. This is the fifth abode of sentient beings.

There are sentient beings that have gone totally beyond perceptions of form. With the ending of perceptions of impingement, not focusing on perceptions of diversity, aware that 'space is infinite', they have been reborn in the dimension of infinite space. This is the sixth abode of sentient beings.

There are sentient beings that have gone totally beyond the dimension of infinite space. Aware that 'consciousness is infinite', they have been reborn in the dimension of infinite consciousness. This is the seventh abode of sentient beings.

There are sentient beings that have gone totally beyond the dimension of infinite consciousness. Aware that 'there is nothing at all', they have been reborn in the dimension of nothingness. This is the eighth abode of sentient beings.

There are sentient beings that have gone totally beyond the dimension of nothingness. They have been reborn in the dimension of neither perception nor non-perception. This is the ninth abode of sentient beings.

Nine lost opportunities for spiritual practice. Firstly, a Realized One has arisen in the world. He teaches the Dhamma leading to peace, extinguishment, awakening, as proclaimed by the Holy One. But a person has been reborn in hell. This is the first lost opportunity for spiritual practice.

Furthermore, a Realized One has arisen in the world. But a person has been reborn in the animal realm. This is the second lost opportunity for spiritual practice.

Furthermore, a Realized One has arisen in the world. But a person has been reborn in the ghost realm. This is the third lost opportunity for spiritual practice.

Furthermore, a Realized One has arisen in the world. But a person has been reborn among the demons. This is the fourth lost opportunity for spiritual practice.

Furthermore, a Realized One has arisen in the world. But a person has been reborn in one of the long-lived orders of gods. This is the fifth lost opportunity for spiritual practice.

Furthermore, a Realized One has arisen in the world. But a person has been reborn in the borderlands, among barbarian tribes, where monks, nuns, laymen, and laywomen do not go. This is the sixth lost opportunity for spiritual practice.

Furthermore, a Realized One has arisen in the world. And a person is reborn in a central country. But they have wrong view and distorted perspective: 'There's no meaning in giving, sacrifice, or offerings. There's no fruit or result of good and bad deeds. There's no afterlife. There are no duties to mother and father. No beings are reborn spontaneously. And there's no ascetic or brahmin who is well attained and practiced, and who describes the afterlife after realizing it with their own insight.' This is the seventh lost opportunity for spiritual practice.

Furthermore, a Realized One has arisen in the world. And a person is reborn in a central country. But they're witless, dull, stupid, and unable to distinguish what is well said from what is poorly said. This is the eighth lost opportunity for spiritual practice.

Furthermore, a Realized One has arisen in the world. But he doesn't teach the Dhamma leading to peace, extinguishment, awakening, as proclaimed by the Holy One. And a person is reborn in a central country. And they're wise, bright, clever, and able to distinguish what is well said from what is poorly said. This is the ninth lost opportunity for spiritual practice.

Nine progressive meditations. A mendicant, quite secluded from sensual pleasures, secluded from unskillful qualities, enters and remains in the first absorption, which has the rapture and bliss born of seclusion, while placing the mind and keeping it connected. As the placing of the mind and keeping it connected are stilled, they enter and remain in the second absorption, which has the rapture and bliss born of immersion, with internal clarity and confidence, and unified mind, without placing the mind and keeping it connected. And with the fading away of rapture, they enter and remain in the third absorption, where they meditate with equanimity, mindful and aware, personally experiencing the bliss of which the noble ones declare, 'Equanimous and mindful, one meditates in bliss.' Giving up pleasure and pain, and ending former happiness and sadness, they enter and remain in the fourth absorption, without pleasure or pain, with pure equanimity and mindfulness. Going totally beyond perceptions of form, with the ending of perceptions of impingement, not focusing on perceptions of diversity, aware that 'space is infinite', they enter and remain in the dimension of infinite space. Going totally beyond the dimension of infinite space, aware that 'consciousness is infinite', they enter and remain in the dimension of infinite consciousness. Going totally beyond the dimension of infinite consciousness, aware that 'there is nothing at all', they enter and remain in the dimension of nothingness. Going totally beyond the dimension of nothingness, they enter and remain in the dimension of neither perception nor non-perception. Going totally beyond the dimension of neither perception nor non-perception, they enter and remain in the cessation of perception and feeling.

Nine progressive cessations. For someone who has attained the first absorption, sensual perceptions have ceased. For someone who has attained the second absorption, the placing of the mind and keeping it connected have ceased. For someone who has attained the third absorption, rapture has ceased. For someone who has attained the fourth absorption, breathing has ceased. For someone who has attained the dimension of infinite space, the perception of form has ceased. For someone who has attained the dimension of infinite consciousness, the perception of the dimension of infinite space has ceased. For someone who has attained the dimension of nothingness, the perception of the dimension of infinite consciousness has ceased. For someone who has attained the dimension of neither perception nor non-perception, the perception of the dimension of nothingness has ceased. For someone who has attained the cessation of perception and feeling, perception and feeling have ceased.

These are the teachings grouped by nine that have been rightly explained by the Buddha. You should all recite these in concert.

Tens

There are teachings grouped by ten that have been rightly explained by the Buddha. You should all recite these in concert. What are the teachings grouped by ten?

Ten qualities that serve as protector. Firstly, a mendicant is ethical, restrained in the monastic code, conducting themselves well and seeking alms in suitable places. Seeing danger in the slightest fault, they keep the rules they've undertaken. This is a quality that serves as protector.

Furthermore, a mendicant is very learned, remembering and keeping what they've learned. These teachings are good in the beginning, good in the middle, and good in the end, meaningful and well-phrased, describing a spiritual practice that's entirely full and pure. They are very learned in such teachings, remembering them, reinforcing them by recitation, mentally scrutinizing them, and comprehending them theoretically. This too is a quality that serves as protector.

Furthermore, a mendicant has good friends, companions, and associates. This too is a quality that serves as protector.

Furthermore, a mendicant is easy to admonish, having qualities that make them easy to admonish. They're patient, and take instruction respectfully. This too is a quality that serves as protector.

Furthermore, a mendicant is deft and tireless in a diverse spectrum of duties for their spiritual companions, understanding how to go about things in order to complete and organize the work. This too is a quality that serves as protector.

Furthermore, a mendicant loves the teachings and is a delight to converse with, being full of joy in the teaching and training. This too is a quality that serves as protector.

Furthermore, a mendicant is content with any kind of robes, alms-food, lodgings, and medicines and supplies for the sick. This too is a quality that serves as protector.

Furthermore, a mendicant lives with energy roused up for giving up unskillful qualities and embracing skillful qualities. They are strong, staunchly vigorous, not slacking off when it comes to developing skillful qualities. This too is a quality that serves as protector.

Furthermore, a mendicant is mindful. They have utmost mindfulness and alertness, and can remember and recall what was said and done long ago. This too is a quality that serves as protector.

Furthermore, a mendicant is wise. They have the wisdom of arising and passing away which is noble, penetrative, and leads to the complete ending of suffering. This too is a quality that serves as protector.

Ten universal dimensions of meditation. Someone perceives the meditation on universal earth above, below, across, non-dual and limitless. They perceive the meditation on universal water … the meditation on universal fire … the meditation on universal air … the meditation on universal blue … the meditation on universal yellow … the meditation on universal red … the meditation on universal white … the meditation on universal space … They perceive the meditation on universal consciousness above, below, across, non-dual and limitless.

Ten ways of doing unskillful deeds: killing living creatures, stealing, and sexual misconduct; speech that's false, divisive, harsh, or nonsensical; covetousness, ill will, and wrong view.

Ten ways of doing skillful deeds: refraining from killing living creatures, stealing, and sexual misconduct; refraining from speech that's false, divisive, harsh, or nonsensical; contentment, good will, and right view.

Ten noble abodes. A mendicant has given up five factors, possesses six factors, has a single guard, has four supports, has eliminated idiosyncratic interpretations of the truth, has totally given up searching, has unsullied intentions, has stilled the physical process, and is well freed in mind and well freed by wisdom.

And how has a mendicant given up five factors? It's when a mendicant has given up sensual desire, ill will, dullness and drowsiness, restlessness and remorse, and doubt. That's how a mendicant has given up five factors.

And how does a mendicant possess six factors? A mendicant, seeing a sight with their eyes, is neither happy nor sad. They remain equanimous, mindful and aware. Hearing a sound with their ears … Smelling an odor with their nose … Tasting a flavor with their tongue … Feeling a touch with their body … Knowing a thought with their mind, they're neither happy nor sad. They remain equanimous, mindful and aware. That's how a mendicant possesses six factors.

And how does a mendicant have a single guard? It's when a mendicant's heart is guarded by mindfulness. That's how a mendicant has a single guard.

And how does a mendicant have four supports? After reflection, a mendicant uses some things, endures some things, avoids some things, and gets rid of some things. That's how a mendicant has four supports.

And how has a mendicant eliminated idiosyncratic interpretations of the truth? Different ascetics and brahmins have different idiosyncratic interpretations of the truth. A mendicant has dispelled, eliminated, thrown out, rejected, let go of, given up, and relinquished all these. That's how a mendicant has eliminated idiosyncratic interpretations of the truth.

And how has a mendicant totally given up searching? It's when they've given up searching for sensual pleasures, for continued existence, and for a spiritual path. That's how a mendicant has totally given up searching.

And how does a mendicant have unsullied intentions? It's when they've given up sensual, malicious, and cruel intentions. That's how a mendicant has unsullied intentions.

And how has a mendicant stilled the physical process? It's when, giving up pleasure and pain, and ending former happiness and sadness, they enter and remain in the fourth absorption, without pleasure or pain, with pure equanimity and mindfulness. That's how a mendicant has stilled the physical process.

And how is a mendicant well freed in mind? It's when a mendicant's mind is freed from greed, hate, and delusion. That's how a mendicant is well freed in mind.

And how is a mendicant well freed by wisdom? It's when a mendicant understands:

'I've given up greed, hate, and delusion, cut them off at the root, made them like a palm stump, obliterated them, so they're unable to arise in the future.' That's how a mendicant's mind is well freed by wisdom.

Ten qualities of an adept: an adept's right view, right thought, right speech, right action, right livelihood, right effort, right mindfulness, right immersion, right knowledge, and right freedom.

Reverends, these are the teachings grouped by ten that have been rightly explained by the Buddha. You should all recite these in concert, without disputing, so that this spiritual path may last for a long time. That would be for the welfare and happiness of the people, for the benefit, welfare, and happiness of gods and humans."

Then the Buddha got up and said to Venerable Sariputta: "Good, good, Sariputta! It's good that you've taught this exposition of the reciting in concert."

That is what Venerable Sariputta said, and the teacher approved. Satisfied, the mendicants were happy with what Sariputta said.

# DASUTTARA SUTTA – UP TO TEN

So I have heard. At one time the Buddha was staying near Campa on the banks of the Gaggara Lotus Pond together with a large Sangha of five hundred mendicants. There Sariputta addressed the mendicants: "Reverends, mendicants!"

"Reverend," they replied. Sariputta said this:

"I will relate the teachings

up to ten for attaining extinguishment,

for making an end of suffering,

the release from all ties.

Groups of One

Reverends, one thing is helpful, one thing should be developed, one thing should be completely understood, one thing should be given up, one thing makes things worse, one thing leads to distinction, one thing is hard to comprehend, one thing should be produced, one thing should be directly known, one thing should be realized.

What one thing is helpful? Diligence in skillful qualities.

What one thing should be developed? Mindfulness of the body that is full of pleasure.

What one thing should be completely understood? Contact, which is accompanied by defilements and is prone to being grasped.

What one thing should be given up? The conceit 'I am'.

What one thing makes things worse? Improper attention.

What one thing leads to distinction? Proper attention.

What one thing is hard to comprehend? The heart's immersion of immediate result.

What one thing should be produced? Unshakable knowledge.

What one thing should be directly known? All sentient beings are sustained by food.

What one thing should be realized? The unshakable heart's release.

So these ten things that are true, real, and accurate, not unreal, not otherwise were rightly awakened to by the Realized One.

Groups of Two

Two things are helpful, two things should be developed, two things should be completely understood, two things should be given up, two things make things worse, two things lead to distinction, two things are hard to comprehend, two things should be produced, two things should be directly known, two things should be realized.

What two things are helpful? Mindfulness and situational awareness.

What two things should be developed? Serenity and discernment.

What two things should be completely understood? Name and form.

What two things should be given up? Ignorance and craving for continued existence.

What two things make things worse? Being hard to admonish and having bad friends.

What two things lead to distinction? Being easy to admonish and having good friends.

What two things are hard to comprehend? What are the causes and conditions for the corruption of sentient beings, and what are the causes and conditions for the purification of sentient beings.

What two things should be produced? Two knowledges: knowledge of ending, and knowledge of non-arising.

What two things should be directly known? Two elements: the conditioned element and the unconditioned element.

What two things should be realized? Knowledge and freedom.

So these twenty things that are true, real, and accurate, not unreal, not otherwise were rightly awakened to by the Realized One.

Groups of Three

Three things are helpful, etc.

What three things are helpful? Associating with good people, listening to the true teaching, and practicing in line with the teaching.

What three things should be developed? Three kinds of immersion. Immersion with placing the mind and keeping it connected. Immersion without placing the mind, but just keeping it connected. Immersion without placing the mind or keeping it connected.

What three things should be completely understood? Three feelings: pleasant, painful, and neutral.

What three things should be given up? Three cravings: craving for sensual pleasures, craving for continued existence, and craving to end existence.

What three things make things worse? Three unskillful roots: greed, hate, and delusion.

What three things lead to distinction? Three skillful roots: non-greed, non-hate, and non-delusion.

What three things are hard to comprehend? Three elements of escape. Renunciation is the escape from sensual pleasures. The formless is the escape from form. Cessation is the escape from whatever is created, conditioned, and dependently originated.

What three things should be produced? Three knowledges: regarding the past, future, and present.

What three things should be directly known? Three elements: sensuality, form, and formlessness.

What three things should be realized? Three knowledges: recollection of past lives, knowledge of the death and rebirth of sentient beings, and knowledge of the ending of defilements.

So these thirty things that are true, real, and accurate, not unreal, not otherwise were rightly awakened to by the Realized One.

Groups of Four

Four things are helpful, etc.

What four things are helpful? Four situations: living in a suitable region, relying on good people, being rightly resolved in oneself, and past merit.

What four things should be developed? The four kinds of mindfulness meditation. A mendicant meditates by observing an aspect of the body — keen, aware, and mindful, rid of desire and aversion for the world. They meditate observing an aspect of feelings … mind … principles — keen, aware, and mindful, rid of desire and aversion for the world.

What four things should be completely understood? Four foods: solid food, whether coarse or fine; contact is the second, mental intention the third, and consciousness the fourth.

What four things should be given up? Four floods: sensuality, desire for rebirth, views, and ignorance.

What four things make things worse? Four bonds: sensuality, desire for rebirth, views, and ignorance.

What four things lead to distinction? Four kinds of detachment: detachment from the bonds of sensuality, desire for rebirth, views, and ignorance.

What four things are hard to comprehend? Four kinds of immersion: immersion liable to decline, stable immersion, immersion that leads to distinction, and immersion that leads to penetration.

What four things should be produced? Four knowledges: knowledge of the present phenomena, inferential knowledge, knowledge of others' minds, and conventional knowledge.

What four things should be directly known? The four noble truths: suffering, the origin of suffering, the cessation of suffering, and the practice that leads to the cessation of suffering.

What four things should be realized? Four fruits of the ascetic life: stream-entry, once-return, non-return, and perfection.

So these forty things that are true, real, and accurate, not unreal, not otherwise were rightly awakened to by the Realized One.

Groups of Five

Five things are helpful, etc.

What five things are helpful? Five factors that support meditation. A mendicant has faith in the Realized One's awakening: 'That Blessed One is perfected, a fully awakened Buddha, accomplished in knowledge and conduct, holy, knower of the world, supreme guide for those who wish to train, teacher of gods and humans, awakened, blessed.' They are rarely ill or unwell. Their stomach digests well, being neither too hot nor too cold, but just right, and fit for meditation. They're not devious or deceitful. They reveal themselves honestly to the Teacher or sensible spiritual companions. They live with energy roused up for giving up unskillful qualities and embracing skillful qualities. They're strong, staunchly vigorous, not slacking off when it comes to developing skillful qualities. They're wise. They have the wisdom of arising and passing away which is noble, penetrative, and leads to the complete ending of suffering.

What five things should be developed? Right immersion with five factors: pervaded with rapture, pervaded with pleasure, pervaded with mind, pervaded with light, and the foundation for reviewing.

What five things should be completely understood? Five grasping aggregates: form, feeling, perception, choices, and consciousness.

What five things should be given up? Five hindrances: sensual desire, ill will, dullness and drowsiness, restlessness and remorse, and doubt.

What five things make things worse? Five kinds of emotional barrenness. Firstly, a mendicant has doubts about the Teacher. They're uncertain, undecided, and lacking confidence. This being so, their mind doesn't incline toward keenness, commitment, persistence, and striving. This is the first kind of emotional barrenness. Furthermore, a mendicant has doubts about the teaching ... the Sangha ... the training ... A mendicant is angry and upset with their spiritual companions, resentful and closed off. This being so, their mind doesn't incline toward keenness, commitment, persistence, and striving. This is the fifth kind of emotional barrenness.

What five things lead to distinction? Five faculties: faith, energy, mindfulness, immersion, and wisdom.

What five things are hard to comprehend? Five elements of escape. A mendicant focuses on sensual pleasures, but their mind isn't eager, confident, settled, and decided about them. But when they focus on renunciation, their mind is eager, confident, settled, and decided about it. Their mind is in a good state, well developed, well risen, well freed, and well detached from sensual pleasures. They're freed from the distressing and feverish defilements that arise because of sensual pleasures, so they don't experience that kind of feeling. This is how the escape from sensual pleasures is explained.

Take another case where a mendicant focuses on ill will, but their mind isn't eager ... But when they focus on good will, their mind is eager ... Their mind is in a good state ... well detached from ill will. They're freed from the distressing and feverish defilements that arise because of ill will, so they don't experience that kind of feeling. This is how the escape from ill will is explained.

Take another case where a mendicant focuses on harming, but their mind isn't eager ... But when they focus on compassion, their mind is eager ... Their mind is in a good state ... well detached from harming. They're freed from the distressing and feverish defilements that arise because of harming, so they don't experience that kind of feeling. This is how the escape from harming is explained.

Take another case where a mendicant focuses on form, but their mind isn't eager ... But when they focus on the formless, their mind is eager ... Their mind is in a good state ... well detached from forms. They're freed from the distressing and feverish defilements that arise because of form, so they don't experience that kind of feeling. This is how the escape from forms is explained.

Take a case where a mendicant focuses on identity, but their mind isn't eager, confident, settled, and decided about it. But when they focus on the ending of identity, their mind is eager, confident, settled, and decided about it. Their mind is in a good state, well developed, well risen, well freed, and well detached from identity. They're freed from the distressing and feverish defilements that arise because of identity, so they don't experience that kind of feeling. This is how the escape from identity is explained.

What five things should be produced? Right immersion with five knowledges. The following knowledges arise for you personally:

'This immersion is blissful now, and results in bliss in the future.'

'This immersion is noble and spiritual.'

'This immersion is not cultivated by sinners.'

'This immersion is peaceful and sublime and tranquil and unified, not held in place by forceful suppression.'

'I mindfully enter into and emerge from this immersion.'

What five things should be directly known? Five opportunities for freedom. Firstly, the Teacher or a respected spiritual companion teaches Dhamma to a mendicant. That mendicant feels inspired by the meaning and the teaching in that Dhamma, no matter how the Teacher or a respected spiritual companion teaches it. Feeling inspired, joy springs up. Being joyful, rapture springs up. When the mind is full of rapture, the body becomes tranquil. When the body is tranquil, one feels bliss. And when blissful, the mind becomes immersed. This is the first opportunity for freedom.

Furthermore, it may be that neither the Teacher nor a respected spiritual companion teaches Dhamma to a mendicant. But the mendicant teaches Dhamma in detail to others as they learned and memorized it. That mendicant feels inspired by the meaning and the teaching in that Dhamma, no matter how they teach it in detail to others as they learned and memorized it. Feeling inspired, joy springs up. Being joyful, rapture springs up. When the mind is full of rapture, the body becomes tranquil. When the body is tranquil, one feels bliss. And when blissful, the mind becomes immersed. This is the second opportunity for freedom.

Furthermore, it may be that neither the Teacher nor … the mendicant teaches Dhamma. But the mendicant recites the teaching in detail as they learned and memorized it. That mendicant feels inspired by the meaning and the teaching in that Dhamma, no matter how they recite it in detail as they learned and memorized it. Feeling inspired, joy springs up. Being joyful, rapture springs up. When the mind is full of rapture, the body becomes tranquil. When the body is tranquil, one feels bliss. And when blissful, the mind becomes immersed. This is the third opportunity for freedom.

Furthermore, it may be that neither the Teacher nor … the mendicant teaches Dhamma … nor does the mendicant recite the teaching. But the mendicant thinks about and considers the teaching in their heart, examining it with the mind as they learned and memorized it. That mendicant feels inspired by the meaning and the teaching in that Dhamma, no matter how they think about and consider it in their heart, examining it with the mind as they learned and memorized it. Feeling inspired, joy springs up. Being joyful, rapture springs up. When the mind is full of rapture, the body becomes tranquil. When the body is tranquil, one feels bliss. And when blissful, the mind becomes immersed. This is the fourth opportunity for freedom.

Furthermore, it may be that neither the Teacher nor … the mendicant teaches Dhamma … nor does the mendicant recite the teaching … or think about it. But a meditation subject as a foundation of immersion is properly grasped, attended, borne in mind, and comprehended with wisdom. That mendicant feels inspired by the meaning and the teaching in that Dhamma, no matter how a meditation subject as a foundation of immersion is properly grasped, attended, borne in mind, and comprehended with wisdom. Feeling inspired, joy springs up. Being joyful, rapture springs up. When the mind is full of rapture, the body becomes tranquil. When the body is tranquil, one feels bliss. And when blissful, the mind becomes immersed. This is the fifth opportunity for freedom.

What five things should be realized? Five spectrums of the teaching: ethics, immersion, wisdom, freedom, and knowledge and vision of freedom.

So these fifty things that are true, real, and accurate, not unreal, not otherwise were rightly awakened to by the Realized One.

Groups of Six

Six things are helpful, etc.

What six things are helpful? Six warm-hearted qualities. Firstly, a mendicant consistently treats their spiritual companions with bodily kindness, both in public and in private. This warm-hearted quality makes for fondness and respect, conducing to inclusion, harmony, and unity, without quarreling.

Furthermore, a mendicant consistently treats their spiritual companions with verbal kindness.

Furthermore, a mendicant consistently treats their spiritual companions with mental kindness.

Furthermore, a mendicant shares without reservation any material possessions they have gained by legitimate means, even the food placed in the alms-bowl, using them in common with their ethical spiritual companions.

Furthermore, a mendicant lives according to the precepts shared with their spiritual companions, both in public and in private. Those precepts are unbroken, impeccable, spotless, and unmarred, liberating, praised by sensible people, not mistaken, and leading to immersion.

Furthermore, a mendicant lives according to the view shared with their spiritual companions, both in public and in private. That view is noble and emancipating, and leads one who practices it to the complete ending of suffering. This warm-hearted quality makes for fondness and respect, conducing to inclusion, harmony, and unity, without quarreling.

What six things should be developed? Six recollections: the recollection of the Buddha, the teaching, the Sangha, ethics, generosity, and the deities.

What six things should be completely understood? Six interior sense fields: eye, ear, nose, tongue, body, and mind.

What six things should be given up? Six classes of craving: craving for sights, sounds, smells, tastes, touches, and thoughts.

What six things make things worse? Six kinds of disrespect. A mendicant lacks respect and reverence for the Teacher, the teaching, and the Sangha, the training, diligence, and hospitality.

What six things lead to distinction? Six kinds of respect. A mendicant has respect and reverence for the Teacher, the teaching, and the Sangha, the training, diligence, and hospitality.

What six things are hard to comprehend? Six elements of escape. Take a mendicant who says: 'I've developed the heart's release by love. I've cultivated it, made it my vehicle and my basis, kept it up, consolidated it, and properly implemented it. Yet somehow ill will still occupies my mind.' They should be told, 'Not so, venerable! Don't say that. Don't misrepresent the Buddha, for misrepresentation of the Buddha is not good. And the Buddha would not say that. It's impossible, reverend, it cannot happen that the heart's release by love has been developed and properly implemented, yet somehow ill will still occupies the mind. For it is the heart's release by love that is the escape from ill will.'

Take another mendicant who says: 'I've developed the heart's release by compassion. I've cultivated it, made it my vehicle and my basis, kept it up, consolidated it, and properly implemented it. Yet somehow the thought of harming still occupies my mind.' They should be told, 'Not so, venerable! ... For it is the heart's release by compassion that is the escape from thoughts of harming.'

Take another mendicant who says: 'I've developed the heart's release by rejoicing. ... Yet somehow negativity still occupies my mind.' They should be told, 'Not so, venerable! ... For it is the heart's release by rejoicing that is the escape from negativity.'

Take another mendicant who says: 'I've developed the heart's release by equanimity. ... Yet somehow desire still occupies my mind.' They should be told, 'Not so, venerable! ... For it is the heart's release by equanimity that is the escape from desire.'

Take another mendicant who says: 'I've developed the signless heart's release. ... Yet somehow my consciousness still follows after signs.' They should be told, 'Not so, venerable! ... For it is the signless release of the heart that is the escape from all signs.'

Take another mendicant who says: 'I'm rid of the conceit "I am". And I don't regard anything as "I am this". Yet somehow the dart of doubt and indecision still occupies my mind.' They should be told, 'Not so, venerable! Don't say that. Don't misrepresent the Buddha, for misrepresentation of the Buddha is not good. And the Buddha would not say that. It's impossible, reverend, it cannot happen that the conceit "I am" has been done away with, and nothing is regarded as "I am this", yet somehow the dart of doubt and indecision still occupy the mind. For it is the uprooting of the conceit "I am" that is the escape from the dart of doubt and indecision.'

What six things should be produced? Six consistent responses. A mendicant, seeing a sight with their eyes, is neither happy nor sad. They remain equanimous, mindful and aware. Hearing a sound with their ears ... Smelling an odor with their nose ... Tasting a flavor with their tongue ... Feeling a touch with their body ... Knowing a thought with their mind, they're neither happy nor sad. They remain equanimous, mindful and aware.

What six things should be directly known? Six unsurpassable things: the unsurpassable seeing, listening, acquisition, training, service, and recollection.

What six things should be realized? Six direct knowledges. A mendicant wields the many kinds of psychic power:

multiplying themselves and becoming one again; appearing and disappearing; going unimpeded through a wall, a rampart, or a mountain as if through space; diving in and out of the earth as if it were water; walking on water as if it were earth; flying cross-legged through the sky like a bird; touching and stroking with the hand the sun and moon, so mighty and powerful; controlling the body as far as the Brahma realm.

With clairaudience that is purified and superhuman, they hear both kinds of sounds, human and divine, whether near or far.

They understand the minds of other beings and individuals, having comprehended them with their own mind.

They recollect many kinds of past lives, with features and details.

With clairvoyance that is purified and superhuman, they see sentient beings passing away and being reborn — inferior and superior, beautiful and ugly, in a good place or a bad place. They understand how sentient beings are reborn according to their deeds.

They realize the undefiled freedom of heart and freedom by wisdom in this very life. And they live having realized it with their own insight due to the ending of defilements.

So these sixty things that are true, real, and accurate, not unreal, not otherwise were rightly awakened to by the Realized One.

Groups of Seven

Seven things are helpful, etc.

What seven things are helpful? Seven kinds of wealth of noble ones: the wealth of faith, ethical conduct, conscience, prudence, learning, generosity, and wisdom.

What seven things should be developed? Seven awakening factors: mindfulness, investigation of principles, energy, rapture, tranquility, immersion, and equanimity.

What seven things should be completely understood? Seven planes of consciousness. There are sentient beings that are diverse in body and diverse in perception, such as human beings, some gods, and some beings in the underworld. This is the first plane of consciousness.

There are sentient beings that are diverse in body and unified in perception, such as the gods reborn in Brahma's Host through the first absorption. This is the second plane of consciousness.

There are sentient beings that are unified in body and diverse in perception, such as the gods of streaming radiance. This is the third plane of consciousness.

There are sentient beings that are unified in body and unified in perception, such as the gods replete with glory. This is the fourth plane of consciousness.

There are sentient beings that have gone totally beyond perceptions of form. With the ending of perceptions of impingement, not focusing on perceptions of diversity, aware that 'space is infinite', they have been reborn in the dimension of infinite space. This is the fifth plane of consciousness.

There are sentient beings that have gone totally beyond the dimension of infinite space. Aware that 'consciousness is infinite', they have been reborn in the dimension of infinite consciousness. This is the sixth plane of consciousness.

There are sentient beings that have gone totally beyond the dimension of infinite consciousness. Aware that 'there is nothing at all', they have been reborn in the dimension of nothingness. This is the seventh plane of consciousness.

What seven things should be given up? Seven underlying tendencies: sensual desire, repulsion, views, doubt, conceit, desire to be reborn, and ignorance.

What seven things make things worse? Seven bad qualities: a mendicant is faithless, shameless, imprudent, uneducated, lazy, unmindful, and witless.

What seven things lead to distinction? Seven good qualities: a mendicant is faithful, conscientious, prudent, learned, energetic, mindful, and wise.

What seven things are hard to comprehend? Seven aspects of the teachings of the good persons: a mendicant knows the teachings, knows the meaning, knows themselves, knows moderation, knows the right time, knows assemblies, and knows people.

What seven things should be produced? Seven perceptions: the perception of impermanence, the perception of not-self, the perception of ugliness, the perception of drawbacks, the perception of giving up, the perception of fading away, and the perception of cessation.

What seven things should be directly known? Seven qualifications for graduation. A mendicant has a keen enthusiasm to undertake the training ... to examine the teachings ... to get rid of desires ... for retreat ... to rouse up energy ... for mindfulness and alertness ... to penetrate theoretically. And they don't lose these desires in the future.

What seven things should be realized? Seven powers of one who has ended the defilements. Firstly, a mendicant with defilements ended has clearly seen with right wisdom all conditions as truly impermanent. This is a power that a mendicant who has ended the defilements relies on to claim: 'My defilements have ended.'

Furthermore, a mendicant with defilements ended has clearly seen with right wisdom that sensual pleasures are truly like a pit of glowing coals. ...

Furthermore, the mind of a mendicant with defilements ended slants, slopes, and inclines to seclusion. They're withdrawn, loving renunciation, and they've totally done with defiling influences. ...

Furthermore, a mendicant with defilements ended has well developed the four kinds of mindfulness meditation. ...

Furthermore, a mendicant with defilements ended has well developed the five faculties. ...

Furthermore, a mendicant with defilements ended has well developed the seven awakening factors. ...

Furthermore, a mendicant with defilements ended has well developed the noble eightfold path. ... This is a power that a mendicant who has ended the defilements relies on to claim: 'My defilements have ended.'

So these seventy things that are true, real, and accurate, not unreal, not otherwise were rightly awakened to by the Realized One.

The first recitation section is finished.

Groups of Eight

Eight things are helpful, etc.

What eight things are helpful? There are eight causes and reasons that lead to acquiring the wisdom fundamental to the spiritual life, and to its increase, growth, development, and fulfillment once it has been acquired. What eight? It's when a mendicant lives relying on the Teacher or a spiritual companion in a teacher's role. And they set up a keen sense of conscience and prudence for them, with warmth and respect. This is the first cause.

When a mendicant lives relying on the Teacher or a spiritual companion in a teacher's role — with a keen sense of conscience and prudence for them, with warmth and respect — from time to time they go and ask them questions: 'Why, sir, does it say this? What does that mean?' Those venerables clarify what is unclear, reveal what is obscure, and dispel doubt regarding the many doubtful matters. This is the second cause.

After hearing that teaching they perfect withdrawal of both body and mind. This is the third cause.

Furthermore, a mendicant is ethical, restrained in the monastic code, conducting themselves well and seeking alms in suitable places. Seeing danger in the slightest fault, they keep the rules they've undertaken. This is the fourth cause.

Furthermore, a mendicant is very learned, remembering and keeping what they've learned. These teachings are good in the beginning, good in the middle, and good in the end, meaningful and well-phrased, describing a spiritual practice that's entirely full and pure. They are very learned in such teachings, remembering them, reinforcing them by recitation, mentally scrutinizing them, and comprehending them theoretically. This is the fifth cause.

Furthermore, a mendicant lives with energy roused up for giving up unskillful qualities and embracing skillful qualities. They are strong, staunchly vigorous, not slacking off when it comes to developing skillful qualities. This is the sixth cause.

Furthermore, a mendicant is mindful. They have utmost mindfulness and alertness, and can remember and recall what was said and done long ago. This is the seventh cause.

Furthermore, a mendicant meditates observing rise and fall in the five grasping aggregates. 'Such is form, such is the origin of form, such is the ending of form. Such is feeling, such is the origin of feeling, such is the ending of feeling. Such is perception, such is the origin of perception, such is the ending of perception. Such are choices, such is the origin of choices, such is the ending of choices. Such is consciousness, such is the origin of consciousness, such is the ending of consciousness.' This is the eighth cause.

What eight things should be developed? The noble eightfold path, that is: right view, right thought, right speech, right action, right livelihood, right effort, right mindfulness, and right immersion.

What eight things should be completely understood? Eight worldly conditions: gain and loss, fame and disgrace, praise and blame, pleasure and pain.

What eight things should be given up? Eight wrong ways: wrong view, wrong thought, wrong speech, wrong action, wrong livelihood, wrong effort, wrong mindfulness, and wrong immersion.

What eight things make things worse? Eight grounds for laziness. Firstly, a mendicant has some work to do. They think: 'I have some work to do. But while doing it my body will get tired. I'd better have a lie down.' They lie down, and don't rouse energy for attaining the unattained, achieving the unachieved, and realizing the unrealized. This is the first ground for laziness.

Furthermore, a mendicant has done some work. They think: 'I've done some work. But while working my body got tired. I'd better have a lie down.' They lie down, and don't rouse energy... This is the second ground for laziness.

Furthermore, a mendicant has to go on a journey. They think: 'I have to go on a journey. But while walking my body will get tired. I'd better have a lie down.'

They lie down, and don't rouse energy... This is the third ground for laziness.

Furthermore, a mendicant has gone on a journey. They think: 'I've gone on a journey. But while walking my body got tired. I'd better have a lie down.' They lie down, and don't rouse energy... This is the fourth ground for laziness.

Furthermore, a mendicant has wandered for alms, but they didn't get to fill up on as much food as they like, coarse or fine. They think: 'I've wandered for alms, but I didn't get to fill up on as much food as I like, coarse or fine. My body is tired and unfit for work. I'd better have a lie down.'... This is the fifth ground for laziness.

Furthermore, a mendicant has wandered for alms, and they got to fill up on as much food as they like, coarse or fine. They think: 'I've wandered for alms, and I got to fill up on as much food as I like, coarse or fine. My body is heavy, unfit for work, like I've just eaten a load of beans. I'd better have a lie down.'... They lie down, and don't rouse energy... This is the sixth ground for laziness.

Furthermore, a mendicant feels a little sick. They think: 'I feel a little sick. Lying down would be good for me. I'd better have a lie down.' They lie down, and don't rouse energy... This is the seventh ground for laziness.

Furthermore, a mendicant has recently recovered from illness. They think: 'I've recently recovered from illness. My body is weak and unfit for work. I'd better have a lie down.' They lie down, and don't rouse energy... This is the eighth ground for laziness.

What eight things lead to distinction? Eight grounds for arousing energy. Firstly, a mendicant has some work to do. They think: 'I have some work to do. While working it's not easy to focus on the instructions of the Buddhas. I'd better preemptively rouse up energy for attaining the unattained, achieving the unachieved, and realizing the unrealized.' They rouse energy for attaining the unattained, achieving the unachieved, and realizing the unrealized. This is the first ground for arousing energy.

Furthermore, a mendicant has done some work. They think: 'I've done some work. While I was working I wasn't able to focus on the instructions of the Buddhas. I'd better preemptively rouse up energy.'... This is the second ground for arousing energy.

Furthermore, a mendicant has to go on a journey. They think: 'I have to go on a journey. While walking it's not easy to focus on the instructions of the Buddhas. I'd better preemptively rouse up energy.'... This is the third ground for arousing energy.

Furthermore, a mendicant has gone on a journey. They think: 'I've gone on a journey. While I was walking I wasn't able to focus on the instructions of the Buddhas. I'd better preemptively rouse up energy.'... This is the fourth ground for arousing energy.

Furthermore, a mendicant has wandered for alms, but they didn't get to fill up on as much food as they like, coarse or fine. They think: 'I've wandered for alms, but I didn't get to fill up on as much food as I like, coarse or fine. My body is light and fit for work. I'd better preemptively rouse up energy.'... This is the fifth ground for arousing energy.

Furthermore, a mendicant has wandered for alms, and they got to fill up on as much food as they like, coarse or fine. They think: 'I've wandered for alms, and I got to fill up on as much food as I like, coarse or fine. My body is strong and fit for work. I'd better preemptively rouse up energy.'... This is the sixth ground for arousing energy.

Furthermore, a mendicant feels a little sick. They think: 'I feel a little sick. It's possible this illness will worsen. I'd better preemptively rouse up energy.'... This is the seventh ground for arousing energy.

Furthermore, a mendicant has recently recovered from illness. They think: 'I've recently recovered from illness. It's possible the illness will come back. I'd better preemptively rouse up energy for attaining the unattained, achieving the unachieved, and realizing the unrealized.' They rouse energy for attaining the unattained, achieving the unachieved, and realizing the unrealized. This is the eighth ground for arousing energy.

What eight things are hard to comprehend? Eight lost opportunities for spiritual practice. Firstly, a Realized One has arisen in the world. He teaches the Dhamma leading to peace, extinguishment, awakening, as proclaimed by the Holy One. But a person has been reborn in hell. This is the first lost opportunity for spiritual practice.

Furthermore, a Realized One has arisen in the world. But a person has been reborn in the animal realm. This is the second lost opportunity for spiritual practice.

Furthermore, a Realized One has arisen in the world. But a person has been reborn in the ghost realm. This is the third lost opportunity for spiritual practice.

Furthermore, a Realized One has arisen in the world. But person has been reborn in one of the long-lived orders of gods. This is the fourth lost opportunity for spiritual practice.

Furthermore, a Realized One has arisen in the world. But a person has been reborn in the borderlands, among barbarian tribes, where monks, nuns, laymen, and laywomen do not go. This is the fifth lost opportunity for spiritual practice.

Furthermore, a Realized One has arisen in the world. And a person is reborn in a central country. But they have wrong view and distorted perspective: 'There's no meaning in giving, sacrifice, or offerings. There's no fruit or result of good and bad deeds. There's no afterlife. There are no duties to mother and father. No beings are reborn spontaneously. And there's no ascetic or brahmin who is well attained and practiced, and who describes the afterlife after realizing it with their own insight.' This is the sixth lost opportunity for spiritual practice.

Furthermore, a Realized One has arisen in the world. And a person is reborn in a central country. But they're witless, dull, stupid, and unable to distinguish what is well said from what is poorly said. This is the seventh lost opportunity for spiritual practice.

Furthermore, a Realized One has arisen in the world. But he doesn't teach the Dhamma leading to peace, extinguishment, awakening, as announced by the Holy One. And a person is reborn in a central country. And they're wise, bright, clever, and able to distinguish what is well said from what is poorly said. This is the eighth lost opportunity for spiritual practice.

What eight things should be produced? Eight thoughts of a great man. 'This teaching is for those of few wishes, not those of many wishes. It's for the contented, not those who lack contentment. It's for the secluded, not those who enjoy company. It's for the energetic, not the lazy. It's for the mindful, not the unmindful. It's for those with immersion, not those without immersion. It's for the wise, not the witless. This teaching is for those who don't enjoy proliferating, not for those who enjoy proliferating.'

What eight things should be directly known? Eight dimensions of mastery. Perceiving form internally, someone sees visions externally, limited, both pretty and ugly. Mastering them, they perceive: 'I know and see.' This is the first dimension of mastery.

Perceiving form internally, someone sees visions externally, limitless, both pretty and ugly. Mastering them, they perceive: 'I know and see.' This is the second dimension of mastery.

Not perceiving form internally, someone sees visions externally, limited, both pretty and ugly. Mastering them, they perceive: 'I know and see.' This is the third dimension of mastery.

Not perceiving form internally, someone sees visions externally, limitless, both pretty and ugly. Mastering them, they perceive: 'I know and see.' This is the fourth dimension of mastery.

Not perceiving form internally, someone sees visions externally that are blue, with blue color, blue hue, and blue tint. They're like a flax flower that's blue, with blue color, blue hue, and blue tint. Or a cloth from Baranasi that's smoothed on both sides, blue, with blue color, blue hue, and blue tint. Mastering them, they perceive: 'I know and see.' This is the fifth dimension of mastery.

Not perceiving form internally, someone sees visions externally that are yellow, with yellow color, yellow hue, and yellow tint. They're like a champak flower that's yellow, with yellow color, yellow hue, and yellow tint. Or a cloth from Baranasi that's smoothed on both sides, yellow, with yellow color, yellow hue, and yellow tint. Mastering them, they perceive: 'I know and see.' This is the sixth dimension of mastery.

Not perceiving form internally, someone sees visions externally that are red, with red color, red hue, and red tint. They're like a scarlet mallow flower that's red, with red color, red hue, and red tint. Or a cloth from Baranasi that's smoothed on both sides, red, with red color, red hue, and red tint. Mastering them, they perceive: 'I know and see.' This is the seventh dimension of mastery.

Not perceiving form internally, someone sees visions externally that are white, with white color, white hue, and white tint. They're like the morning star that's white, with white color, white hue, and white tint. Or a cloth from Baranasi that's smoothed on both sides, white, with white color, white hue, and white tint. This is the eighth dimension of mastery.

What eight things should be realized? Eight liberations. Having physical form, they see visions. This is the first liberation.

Not perceiving physical form internally, someone see visions externally. This is the second liberation.

They're focused only on beauty. This is the third liberation.

Going totally beyond perceptions of form, with the ending of perceptions of impingement, not focusing on perceptions of diversity, aware that 'space is infinite', they enter and remain in the dimension of infinite space. This is the fourth liberation.

Going totally beyond the dimension of infinite space, aware that 'consciousness is infinite', they enter and remain in the dimension of infinite consciousness. This is the fifth liberation.

Going totally beyond the dimension of infinite consciousness, aware that 'there is nothing at all', they enter and remain in the dimension of nothingness. This is the sixth liberation.

Going totally beyond the dimension of nothingness, they enter and remain in the dimension of neither perception nor non-perception. This is the seventh liberation.

Going totally beyond the dimension of neither perception nor non-perception, they enter and remain in the cessation of perception and feeling. This is the eighth liberation.

So these eighty things that are true, real, and accurate, not unreal, not otherwise were rightly awakened to by the Realized One.

Groups of Nine

Nine things are helpful, etc.

What nine things are helpful? Nine things rooted in proper attention. When you attend properly, joy springs up. When you're joyful, rapture springs up. When the mind is full of rapture, the body becomes tranquil. When the body is tranquil, you feel bliss. And when you're blissful, the mind becomes immersed. When your mind is immersed, you truly know and see. When you truly know and see, you grow disillusioned. Being disillusioned, desire fades away. When desire fades away you're freed.

What nine things should be developed? Nine factors of trying to be pure. The factors of trying to be pure in ethics, mind, view, overcoming doubt, knowledge and vision of the variety of paths, knowledge and vision of the practice, knowledge and vision, wisdom, and freedom.

What nine things should be completely understood? Nine abodes of sentient beings. There are sentient beings that are diverse in body and diverse in perception, such as human beings, some gods, and some beings in the underworld. This is the first abode of sentient beings.

There are sentient beings that are diverse in body and unified in perception, such as the gods reborn in Brahma's Host through the first absorption. This is the second abode of sentient beings.

There are sentient beings that are unified in body and diverse in perception, such as the gods of streaming radiance. This is the third abode of sentient beings.

There are sentient beings that are unified in body and unified in perception, such as the gods replete with glory. This is the fourth abode of sentient beings.

There are sentient beings that are non-percipient and do not experience anything, such as the gods who are non-percipient beings. This is the fifth abode of sentient beings.

There are sentient beings that have gone totally beyond perceptions of form. With the ending of perceptions of impingement, not focusing on perceptions of diversity, aware that 'space is infinite', they have been reborn in the dimension of infinite space. This is the sixth abode of sentient beings.

There are sentient beings that have gone totally beyond the dimension of infinite space. Aware that 'consciousness is infinite', they have been reborn in the dimension of infinite consciousness. This is the seventh abode of sentient beings.

There are sentient beings that have gone totally beyond the dimension of infinite consciousness. Aware that 'there is nothing at all', they have been reborn in the dimension of nothingness. This is the eighth abode of sentient beings.

There are sentient beings that have gone totally beyond the dimension of nothingness. They have been reborn in the dimension of neither perception nor non-perception. This is the ninth abode of sentient beings.

What nine things should be given up? Nine things rooted in craving. Craving is a cause for seeking. Seeking is a cause for gaining material possessions. Gaining material possessions is a cause for assessing. Assessing is a cause for desire and lust. Desire and lust is a cause for attachment. Attachment is a cause for possessiveness. Possessiveness is a cause for stinginess. Stinginess is a cause for safeguarding. Owing to safeguarding, many bad, unskillful things come to be:

taking up the rod and the sword, quarrels, arguments, fights, accusations, divisive speech, and lies.

What nine things make things worse? Nine grounds for resentment. Thinking: 'They did wrong to me,' you harbor resentment. Thinking: 'They are doing wrong to me' ... 'They will do wrong to me' ... 'They did wrong by someone I love' ... 'They are doing wrong by someone I love' ... 'They will do wrong by someone I love' ... 'They helped someone I dislike' ... 'They are helping someone I dislike' ... Thinking: 'They will help someone I dislike,' you harbor resentment.

What nine things lead to distinction? Nine methods to get rid of resentment. Thinking: 'They did wrong to me, but what can I possibly do?' you get rid of resentment. Thinking: 'They are doing wrong to me ...' ... 'They will do wrong to me ...' ... 'They did wrong by someone I love ...' ... 'They are doing wrong by someone I love ...' ... 'They will do wrong by someone I love ...' ... 'They helped someone I dislike ...' ... 'They are helping someone I dislike ...' ... Thinking: 'They will help someone I dislike, but what can I possibly do?' you get rid of resentment.

What nine things are hard to comprehend? Nine kinds of diversity. Diversity of elements gives rise to diversity of contacts. Diversity of contacts gives rise to diversity of feelings. Diversity of feelings gives rise to diversity of perceptions. Diversity of perceptions gives rise to diversity of intentions. Diversity of intentions gives rise to diversity of desires. Diversity of desires gives rise to diversity of passions. Diversity of passions gives rise to diversity of searches. Diversity of searches gives rise to diversity of gains.

What nine things should be produced? Nine perceptions: the perceptions of ugliness, death, repulsiveness in food, dissatisfaction with the whole world, impermanence, suffering in impermanence, not-self in suffering, giving up, and fading away.

What nine things should be directly known? Nine progressive meditations. A mendicant, quite secluded from sensual pleasures, secluded from unskillful qualities, enters and remains in the first absorption ... second absorption ... third absorption ... fourth absorption. Going totally beyond perceptions of form, with the ending of perceptions of impingement, not focusing on perceptions of diversity, aware that 'space is infinite', they enter and remain in the dimension of infinite space. Going totally beyond the dimension of infinite space, aware that 'consciousness is infinite', they enter and remain in the dimension of infinite consciousness. Going totally beyond the dimension of infinite consciousness, aware that 'there is nothing at all', they enter and remain in the dimension of nothingness. Going totally beyond the dimension of nothingness, they enter and remain in the dimension of neither perception nor non-perception. Going totally beyond the dimension of neither perception nor non-perception, they enter and remain in the cessation of perception and feeling.

What nine things should be realized? Nine progressive cessations. For someone who has attained the first absorption, sensual perceptions have ceased. For someone who has attained the second absorption, the placing of the mind and keeping it connected have ceased. For someone who has attained the third absorption, rapture has ceased. For someone who has attained the fourth absorption, breathing has ceased. For someone who has attained the dimension of infinite space, the perception of form has ceased. For someone who has attained the dimension of infinite consciousness, the perception of the dimension of infinite space has ceased. For someone who has attained the dimension of nothingness, the perception of the dimension of infinite consciousness has ceased. For someone who has attained the dimension of neither perception nor non-perception, the perception of the dimension of nothingness has ceased. For someone who has attained the cessation of perception and feeling, perception and feeling have ceased.

So these ninety things that are true, real, and accurate, not unreal, not otherwise were rightly awakened to by the Realized One.

Groups of Ten

Ten things are helpful, ten things should be developed, ten things should be completely understood, ten things should be given up, ten things make things worse, ten things lead to distinction, ten things are hard to comprehend, ten things should be produced, ten things should be directly known, ten things should be realized.

What ten things are helpful? Ten qualities that serve as protector. First, a mendicant is ethical, restrained in the monastic code, conducting themselves well and seeking alms in suitable places. Seeing danger in the slightest fault, they keep the rules they've undertaken. This is a quality that serves as protector.

Furthermore, a mendicant is learned. This too is a quality that serves as protector.

Furthermore, a mendicant has good friends, companions, and associates. This too is a quality that serves as protector.

Furthermore, a mendicant is easy to admonish, having qualities that make them easy to admonish. They're patient, and take instruction respectfully. This too is a quality that serves as protector.

Furthermore, a mendicant is deft and tireless in a diverse spectrum of duties for their spiritual companions, understanding how to go about things in order to complete and organize the work. This too is a quality that serves as protector.

Furthermore, a mendicant loves the teachings and is a delight to converse with, being full of joy in the teaching and training. This too is a quality that serves as protector.

Furthermore, a mendicant is content with any kind of robes, alms-food, lodgings, and medicines and supplies for the sick. This too is a quality that serves as protector.

Furthermore, a mendicant is energetic. This too is a quality that serves as protector.

Furthermore, a mendicant is mindful. They have utmost mindfulness and alertness, and can remember and recall what was said and done long ago. This too is a quality that serves as protector.

Furthermore, a mendicant is wise. They have the wisdom of arising and passing away which is noble, penetrative, and leads to the complete ending of suffering. This too is a quality that serves as protector.

What ten things should be developed? Ten universal dimensions of meditation. Someone perceives the meditation on universal earth above, below, across, non-dual and limitless. They perceive the meditation on universal water ... the meditation on universal fire ... the meditation on universal air ... the meditation on universal blue ... the meditation on universal yellow ... the meditation on universal red ... the meditation on universal white ... the meditation on universal space ... They perceive the meditation on universal consciousness above, below, across, non-dual and limitless.

What ten things should be completely understood? Ten sense fields: eye and sights, ear and sounds, nose and smells, tongue and tastes, body and touches.

What ten things should be given up? Ten wrong ways: wrong view, wrong thought, wrong speech, wrong action, wrong livelihood, wrong effort, wrong mindfulness, wrong immersion, wrong knowledge, and wrong freedom.

What ten things make things worse? Ten ways of doing unskillful deeds: killing living creatures, stealing, and sexual misconduct; speech that's false, divisive, harsh, or nonsensical; covetousness, ill will, and wrong view.

What ten things lead to distinction? Ten ways of doing skillful deeds: refraining from killing living creatures, stealing, and sexual misconduct; avoiding speech that's false, divisive, harsh, or nonsensical; contentment, good will, and right view.

What ten things are hard to comprehend? Ten noble abodes. A mendicant has given up five factors, possesses six factors, has a single guard, has four supports, has eliminated idiosyncratic interpretations of the truth, has totally given up searching, has unsullied intentions, has stilled the physical process, and is well freed in mind and well freed by wisdom.

And how has a mendicant given up five factors? It's when a mendicant has given up sensual desire, ill will, dullness and drowsiness, restlessness and remorse, and doubt. That's how a mendicant has given up five factors.

And how does a mendicant possess six factors? A mendicant, seeing a sight with their eyes, is neither happy nor sad. They remain equanimous, mindful and aware. Hearing a sound with their ears ... Smelling an odor with their nose ... Tasting a flavor with their tongue ... Feeling a touch with their body ... Knowing a thought with their mind, they're neither happy nor sad. They remain equanimous, mindful and aware. That's how a mendicant possesses six factors.

And how does a mendicant have a single guard? It's when a mendicant's heart is guarded by mindfulness. That's how a mendicant has a single guard.

And how does a mendicant have four supports? After reflection, a mendicant uses some things, endures some things, avoids some things, and gets rid of some things. That's how a mendicant has four supports.

And how has a mendicant eliminated idiosyncratic interpretations of the truth? Different ascetics and brahmins have different idiosyncratic interpretations of the truth. A mendicant has dispelled, eliminated, thrown out, rejected, let go of, given up, and relinquished all these. That's how a mendicant has eliminated idiosyncratic interpretations of the truth.

And how has a mendicant totally given up searching? It's when they've given up searching for sensual pleasures, for continued existence, and for a spiritual path. That's how a mendicant has totally given up searching.

And how does a mendicant have unsullied intentions? It's when they've given up sensual, malicious, and cruel intentions. That's how a mendicant has unsullied intentions.

And how has a mendicant stilled the physical process? Giving up pleasure and pain, and ending former happiness and sadness, they enter and remain in the fourth absorption, without pleasure or pain, with pure equanimity and mindfulness. That's how a mendicant has stilled the physical process.

And how is a mendicant well freed in mind? It's when a mendicant's mind is freed from greed, hate, and delusion. That's how a mendicant is well freed in mind.

And how is a mendicant well freed by wisdom? It's when a mendicant understands: 'I've given up greed, hate, and delusion, cut them off at the root, made them like a palm stump, obliterated them, so they're unable to arise in the future.' That's how a mendicant's mind is well freed by wisdom.

What ten things should be produced? Ten perceptions: the perceptions of ugliness, death, repulsiveness in food, dissatisfaction with the whole world, impermanence, suffering in impermanence, not-self in suffering, giving up, fading away, and cessation.

What ten things should be directly known? Ten grounds for wearing away. For one of right view, wrong view is worn away. And the many bad, unskillful qualities that arise because of wrong view are worn away. For one of right intention, wrong intention is worn away. ... For one of right speech, wrong speech is worn away. ... For one of right action, wrong action is worn away. ... For one of right livelihood, wrong livelihood is worn away. ... For one of right effort, wrong effort is worn away. ... For one of right mindfulness, wrong mindfulness is worn away. ... For one of right immersion, wrong immersion is worn away. ... For one of right knowledge, wrong knowledge is worn away. ... For one of right freedom, wrong freedom is worn away. And the many bad, unskillful qualities that arise because of wrong freedom are worn away.

What ten things should be realized? Ten qualities of an adept: an adept's right view, right thought, right speech, right action, right livelihood, right effort, right mindfulness, right immersion, right knowledge, and right freedom.

So these hundred things that are true, real, and accurate, not unreal, not otherwise were rightly awakened to by the Realized One."

This is what Venerable Sariputta said. Satisfied, the mendicants were happy with what Sariputta said.

# KHUDDAPATHA

# 1 SARANATTAYA:

# THE THREE REFUGES

Homage to that Blessed One, the perfected one, the fully awakened Buddha!

I take refuge in the Buddha,

I take refuge in the Teaching,

I take refuge in the Sangha.

For the second time I take refuge in the Buddha,

for the second time I take refuge in the Teaching,

for the second time I take refuge in the Sangha.

For the third time I take refuge in the Buddha,

for the third time I take refuge in the Teaching,

for the third time I take refuge in the Sangha.

# 2 DASASIKKHAPADA:

# THE TEN PRECEPTS

I undertake the precept to refrain from killing living creatures.

I undertake the precept to refrain from stealing.

I undertake the precept to refrain from sexual activity.

I undertake the precept to refrain from lying.

I undertake the precept to refrain from taking alcoholic drinks that cause negligence.

I undertake the precept to refrain from food at the wrong time.

I undertake the precept to refrain from dancing, singing, music, and seeing shows.

I undertake the precept to refrain from beautifying and adorning myself with garlands, perfumes, and makeup.

I undertake the precept to refrain from high and luxurious beds.

I undertake the precept to refrain from receiving gold and money.

# 3 DVATTIṀSAKARA:

# THE THIRTY-TWO PARTS OF THE BODY

"In this body there is head hair, body hair, nails, teeth, skin, flesh, sinews, bones, bone marrow, kidneys, heart, liver, diaphragm, spleen, lungs, intestines, mesentery, undigested food, feces, brain, bile, phlegm, pus, blood, sweat, fat, tears, grease, saliva, snot, synovial fluid, urine."

# 4 KUMARAPANHA:

# THE BOY'S QUESTIONS

What is the one? All sentient beings are sustained by food.

What is the two? Name and form.

What is the three? Three feelings.

What is the four? Four noble truths.

What is the five? Five grasping aggregates.

What is the six? Six interior sense fields.

What is the seven? Seven awakening factors.

What is the eight? The noble eightfold path.

What is the nine? Nine abodes of sentient beings.

What is the ten? One endowed with ten factors is called "perfected".

# 5 MAṄGALASUTTA:

# BLESSINGS

So I have heard. At one time the Buddha was staying near Savatthi in Jeta's Grove, Anathapindika's monastery. Then, late at night, a glorious deity, lighting up the entire Jeta's Grove, went up to the Buddha, bowed, and stood to one side. That deity addressed the Buddha in verse:

"Many gods and humans

have thought about blessings

desiring well-being:

declare the highest blessing."

"Not to fraternize with fools,

but to fraternize with the wise,

and honoring those worthy of honor:

this is the highest blessing.

Living in a suitable region,

having made merit in the past,

being rightly resolved in oneself,

this is the highest blessing.

Education and a craft,

discipline and training,

and well-spoken speech:

this is the highest blessing.

Caring for mother and father,

kindness to children and partners,

and unstressful work:

this is the highest blessing.

Giving and righteous conduct,

kindness to relatives,

blameless deeds:

this is the highest blessing.

Desisting and abstaining from evil,

avoiding alcoholic drinks,

diligence in good qualities:

this is the highest blessing.

Respect and humility,

contentment and gratitude,

and timely listening to the teaching:

this is the highest blessing.

Patience, being easy to admonish,

the sight of ascetics,

and timely discussion of the teaching:

this is the highest blessing.

Austerity and celibacy

seeing the noble truths,

and realization of extinguishment:

this is the highest blessing.

Though touched by worldly conditions,

their mind does not tremble;

sorrowless, stainless, secure:

this is the highest blessing.

Having completed these things,

undefeated everywhere;

everywhere they go in safety:

# THIS IS THEIR HIGHEST BLESSING."

## 6 RATANASUTTA:

Gems

Whatever beings have gathered here,

on the ground or in the sky,

may beings all be of happy heart,

and listen carefully to what is said.

So pay heed, all you beings,

have love for humankind,

who day and night bring offerings;

please protect them diligently.

There's no wealth here or beyond,

no sublime gem in the heavens,

that equals the Realized One.

This sublime gem is in the Buddha:

by this truth, may you be well!

Ending, dispassion, the undying, the sublime,

attained by the Sakyan Sage immersed in samadhi;

there is nothing equal to that Dhamma.

This sublime gem is in the Dhamma:

by this truth, may you be well!

The purity praised by the highest Buddha,

is said to be the "immersion with immediate fruit";

no equal to that immersion is found.

This sublime gem is in the Dhamma:

by this truth, may you be well!

The eight individuals praised by the good,

are the four pairs of the Holy One's disciples;

they are worthy of religious donations,

what's given to them is very fruitful.

This sublime gem is in the Saṅgha:

by this truth, may you be well!

Dedicated to Gotama's dispensation,

strong-minded, free of sense desire,

they've attained the goal, plunged into the deathless,

and enjoy the quenching they've freely gained.

This sublime gem is in the Saṅgha:

by this truth, may you be well!

As a well planted boundary-pillar

is not shaken by the four winds,

I say a good person is like this,

who sees the noble truths in experience.

This sublime gem is in the Saṅgha:

by this truth, may you be well!

Those who fathom the noble truths

taught by the one of deep wisdom,

do not take an eighth life,

even if they are hugely negligent.

This sublime gem is in the Saṅgha:

by this truth, may you be well!

When they attain to vision

they give up three things:

identity view, doubt, and any

attachment to precepts and observances.

They're freed from the four places of loss,

and unable to perform the six grave crimes.

This sublime gem is in the Saṅgha:

by this truth, may you be well!

Even if they do a bad deed

by body, speech, or mind,

they are unable to conceal it;

they say this inability applies to one who has seen the truth.

This sublime gem is in the Saṅgha:

by this truth, may you be well!

Like a tall forest tree crowned with flowers

in the first month of summer;

that's how he taught the superb Dhamma,

leading to quenching, the ultimate benefit.

This sublime gem is in the Buddha:

by this truth, may you be well!

The superb, knower of the superb, giver of the superb, bringer of the superb;

taught the superb Dhamma supreme.

This sublime gem is in the Buddha:

by this truth, may you be well!

The old is ended, nothing new is produced.

their minds have no desire for future rebirth.

Withered are the seeds, there's no desire for growth,

those wise ones are extinguished just like this lamp.

This sublime gem is in the Saṅgha:

by this truth, may you be well!

Whatever beings have gathered here,

on the ground or in the sky:

the Realized One is honored by gods and humans!

We bow to the Buddha! May you be safe!

Whatever beings have gathered here,

on the ground or in the sky:

the Realized One is honored by gods and humans!

We bow to the Dhamma! May you be safe!

Whatever beings have gathered here,

on the ground or in the sky:

the Realized One is honored by gods and humans!

We bow to the Saṅgha! May you be safe!

# 7 TIROKUTTASUTTA:

# OUTSIDE THE WALLS

Outside the walls they stand and wait,

at the junctions and the crossroads.

Returning to their former homes

they wait beside the door posts.

But when lavish food and drink

of many kinds is set out,

no-one remembers them at all,

because of those beings's deeds.

That's why those who have compassion

give to their relatives

food and drink at the right time,

that's clean, delicious, and suitable.

"May this be for our relatives!

May our relatives be happy!"

Those ghosts who have gathered there,

the departed relatives who have come

for the lavish food and drink

gratefully express appreciation:

"May our relatives live long!

For those to whom we owe this gain,

who have given honor to us,

it will not be fruitless for the donor."

There is no farming there,

no cow pasture can be found;

likewise there's no trading,

and no commerce in gold.

The departed, the dead in that place

live on what is given here.

Just as water that rains on high

flows down to the plains,

so too what is given here

aids the departed ghosts.

Just as the rivers full

swell the ocean seas

so too what is given here

aids the departed ghosts.

Thinking: "They gave to me, they did for me,

they were my family, friend, companion",

give offerings to departed kin,

remembering past deeds.

For neither tears nor grief

or other lamentations

are of any use to the departed,

so long as their relatives stay like this.

This offering that has been given,

well placed in the Saṅgha,

is for their lasting welfare,

and aids them right away.

The relative's duty has now been shown:

how high honor to departed is performed,

how the mendicants can be kept healthy,

and how no little merit is produced by you.

# 8 NIDHIKANDASUTTA:

# A HIDDEN TREASURE

A person stores away their savings

in a deep pit by the water's edge:

"When need arises

it will be there to help

free me from rulers if I am slandered,

or from bandits if harassed,

or to release me from debt,

or in case of famine or losses."

What the world calls savings

get stored away for such reasons.

But no matter how well stored away they are

in a deep pit by the water's edge,

all their savings will fail

to aid them all the time.

For perhaps those savings are removed from there,

or they forget what marks the site,

or dragons make off with them,

or spirits carry them away,

or unloved heirs

secretly unearth them.

When their merit is used up,

all of that will vanish.

But by giving and morality,

restraint and self-control,

a women or man

keeps their savings safe.

At a shrine or with the Saṅgha,

with mother or father,

or else an elder sibling,

those savings are kept safe,

they stay with you, undecaying.

We must go on leaving all behind,

only this you take when you go.

You don't have to divide it with others,

no thief makes off with your savings.

A wise person would make merit,

the savings that stay with you.

Such savings grant every desire

of gods and humans too.

Whatever it is that they wish for

through this they have it all.

Good looks, a sweet voice,

a good shape, and good appearance,

leadership and followers:

through this they have it all.

Sovereignty of a local kingdom,

the happiness of a Wheel-Turning Monarch,

even divine kingship in the heavens:

through this they have it all.

Human success,

heavenly delight,

attaining extinguishment:

through this they have it all.

Relying on having good friends,

proper application of effort,

mastery of knowledge and freedom:

through this they have it all.

Analytical knowledge, the liberations,

the perfections of the disciple,

the plane of a Buddha awakened for themselves:

through this they have it all.

This accomplishment in merit

is so very beneficial.

That's why the wise and the astute

praise the making of merit.

# 9 METTASUTTA:

# THE DISCOURSE ON LOVE

Those who are skilled in the meaning of scripture

should practice like this so as to realize the state of peace.

Let them be able and upright, very upright,

easy to speak to, gentle and humble;

content and unburdensome,

unbusied, living lightly,

alert, with senses calmed,

courteous, not fawning on families.

Let them not do the slightest thing

that others might blame with reason.

May they be happy and safe!

May all beings be happy!

Whatever living creatures there are

with not a one left out—

frail or firm, long or large,

medium, small, tiny or round,

visible or invisible,

living far or near,

those born or to be born—

may all beings be happy!

Let none turn from another,

nor look down on anyone anywhere.

Though provoked or aggrieved,

let them not wish pain on each other.

Even as a mother would protect with her life

her child, her only child,

so too for all creatures

unfold a boundless heart.

With love for the whole world,

unfold a boundless heart:

above, below, all round,

unconstricted, without enemy or foe.

When standing, walking, sitting,

or lying down while yet unweary,

keep this ever in mind;

for this, they say, is a meditation of Brahma in this life.

Avoiding harmful views,

virtuous, accomplished in insight,

with sensual desire dispelled,

they never return to a womb again.

# ITIVUTTAKA

# SO IT WAS SAID

# THE SECTION OF THE ONES

1. Greed

This was said by the Lord, said by the Arahant, so I heard:

"Abandon one thing, bhikkhus, and I guarantee you non-returning. What is that one thing? Greed is that one thing, bhikkhus. Abandon that and I guarantee you non-returning."

This is the meaning of what the Lord said. So in regard to this it was said:

Beings coveting with greed

Go to rebirth in a bad bourn.

But having rightly understood greed,

Those with insight abandon it.

By abandoning it they never come

Back to this world again.

This too is the meaning of what was said by the Lord, so I heard.

2. Hate

This was said by the Lord, said by the Arahant, so I heard:

"Abandon one thing, bhikkhus, and I guarantee you non-returning. What is that one thing? Hate is that one thing, bhikkhus. Abandon that and I guarantee you non-returning."

This is the meaning of what the Lord said. So in regard to this it was said:

Beings corrupted by hate

Go to rebirth in a bad bourn.

But having rightly understood hate,

Those with insight abandon it.

By abandoning it they never come

Back to this world again.

This too is the meaning of what was said by the Lord, so I heard.

3. Delusion

This was said by the Lord, said by the Arahant, so I heard:

"Abandon one thing, bhikkhus, and I guarantee you non-returning. What is that one thing? Delusion is that one thing, bhikkhus. Abandon that and I guarantee you non-returning."

This is the meaning of what the Lord said. So in regard to this it was said:

Beings confused by delusion

Go to rebirth in a bad bourn.

But having rightly understood delusion,

Those with insight abandon it.

By abandoning it they never come

Back to this world again.

This too is the meaning of what was said by the Lord, so I heard.

4. Anger

This was said by the Lord, said by the Arahant, so I heard:

"Abandon one thing, bhikkhus, and I guarantee you non-returning. What is that one thing? Anger is that one thing, bhikkhus. Abandon that and I guarantee you non-returning."

This is the meaning of what the Lord said. So in regard to this it was said:

Beings enraged with anger

Go to rebirth in a bad bourn.

But having rightly understood anger,

Those with insight abandon it.

By abandoning it they never come

Back to this world again.

This too is the meaning of what was said by the Lord, so I heard.

5. Contempt

This was said by the Lord, said by the Arahant, so I heard:

"Abandon one thing, bhikkhus, and I guarantee you non-returning. What is that one thing? Contempt is that one thing, bhikkhus. Abandon that and I guarantee you non-returning."

This is the meaning of what the Lord said. So in regard to this it was said:

Beings despising others with contempt

Go to rebirth in a bad bourn.

But having rightly understood contempt,

Those with insight abandon it.

By abandoning it they never come

Back to this world again.

This too is the meaning of what was said by the Lord, so I heard.

6. Conceit

This was said by the Lord, said by the Arahant, so I heard:

"Abandon one thing, bhikkhus, and I guarantee you non-returning. What is that one thing? Conceit is that one thing, bhikkhus. Abandon that and I guarantee you non-returning."

This is the meaning of what the Lord said. So in regard to this it was said:

Beings puffed up with conceit

Go to rebirth in a bad bourn.

But having rightly understood conceit,

Those with insight abandon it.

By abandoning it they never come

Back to this world again.

This too is the meaning of what was said by the Lord, so I heard.

7. Understanding the All

This was said by the Lord, said by the Arahant, so I heard:

"Bhikkhus, one who has not directly known and fully understood the 'All,' who has not detached his mind from it and abandoned it, is incapable of destroying suffering. But one who has directly known and fully understood the 'All,' and who has detached his mind from it and abandoned it, is capable of destroying suffering."

This is the meaning of what the Lord said. So in regard to this it was said:

One who knows the "All" in every way,

Who is not attached to anything,

Having fully understood the "All,"

Has overcome all suffering.

This too is the meaning of what was said by the Lord, so I heard.

8. Understanding Conceit

This was said by the Lord, said by the Arahant, so I heard:

"Bhikkhus, one who has not directly known and fully understood conceit, who has not detached his mind from it and abandoned it, is incapable of destroying suffering. But one who has directly known and fully understood conceit, and who has detached his mind from it and abandoned it, is capable of destroying suffering."

This is the meaning of what the Lord said. So in regard to this it was said:

Humankind is possessed by conceit,

Bound by conceit and delighted with being;

Not fully understanding conceit,

They come again to renewal of being.

But those who have abandoned conceit,

And who by destroying conceit are freed,

Have conquered the bondage of conceit

And overcome all suffering.

This too is the meaning of what was said by the Lord, so I heard.

9. Understanding Greed

This was said by the Lord, said by the Arahant, so I heard:

"Bhikkhus, one who has not directly known and fully understood greed, who has not detached his mind from it and abandoned it, is incapable of destroying suffering. But one who has directly known and fully understood greed, and who has detached his mind from it and abandoned it, is capable of destroying suffering."

This is the meaning of what the Lord said. So in regard to this it was said:

Humankind is possessed by greed,

Bound by greed and delighted with being;

Not fully understanding greed,

They come again to renewal of being.

But those who have abandoned greed,

And who by destroying greed are freed,

Have conquered the bondage of greed

And overcome all suffering.

This too is the meaning of what was said by the Lord, so I heard.

10. Understanding Hate

This was said by the Lord, said by the Arahant, so I heard:

"Bhikkhus, one who has not directly known and fully understood hate, who has not detached his mind from it and abandoned it, is incapable of destroying suffering. But one who has directly known and fully understood hate, and who has detached his mind from it and abandoned it, is capable of destroying suffering."

This is the meaning of what the Lord said. So in regard to this it was said:

Humankind is possessed by hate,

Bound by hate and delighted with being;

Not fully understanding hate,

They come again to renewal of being.

But those who have abandoned hate,

And who by destroying hate are freed,

Have conquered the bondage of hate

And overcome all suffering.

This too is the meaning of what was said by the Lord, so I heard.

11. Understanding Delusion

This was said by the Lord, said by the Arahant, so I heard:

"Bhikkhus, one who has not directly known and fully understood delusion, who has not detached his mind from it and abandoned it, is incapable of destroying suffering. But one who has directly known and fully understood delusion, and who has detached his mind from it and abandoned it, is capable of destroying suffering."

This is the meaning of what the Lord said. So in regard to this it was said:

Humankind is possessed by delusion,

Bound by delusion and delighted with being;

Not fully understanding delusion,

They come again to renewal of being.

But those who have abandoned delusion,

And who by destroying delusion are freed,

Have conquered the bondage of delusion

And overcome all suffering.

This too is the meaning of what was said by the Lord, so I heard.

12. Understanding Anger

This was said by the Lord, said by the Arahant, so I heard:

"Bhikkhus, one who has not directly known and fully understood anger, who has not detached his mind from it and abandoned it, is incapable of destroying suffering. But one who has directly known and fully understood anger, and who has detached his mind from it and abandoned it, is capable of destroying suffering."

This is the meaning of what the Lord said. So in regard to this it was said:

Humankind is possessed by anger,

Bound by anger and delighted with being;

Not fully understanding anger,

They come again to renewal of being.

But those who have abandoned anger,

And who by destroying anger are freed,

Have conquered the bondage of anger

And overcome all suffering.

This too is the meaning of what was said by the Lord, so I heard.

13. Understanding Contempt

This was said by the Lord, said by the Arahant, so I heard:

"Bhikkhus, one who has not directly known and fully understood contempt, who has not detached his mind from it and abandoned it, is incapable of destroying suffering. But one who has directly known and fully understood contempt, and who has detached his mind from it and abandoned it, is capable of destroying suffering."

This is the meaning of what the Lord said. So in regard to this it was said:

Humankind is possessed by contempt,

Bound by contempt and delighted with being;

Not fully understanding contempt,

They come again to renewal of being.

But those who have abandoned contempt,

And who by destroying contempt are freed,

Have conquered the bondage of contempt

And overcome all suffering.

This too is the meaning of what was said by the Lord, so I heard.

14. Ignorance

This was said by the Lord, said by the Arahant, so I heard:

"Bhikkhus, I do not perceive any single hindrance other than the hindrance of ignorance by which humankind is so obstructed and for so long a time runs on and wanders in saṃsara. It is indeed through the hindrance of ignorance that humankind is obstructed and for a long time runs on and wanders in saṃsara."

This is the meaning of what the Lord said. So in regard to this it was said:

No other single thing exists

Like the hindrance of delusion,

Which so obstructs humankind

And makes it wander on forever.

Those who have abandoned delusion,

Cleaving through this mass of darkness,

No longer roam and wander on;

In them the cause is found no more.

This too is the meaning of what was said by the Lord, so I heard.

15. Craving

This was said by the Lord, said by the Arahant, so I heard:

"Bhikkhus, I do not perceive any single fetter other than the fetter of craving by which beings are so tied and for so long a time run on and wander in saṃsara. It is indeed through the fetter of craving that beings are tied and for a long time run on and wander in saṃsara."

This is the meaning of what the Lord said. So in regard to this it was said:

A man companioned by craving

Wanders on this long journey;

He cannot go beyond saṃsara

In this state of being or another.

Having understood the danger thus—

That craving is the origin of suffering—

A bhikkhu should wander mindfully,

Free from craving, without grasping.

This too is the meaning of what was said by the Lord, so I heard.

16. The Learner

This was said by the Lord, said by the Arahant, so I heard:

"Bhikkhus, in regard to internal factors, I do not perceive another single factor so helpful as wise attention for a bhikkhu who is a learner, who has not attained perfection but lives aspiring for the supreme security from bondage. Bhikkhus, a bhikkhu who wisely attends abandons what is unwholesome and develops what is wholesome."

This is the meaning of what the Lord said. So in regard to this it was said:

For a bhikkhu who is a learner

There is no other thing so helpful

For reaching the highest goal

As the factor wise attention.

Wisely striving a bhikkhu may attain

The destruction of all suffering.

This too is the meaning of what was said by the Lord, so I heard.

17. The Good Friend

This was said by the Lord, said by the Arahant, so I heard:

"Bhikkhus, in regard to external factors, I do not perceive another single factor so helpful as good friendship for a bhikkhu who is a learner, who has not attained perfection but lives aspiring for the supreme security from bondage. Bhikkhus, a bhikkhu who has a good friend abandons what is unwholesome and develops what is wholesome."

This is the meaning of what the Lord said. So in regard to this it was said:

When a bhikkhu has good friends,

And is reverential and respectful,

Doing what his friends advise,

Clearly comprehending and mindful,

He may progressively attain

The destruction of all fetters.

This too is the meaning of what was said by the Lord, so I heard.

18. Disunity in the Sangha

This was said by the Lord, said by the Arahant, so I heard:

"There is one thing, bhikkhus, which, when it appears in the world, appears for the detriment of many people, for the misery of many people, for the loss, detriment, and suffering of devas and humans. What is that one thing? It is disunity in the Sangha. When the Sangha is divided there are mutual quarrels, mutual recriminations, mutual denigrations, and mutual expulsions. In this situation those who are unsympathetic are not converted and some who are sympathetic change their minds."

This is the meaning of what the Lord said. So in regard to this it was said:

One who divides the Sangha

Abides in a state of misery, in hell,

For the aeon's full duration.

Delighting in dissent, unrighteous,

He is deprived of security from bondage;

By dividing a unified Sangha

He suffers in hell for an aeon.

This too is the meaning of what was said by the Lord, so I heard.

19. Unity in the Sangha

This was said by the Lord, said by the Arahant, so I heard:

"There is one thing, bhikkhus, which, when it appears in the world, appears for the welfare of many people, for the happiness of many people, for the good, welfare, and happiness of devas and humans. What is that one thing? It is unity in the Sangha. When the Sangha is united there are no mutual quarrels, mutual recriminations, mutual denigrations, and mutual expulsions. In this situation those who are unsympathetic are converted and those who are sympathetic increase in faith."

This is the meaning of what the Lord said. So in regard to this it was said:

Pleasant is unity in the Sangha.

One who helps those in unity,

Who delights in unity and is righteous,

Is not deprived of security from bondage.

By making the Sangha united

He rejoices in heaven for an aeon.

This too is the meaning of what was said by the Lord, so I heard.

20. A Corrupt Mind

This was said by the Lord, said by the Arahant, so I heard:

"Here, bhikkhus, some person has a corrupt mind. Having examined his mind with my mind, I know that if this person were to die at this time, as if carried there he would be placed in hell. What is the reason for that? It is because his mind is corrupt. It is because of the mind's corruption that some beings here, when the body perishes, are reborn after death in a state of misery, a bad bourn, a state of ruin, hell."

This is the meaning of what the Lord said. So in regard to this it was said:

Understanding the corrupt mind

Of some person dwelling here,

The Buddha explained its meaning

In the presence of the bhikkhus.

If that person were to die

At this very moment now,

He would be reborn in hell

Because of his corrupt mind.

As if they were carried off

And placed there, thus

Beings go to a bad bourn

Because of mind's corruption.

This too is the meaning of what was said by the Lord, so I heard.

21. A Confident Mind

This was said by the Lord, said by the Arahant, so I heard:

"Here, bhikkhus, some person has a confident mind. Having examined his mind with my mind, I know that if this person were to die at this time, as if carried there he would be placed in heaven. What is the reason for that? It is because his mind is confident. It is because of the mind's confidence that some beings here, when the body perishes, are reborn after death in a good bourn, in a heavenly world."

This is the meaning of what the Lord said. So in regard to this it was said:

Understanding the confident mind

Of some person dwelling here,

The Buddha explained its meaning

In the presence of the bhikkhus.

If that person were to die

At this very moment now,

He would arise in a good bourn

Because of his confident mind.

As if they were carried off

And placed there, thus

Beings go to a good bourn

Because of mind's confidence.

This too is the meaning of what was said by the Lord, so I heard.

22. Meritorious Deeds

This was said by the Lord, said by the Arahant, so I heard:

"Bhikkhus, do not fear meritorious deeds. This is an expression denoting happiness, what is desirable, wished for, dear and agreeable, that is, 'meritorious deeds.' For I know full well, bhikkhus, that for a long time I experienced desirable, wished for, dear and agreeable results from often performing meritorious deeds.

"Having cultivated for seven years a mind of loving-kindness, for seven aeons of contraction and expansion I did not return to this world. Whenever the aeon contracted I reached the plane of Streaming Radiance, and when the aeon expanded I arose in an empty Brahma-mansion. And there I was a Brahma, the Great Brahma, the Unvanquished Victor, the All-seeing, the All-powerful. Thirty-six times I was Sakka, the ruler of the devas. And many hundreds of times I was a Wheel-turning Monarch, righteous, a king of righteousness, conqueror of the four quarters of the earth, maintaining stability in the land, in possession of the seven jewels. What need is there to speak of mere local kingship?

"It occurred to me, bhikkhus, to wonder: 'Of what kind of deed of mine is this the fruit? Of what deed's ripening is it that I am now of such great accomplishment and power?' And then it occurred to me: 'It is the fruit of three kinds of deeds of mine, the ripening of three kinds of deeds that I am now of such great accomplishment and power: deeds of giving, of self-mastery, and of refraining.'"

This is the meaning of what the Lord said. So in regard to this it was said:

One should train in deeds of merit

That yield long-lasting happiness:

Generosity, a balanced life,

Developing a loving mind.

By cultivating these three things,

Deeds yielding happiness,

The wise person is reborn in bliss

In an untroubled happy world.

This too is the meaning of what was said by the Lord, so I heard.

23. Diligence

This was said by the Lord, said by the Arahant, so I heard:

"There is one thing, bhikkhus, developed and continually practised, by which both kinds of welfare are acquired and maintained: welfare here and now, and that pertaining to the future. What is that one thing? It is diligence in wholesome states. This is that one thing, bhikkhus, developed and continually practised, by which both kinds of welfare are acquired and maintained: welfare here and now, and that pertaining to the future."

This is the meaning of what the Lord said. So in regard to this it was said:

The wise praise diligence

In doing deeds of merit;

For one who is wise and diligent

Obtains a twofold benefit:

Welfare in the here and now

And welfare in a future life.

And because one has realized the good,

The wise person is called a sage.

This too is the meaning of what was said by the Lord, so I heard.

24. A Heap of Bones

This was said by the Lord, said by the Arahant, so I heard:

"Bhikkhus, the skeletons of a single person, running on and wandering in saṃsara for an aeon, would make a heap of bones, a quantity of bones as large as this Mount Vepulla, if there were someone to collect them and if the collection were not destroyed."

This is the meaning of what the Lord said. So in regard to this it was said:

The bones of a single person

Accumulated in a single aeon

Would make a heap like a mountain—

So said the Great Sage.

He declared it to be

As great as Mount Vepulla

To the north of Vulture's Peak

In the hill-fort of Magadha.

But when one sees with perfect wisdom

The four noble truths as they are—

Suffering, the origin of suffering,

The overcoming of suffering,

And the noble eightfold path

Leading to relief from suffering—

Having merely run on

Seven times at the most,

By destroying all fetters

One makes an end of suffering.

This too is the meaning of what was said by the Lord, so I heard.

25. Lying

This was said by the Lord, said by the Arahant, so I heard:

"Bhikkhus, I say that for an individual who transgresses in one thing, there is no evil deed whatsoever he would not do. What is that one thing? It is this, bhikkhus: deliberately telling a lie."

This is the meaning of what the Lord said. So in regard to this it was said:

There is no evil that cannot be done

By a person who deliberately lies,

Who transgresses in one thing,

Taking no account of the next world.

This too is the meaning of what was said by the Lord, so I heard.

26. Giving

This was said by the Lord, said by the Arahant, so I heard:

"Bhikkhus, if beings knew, as I know, the result of giving and sharing, they would not eat without having given, nor would they allow the stain of meanness to obsess them and take root in their minds. Even if it were their last morsel, their last mouthful, they would not eat without having shared it, if there were someone to share it with. But, bhikkhus, as beings do not know, as I know, the result of giving and sharing, they eat without having given, and the stain of meanness obsesses them and takes root in their minds."

This is the meaning of what the Lord said. So in regard to this it was said:

If beings only knew—

So said the Great Sage—

How the result of sharing

Is of such great fruit,

With a gladdened mind,

Rid of the stain of meanness,

They would duly give to noble ones

Who make what is given fruitful.

Having given much food as offerings

To those most worthy of offerings,

The donors go to heaven

On departing the human state.

Having gone to heaven they rejoice,

And enjoying pleasures there,

The unselfish experience the result

Of generously sharing with others.

This too is the meaning of what was said by the Lord, so I heard.

27. The Development of Loving-kindness

This was said by the Lord, said by the Arahant, so I heard:

"Bhikkhus, whatever grounds there are for making merit productive of a future birth, all these do not equal a sixteenth part of the mind-release of loving-kindness. The mind-release of loving-kindness surpasses them and shines forth, bright and brilliant.

"Just as the radiance of all the stars does not equal a sixteenth part of the moon's radiance, but the moon's radiance surpasses them and shines forth, bright and brilliant, even so, whatever grounds there are for making merit productive of a future birth, all these do not equal a sixteenth part of the mind-release of loving-kindness...

"Just as in the last month of the rainy season, in the autumn, when the sky is clear and free of clouds, the sun, on ascending, dispels the darkness of space and shines forth, bright and brilliant, even so, whatever grounds there are for making merit productive of a future birth, all these do not equal a sixteenth part of the mind-release of loving-kindness...

"And just as in the night, at the moment of dawn, the morning star shines forth, bright and brilliant, even so, whatever grounds there are for making merit productive of a future birth, all these do not equal a sixteenth part of the mind-release of loving-kindness. The mind-release of loving-kindness surpasses them and shines forth, bright and brilliant."

This is the meaning of what the Lord said. So in regard to this it was said:

For one who mindfully develops

Boundless loving-kindness

Seeing the destruction of clinging,

The fetters are worn away.

If with an uncorrupted mind

He pervades just one being

With loving kindly thoughts,

He makes some merit thereby.

But a noble one produces

An abundance of merit

By having a compassionate mind

Towards all living beings.

Those royal seers who conquered

The earth crowded with beings

Went about performing sacrifices:

The horse sacrifice, the man sacrifice,

The water rites, the soma sacrifice,

And that called "the Unobstructed."

But these do not share even a sixteenth part

Of a well cultivated mind of love,

Just as the entire starry host

Is dimmed by the moon's radiance.

One who does not kill

Nor cause others to kill,

Who does not conquer

Nor cause others to conquer,

Kindly towards all beings—

He has enmity for none.

This too is the meaning of what was said by the Lord, so I heard.

# THE SECTION OF THE TWOS

28. Living in Discomfort

This was said by the Lord, said by the Arahant, so I heard:

"Bhikkhus, possessed of two things, a bhikkhu lives in discomfort here and now, bringing upon himself vexation, trouble, and distress, and when the body perishes after death a bad bourn is to be expected. What are the two? Being unguarded regarding the doors of the senses and being immoderate in eating. These are the two things possessed of which a bhikkhu lives in discomfort..."

This is the meaning of what the Lord said. So in regard to this it was said:

The eye, ear, nose, tongue,

Body and likewise the mind—

A bhikkhu who leaves these doors

Unguarded here,

Immoderate in eating,

Of uncontrolled senses,

Experiences suffering

Both bodily and mental.

Being tormented by body,

And tormented by mind,

Such a one lives in discomfort

Both by day and by night.

This too is the meaning of what was said by the Lord, so I heard.

29. Living in Comfort

This was said by the Lord, said by the Arahant, so I heard:

"Bhikkhus, possessed of two things a bhikkhu lives in comfort here and now, not bringing upon himself vexation, trouble, and distress, and when the body perishes after death a good bourn is to be expected. What are the two? Being guarded regarding the doors of the senses and being moderate in eating. These are the two things, possessed of which, a bhikkhu lives in comfort here and now, not bringing upon himself vexation, trouble, and distress, and when the body perishes after death a good bourn is to be expected."

This is the meaning of what the Lord said. So in regard to this it was said:

The eye, ear, nose, tongue,

Body and likewise the mind—

A bhikkhu who has these doors

Well guarded here,

Moderate in eating,

Of controlled senses,

Experiences happiness

Both bodily and mental.

Not tormented by body,

Nor tormented by mind,

Such a one lives in comfort

Both by day and by night.

This too is the meaning of what was said by the Lord, so I heard.

30. Remorse

This was said by the Lord, said by the Arahant, so I heard:

"There are two things, bhikkhus, causing remorse. What are the two? Here someone has not done what is good, not done what is wholesome, not done what is beneficial, but has done evil, callous, wrongful deeds. He is remorseful on thinking, 'I have not done good,' and is remorseful on thinking, 'I have done evil.' These, bhikkhus, are the two things causing remorse."

This is the meaning of what the Lord said. So in regard to this it was said:

Having performed misconduct

By body, misconduct by speech,

Misconduct by mind, and whatever else

Is reckoned a fault—

Not having done a good deed

And done much that is bad—

When his body perishes

That foolish one is reborn in hell.

This too is the meaning of what was said by the Lord, so I heard.

31. Non-remorse

This was said by the Lord, said by the Arahant, so I heard:

"There are two things, bhikkhus, causing no remorse. What are the two? Here someone has done what is good, done what is wholesome, done what is beneficial, and has not done evil, callous, wrongful deeds. He is not remorseful on thinking, 'I have done good,' and is not remorseful on thinking, 'I have done no evil.' These, bhikkhus, are the two things causing no remorse."

This is the meaning of what the Lord said. So in regard to this it was said:

Having abandoned misconduct

By body, misconduct by speech,

Misconduct by mind, and whatever else

Is reckoned a fault—

Not having done a bad deed

And done much that is good—

When his body perishes

That wise one is reborn in heaven.

This too is the meaning of what was said by the Lord, so I heard.

32. Behaviour (1)

This was said by the Lord, said by the Arahant, so I heard:

"Possessing two things, bhikkhus, a person is placed in hell as if carried there. What are the two things? Bad behaviour and a bad view. These, bhikkhus, are the two things, possessed of which, a person is placed in hell as if carried there."

This is the meaning of what the Lord said. So in regard to this it was said:

If a person possesses these two things—

Bad behaviour and a bad view—

When his body perishes

That foolish one is reborn in hell.

This too is the meaning of what was said by the Lord, so I heard.

33. Behaviour (2)

This was said by the Lord, said by the Arahant, so I heard:

"Possessing two things, bhikkhus, a person is placed in heaven as if carried there. What are the two things? Good behaviour and a good view. These are the two things, possessed of which, a person is placed in heaven as if carried there."

This is the meaning of what the Lord said. So in regard to this it was said:

If a person possesses these two things—

Good behaviour and a good view—

When his body perishes

That wise one is reborn in heaven.

This too is the meaning of what was said by the Lord, so I heard.

34. Ardour

This was said by the Lord, said by the Arahant, so I heard:

"Bhikkhus, a bhikkhu who is without ardour and without fear of wrongdoing is incapable of attaining enlightenment, incapable of attaining Nibbana, incapable of attaining the supreme security from bondage. But a bhikkhu who has ardour and fear of wrongdoing is capable of doing so."

This is the meaning of what the Lord said. So in regard to this it was said:

One who is not ardent, reckless,

Lazy, and of little vigour,

Full of lethargy and torpor,

Shameless and without respect—

Such a bhikkhu cannot attain

Enlightenment which is supreme.

But a mindful and discerning meditator,

Ardent, scrupulous, and diligent,

Having severed the fetters of birth and decay,

Can attain for himself right here and now

Enlightenment which is supreme.

This too is the meaning of what was said by the Lord, so I heard.

35. Not Deceiving (1)

This was said by the Lord, said by the Arahant, so I heard:

"Bhikkhus, this holy life is not lived for the sake of deceiving people, for the sake of cajoling people, for the sake of profiting in gain, honour, and fame, nor with the idea, 'Let people know me thus.' This holy life, bhikkhus, is lived for the sake of restraint and abandoning."

This is the meaning of what the Lord said. So in regard to this it was said:

The Lord taught a holy life

Not based on tradition,

For restraint and abandoning,

Leading to and merging in Nibbana.

This is the path followed by the great,

Pursued by the lofty sages.

Those who enter that course

As taught by the Enlightened One,

Heeding the Teacher's instruction,

Will make an end of suffering.

This too is the meaning of what was said by the Lord, so I heard.

36. Not Deceiving (2)

This was said by the Lord, said by the Arahant, so I heard:

"Bhikkhus, this holy life is not lived for the sake of deceiving people, for the sake of cajoling people, for the sake of profiting in gain, honour, and fame, nor with the idea, 'Let people know me thus.' This holy life, bhikkhus, is lived for the sake of direct knowledge and full understanding."

This is the meaning of what the Lord said. So in regard to this it was said:

The Lord taught a holy life

Not based on tradition,

For knowledge and understanding,

Leading to and merging in Nibbana.

This is the path followed by the great,

Pursued by the lofty sages.

Those who enter that course

As taught by the Enlightened One,

Heeding the Teacher's instruction,

Will make an end of suffering.

This too is the meaning of what was said by the Lord, so I heard.

37. Happiness

This was said by the Lord, said by the Arahant, so I heard:

"Bhikkhus, possessing two things a bhikkhu lives here and now with much pleasure and happiness and is properly motivated for the destruction of the taints. What are the two things? Being moved by a sense of urgency on occasions for urgency, and, being moved, making a proper endeavour. These, bhikkhus, are the two things, possessing which, a bhikkhu lives here and now with much pleasure and happiness and is properly motivated for the destruction of the taints."

This is the meaning of what the Lord said. So in regard to this it was said:

A wise person should be urgently moved

On occasions that make for urgency;

As an ardent discerning bhikkhu

He should investigate with wisdom.

One living ardent thus,

Of peaceful conduct, not proud,

Practising tranquillity of mind,

May attain the destruction of suffering.

This too is the meaning of what was said by the Lord, so I heard.

38. Often Occurring Thoughts

This was said by the Lord, said by the Arahant, so I heard:

"Bhikkhus, two thoughts often occur to the Tathagata, the Arahant, the Fully Enlightened One: the thought of security (for beings) and the thought of solitude.

"The Tathagata, bhikkhus, is one who delights in and enjoys non-ill will. As the Tathagata delights in and enjoys non-ill will, this thought often occurs to him: 'By this behaviour I do not oppress anyone either frail or firm.' The Tathagata, bhikkhus, is one who delights in and enjoys solitude. As the Tathagata delights in and enjoys solitude, this thought often occurs to him: 'What is unwholesome has been abandoned.'

"Therefore, bhikkhus, I say, you too must live delighting in and enjoying non-ill will. As you so live this thought will often occur to you: 'By this behaviour we do not oppress anyone either frail or firm.'

"Bhikkhus, you too must live delighting in and enjoying solitude. As you so live this thought will often occur to you: 'What is unwholesome? What has not been abandoned? What have we abandoned?'"

This is the meaning of what the Lord said. So in regard to this it was said:

Two thoughts occur to him,

The Tathagata, the Awakened One

Who endured what is beyond endurance:

Security (for beings) was the first thought spoken of,

Solitude was the second announced.

The dispeller of darkness, gone beyond,

The great sage who has reached attainment,

Become a master, freed from taints,

Who has crossed over entirely,

Released by the destruction of craving—

That sage bears his final body,

And having left behind Mara, I say,

He has gone beyond decay.

As one standing on a mountain peak

Might see all round the people down below,

So having ascended the Dhamma-palace,

The vastly wise one, all-seeing,

Views the people of the world.

The sorrowless one views below

Those still immersed in sorrow,

Overwhelmed by birth and decay.

This too is the meaning of what was said by the Lord, so I heard.

39. Dhamma-teachings

This was said by the Lord, said by the Arahant, so I heard:

"There are, bhikkhus, two successive Dhamma-teachings of the Tathagata, the Arahant, the Fully Enlightened One. What are the two? 'See evil as evil'— this is the first Dhamma-teaching. 'Having seen evil as evil, be rid of it, be detached from it, be freed from it'—this is the second Dhamma-teaching. These, bhikkhus, are the two successive Dhamma-teachings of the Tathagata, the Arahant, the Fully Enlightened One."

This is the meaning of what the Lord said. So in regard to this it was said:

Regard the ordered words he spoke,

The Tathagata, the Awakened One,

Compassionate for all beings,

And the two things he proclaimed:

"See what is evil" is one,

The other "Be detached from it."

With a mind become detached from evil

You will make an end of suffering.

This too is the meaning of what was said by the Lord, so I heard.

40. Knowledge

This was said by the Lord, said by the Arahant, so I heard:

"Ignorance, bhikkhus, precedes and leads to unwholesome states, and shamelessness and lack of fear of wrongdoing follow after. Knowledge, bhikkhus, precedes and leads to wholesome states, and shame and fear of wrongdoing follow after."

This is the meaning of what the Lord said. So in regard to this it was said:

Whatever bad bourns there are

In this world and hereafter,

All are rooted in ignorance,

Constructed by desire and greed.

Since one of evil desires

Is shameless and disrespectful,

From that evil flows forth

And he goes to a state of misery.

Thus by discarding desire and greed,

Along with ignorance as well,

A bhikkhu arouses knowledge

And abandons all bad bourns.

This too is the meaning of what was said by the Lord, so I heard.

41. Deprived of Wisdom

This was said by the Lord, said by the Arahant, so I heard:

"Bhikkhus, those beings are thoroughly deprived who are deprived of noble wisdom. They live in discomfort even here and now, with vexation, trouble, and distress, and when the body perishes at death a bad bourn is to be expected.

"Those beings are not deprived who are not deprived of noble wisdom. They live in comfort here and now, without vexation, trouble, or distress, and when the body perishes at death a good bourn is to be expected."

This is the meaning of what the Lord said. So in regard to this it was said:

See the world with its devas,

Destitute of wisdom,

Established in name-and-form,

Conceiving this to be the truth.

Wisdom which leads to penetration

Is the best thing in the world;

By this one completely understands

The ending of both birth and being.

Devas and human beings hold dear

Those awakened ones ever mindful,

Possessing joyous wisdom,

Bearing their final bodies.

This too is the meaning of what was said by the Lord, so I heard.

42. The Bright Protectors

This was said by the Lord, said by the Arahant, so I heard:

"Bhikkhus, these two bright principles protect the world. What are the two? Shame and fear of wrongdoing. If, bhikkhus, these two bright principles did not protect the world, there would not be discerned respect for mother or maternal aunt or maternal uncle's wife or a teacher's wife or the wives of other honoured persons, and the world would have fallen into promiscuity, as with goats, sheep, chickens, pigs, dogs, and jackals. But as these two bright principles protect the world, there is discerned respect for mother or maternal aunt or maternal uncle's wife or a teacher's wife, and the wives of other honoured persons."

This is the meaning of what the Lord said. So in regard to this it was said:

Those in whom shame and fear of wrong

Are not consistently found

Have deviated from the bright root

And are led back to birth and death.

But those in whom shame and fear of wrong

Are consistently ever present,

Peaceful, mature in the holy life,

They put an end to renewal of being.

This too is the meaning of what was said by the Lord, so I heard.

43. The Not-born

This was said by the Lord, said by the Arahant, so I heard:

"There is, bhikkhus, a not-born, a not-brought-to-being, a not-made, a not-conditioned. If, bhikkhus, there were no not-born, not-brought-to-being, not-made, not-conditioned, no escape would be discerned from what is born, brought-to-being, made, conditioned. But since there is a not-born, a not-brought-to-being, a not-made, a not-conditioned, therefore an escape is discerned from what is born, brought-to-being, made, conditioned."

This is the meaning of what the Lord said. So in regard to this it was said:

The born, come-to-be, produced,

The made, the conditioned, the transient,

Conjoined with decay and death,

A nest of disease, perishable,

Sprung from nutriment and craving's cord—

That is not fit to take delight in.

The escape from that, the peaceful,

Beyond reasoning, everlasting,

The not-born, the unproduced,

The sorrowless state that is void of stain,

The cessation of states linked to suffering,

The stilling of the conditioned—bliss.

This too is the meaning of what was said by the Lord, so I heard.

44. The Nibbana-element

This was said by the Lord, said by the Arahant, so I heard:

"Bhikkhus, there are these two Nibbana-elements. What are the two? The Nibbana-element with residue left and the Nibbana-element with no residue left.

"What, bhikkhus, is the Nibbana-element with residue left? Here a bhikkhu is an arahant, one whose taints are destroyed, the holy life fulfilled, who has done what had to be done, laid down the burden, attained the goal, destroyed the fetters of being, completely released through final knowledge. However, his five sense faculties remain unimpaired, by which he still experiences what is agreeable and disagreeable and feels pleasure and pain. It is the extinction of attachment, hate, and delusion in him that is called the Nibbana-element with residue left.

"Now what, bhikkhus, is the Nibbana-element with no residue left? Here a bhikkhu is an arahant, one whose taints are destroyed, the holy life fulfilled, who has done what had to be done, laid down the burden, attained the goal, destroyed the fetters of being, completely released through final knowledge. For him, here in this very life, all that is experienced, not being delighted in, will be extinguished. That, bhikkhus, is called the Nibbana-element with no residue left.

"These, bhikkhus, are the two Nibbana-elements."

This is the meaning of what the Lord said. So in regard to this it was said:

These two Nibbana-elements were made known

By the Seeing One, stable and unattached:

One is the element seen here and now

With residue, but with the cord of being destroyed;

The other, having no residue for the future,

Is that wherein all modes of being utterly cease.

Having understood the unconditioned state,

Released in mind with the cord of being destroyed,

They have attained to the Dhamma-essence.

Delighting in the destruction (of craving),

Those stable ones have abandoned all being.

This too is the meaning of what was said by the Lord, so I heard.

45. Living in Seclusion

This was said by the Lord, said by the Arahant, so I heard:

"Live enjoying seclusion, bhikkhus; live delighting in seclusion, engage in practising inner mental tranquillity, not neglecting meditation, possessing insight, and frequenting empty places. If you live enjoying seclusion, bhikkhus, live delighting in seclusion, engage in practising inner mental tranquillity, not neglecting meditation, possessing insight, and frequenting empty places, one of two fruits is to be expected: final knowledge here and now or, there being some residual defilement, the state of non-returning."

This is the meaning of what the Lord said. So in regard to this it was said:

Those of peaceful mind, discerning,

Mindful, given to meditation,

Clearly see things rightly

And long not for sensual pleasures.

Those peaceful ones, delighting in diligence,

Who see fear in negligence,

Are incapable of falling away

And are close to Nibbana.

This too is the meaning of what was said by the Lord, so I heard.

46. The Benefits of the Training

This was said by the Lord, said by the Arahant, so I heard:

"Bhikkhus, live so as to realize the benefits of the training, the attainment of higher wisdom, the essence of release, and the control of mindfulness. Bhikkhus, if you live to realize the benefits of the training, the attainment of higher wisdom, the essence of release, and the control of mindfulness, one of two fruits is to be expected: final knowledge here and now or, there being some residual defilement, the state of non-returning."

This is the meaning of what the Lord said. So in regard to this it was said:

One who has completed the training,

Incapable of falling away,

Attained to the higher wisdom,

A seer of the end of birth—

That sage bears his final body,

And having left behind conceit,

He has gone beyond decay, I say.

Therefore ever delighting in meditation,

Concentrated, with ardent energy,

Seeing the end of birth, O bhikkhus,

Conquer Mara and his host,

And go beyond all birth and death.

This too is the meaning of what was said by the Lord, so I heard.

47. Vigilance

This was said by the Lord, said by the Arahant, so I heard:

"Bhikkhus, a bhikkhu should be vigilant; he should live mindful, clearly comprehending, concentrated, happy and calm, and should know when it is suitable to cultivate those things that are wholesome. Bhikkhus, for a bhikkhu who is vigilant and living thus, one of two fruits is to be expected: final knowledge here and now or, there being some residual defilement, the state of non-returning."

This is the meaning of what the Lord said. So in regard to this it was said:

You vigilant ones hear this:

Wake up, you who are asleep!

Vigilance is better than sleep:

There is no fear for the vigilant.

One who is vigilant and mindful,

Comprehending and concentrated,

Joyful and calm in his thoughts,

By rightly investigating the Dhamma

With unified mind, will in time

Destroy the darkness of ignorance.

Therefore be devoted to vigilance,

An ardent, discerning, meditative bhikkhu.

Having severed the fetter of birth and decay,

One may here and now attain

Enlightenment which is supreme.

This too is the meaning of what was said by the Lord, so I heard.

48. A State of Misery

This was said by the Lord, said by the Arahant, so I heard:

"Bhikkhus, these two will go to a state of misery, to hell, by not giving up such conduct as this. What two? One who while no liver of the holy life pretends to be one who lives the holy life, and one who falsely accuses another who lives the holy life in complete purity of not living it. These two will go to a state of misery, to hell, by not giving up such conduct as this."

This is the meaning of what the Lord said. So in regard to this it was said:

The false-accuser goes to hell

And also one who denies the deed he did;

Both these become equal hereafter,

Persons of base actions in the world beyond.

Many imposters wear the yellow robe

Though evil-natured and uncontrolled.

Because of their evil deeds,

Those evil ones are born in hell.

Far better for him to swallow

A fiery hot iron ball

Than that immoral and uncontrolled

He should eat the country's alms.

This too is the meaning of what was said by the Lord, so I heard.

49. Held by Views

This was said by the Lord, said by the Arahant, so I heard:

"Bhikkhus, held by two kinds of views, some devas and

human beings hold back and some overreach; only those with vision see.

"And how, bhikkhus, do some hold back? Devas and humans enjoy being, delight in being, are satisfied with being. When Dhamma is taught to them for the cessation of being, their minds do not enter into it or acquire confidence in it or settle upon it or become resolved upon it. Thus, bhikkhus, do some hold back.

"How, bhikkhus, do some overreach? Now some are troubled, ashamed, and disgusted by this very same being and they rejoice in (the idea of) non-being, asserting: 'In as much as this self, good sirs, when the body perishes at death, is annihilated and destroyed and does not exist after death—this is peaceful, this is excellent, this is reality!' Thus, bhikkhus, do some overreach.

"How, bhikkhus, do those with vision see? Herein a bhikkhu sees what has come to be as having come to be. Having seen it thus, he practises the course for turning away, for dispassion, for the cessation of what has come to be. Thus, bhikkhus, do those with vision see."

This is the meaning of what the Lord said. So in regard to this it was said:

Having seen what has come to be

As having come to be,

Passing beyond what has come to be,

They are released in accordance with truth

By exhausting the craving for being.

When a bhikkhu has fully understood

That which has come to be as such,

Free from craving to be this or that,

By the extinction of what has come to be

He comes no more to renewal of being.

This too is the meaning of what was said by the Lord, so I heard.

# THE SECTION OF THE THREES

50. Roots

This was said by the Lord, said by the Arahant, so I heard:

"Bhikkhus, there are these three unwholesome roots. What three? The unwholesome root greed, the unwholesome root hate, and the unwholesome root delusion. These are the three."

This is the meaning of what the Lord said. So in regard to this it was said:

Greed and hate and delusion,

Arisen from within himself,

Harm an evil-minded person

As its own fruit destroys the bamboo tree.

This too is the meaning of what was said by the Lord, so I heard.

51. Elements

This was said by the Lord, said by the Arahant, so I heard:

"Bhikkhus, there are these three elements. What three? The form element, the formless element, and the element of cessation. These are the three."

This is the meaning of what the Lord said. So in regard to this it was said:

By fully understanding the form element

Without getting stuck in the formless,

They are released into cessation

And leave Death far behind them.

Having touched with his own person

The deathless element free from clinging,

Having realized the relinquishment of clinging

His taints all gone,

The Fully Enlightened One proclaims

The sorrowless state that is void of stain.

This too is the meaning of what was said by the Lord, so I heard.

52. Feelings (1)

This was said by the Lord, said by the Arahant, so I heard:

"Bhikkhus, there are these three feelings. What three? Pleasant feeling, painful feeling, and neither-pleasant-nor-painful feeling. These are the three."

This is the meaning of what the Lord said. So in regard to this it was said:

A disciple of the Buddha,

Concentrated, clearly comprehending

And mindful, knows feelings

And the origin of feelings,

Where they cease and the path

That leads to their full destruction.

With the destruction of feelings a bhikkhu,

Without longing, has attained Nibbana.

This too is the meaning of what was said by the Lord, so I heard.

53. Feelings (2)

This was said by the Lord, said by the Arahant, so I heard:

"Bhikkhus, there are these three feelings. What three? Pleasant feeling, painful feeling, and neither-pleasant-nor-painful feeling. Pleasant feeling, bhikkhus, should be seen as suffering, painful feeling should be seen as a dart, neither-pleasant-nor-painful feeling should be seen as impermanent.

"When a bhikkhu has seen these three feelings thus, he is said to be a noble one who sees rightly. He has cut off craving, destroyed the fetters, and by thoroughly understanding conceit, he has made an end of suffering."

This is the meaning of what the Lord said. So in regard to this it was said:

One sees pleasure as suffering

And sees pain as a dart.

One sees as impermanent the peaceful feeling

That is neither pleasant nor painful.

Such a bhikkhu who sees rightly

Is thereby well released.

Accomplished in knowledge, at peace,

That sage has overcome all bonds.

This too is the meaning of what was said by the Lord, so I heard.

54. Search (1)

This was said by the Lord, said by the Arahant, so I heard:

"Bhikkhus, there are these three kinds of search. What three? The search for sensual gratification, the search for being, and the search for a holy life. These are the three."

This is the meaning of what the Lord said. So in regard to this it was said:

A disciple of the Buddha,

Concentrated, clearly comprehending

And mindful, knows searches

And the origin of searches,

Where they cease and the path

That leads to their full destruction.

With the destruction of searches a bhikkhu,

Without longing, has attained Nibbana.

This too is the meaning of what was said by the Lord, so I heard.

55. Search (2)

This was said by the Lord, said by the Arahant, so I heard:

"Bhikkhus, there are these three kinds of search. What three? The search for sensual gratification, the search for being, and the search for a holy life. These are the three."

This is the meaning of what the Lord said. So in regard to this it was said:

Sensual search, the search for being,

The search for a holy life of one

Who takes his stand upon a view

And holds it tightly as the truth—

These are heapings of defilements.

For a bhikkhu wholly dispassionate

And freed by the destruction of craving,

Searches have been relinquished

And uprooted the standpoint of views.

With the destruction of searches a bhikkhu

Is free from desire and doubt.

This too is the meaning of what was said by the Lord, so I heard.

56. Taints (1)

This was said by the Lord, said by the Arahant, so I heard:

"Bhikkhus, there are these three taints. What three? The taint of sensual desire, the taint of being, and the taint of ignorance. These are the three."

This is the meaning of what the Lord said. So in regard to this it was said:

A disciple of the Buddha,

Concentrated, clearly comprehending

And mindful, knows the taints

And the origin of taints,

Where they cease and the path

That leads to their full destruction.

With the destruction of the taints a bhikkhu,

Without longing, has attained Nibbana.

This too is the meaning of what was said by the Lord, so I heard.

57. Taints (2)

This was said by the Lord, said by the Arahant, so I heard:

"Bhikkhus, there are these three taints. What three? The taint of sensual desire, the taint of being, and the taint of ignorance. These are the three."

This is the meaning of what the Lord said. So in regard to this it was said:

One for whom the taint of desire

For sensual pleasures has been destroyed,

Who has eliminated ignorance

And exhausted the taint of being—

Such a one is released without clinging.

Having conquered Mara and his mount,

He bears his final body.

This too is the meaning of what was said by the Lord, so I heard.

58. Craving

This was said by the Lord, said by the Arahant, so I heard:

"Bhikkhus, there are these three cravings. What three? The craving for sensual pleasures, the craving for being, and the craving for non-being. These are the three."

This is the meaning of what the Lord said. So in regard to this it was said:

Those fettered by the bond of craving,

Whose minds delight in being this or that,

Are people in the bondage of Mara

Who enjoy no security from bondage.

Such beings continue in saṃsara,

Going on from birth to death.

But those who have abandoned craving,

Free from craving for being this or that,

Having attained the taints' destruction,

Though in the world, have gone beyond.

This too is the meaning of what was said by the Lord, so I heard.

59. Mara's Domain

This was said by the Lord, said by the Arahant, so I heard:

"Bhikkhus, being in possession of three things, a bhikkhu has passed beyond the domain of Mara and shines like the sun. What are the three? Herein a bhikkhu is in possession of the non-learner's aggregate of virtue, the non-learner's aggregate of concentration, and the non-learner's aggregate of wisdom. These are the three things in possession of which a bhikkhu has passed beyond the domain of Mara and shines like the sun."

This is the meaning of what the Lord said. So in regard to this it was said:

Virtue, concentration, and wisdom—

One in whom these are fully developed,

On passing beyond Mara's domain,

Shines forth like the sun.

This too is the meaning of what was said by the Lord, so I heard.

60. Grounds for Making Merit

This was said by the Lord, said by the Arahant, so I heard:

"Bhikkhus, there are these three grounds for making merit. What three? The ground for making merit consisting in giving, the ground for making merit consisting in virtue, and the ground for making merit consisting in mind-development. These are the three."

This is the meaning of what the Lord said. So in regard to this it was said:

One should train in deeds of merit

That yield long-lasting happiness:

Generosity, a balanced life,

Developing a loving mind.

By cultivating these three things,

Deeds yielding happiness,

The wise person is reborn in bliss

In an untroubled happy world.

This too is the meaning of what was said by the Lord, so I heard.

61. Eyes

This was said by the Lord, said by the Arahant, so I heard:

"Bhikkhus, there are these three eyes. What three? The fleshly eye, the divine eye, and the wisdom eye. These, bhikkhus, are the three eyes."

This is the meaning of what the Lord said. So in regard to this it was said:

The fleshly eye, the divine eye,

And the unsurpassed wisdom eye—

These three eyes were described

By the Buddha, supreme among men.

The arising of the fleshly eye

Is the path to the divine eye,

But the unsurpassed wisdom eye

Is that from which knowledge arises.

By obtaining such an eye

One is released from all suffering.

This too is the meaning of what was said by the Lord, so I heard.

62. Faculties

This was said by the Lord, said by the Arahant, so I heard:

"Bhikkhus, there are these three faculties. What three? The faculty of the assurance: 'I shall come to finally know what is as yet not finally known'; the faculty of final knowledge; and the faculty of one who has finally known. These, bhikkhus, are the three faculties."

This is the meaning of what the Lord said. So in regard to this it was said:

For a learner who is training

In conformity with the direct path,

The knowledge of destruction arises first,

And final knowledge immediately follows.

Freed by that final knowledge,

By destroying the fetters of being

The serene one has the certainty:

"Unshakeable is my release."

Endowed with this faculty

The peaceful one delights in the peaceful state.

Having conquered Mara and his mount,

He bears his final body.

This too is the meaning of what was said by the Lord, so I heard.

63. Time

This was said by the Lord, said by the Arahant, so I heard:

"Bhikkhus, these are the three times. What three? Past time, future time, and present time. These, bhikkhus, are the three times."

This is the meaning of what the Lord said. So in regard to this it was said:

Perceiving what can be expressed through concepts,

Beings take their stand on what is expressed.

Not fully understanding the expressed,

They come under the bondage of Death.

But by fully understanding what is expressed

One does not misconceive the speaker.

His mind has attained to freedom,

The unsurpassed state of peace.

Understanding what is expressed,

The peaceful one delights in the peaceful state.

Standing on Dhamma, perfect in knowledge,

He freely makes use of concepts

But no more enters into concept's range.

This too is the meaning of what was said by the Lord, so I heard.

64. Misconduct

This was said by the Lord, said by the Arahant, so I heard:

"Bhikkhus, there are these three kinds of misconduct. What are the three? Misconduct by body, misconduct by speech, and misconduct by mind. These are the three."

This is the meaning of what the Lord said. So in regard to this it was said:

Having performed misconduct

By body, misconduct by speech,

Misconduct by mind, and whatever else

Is reckoned a fault—

Not having done a good deed

And done much that is bad—

When his body perishes

That foolish one is reborn in hell.

This too is the meaning of what was said by the Lord, so I heard.

65. Good Conduct

This was said by the Lord, said by the Arahant, so I heard:

"Bhikkhus, there are these three kinds of good conduct. What are the three? Good conduct by body, good conduct by speech, and good conduct by mind. These are the three."

This is the meaning of what the Lord said. So in regard to this it was said:

Having abandoned misconduct

By body, misconduct by speech,

Misconduct by mind, and whatever else

Is reckoned a fault—

Not having done a bad deed

And done much that is good—

When his body perishes

That wise one is reborn in heaven.

This too is the meaning of what was said by the Lord, so I heard.

66. Purity

This was said by the Lord, said by the Arahant, so I heard:

"Bhikkhus, there are these three kinds of purity. What are the three? Purity of body, purity of speech, and purity of mind. These are the three."

This is the meaning of what the Lord said. So in regard to this it was said:

Bodily pure, pure of speech,

Mentally pure and taintless—

A pure one possessing such purity

Is called one who has abandoned all.

This too is the meaning of what was said by the Lord, so I heard.

67. Perfection

This was said by the Lord, said by the Arahant, so I heard:

"Bhikkhus, there are these three kinds of perfection. What are the three? Perfection of body, perfection of speech, and perfection of mind. These are the three."

This is the meaning of what the Lord said. So in regard to this it was said:

Bodily perfect, perfect of speech,

Mentally perfect and taintless;

A sage possessing such perfection

Is called one cleansed of evil.

This too is the meaning of what was said by the Lord, so I heard.

68. Attachment (1)

This was said by the Lord, said by the Arahant, so I heard:

"Bhikkhus, one in whom attachment is not abandoned, hate is not abandoned, and delusion is not abandoned, is said to be in the bondage of Mara; he is caught in Mara's noose and at the mercy of the Evil One.

"Bhikkhus, one in whom attachment is abandoned, hate is abandoned, and delusion is abandoned, is said to be free from the bondage of Mara; he has cast off Mara's noose and is not at the mercy of the Evil One."

This is the meaning of what the Lord said. So in regard to this it was said:

One who has destroyed attachment

Along with hate and ignorance

Is called one inwardly developed,

A Tathagata become supreme,

Awakened, past enmity and fear,

One who has abandoned all.

This too is the meaning of what was said by the Lord, so I heard.

69. Attachment (2)

This was said by the Lord, said by the Arahant, so I heard:

"Bhikkhus, any bhikkhu or bhikkhuni in whom attachment is not abandoned, hate is not abandoned, and delusion is not abandoned, is said to be one who has not crossed the ocean with its waves, breakers, and eddies, with its sharks and demons. But any bhikkhu or bhikkhuni in whom attachment is abandoned, hate is abandoned, and delusion is abandoned, is said to be one who has crossed the ocean with its waves, breakers, and eddies, its sharks and demons—one of whom it is said: 'Crossed over, gone beyond, the brahmin stands on dry ground.'"

This is the meaning of what the Lord said. So in regard to this it was said:

One who has destroyed attachment

Along with hate and ignorance

Has crossed this ocean

With its sharks and demons,

Its fearful waves so hard to cross.

He has surmounted every tie,

Left Death behind,

Become free from clinging,

Forsaken suffering and renewal of being.

Vanished, he cannot be defined, I say—

He has bewildered the King of Death.

This too is the meaning of what was said by the Lord, so I heard.

70. Wrong View

This was said by the Lord, said by the Arahant, so I heard:

"Bhikkhus, I have seen beings who practise misconduct by body, speech, and mind, who vilify the noble ones, who hold wrong view and perform various deeds because of their wrong view. When the body perishes, those beings are reborn after death in a state of misery, a bad bourn, a state of ruin, in hell. I say this, bhikkhus, without having learnt it from another recluse or brahmin. It is just because I myself have known it, seen it, and observed it that I say: 'Bhikkhus, I have seen beings who practise misconduct by body, speech, and mind, who vilify the noble ones, who hold wrong view and perform various deeds because of their wrong view. When the body perishes, those beings are reborn after death in a state of misery, a bad bourn, a state of ruin, in hell.'"

This is the meaning of what the Lord said. So in regard to this it was said:

An individual here with

A wrongly directed mind

Who utters wrong speech

And performs wrong deeds,

One of little learning,

Who does demerit in this short life—

Upon the perishing of the body

That foolish one is reborn in hell.

This too is the meaning of what was said by the Lord, so I heard.

71. Right View

This was said by the Lord, said by the Arahant, so I heard:

"Bhikkhus, I have seen beings who practise good conduct by body, speech, and mind, who do not vilify the noble ones, who hold right view and perform various deeds because of their right view. When the body perishes, those beings are reborn after death in a good bourn, a heavenly world. I say this, bhikkhus, without having learnt it from another recluse or brahmin. It is just because I myself have known it, seen it, and observed it that I say: 'Bhikkhus, I have seen beings who practise good conduct by body, speech, and mind … reborn after death in a good bourn, a heavenly world.'"

This is the meaning of what the Lord said. So in regard to this it was said:

An individual here with

A rightly directed mind

Who utters right speech

And performs right deeds,

One of much learning,

Who does much merit in this short life—

Upon the perishing of the body

That wise one is reborn in heaven.

This too is the meaning of what was said by the Lord, so I heard.

72. Escape

This was said by the Lord, said by the Arahant, so I heard:

"Bhikkhus, there are these three elements of escape. What three? The escape from sensual desires, that is, renunciation; the escape from form, that is, the formless; and the escape from whatever has come to be, from whatever is conditioned and dependently arisen, that is, cessation. These, bhikkhus, are the three elements of escape."

This is the meaning of what the Lord said. So in regard to this it was said:

Having known the escape from sensual desires

And the overcoming of forms,

One whose energy is always ardent

Reaches the stilling of all formations.

Such a bhikkhu who sees rightly

Is thereby well released.

Accomplished in knowledge, at peace,

That sage has overcome all bonds.

This too is the meaning of what was said by the Lord, so I heard.

73. More Peaceful

This was said by the Lord, said by the Arahant, so I heard:

"Bhikkhus, the formless is more peaceful than the form realm, and cessation is more peaceful than the formless."

This is the meaning of what the Lord said. So in regard to this it was said:

Those beings who reach the form realm

And those established in the formless,

If they do not know cessation

Come back to renewal of being.

Those who fully understand forms

Without getting stuck in the formless,

Are released into cessation

And leave Death far behind them.

Having touched with his own person

The deathless element free from clinging,

Having realized the relinquishment of clinging,

His taints all gone,

The Fully Enlightened One proclaims

The sorrowless state that is void of stain.

This too is the meaning of what was said by the Lord, so I heard.

74. Sons

This was said by the Lord, said by the Arahant, so I heard:

"Bhikkhus, these three kinds of sons are found existing in the world. What three? The superior kind, the similar kind, and the inferior kind.

"Now what, bhikkhus, is the superior kind of son? In this instance a son has a mother and father who have not gone for refuge to the Buddha, to the Dhamma, and to the Sangha; who do not abstain from taking life, from taking what has not been given, from wrong conduct in sensual desires, from false speech, and from intoxicating drink leading to negligence; who are unvirtuous and of bad conduct. But the son is one who has gone for refuge to the Buddha, to the Dhamma, and to the Sangha; who abstains from taking life, from taking what has not been given, from wrong conduct in sensual desires, from false speech, and from intoxicating drink leading to negligence; who is virtuous and of good conduct. This, bhikkhus, is the superior kind of son.

"Now what, bhikkhus, is the similar kind of son? In this instance a son has a mother and father who have gone for refuge to the Buddha … who abstain from taking life … who are virtuous and of good conduct. And the son also is one who has gone for refuge to the Buddha … who abstains from taking life … who is virtuous and of good conduct. This, bhikkhus, is the similar kind of son.

"Now what, bhikkhus, is the inferior kind of son? In this instance a son has a mother and father who have gone for refuge to the Buddha … who abstain from taking life … who are virtuous and of good conduct. But the son is one who has not gone for refuge to the Buddha … who does not abstain from taking life … who is unvirtuous and of bad conduct. This, bhikkhus, is the inferior kind of son.

"These, bhikkhus, are the three kinds of sons found existing in the world."

This is the meaning of what the Lord said. So in regard to this it was said:

The wise wish for a son

Who is superior or similar.

They do not wish for an inferior son,

One who disgraces the family.

But such sons in the world

Who are devoted lay followers,

Excelling in faith and virtue,

Liberal, without selfishness,

Shine forth in assemblies

Like the moon freed from clouds.

This too is the meaning of what was said by the Lord, so I heard.

75. A Rainless Cloud

This was said by the Lord, said by the Arahant, so I heard:

"Bhikkhus, these three kinds of persons are found existing in the world. What three? One who is like a rainless cloud, one who rains locally, and one who rains everywhere.

"Now what kind of person, bhikkhus, is like a rainless cloud? Here, a certain person is not a giver to anyone; he does not give food, drink, clothing, vehicles, garlands, scents, ointments, beds, lodging, and lamps to recluses and brahmins, to the poor, destitute, and needy. This kind of person is like a rainless cloud.

"Now what, bhikkhus, is the kind of person who rains locally? Here, a certain person is a giver to some but not a giver to others. Food, drink, clothing, vehicles, garlands, scents, ointments, beds, lodging, and lamps he gives only to some recluses and brahmins, to some of the poor, destitute, and needy, but not to others. This is the kind of person who rains locally.

"Now what, bhikkhus, is the kind of person who rains everywhere? Here, a certain person gives to all. He gives food, drink, clothing, vehicles, garlands, scents, ointments, beds, lodging, and lamps to all recluses and brahmins, to the poor, destitute, and needy. This is the kind of person who rains everywhere.

"These, bhikkhus, are the three kinds of persons found existing in the world."

This is the meaning of what the Lord said. So in regard to this it was said:

Neither to recluses nor brahmins

Nor to the poor and destitute

Does he distribute his store

Of food and drink and goods;

That base person is called

"One like a rainless cloud."

To some he does not give,

To some he offers alms;

That one wise people call

"One who rains only locally."

A person renowned for his bounty,

Compassionate towards all beings,

Distributes alms gladly.

"Give! Give!" he says.

Like a great storm cloud

That thunders and rains down

Filling the levels and hollows,

Saturating the earth with water,

Even so is such a person.

Having righteously gathered wealth

Which he obtains by his own effort,

He fully satisfies with food and drink

Whatever beings live in need.

This too is the meaning of what was said by the Lord, so I heard.

76. Aspiring for Happiness

This was said by the Lord, said by the Arahant, so I heard:

"Bhikkhus, aspiring for these three kinds of happiness, a wise person should guard virtuous conduct. What are the three?

Aspiring 'May praise come to me,' a wise person should guard virtuous conduct. Aspiring 'May I become wealthy,' a wise person should guard virtuous conduct. Aspiring 'Upon the perishing of the body at death may I be reborn in a good bourn, in a heavenly world,' a wise person should guard virtuous conduct. These are the three kinds of happiness aspiring for which a wise person should guard virtuous conduct."

This is the meaning of what the Lord said. So in regard to this it was said:

Aspiring for three kinds of happiness

The wise person should guard virtue:

Praise, the obtaining of property,

Rejoicing in heaven hereafter.

If one who does no evil

Associates with an evil-doer,

He is suspected of evil

And his disrepute grows.

Whatever person one befriends,

Whomever one associates with,

One becomes of like quality,

One becomes like one's companion.

The follower and the followed,

One who contacts and one contacted,

Are like an arrow coated with poison

That contaminates its quiver.

Fearing contamination the wise person

Should not have evil friends.

A man who ties up putrid fish

With some blades of kusa-grass

Makes the kusa-grass smell putrid;

So it is with those who follow fools.

But a man who wraps tagara powder

In the broad leaf of a tree

Makes the leaf smell fragrant;

So it is with those who follow sages.

Therefore as with the leaf-container,

Understanding the outcome for oneself,

The unvirtuous should not be followed,

A wise person should follow the virtuous.

The unvirtuous lead one to hell,

The virtuous help one reach heaven.

This too is the meaning of what was said by the Lord, so I heard.

77. Perishable

This was said by the Lord, said by the Arahant, so I heard:

"This body, bhikkhus, is perishable, consciousness is of a nature to dissolve, and all objects of clinging are impermanent, suffering, and subject to change."

This is the meaning of what the Lord said. So in regard to this it was said:

Having known the body as perishable

And consciousness as bound to dissolve,

Having seen fear in objects of clinging,

He has gone beyond birth and death;

Having attained supreme peace,

With composed mind he bides his time.

This too is the meaning of what was said by the Lord, so I heard.

78. Like Elements

This was said by the Lord, said by the Arahant, so I heard:

"Bhikkhus, it is according to like elements that beings associate with each other and come together. Beings of low disposition associate and come together with beings of low disposition. Beings of good disposition associate and come together with beings of good disposition. It was so in the past, it will be so in the future, and it is so in the present."

This is the meaning of what the Lord said. So in regard to this it was said:

Desire born of association

Is severed by non-association.

As one riding on a wooden plank

Would sink in the mighty ocean,

Even so one of virtuous life

Sinks by consorting with an idler.

Therefore shun an idle person,

One who makes little effort.

Live with those who dwell secluded,

The noble ones resolved and meditative,

Who are ever strenuous and wise.

This too is the meaning of what was said by the Lord, so I heard.

79. Falling Away

This was said by the Lord, said by the Arahant, so I heard:

"Three things, bhikkhus, lead to the falling away of a learner bhikkhu. What are the three? Here, a learner bhikkhu enjoys activity, is fond of activity, enjoys indulging in activity. He enjoys gossip, is fond of gossip, enjoys indulging in gossip. He enjoys sleep, is fond of sleep, enjoys indulging in sleep. These are the three things that lead to the falling away of a learner bhikkhu.

"Three things, bhikkhus, protect a learner bhikkhu from falling away. What are the three? Here, a learner bhikkhu does not enjoy activity, is not fond of activity, does not enjoy indulging in activity. He does not enjoy gossip, is not fond of gossip, does not enjoy indulging in gossip. He does not enjoy sleep, is not fond of sleep, does not enjoy indulging in sleep. These are the three things that protect a learner bhikkhu from falling away."

This is the meaning of what the Lord said. So in regard to this it was said:

A bhikkhu who enjoys activity,

Restless, fond of gossip and sleep,

Will never be able to attain

Enlightenment which is supreme.

Thus let him restrict his duties,

Give up sloth and restlessness;

Such a bhikkhu can attain

Enlightenment which is supreme.

This too is the meaning of what was said by the Lord, so I heard.

80. Unwholesome Thoughts

This was said by the Lord, said by the Arahant, so I heard:

"Bhikkhus, there are these three kinds of unwholesome thoughts. What three? A thought concerned with not being despised; a thought concerned with gain, honour, and fame; a thought concerned with involvement in the affairs of others. These, bhikkhus, are the three kinds of unwholesome thoughts."

This is the meaning of what the Lord said. So in regard to this it was said:

One concerned with not being despised,

With gain, honour, and esteem,

And who delights in companionship

Is far from the destruction of fetters.

But having abandoned sons and herds

Family life and possessions,

Such a bhikkhu can attain

Enlightenment which is supreme.

This too is the meaning of what was said by the Lord, so I heard.

81. Homage

This was said by the Lord, said by the Arahant, so I heard:

"Bhikkhus, I have seen beings, overwhelmed and with minds obsessed by receiving homage, upon the perishing of the body after death take rebirth in a state of misery, a bad bourn, a state of ruin, hell. I have seen beings, overwhelmed and with minds obsessed by not receiving homage, upon the perishing of the body after death take rebirth in a state of misery, a bad bourn, a state of ruin, hell. I have seen beings, overwhelmed and with minds obsessed by both receiving homage and (later) not receiving homage, upon the perishing of the body after death take rebirth in a state of misery, a bad bourn, a state of ruin, hell.

"I say this, bhikkhus, without having learnt it from another recluse or brahmin… It is just because I myself have known it, seen it, and observed it, that I say: I have seen beings, overwhelmed and with minds obsessed by receiving homage, upon the perishing of the body after death take rebirth in a state of misery, a bad bourn, a state of ruin, hell. I have seen beings, overwhelmed and with minds obsessed by not receiving homage, upon the perishing of the body after death take rebirth in a state of misery, a bad bourn, a state of ruin, hell. I have seen beings, overwhelmed and with minds obsessed by both receiving homage and (later) not receiving homage, upon the perishing of the body after death take rebirth in a state of misery, a bad bourn, a state of ruin, hell."

This is the meaning of what the Lord said. So in regard to this it was said:

He is one who lives diligently

With concentration undisturbed,

Both when homage is paid to him

And when he receives no homage.

Meditating continuously, gifted

With subtle view and insight,

Enjoying the destruction of grasping—

They call such a one a "true man."

This too is the meaning of what was said by the Lord, so I heard.

82. Joyous Utterances

This was said by the Lord, said by the Arahant, so I heard:

"Bhikkhus, among the devas these three joyous utterances are proclaimed from time to time upon certain occasions. What three?

"At the time when a noble disciple, having had his hair and beard shaved off and having clothed himself in the yellow robe, intends going forth from home into homelessness, at that time among the devas the joyous utterance is proclaimed: 'A noble disciple intends to do battle with Mara.' This is the first joyous utterance proclaimed among the devas from time to time upon a certain occasion.

"Again, bhikkhus, at the time when a noble disciple lives engaged in cultivating the seven groups of the requisites of enlightenment, at that time among the devas the joyous utterance is proclaimed: 'A noble disciple is doing battle with Mara.' This is the second joyous utterance proclaimed among the devas from time to time upon a certain occasion.

"And again, bhikkhus, at the time when a noble disciple, through realization by his own direct knowledge, here and now enters and abides in the mind-release and wisdom-release that is taintless by the destruction of the taints, at that time among the devas the joyous utterance is proclaimed: 'A noble disciple has won the battle. He was in the forefront of the fight and he now dwells victorious.' This, bhikkhus, is the third joyous utterance proclaimed among the devas from time to time upon a certain occasion.

"These, bhikkhus, are the three joyous utterances proclaimed from time to time upon certain occasions."

This is the meaning of what the Lord said. So in regard to this it was said:

On seeing that he has won the battle,

Even the devas honour him,

The Fully Enlightened One's disciple,

A great one free from diffidence:

"We salute you, O thoroughbred man,

You who have won a difficult conquest.

Having routed the army of Death,

You are unhindered in liberation."

Thus do the devas extol him,

The one who has attained the goal,

For they do not perceive in him

Ground for subjection to Death's control.

This too is the meaning of what was said by the Lord, so I heard.

83. The Five Prognostic Signs

This was said by the Lord, said by the Arahant, so I heard:

"Bhikkhus, when a deva is due to pass away from a company of devas, five prognostic signs appear: his flower-garlands wither, his clothes become soiled, sweat is released from his armpits, his bodily radiance fades, and the deva takes no delight in his heavenly throne. The devas, observing the prognostic signs that this deva is due to pass away, encourage him in three things with the words: 'Go from here, friend, to a good bourn. Having gone to a good bourn, gain that which is good to gain. Having gained that which is good to gain, become firmly established in it.'"

When this was said, a certain bhikkhu asked the Lord: "Venerable sir, what is reckoned by the devas to be a good bourn? What is reckoned by the devas to be a gain that is good to gain? What is reckoned by the devas to be firmly established?"

"It is human existence, bhikkhus, that is reckoned by the devas to be a good bourn. When a human being acquires faith in the Dhamma-and-Discipline taught by the Tathagata, this is reckoned by the devas to be a gain that is good to gain. When faith is steadfast in him, firmly rooted, established and strong, not to be destroyed by any recluse or brahmin or deva or Mara or Brahma or by anyone else in the world, this is reckoned by the devas to be firmly established."

This is the meaning of what the Lord said. So in regard to this it was said:

When a deva whose life is exhausted

Passes away from a deva-company,

The devas encourage him

In three ways with the words:

"Go, friend, to a good bourn,

To the fellowship of humans.

On becoming human acquire faith

Unsurpassed in the true Dhamma.

That faith made steadfast,

Become rooted and standing firm,

Will be unshakeable for life

In the true Dhamma well proclaimed.

Having abandoned misconduct by body,

Misconduct by speech as well,

Misconduct by mind, and whatever else

Is reckoned as a fault,

Having done much that is good

Both by body and by speech,

And done good with a mind

That is boundless and free from clinging,

With that merit as a basis

Made abundant by generosity,

You should establish other people

In the true Dhamma and the holy life."

When the devas know that a deva

Is about to pass from their midst,

Out of compassion they encourage him:

"Return here, deva, again and again."

This too is the meaning of what was said by the Lord, so I heard.

84. For the Welfare of Many

This was said by the Lord, said by the Arahant, so I heard:

"Bhikkhus, these three persons appearing in the world appear for the welfare of many people, for the happiness of many people, out of compassion for the world, for the good, welfare, and happiness of devas and humans. What three?

"Here, bhikkhus, a Tathagata appears in the world, an Arahant, a Fully Enlightened One, possessing perfect knowledge and conduct, a sublime one, a world-knower, an unsurpassed leader of persons to be tamed, a teacher of devas and humans, an enlightened one, a Lord. He teaches Dhamma that is good at the outset, good in the middle, and good at the end, with its correct meaning and wording, and he proclaims the holy life in its fulfilment and complete purity. This, bhikkhus, is the first person appearing in the world who appears for the welfare of many people, for the happiness of many people, out of compassion for the world, for the good, welfare, and happiness of devas and humans.

"Next, bhikkhus, there is a disciple of that teacher, an arahant, one whose taints are destroyed, the holy life fulfilled, who has done what had to be done, laid down the burden, attained the goal, destroyed the fetters of being, and is completely released through final knowledge. He teaches Dhamma that is good at the outset, good in the middle, and good at the end, with its correct meaning and wording, and he proclaims the holy life in its fulfilment and complete purity. This, bhikkhus, is the second person appearing in the world who appears for the welfare of many people, for the happiness of many people, out of compassion for the world, for the good, welfare, and happiness of devas and humans.

"And next, bhikkhus, there is a disciple of that teacher, a learner who is following the path, who has learnt much and is of virtuous conduct. He teaches Dhamma that is good at the outset, good in the middle, and good at the end, with its correct meaning and wording, and he proclaims the holy life in its fulfilment and complete purity. This, bhikkhus, is the third person appearing in the world who appears for the welfare of many people, for the happiness of many people, out of compassion for the world, for the good, welfare, and happiness of devas and humans.

"These, bhikkhus, are the three persons appearing in the world who appear for the welfare of many people, for the happiness of many people, out of compassion for the world, for the good, welfare, and happiness of devas and humans."

This is the meaning of what the Lord said. So in regard to this it was said:

The teacher, the great sage,

Is the first in the world;

Following him is the disciple

Whose composure is perfected;

And then the learner training on the path,

One who has learnt much and is virtuous.

These three are chief amongst devas and humans:

Illuminators, preaching Dhamma,

Opening the door to the Deathless,

They free many people from bondage.

Those who follow the path

Well taught by the unsurpassed

Caravan-leader, who are diligent

In the Sublime One's dispensation,

Make an end of suffering

Within this very life itself.

This too is the meaning of what was said by the Lord, so I heard.

85. Contemplating Foulness

This was said by the Lord, said by the Arahant, so I heard:

"Bhikkhus, live contemplating the foulness of the body. Let mindfulness of breathing be inwardly well established before you. Live contemplating the impermanence of all formations.

"For those who live contemplating foulness in the body, the tendency to lust with regard to the element of beauty is abandoned. When mindfulness of breathing is inwardly well established before one, the tendencies of extraneous thoughts to produce vexation of mind remain no more. For those who live contemplating the impermanence of all formations, ignorance is abandoned and knowledge arises."

This is the meaning of what the Lord said. So in regard to this it was said:

Contemplating foulness in the body,

Being mindful of in-and-out breathing,

Ever ardent and seeing clearly

The calming down of all formations:

Such a bhikkhu who sees rightly

Is thereby well released.

Accomplished in knowledge, at peace,

That sage has overcome all bonds.

This too is the meaning of what was said by the Lord, so I heard.

86. Practice According to Dhamma

This was said by the Lord, said by the Arahant, so I heard:

"When referring to a bhikkhu who practises according to Dhamma, this is the proper way of defining 'practice according to Dhamma.' When speaking he speaks only Dhamma, not non-Dhamma. When thinking he thinks only thoughts of Dhamma, not thoughts of non-Dhamma. By avoiding these two he lives with equanimity, mindful and clearly comprehending."

This is the meaning of what the Lord said. So in regard to this it was said:

A bhikkhu enjoying the Dhamma

And delighting in the Dhamma,

Reflecting upon the Dhamma,

Does not fall from the true Dhamma.

Whether walking or standing,

Sitting or lying down,

With mind inwardly restrained,

He attains to lasting peace.

This too is the meaning of what was said by the Lord, so I heard.

87. Producing Blindness

This was said by the Lord, said by the Arahant, so I heard:

"Bhikkhus, these three kinds of unwholesome thoughts produce blindness, lack of vision, and absence of knowledge; they obstruct wisdom, lead to vexation, and are not conducive to Nibbana. What are the three? A sensual thought, a thought of ill will, and an aggressive thought. These, bhikkhus, are the three kinds of unwholesome thoughts that produce blindness, lack of vision, and absence of knowledge; they obstruct wisdom, lead to vexation, and are not conducive to Nibbana.

"Bhikkhus, these three kinds of wholesome thoughts remove blindness and produce vision, knowledge, and the growth of wisdom; they do not lead to vexation and are conducive to Nibbana. What are the three? A thought of renunciation, a thought of friendliness, and a thought of harmlessness. These, bhikkhus, are the three kinds of wholesome thoughts that remove blindness, lack of vision, and absence of knowledge; they obstruct wisdom, lead to vexation, and are conducive to Nibbana."

This is the meaning of what the Lord said. So in regard to this it was said:

Three wholesome thoughts should be entertained,

Three unwholesome thoughts rejected.

One who stops such trains of thought

As a shower settles a cloud of dust,

With a mind that has quelled such thoughts

Attains in this life the state of peace.

This too is the meaning of what was said by the Lord, so I heard.

88. Inner Stains

This was said by the Lord, said by the Arahant, so I heard:

"Bhikkhus, these three are inner stains, inner enemies, inner foes, inner murderers, inner adversaries. What three? Greed, bhikkhus, is an inner stain, an inner enemy, an inner foe, an inner murderer, an inner adversary. Hate is an inner stain, an inner enemy, an inner foe, an inner murderer, an inner adversary. Delusion is an inner stain, an inner enemy, an inner foe, an inner murderer, an inner adversary. These are the three."

This is the meaning of what the Lord said. So in regard to this it was said:

Greed is a cause of misfortune,

Greed agitates the mind;

People do not understand this

As a danger produced within.

A greedy person does not know the good,

A greedy person does not see the Dhamma;

Blinding darkness then prevails

When greed overwhelms a person.

But one who has abandoned greed

Longs not for what invites cupidity.

Greed slips away from him

As a water drop from a lotus leaf.

Hate is a cause of misfortune,

Hate agitates the mind;

People do not understand this

As a danger produced within.

A hater does not know the good,

A hater does not see the Dhamma;

Blinding darkness then prevails

When hate overwhelms a person.

But one who has abandoned hate

Is not angered by what incites to anger.

Hate drops away from him

As a palmyra fruit from its stalk.

Delusion is a cause of misfortune,

Delusion agitates the mind;

People do not understand this

As a danger produced within.

One deluded does not know the good,

One deluded does not see the Dhamma;

Blinding darkness then prevails

When delusion overwhelms a person.

But one who has abandoned delusion

Is not bewildered by confusing things.

He puts an end to all delusion

As the sunrise dispels the dark.

This too is the meaning of what was said by the Lord, so I heard.

89. Devadatta

This was said by the Lord, said by the Arahant, so I heard:

"Bhikkhus, overcome with his mind obsessed by three kinds of wickedness, Devadatta will inevitably go to a state of misery, to hell, for the duration of the aeon. What are the three? Overcome with his mind obsessed by evil desires, Devadatta will inevitably go to a state of misery, to hell, for the duration of the aeon; overcome with his mind obsessed by evil friends, Devadatta will inevitably go to a state of misery, to hell, for the duration of the aeon; and although there was more that should have been done, he stopped halfway through gaining a trifling attainment of distinction. These, bhikkhus, are the three."

This is the meaning of what the Lord said. So in regard to this it was said:

Surely no one of evil desires

Is born again into this world.

Know that he goes to the bourn of those

Who live in the grip of evil desires.

I heard how Devadatta was

Regarded as a wise man,

One developed in meditation

Who shone as it were with fame.

Having thought himself his equal,

He assaulted the Tathagata

And went to the four-doored frightful place,

Avici the Unremitting Hell.

When one plots against an innocent

Who has done no evil deed,

That evil merely affects the one

Corrupt of mind and disrespectful.

One who thinks he could pollute

The ocean with a pot of poison

Would not be able to pollute it—

Awesome is that mass of water.

It is similar in attacking with abuse

The Tathagata who has reached perfection

And ever dwells with peaceful mind—

Abuse has no effect on him.

A wise man should befriend such a one

And constantly follow after him.

A bhikkhu who goes along his path

Can reach the end of suffering.

This too is the meaning of what was said by the Lord, so I heard.

90. Foremost Faith

This was said by the Lord, said by the Arahant, so I heard:

"Bhikkhus, there are these three foremost kinds of faith. What are the three?

"Whatever beings there are, whether footless or two-footed or four-footed, with form or without form, percipient or non-percipient or neither-percipient-nor-non-percipient, of these the Tathagata is reckoned foremost, the Arahant, the Fully Enlightened One. Those who have faith in the Buddha have faith in the foremost, and for those with faith in the foremost the result will be foremost.

"Whatever states there are, whether conditioned or unconditioned, of these detachment is reckoned foremost, that is, the subduing of vanity, the elimination of thirst, the removal of reliance, the termination of the round (of rebirths), the destruction of craving, detachment, cessation, Nibbana. Those who have faith in the Dhamma of detachment have faith in the foremost, and for those with faith in the foremost the result will be foremost.

"Whatever communities or groups there are, bhikkhus, of these the Sangha of the Tathagata's disciples is reckoned foremost, that is, the four pairs of persons, the eight individuals. This Sangha of the Lord's disciples is worthy of gifts, worthy of hospitality, worthy of offerings, worthy of reverential salutation, the unsurpassable field of merit for the world. Those who have faith in the Sangha have faith in the foremost, and for those with faith in the foremost the result will be foremost.

"These, bhikkhus, are the three foremost kinds of faith."

This is the meaning of what the Lord said. So in regard to this it was said:

This is foremost for those with faith,

For those who know the foremost Dhamma:

Having faith in the Buddha as foremost,

Worthy of offerings, unsurpassed;

Having faith in the Dhamma as foremost,

The peace of detachment, bliss;

Having faith in the Sangha as foremost,

A field of merit unsurpassed.

Distributing gifts among the foremost,

Foremost is the merit that accrues;

Foremost their life and beauty,

Fame, reputation, happiness, and strength.

The wise one who gives to the foremost,

Concentrated on the foremost Dhamma,

Whether he becomes a deva or a human,

Rejoices in his foremost attainment.

This too is the meaning of what was said by the Lord, so I heard.

91. A Means of Subsistence

This was said by the Lord, said by the Arahant, so I heard:

"Bhikkhus, this is a contemptible means of subsistence, this gathering of alms. In the world, bhikkhus, it is a form of abuse to say, 'You alms-gatherer! Wandering about clutching a bowl!' Yet this means of subsistence has been taken up by young men of good family for a reason, for a purpose. They have not been reduced to it by kings nor by robbers nor because of debt nor through fear nor from loss of an alternative means of livelihood, but with the thought: 'We are beset by birth, ageing and death, by sorrow, lamentation, pain, grief, and despair; overcome by suffering, afflicted by suffering. Perhaps an end can be discerned of this whole mass of suffering!'

"So this young man of good family has gone forth (into homelessness), but he may be covetous for objects of desire, strongly passionate, malevolent, corrupt in thought, unmindful, uncomprehending, unconcentrated, of wandering mind and uncontrolled faculties. Just as a brand from a funeral pyre, burnt at both ends and in the middle smeared with excrement, can be used as timber neither in the village nor in the forest, so by such a simile do I speak about this person: he has missed out on the enjoyments of a householder, yet he does not fulfil the purpose of recluseship."

This is the meaning of what the Lord said. So in regard to this it was said:

He has missed both a layman's pleasure

And his recluseship, too, the luckless man!

Ruining it, he throws it away

And perishes like a funerary brand.

Far better for him to swallow

A fiery hot iron ball

Than that immoral and uncontrolled

He should eat the country's alms.

This too is the meaning of what was said by the Lord, so I heard.

92. The Hem of the Robe

This was said by the Lord, said by the Arahant, so I heard:

"Bhikkhus, even though a bhikkhu might hold on to the hem of my robe and follow close behind me step by step, if he is covetous for objects of desire, strongly passionate, malevolent, corrupt in thought, unmindful, uncomprehending, unconcentrated, of wandering mind and uncontrolled faculties, he is far from me and I am far from him. What is the reason? That bhikkhu does not see Dhamma. Not seeing Dhamma, he does not see me.

"Bhikkhus, even though a bhikkhu might live a hundred leagues away, if he is not covetous for objects of desire, not strongly passionate, not malevolent, uncorrupt in thought, with mindfulness established, clearly comprehending, concentrated, of unified mind and controlled faculties, he is close to me and I am close to him. What is the reason? That bhikkhu sees Dhamma. Seeing Dhamma, he sees me."

This is the meaning of what the Lord said. So in regard to this it was said:

Though closely following behind,

Full of longings and resentment,

See how far away he is—

The desirous one from the desireless,

One unquenched from the quenched,

A greedy one from the one without greed.

But a wise person who by direct knowledge

Has fully understood the Dhamma,

Becomes desireless and tranquil

Like a calm unruffled lake.

See how close he is to him—

A desireless one to the desireless,

One quenched to the quenched,

The greedless one to the one without greed.

This too is the meaning of what was said by the Lord, so I heard.

93. The Fires

This was said by the Lord, said by the Arahant, so I heard:

"Bhikkhus, there are these three fires. What three? The fire of lust, the fire of hate, and the fire of delusion. These, bhikkhus, are the three fires."

This is the meaning of what the Lord said. So in regard to this it was said:

The fire of lust burns mortals

Infatuated by sensual pleasures;

The fire of hate burns malevolent people

Who kill other living beings;

The fire of delusion burns the bewildered,

Ignorant of the Noble One's Dhamma.

Being unaware of these three fires,

Humankind delights in personal existence.

Unfree from the bonds of Mara

They swell the ranks of hell,

Existence in the animal realm,

Asura-demons and the sphere of ghosts.

But those engaged in practising

The Buddha's teaching day and night

Ever perceiving the body's foulness,

Extinguish the fire of lust.

Those best of humans by loving-kindness

Extinguish the fire of hate,

And they extinguish the fire of delusion

By wisdom that leads to penetration.

Having extinguished these fires,

Unwearied night and day,

Those discerning ones attain Nibbana

And overcome all suffering.

The noble seers, masters of knowledge,

Wise ones with perfect understanding,

By directly knowing the end of birth

Come no more to renewal of being.

This too is the meaning of what was said by the Lord, so I heard.

94. Investigating

This was said by the Lord, said by the Arahant, so I heard:

"Bhikkhus, a bhikkhu should so investigate that as he investigates, his consciousness is not distracted and diffused externally, and internally is not fixed, and by not grasping anything he should remain undisturbed. If his consciousness is not distracted and diffused externally, and internally is not fixed, and if by not grasping anything he remains undisturbed, then there is no coming into existence of birth, ageing, death, and suffering in the future."

This is the meaning of what the Lord said. So in regard to this it was said:

When a bhikkhu has abandoned

The seven ties and cut the cord,

His wandering on in births is finished:

There is no renewal of being for him.

This too is the meaning of what was said by the Lord, so I heard.

95. Sensual Desire

This was said by the Lord, said by the Arahant, so I heard:

"Bhikkhus, there are these three ways of obtaining the objects of sensual desire. What three? There are those objects of sensual desire already existent; there is the way of those who delight in creating them; and there is the way of those who gain control over objects created by others. These are the three ways of obtaining the objects of sensual desire."

This is the meaning of what the Lord said. So in regard to this it was said:

Those who enjoy what exists,

Those devas exercising control,

Those who delight in creating,

And others who enjoy sense-objects—

Being in this state or another

They cannot pass beyond saṃsara.

Understanding this danger

In objects of sensual enjoyment,

Let the wise person abandon all sense pleasures,

Those both heavenly and human.

By severing the flow of craving,

The flow so difficult to overcome

Of greed for pleasing, enticing forms,

They attain to final Nibbana

And overcome all suffering.

The noble seers, masters of knowledge,

Wise ones with perfect understanding,

By directly knowing the end of birth

Come no more to renewal of being.

This too is the meaning of what was said by the Lord, so I heard.

96. The Bonds

This was said by the Lord, said by the Arahant, so I heard:

"Bhikkhus, one bound by the bond of sensual desire and by the bond of being is a returner, one who comes back to this state. One freed from the bond of sensual desire but still bound by the bond of being is a non-returner, one who does not come back to this state. One freed from the bond of sensual desire and freed from the bond of being is an arahant, one in whom the taints are destroyed."

This is the meaning of what the Lord said. So in regard to this it was said:

Fettered by both these bonds—

The sensual bond and the bond of being—

Living beings continue in saṃsara,

Journeying on to birth and death.

Those who abandon sensual desires

But have not reached the taints' destruction,

Fettered by the bondage of being,

Are declared to be non-returners.

But those who have cut off doubts,

Destroyed conceit and renewal of being,

Who reach the taints' full destruction,

Though in the world, have gone beyond.

This too is the meaning of what was said by the Lord, so I heard.

97. Lovely Behaviour

This was said by the Lord, said by the Arahant, so I heard:

"Bhikkhus, a bhikkhu who is of lovely behaviour, lovely nature, and lovely wisdom is called in this Dhamma-and-Discipline one who is fully accomplished, who has reached fulfilment, the supreme among humans.

"And how is a bhikkhu of lovely behaviour? Here, a bhikkhu is virtuous, he lives restrained by the restraint of the rules of discipline, endowed with perfect conduct and resort; seeing danger in the slightest faults, he undertakes the rules of training and trains in them. In this way a bhikkhu is one who is of lovely behaviour. Thus he is of lovely behaviour.

"And how is he of lovely nature? Here, a bhikkhu lives engaged in cultivating the seven groups of the requisites of enlightenment. In this way a bhikkhu is one who is of lovely nature. Thus he is of lovely behaviour and lovely nature.

"And how is he of lovely wisdom? Here, through realization by his own direct knowledge, a bhikkhu here and now enters and abides in the mind-release and wisdom-release that is taintless by the destruction of the taints. In this way a bhikkhu is one who is of lovely wisdom.

"Thus he is of lovely behaviour, lovely nature, and lovely wisdom. In this Dhamma-and-Discipline he is called one who is fully accomplished, who has reached fulfilment and is supreme among humans."

This is the meaning of what the Lord said. So in regard to this it was said:

A conscientious bhikkhu

Who never does wrong in any way,

Neither by body, speech, or mind,

Is called "one of lovely behaviour."

An unassuming bhikkhu

Who has cultivated well the states

That lead to enlightenment

Is called "one of lovely nature."

A taintless bhikkhu

Who understands for himself

The end of suffering here

Is called "one of lovely wisdom."

He who excels in these three things,

Untroubled, with doubt destroyed,

Unattached in all the world,

Is called "one who has abandoned all."

This too is the meaning of what was said by the Lord, so I heard.

98. Giving

This was said by the Lord, said by the Arahant, so I heard:

"Bhikkhus, there are these two kinds of giving: the giving of material things and the giving of the Dhamma. Of these two kinds of giving, this is the foremost, namely, the giving of the Dhamma. There are these two kinds of sharing: the sharing of material things and the sharing of the Dhamma. Of these two kinds of sharing, this is the foremost, namely, the sharing of the Dhamma. There are these two kinds of help: help with material things and help with the Dhamma. Of these two kinds of help, this is the foremost, namely, help with the Dhamma."

This is the meaning of what the Lord said. So in regard to this it was said:

When they say that giving

Is supreme and unsurpassed,

And the Lord himself has extolled sharing,

Who, wise and knowing,

Confident in that foremost field of merit,

Would not give at the appropriate time?

Both for those who proclaim it

And for those who listen to it,

Confident in the Sublime One's teaching,

The supreme good is fully purified

As they live diligently in the teaching.

This too is the meaning of what was said by the Lord, so I heard.

99. The Threefold Knowledge

This was said by the Lord, said by the Arahant, so I heard:

"Bhikkhus, I declare that it is through the Dhamma that one becomes a brahmin possessing the threefold knowledge: (I do not say this) of another merely because he can talk persuasively and recite. And how do I declare that it is through the Dhamma that one becomes a brahmin possessing the threefold knowledge?

"Here, bhikkhus, a bhikkhu recollects a variety of former lives, that is, one birth, two births, three births, four births, five births, ten births, twenty births, thirty births, forty births, fifty births, a hundred births, a thousand births, a hundred thousand births; many aeons of world-contraction, many aeons of world-expansion, many aeons of both world-contraction and expansion. He recollects in a particular life being such a one by name, of such a clan, of such an appearance, having this kind of nutriment, experiencing these kinds of pleasure and pain, having this lifespan; and deceasing from there he arose here. Thus with all their details and particulars he recollects a variety of former lives. This is the first knowledge attained by him. Ignorance is dispelled, knowledge has arisen; darkness is dispelled, light has arisen, as happens in one who lives diligent, ardent, and resolute.

"Then again, bhikkhus, with the divine eye, purified and surpassing the human, a bhikkhu sees beings passing away and reappearing, inferior and superior, fair and ugly, fortunate and unfortunate, and he understands how beings pass on according to their deeds thus: 'Those worthy beings practising misconduct by body, speech, and mind, insulters of the noble ones, of wrong view and undertaking deeds in consequence of wrong view, when the body perishes have been reborn after death in a state of misery, a bad bourn, a state of ruin, hell. But those worthy beings practising good conduct by body, speech, and mind, not insulters of the noble ones, of right view and undertaking deeds in consequence of right view, when the body perishes, have been reborn after death in a good bourn, a heavenly world.' Thus he sees this with the divine eye and he understands how beings pass on according to their deeds. This is the second knowledge attained by him. Ignorance is dispelled, knowledge has arisen; darkness is dispelled, light has arisen, as happens in one who lives diligent, ardent, and resolute.

"Then again, bhikkhus, a bhikkhu, through realization by his own direct knowledge, here and now enters and abides in the mind-release and wisdom-release that is taintless by the destruction of the taints. This is the third knowledge attained by him. Ignorance is dispelled, knowledge has arisen; darkness is dispelled, light has arisen, as happens in one who lives diligent, ardent, and resolute.

"Thus, bhikkhus, do I declare that it is through the Dhamma that one becomes a brahmin possessing the threefold knowledge; (I do not say this) of another merely because he can talk persuasively and recite."

This is the meaning of what the Lord said. So in regard to this it was said:

He who knows his former lives,

Who sees heaven and states of woe,

Who reaches the end of birth,

A sage and master of direct knowledge—

By these three ways of knowing one becomes

A brahmin having the threefold knowledge.

That is what I call the threefold knowledge,

Not another's babbling and reciting.

This too is the meaning of what was said by the Lord, so I heard.

# THE SECTION OF THE FOURS

100. The Dhamma-offering

This was said by the Lord, said by the Arahant, so I heard:

"Bhikkhus, I am a brahmin, ever accessible to entreaties, open-handed, one bearing his last body, an unsurpassed physician and surgeon. You are my own legitimate sons, born from my mouth, born of Dhamma, fashioned by Dhamma, heirs of Dhamma, not heirs of material things.

"Bhikkhus, there are these two kinds of giving: the giving of material things and the giving of the Dhamma. Of these two kinds of giving, this is the foremost, namely, the giving of the Dhamma. There are these two kinds of sharing: the sharing of material things and the sharing of the Dhamma. Of these two kinds of sharing, this is the foremost, namely, the sharing of the Dhamma. There are these two kinds of help: the help of material things and the help of the Dhamma. Of these two kinds of help, this is the foremost, namely, the help of the Dhamma. There are these two kinds of offerings: the offering of material things and the offering of the Dhamma. Of these two kinds of offering, this is the foremost, namely, the offering of the Dhamma."

This is the meaning of what the Lord said. So in regard to this it was said:

The Tathagata has made the Dhamma-offering,

Unselfish, compassionate towards all beings;

Living beings revere such a one,

Gone beyond being, as chief of devas and humans.

This too is the meaning of what was said by the Lord, so I heard.

101. Easily Obtained

This was said by the Lord, said by the Arahant, so I heard:

"These four, bhikkhus, are trifling things, easily obtained and blameless. What four? A robe made of cast-off rags is a trifling thing, easily obtained and blameless. Food gathered on alms round is a trifling thing, easily obtained and blameless. The root of a tree as a dwelling place is a trifling thing, easily obtained and blameless. Medicine consisting of putrid cow urine is a trifling thing, easily obtained and blameless. These, bhikkhus, are the four trifling things, easily obtained and blameless. When a bhikkhu is content with these things that are trifling and easily obtained, I say of him that he has the requisites for recluseship."

This is the meaning of what the Lord said. So in regard to this it was said:

One content with what is blameless,

Things trifling and easily obtained,

Does not become vexed in mind

When not obtaining a place to live,

A robe to wear, and food and drink;

He has no resentment in any quarter.

These are the things declared to be

Suitable for a recluse's life

By possession of which a bhikkhu

May abide content and diligent.

This too is the meaning of what was said by the Lord, so I heard.

102. The Destruction of the Taints

This was said by the Lord, said by the Arahant, so I heard:

"For one knowing and seeing, bhikkhus, I say there is the destruction of the taints, not for one not knowing and not seeing. But for one knowing what, seeing what, is there the destruction of the taints? For one knowing and seeing, 'This is suffering,' there is the destruction of the taints. For one knowing and seeing, 'This is the origin of suffering' there is the destruction of the taints. For one knowing and seeing, 'This is the cessation of suffering' there is the destruction of the taints. For one knowing and seeing, 'This is the course leading to the cessation of suffering,' there is the destruction of the taints. Thus it is, bhikkhus, that for one knowing and seeing there is the destruction of the taints."

This is the meaning of what the Lord said. So in regard to this it was said:

For a learner who is training

In conformity with the direct path,

The knowledge of destruction arises first,

And final knowledge immediately follows.

To one freed by that final knowledge,

The topmost knowledge of freedom,

There arises the knowledge of destruction:

"Thus the fetters are destroyed."

Certainly not by the lazy person

Nor by the uncomprehending fool

Is Nibbana to be attained,

The loosening of all worldly ties.

This too is the meaning of what was said by the Lord, so I heard.

103. Recluses and Brahmins

This was said by the Lord, said by the Arahant, so I heard:

"Bhikkhus, whatever recluses and brahmins do not understand as it actually is: 'This is suffering'; 'This is the origin of suffering'; 'This is the cessation of suffering'; 'This is the course leading to the cessation of suffering'—these recluses and brahmins are not considered by me to be true recluses among recluses, to be true brahmins among brahmins. These venerable ones live without having realized and achieved here and now by their own direct knowledge the aim of being a recluse, the aim of being a brahmin.

"But, bhikkhus, whatever recluses and brahmins understand as it actually is: 'This is suffering'; 'This is the origin of suffering'; 'This is the cessation of suffering'; 'This is the course leading to the cessation of suffering'—these recluses and brahmins are considered by me to be true recluses among recluses, to be true brahmins among brahmins. These venerable ones indeed live having achieved and realized here and now by their own direct knowledge the aim of being a recluse, the aim of being a brahmin."

This is the meaning of what the Lord said. So in regard to this it was said:

Those who do not understand suffering,

Or how suffering is produced,

Or where suffering finally stops

Altogether without remainder,

And who do not know that path

Leading to relief from suffering—

They are destitute of mind-release

And lack release by wisdom too;

Unable to make an end of it,

They fare on in birth and decay.

But those who understand suffering,

And how suffering is produced,

And where suffering finally stops

Altogether without remainder,

And who also know that path

Leading to relief from suffering—

They possess that mind-release

And the release by wisdom too;

Able to make an end of it

They never come back to birth and decay.

This too is the meaning of what was said by the Lord, so I heard.

104. Excelling in Virtue

This was said by the Lord, said by the Arahant, so I heard:

"Bhikkhus, as to those bhikkhus who excel in virtue, excel in concentration, excel in wisdom, excel in release, excel in the knowledge and vision of release, who are advisors, instructors, and demonstrators, who can exhort, inspire, and encourage, and who are competent teachers of the true Dhamma—seeing those bhikkhus is very helpful, I say; listening to those bhikkhus, approaching them, attending upon them, remembering them, and following their example in going forth into homelessness is very helpful, I say. For what reason?

"By following such bhikkhus, by associating with them and attending upon them, the aggregate of virtue as yet incomplete reaches completion of development, the aggregate of concentration, of wisdom, of release, and of knowledge and vision of release as yet incomplete reaches completion of development. Such bhikkhus as these are called teachers, caravan-leaders, fault-abandoners, dispellers of darkness, light-bringers, makers of radiance, luminaries, torch-bearers, bringers of illumination, noble ones, possessors of vision."

This is the meaning of what the Lord said. So in regard to this it was said:

For those who are knowledgeable

This is a state making for joy—

Living the life of Dhamma

Under the noble ones perfected in mind.

They clarify the true Dhamma,

Shining forth and illuminating it,

Those light-bringers, heroic sages,

Endowed with vision, dispelling faults.

Having heard their teaching,

The wise with perfect understanding

By directly knowing the end of birth

Come no more to renewal of being.

This too is the meaning of what was said by the Lord, so I heard.

105. Arousing Craving

This was said by the Lord, said by the Arahant, so I heard:

"Bhikkhus, there are four things that arouse craving whereby the craving that has arisen in a bhikkhu arises. What are the four? Because of robes, because of almsfood, because of a dwelling place, because of gaining this or losing that the craving that has arisen in a bhikkhu arises. These, bhikkhus, are the four things that arouse craving whereby the craving that has arisen in a bhikkhu arises."

This is the meaning of what the Lord said. So in regard to this it was said:

A person companioned by craving

Wanders on the long journey

In this state of being or another

And cannot go beyond saṃsara.

Having understood the danger thus,

That craving is the origin of suffering,

A bhikkhu should wander mindfully,

Free from craving, without grasping.

This too is the meaning of what was said by the Lord, so I heard.

106. With Brahma

This was said by the Lord, said by the Arahant, so I heard:

"Living with Brahma are those families where, within the home, mother and father are respected by their children. Living with the early devas are those families where, within the home, mother and father are respected by their children. Living with the early teachers are those families where, within the home, mother and father are respected by their children. Living with those worthy of adoration are those families where, within the home, mother and father are respected by their children. 'Brahma,' bhikkhus, is a term for mother and father. 'Early devas' and 'early teachers' and 'those worthy of veneration' are terms for mother and father. For what reason? Because mother and father are very helpful to their children, they take care of them and bring them up and teach them about the world."

This is the meaning of what the Lord said. So in regard to this it was said:

Mother and father are called

"Brahma," "early teachers"

And "worthy of veneration,"

Being compassionate towards

Their family of children.

Thus the wise should venerate them,

Pay them due honour,

Provide them with food and drink,

Give them clothing and a bed,

Anoint and bathe them

And also wash their feet.

When he performs such service

For his mother and his father,

They praise that wise person even here

And hereafter he rejoices in heaven.

This too is the meaning of what was said by the Lord, so I heard.

107. Very Helpful

This was said by the Lord, said by the Arahant, so I heard:

"Bhikkhus, brahmins and householders are very helpful to you. They provide you with the requisites of robes, almsfood, lodgings, and medicine in time of sickness. And you, bhikkhus, are very helpful to brahmins and householders, as you teach them the Dhamma that is good at the outset, good in the middle, and good at the end, with its correct meaning and wording, and you proclaim the holy life in its fulfilment and complete purity. Thus, bhikkhus, this holy life is lived with mutual support for the purpose of crossing the flood and making a complete end of suffering."

This is the meaning of what the Lord said. So in regard to this it was said:

Householders and homeless alike,

Each a support for the other,

Both accomplish the true Dhamma—

The unsurpassed security from bondage.

From householders the homeless receive

These basic necessities of life,

Robes to wear and a place to dwell

Dispelling the hardships of the seasons.

And by relying on one of good conduct,

Home-loving layfolk dwelling in a house

Place faith in those worthy ones

Of noble wisdom and meditative.

Practising the Dhamma in this life,

The path leading to a good bourn,

Those wishing for pleasure rejoice

In the delights of the deva world.

This too is the meaning of what was said by the Lord, so I heard.

108. Deceitful

This was said by the Lord, said by the Arahant, so I heard:

"Bhikkhus, whatever bhikkhus are deceitful, stubborn, mere talkers, frauds, arrogant, and unconcentrated, these bhikkhus are no followers of mine. They have turned aside from this Dhamma-and-Discipline and will not achieve growth, progress, or development within it.

"But whatever bhikkhus are not deceitful, not mere talkers, wise, adaptable, and well concentrated, these bhikkhus are indeed my followers. They have not turned aside from this Dhamma-and-Discipline and will achieve growth, progress, and development within it."

This is the meaning of what the Lord said. So in regard to this it was said:

Deceitful, stubborn, mere talkers,

Frauds, arrogant, unconcentrated—

These make no progress in the Dhamma

Taught by the Fully Enlightened One.

Undeceitful, not talkative, wise,

Adaptable, well concentrated—

Such as these progress in the Dhamma

Taught by the Fully Enlightened One.

This too is the meaning of what was said by the Lord, so I heard.

109. The River Current

This was said by the Lord, said by the Arahant, so I heard:

"Suppose, bhikkhus, a man was being borne along by the current of a river that seemed pleasant and agreeable. But upon seeing him, a keen-sighted man standing on the bank would call out to him: 'Hey, good man! Although you are being borne along by the current of a river that seems pleasant and agreeable, lower down there is a pool with turbulent waves and swirling eddies, with monsters and demons. On reaching that pool you will die or suffer close to death.' Then, bhikkhus, upon hearing the words of that person, that man would struggle against the current with hands and feet.

"I have made use of this simile, bhikkhus, to illustrate the meaning. And this is the meaning here: 'The current of the river' is a synonym for craving. 'Seeming pleasant and agreeable' is a synonym for the six internal sense-bases. 'The pool lower down' is a synonym for the five lower fetters.'Turbulent waves' is a synonym for anger and frustration. 'Swirling eddies' is a synonym for the five strands of sensual pleasure. 'Monsters and demons' is a synonym for womenfolk. 'Against the current' is a synonym for renunciation. 'Struggling with hands and feet' is a synonym for instigating energy. 'The keen-sighted man standing on the bank' is a synonym for the Tathagata, the Arahant, the Fully Enlightened One."

This is the meaning of what the Lord said. So in regard to this it was said:

Desiring future security from bondage

One should abandon sensual desire

However painful this may be.

Rightly comprehending with wisdom,

Possessing a mind that is well released,

One may reach freedom step by step.

One who is a master of knowledge,

Who has lived the holy life,

Is called one gone to the world's end,

One who has reached the further shore.

This too is the meaning of what was said by the Lord, so I heard.

110. While Walking

This was said by the Lord, said by the Arahant, so I heard:

"Bhikkhus, if while walking a sensual thought or a thought of ill will or an aggressive thought arises in a bhikkhu, and if he tolerates it and does not reject it, does not dispel it and get rid of it and bring it to an end, that bhikkhu—who in such a manner is lacking in ardour and unafraid of wrongdoing—is called constantly lazy and indolent. If while standing a sensual thought or a thought of ill will or an aggressive thought arises in a bhikkhu, and if he tolerates it and does not reject it, does not dispel it and get rid of it and bring it to an end, that bhikkhu—who in such a manner is lacking in ardour and unafraid of wrongdoing—is called constantly lazy and indolent. If while sitting a sensual thought or a thought of ill will or an aggressive thought arises in a bhikkhu, and if he tolerates it and does not reject it, does not dispel it and get rid of it and bring it to an end, that bhikkhu—who in such a manner is lacking in ardour and unafraid of wrongdoing—is called constantly lazy and indolent. If while lying down a sensual thought or a thought of ill will or an aggressive thought arises in a bhikkhu, and if he tolerates it and does not reject it a sensual thought or a thought of ill will or an aggressive thought arises in a bhikkhu, and if he tolerates it and does not reject it, does not dispel it and get rid of it and bring it to an end, that bhikkhu—who in such a manner is lacking in ardour and unafraid of wrongdoing—is called constantly lazy and indolent. that bhikkhu is called constantly lazy and indolent.

"But if while walking … standing … sitting … lying down a sensual thought or a thought of ill will or an aggressive thought arises in a bhikkhu and he does not tolerate it, but rejects it, dispels it, gets rid of it, and brings it to an end, that bhikkhu—who in such a manner is ardent and afraid of wrongdoing—is called constantly energetic and resolute."

This is the meaning of what the Lord said. So in regard to this it was said:

Whether walking or standing,

Sitting or lying down

Whoever thinks such thoughts

That are evil and worldly—

He is following a wrong path,

Infatuated with delusive things.

Such a bhikkhu cannot reach

Enlightenment which is supreme.

Whether walking or standing,

Sitting or lying down,

Whoever overcomes these thoughts,

Delighting in the quelling of thoughts—

Such a bhikkhu is able to reach

Enlightenment which is supreme.

This too is the meaning of what was said by the Lord, so I heard.

111. Perfect in Virtue

This was said by the Lord, said by the Arahant, so I heard:

"Bhikkhus, you should live perfect in virtue, perfect in the practice of the rules of discipline, and be restrained by the restraint of the rules. Perfect in conduct and resort, seeing danger in the slightest faults, you should train in the rules of training you have undertaken. Living perfect in virtue, bhikkhus, … and training in the rules of training you have undertaken, what is there further that should be done?

"If while he is walking, standing, sitting, and lying down a bhikkhu is free from covetousness and ill will, free from sloth and torpor, free from restlessness and worry, and has abandoned doubts, his energy becomes strong and unflagging, his mindfulness is alert and unclouded, his body is calm and undistressed, his mind concentrated and one-pointed. A bhikkhu who in such a manner is ardent and afraid of wrongdoing is called constantly energetic and resolute."

This is the meaning of what the Lord said. So in regard to this it was said:

Controlled while walking,

Controlled while standing,

Controlled while sitting,

Controlled while reclining,

Controlled in bending and

Stretching his limbs—

Above, across, and below,

As far as the world extends,

A bhikkhu observes how things occur,

The arising and passing of the aggregates.

Living thus ardently,

Of calm and quiet conduct,

Ever mindful, he trains in the course

Of calm tranquillity of mind.

Such a bhikkhu is said to be

One who is ever resolute.

This too is the meaning of what was said by the Lord, so I heard.

112. The World

This was said by the Lord, said by the Arahant, so I heard:

"Bhikkhus, the world has been fully understood by the Tathagata; the Tathagata is released from the world. The origin of the world has been fully understood by the Tathagata; the origin of the world has been abandoned by the Tathagata. The cessation of the world has been fully understood by the Tathagata; the cessation of the world has been realized by the Tathagata. The course leading to the cessation of the world has been fully understood by the Tathagata; the course leading to the cessation of the world has been developed by the Tathagata.

"Bhikkhus, in the world with its devas, maras, and brahmas, with its recluses and brahmins, among humankind with its princes and people, whatever is seen, heard, sensed, cognized, attained, sought, and reflected upon by the mind—that is fully understood by the Tathagata: therefore he is called the Tathagata.

"Bhikkhus, from the night when the Tathagata awakened to unsurpassed full enlightenment until the night when he passes away into the Nibbana-element with no residue left, whatever he speaks, utters, and explains—all that is just so and not otherwise: therefore he is called the Tathagata.

"As the Tathagata says, so he does; as the Tathagata does, so he says: therefore he is called the Tathagata.

"In the world with its devas, maras, and brahmas, with its recluses and brahmins, among humankind with its princes and people, the Tathagata is the conqueror, unvanquished, all-seer, wielding power: therefore he is called the Tathagata."

This is the meaning of what the Lord said. So in regard to this it was said:

By knowledge of the whole world,

The whole world as it truly is,

He is released from all the world,

In all the world he is unattached.

The all-conquering heroic sage,

Freed from every bond is he;

He has reached that perfect peace,

Nibbana which is free from fear.

Rid of taints, he is enlightened,

Trouble-free, with doubts destroyed,

Reached the final end of deeds,

Released by clinging's full destruction.

The Enlightened One, the Lord,

A lion is he, unsurpassed;

For in the world together with its devas

He set the Brahma-wheel in motion.

Thus those devas and human beings,

Gone for refuge to the Buddha,

On meeting him pay homage to him,

The great one free from diffidence.

Tamed, of the tamed he is the best;

Calmed, of the calmed he is the seer;

Freed, of the freed he is the foremost;

Crossed, of the crossed he is the chief.

Thus do they pay him due homage,

The great one free from diffidence:

"In the world together with its devas

There is no person equalling you."

This too is the meaning of what was said by the Lord, so I heard.


The Book of the Buddha's Sayings is Finished.